Kaleidoscope Eyes

Kaleidoscope Eyes

Psychedelic Rock From the '60s to the '90s

JIM DEROGATIS

A CITADEL PRESS BOOK

Published by Carol Publishing Group

A Citadel Press Book
Published by Carol Publishing Group
Citadel Press is a registered trademark of Carol Communications, Inc.
Editorial, sales and distrtibution, rights and permissions inquiries should be addressed
to Carol Publishing Group, 120 Enterprise Avenue, Secaucus, N.J. 07094
In Canada: Canadian Manda Group, One Atlantic Avenue, Suite 105, Toronto, Ontario
 M6K 3E7

Carol Publishing Group books are available at special discounts for
bulk purchases, sales promotion, fund-raising, or educational
purposes. Special editions can be created to specifications. For
details, contact: Special Sales Department, Carol Publishing
Group, 120 Enterprise Avenue, Secaucus, N.J. 07094

Designed by Jessica Shatan
Manufactured in the United States of America

10 9 8 7 6 5 4 3 2 1

Library of Congress Cataloging-in-Publication Data
DeRogatis, Jim.
    Kaleidoscope eyes : psychedelic rock from the '60s to the '90s /
Jim DeRogatis.
       p.   cm.
    "A Citadel Press book."
    ISBN 0-8065-1788-3 (pbk.)
    1. Psychedelic rock music—History and criticism.   I. Title.
ML3534.D47   1996
781.66—dc20   95-49767
                                                       CIP
                                                       MN

To my wife, Kim:
God only knows what I'd be without you.

Contents

Acknowledgments   ix
Introduction   xi

1   My White Bicycle: The Origins and Hallmarks of
Psychedelic Rock   3

2   Why Don't We Sing This Song All Together? The
Psychedelic Beach Boys, Beatles, and Rolling Stones   17

3   Drugs, Dementia, and Amplified Jugs: Psychedelic Punk   32

4   Eight Miles High: Folk Rock Turns Psychedelic   47

5   Pipers at the Gates of Dawn: The Pink Floyd   63

6   The 14-Hour Technicolour Dream and the Art-Rock
Nightmare   78

7   Just Say Yes: Psychedelia Stretches Out   93

8   Broken Head (Quiet, Super Genius at Work)   108

9   Yoo Doo Right: The Krautrock Invasion   124

10   An Evening of Fun in the Metropolis of Your Dreams:
     Psychedelic Punk Return   141

11   Passionate Friends: The English Psychedelic Eccentrics   154

12   Retrodelic: The American Psychedelic Revival   170

13   Bad Trips and One-Hit Wonders   182

14   Reality Used to Be a Friend of Mine: Psychedelic
     Hip-Hop   194

15   Raving and Drooling: Psychedelic
     Dance Music   203

16   Pigfuckers and Shoegazers: Psychedelic Guitar Bands
     in the '80s and '90s   216

     A Select Psychedelic-Rock Discography   234
     Endnotes   259
     Bibliography   265
     Index   269

Acknowledgments

Kaleidoscope Eyes was an ambitious project, and it couldn't have been completed without the help of a lot of people. First and foremost, I'm grateful to the interview subjects who offered insights and information, including Tony Banks, Geoff Barrow, Joe Boyd, John Cale, George Clinton, Phil Collins, Stu Cook, Julian Cope, Wayne Coyne, John Drake, Steven Drozd, Brian Eno, Roky Erickson, Bryan Ferry, John Frankovic, Peter Gabriel, Tim Gane, Bruce Gilbert, Robert Gotobed, David Gilmour, Robyn Hitchcock, Steve Howe, Michael Ivins, Bruce Johnston, John Paul Jones, Ronald Jones, Lenny Kaye, Damon Krukowski, Graham Lewis, Mick London, Nick Mason, Alan McGee, Terence McKenna, Glenn Mercer, Bill Million, Colin Newman, Mike Oldfield, Alex Patterson, Jason Pierce, Prince Be, Simon Raymonde, Lou Reed, Glenn Rehse, Keith Richards, Steven Roback, Mike Rutherford, Laetitia Sadier, Kevin Shields, David Thomas, Mike Thorne, Nik Turner, Dean Wareham, and Dave Weckerman.

Publicists and managers who helped arrange these interviews or fill in the gaps in my discography included Bill Bentley, Deb Bernadini, Scott Booker, Kerry Cooley, David Dorn, Rick Gershon, Michele Guttenstein, Regina Joskow-Dunton, Roni Kairey, Andy Karlick, Mark Linn, Joecelynn Loebl, Maria Malta, Casey Monahan, Jim Merlis, David Millman, Frances Pennington, Stephen K. Peeples, Rene Pfeffer, Michele Roche, Marci Rondan, Chad Schultz, Jodi Smith, Carrie Anne Svingen, Gina Warren, Ken Weinstein, Sarah Weinstein, and Doug Wygal.

Among the astute friends and fellow enthusiasts who loaned me tapes, books, ideas, and/or advice were Ed Ackerson, Greg Beaudoin, Pat Daly, Jon-Henri Damski, A. J. DiMurro, David Dunton, Jory Farr, Bruce Gallanter, Larry Grogan, Michael Hale, Bill Holdship, Chris Holmes, Don Jackson, Jeff Jensen, Steve Kaye, John Kass, David Leaf, Peter Margasak, Don McLeese, Drew Miller, Rick Mitchell, John Neilson, Rob Patterson, Eric Puls, Ira Robbins, Doug Rushkoff, Scott Rutherford, Bill Ryan, Bud Scoppa, Siyabonga Sithole, David Sprague, Mike Stark, Jim Testa, Michael Weinstein, Paul Williams and my radio partner, Bill Wyman, who for two years listened to me wax rhapsodic about a lot of this music on our weekly radio show, *Sound Opinions*. I'd also like to thank my parents, Helene and Harry Reynolds, as well as all of the family members (DeRogatis and Kotars) who offered encouragement.

Articles about some of these artists originally appeared in *Request* magazine and the *Chicago Sun-Times*. I'd like to thank everybody I worked with at those publications, but particularly Keith Moerer and Mark Nadler. Phil Velasquez and Robin Daughtridge lent their photo expertise, and rock gods Andy Peters and Marty Perez contributed original work. Very special thanks are due the perceptive readers and volunteer editors who offered guidance along the way: Brian Beck, riot mom Susan Hamre, Jed Mayer, Jay Orff, and David Prince are good friends and excellent critics. Though I never took a course with her, Professor Deena Weinstein is one of the best teachers I've ever had, and hers was the voice in the back of my head forcing me to sharpen my thinking; the book would not have been possible without her help. Last but not least, I am indebted to my agent, David Vigliano; my editor, Kevin McDonough; copy editor and query queen Patricia Romanowski; production editor Renata Somogyi, and all at Citadel Press/Carol Publishing.

Introduction

During the punk explosion of the mid-'70s, critic Lester Bangs drew a
new line through rock history that connected the three-chord drive and
amped-up attitude of Ritchie Valens's "La Bamba" to the Kingsmen's
"Louie Louie," the Stooges' "No Fun," the Ramones' "Blitzkrieg Bop,"
and—I would add now—Nirvana's "Smells Like Teen Spirit." Critics have
rarely attempted this sort of overview with psychedelia, perhaps because
of the complex technology behind the music, its non-verbal nature, the
fringe position it occupies in the business of selling music, or the myopia
that infects those cultural observers who believe the style was limited to
the '60s. The history books tell us that the high point of psychedelic
rock was the Haight-Ashbury scene of 1967, but the genre didn't start
in San Francisco, and its evolution didn't end there. A line can be drawn
from the hypnotic drone of the Velvet Underground to the disorienting
swirl of My Bloody Valentine; from the artful experiments of the Beatles to the flowing, otherworldly samples of rappers PM Dawn; from the
dementia of the 13th Floor Elevators to the grungy lunacy of the Flaming Lips, and from the sounds and sights at Ken Kesey's '60s Acid Tests
to those at '90s raves.

This book is an attempt to connect the dots.

In the beginning were the drugs. Chapter 1 starts with an account
of the discovery of LSD, the drug that brought psychedelic conscious-

ness into the mainstream of Western culture in the mid-'60s. But *Kaleidoscope Eyes* is a book about music, not drugs. As psychedelic rock evolved, it developed a code of sonic requirements that mark a particular song as part of the genre. It works first and foremost as great rock 'n' roll, but then there is the added dimension of an artist attempting to transport the listener to a place that he or she has never been before, to transcend the everyday and experience the extraordinary. Some artists used drugs in the process of making these sounds, and some did not. A discussion of the characteristics that *are* necessary to make rock 'n' roll "mind revealing" or "soul-manifesting"—the root meanings of the word "psychedelic"—comprises the second half of chapter 1, while the rest of the book traces the development of the genre in more or less chronological order, pausing from time to time to focus on artists whose work was particularly important, influential, or inspirational, or whose stories illustrate the experiences of a group of artists working in a similar style at the same time or place.

Like any history, this one is subjective. Another account of psychedelic rock could be written emphasizing an entirely different set of artists, and I would enjoy reading it. In addition to making the case that the genre didn't end with the '60s, my goal was to share my enthusiasm for music that I consider to be some of the finest that rock has produced. The book leads up to a discography that works as a sort of psychedelic rock record collection waiting to happen. If any part of *Kaleidoscope Eyes* sends you rushing to the CD player or the record store, then I've succeeded at what I set out to do.

kaleidoscope Eyes

CHAPTER ONE

My White Bicycle: The Origins and Hallmarks of Psychedelic Rock

A psychedelic drug is one which, without causing physical addiction, craving, major physiological disturbances, delirium, disorientation, or amnesia, more or less reliably produces thought, mood, and perceptual changes otherwise rarely experienced except in dreams, contemplative and religious exaltations, flashes of vivid involuntary memory, and acute psychoses.

—Lester Grinspoon and James B. Bakalar[1]

Since prehistoric times, members of all societies have discovered and ritualized the use of plants that enlarge the scope of the mind in ways that appear both healing and transcendent. In the nineteenth century, scientists began synthesizing chemicals with these same properties in the laboratory: mescaline, LSD, psilocybin, Ecstasy. Musicians have sampled all of these drugs, and each has had some impact on rock 'n' roll. But it was the collision between rock and LSD that ushered in the genre of psychedelic rock and brought psychedelic thought into mainstream consciousness, and so it is with a Swiss chemist's wild bicycle ride that this book must start.

In the spring of 1943, Albert Hofmann was a close-cropped, bespectacled professional and a thirty-seven-year-old father of three. He had been working as a research chemist at the Sandoz Company in Basel, Switzerland, for fourteen years, the last eight spent researching the medicinal properties of ergot, a fungus that grows on rye. During the Middle Ages, ergot-contaminated rye bread caused outbreaks of St. Anthony's Fire, a nasty disease that caused the fingers and toes to turn black and fall off, eventually causing death through violent convulsions. In the 1500s midwives discovered that small amounts of ergot could help during childbirth by speeding uterine contractions and slowing the flow of blood. Hofmann's work involved synthesizing variations of lysergic acid, the key ingredient in the ergot alkaloid, in the hope that it could be used as a cure for migraines. The chemist produced his twenty-fifth synthesis, lysergic acid diethylamide (LSD-25), in 1938, but when it was tested by Sandoz pharmacologists, they didn't notice anything special, and work moved on to other molecular combinations.

Five years later, Hofmann had an odd premonition that Sandoz staffers had overlooked something unique about LSD-25. In the '60s, hippies looking for cosmic coincidences would point out that this notion struck the good doctor only weeks after scientists first achieved nuclear fission under a football field at the University of Chicago. New Age thinking holds that nature simultaneously gave humanity the tool to destroy itself (the atom bomb) and the key to open the door to a higher and more peaceful level of consciousness (LSD). Of course Hofmann couldn't have known about any of that. On April 16, 1943, he synthesized a new batch of LSD-25. As he finished his work, he began to feel dizzy. Thinking he had a touch of the flu, he closed his lab for the weekend and went home, and there he embarked on the first acid trip. "I perceived an uninterrupted stream of fantastic pictures, extraordinary shapes with intense, kaleidoscopic play of colors," he wrote. "After some two hours, this condition faded away."[2]

Reflecting on these gentle hallucinations over the weekend, he decided that they had been caused by the drug, which he had handled without wearing gloves. Late on the afternoon of April 19 he tested his theory. Hofmann dissolved 250 millionths of a gram of LSD in a glass of water and, in the name of science, drank it down. After forty minutes, he began to feel dizzy and anxious. He hopped on his beaten-up bicycle—the only form of transportation available in wartime Switzerland—and started the four-mile trip home. He felt as if he was barely moving, but the assistant who followed him on another bicycle reported that they pedaled at a furious pace. The road before him rose and fell like the swells of a turbulent sea, and the buildings that lined the streets bulged and contracted like objects thrust before a fun-house mirror. When Hofmann finally reached home, he was in the middle of the first *bad* acid trip. His world wouldn't stop spinning, the furniture took on grotesque forms, and the neighbor who offered him a glass of milk turned into a horrible witch. He calmed down only when his physician arrived. "Now, little by little I could begin to enjoy the unprecedented colors and shapes that persisted behind my closed eyes," he wrote. "Kaleidoscopic, fantastic images surged in on me . . . exploding in colored fountains."[3]

Hofmann's bike ride would be commemorated (consciously or not) in several early psychedelic-rock songs, including "I Just Wasn't Made for These Times" by the Beach Boys, "Bike" by Pink Floyd, and "My White Bicycle" by Tomorrow. But it took two decades for his surprising discovery to make its way from the laboratory to the recording studio.

The morning after his second LSD experience, Hofmann woke up clear and refreshed, and a sensation of well-being and renewed life flowed through him. Research began almost immediately. Sandoz wanted to test the drug's toxicity on cats, mice, and chimpanzees, but Hofmann and members of his staff were impatient, and they began taking it themselves and recording their hallucinatory visions. Dr. Werner Stoll, the son of Hofmann's boss, took the drug and found himself swept away by images of Edgar Allan Poe's maelstrom. The experience convinced Stoll that LSD could be useful in psychotherapy, and he began studying its effects on schizophrenics at the University of Zurich psychiatry clinic. In 1947 he published some encouraging findings, and Sandoz started offering the drug to clinical psychiatrists around the world, "literature available on request."

British psychiatrist Humphry Osmond studied the effects of mescaline and LSD on alcoholics in Saskatchewan, Canada. In 1953 he published a paper stating that the drugs prompted a kind of artificial schizophrenia, mimicking the chemical reactions that happened in actual schizophrenics. Curious about mind-altering drugs—he had written about the fictional "soma" in his novel, *Brave New World*—English author Aldous Huxley corresponded with Osmond, and from these letters came a word to describe the drugs' effects. Huxley originally proposed "phanerothyme," from roots relating to "spirit" or "soul." He illustrated its use in a letter to Osmond: "To make this trivial world sublime, take half a gram of phanerothyme." Osmond thought the word was too pretty—he wasn't

Psychedelic pioneers Allen Ginsberg, Timothy Leary, and Ralph Metzner hype the League for Spiritual Discovery (LSD) in 1967.

convinced that *every* psychedelic experience was sublime—and he suggested a new one from the Greek *psyche* (soul or mind) and *delein* (to make manifest) or *deloun* (to show or reveal). "To fathom hell or soar angelic, just take a pinch of psychedelic," he wrote.[4]

Under Osmond's supervision, Huxley took mescaline in 1953 at his home in Hollywood Hills, California. He described his beatific vision—a journey toward "the white light"—in *The Doors of Perception*. (The book's title was inspired by the 18th century poet William Blake, who wrote that, "If the doors of perception were cleansed, everything would appear to man as it is—infinite.") Huxley went on to take LSD as part of a group of curious intellectuals that included Los Angeles psychiatrist Oscar Janiger and philosopher Alan Watts. Janiger had been interested in LSD since reading Stoll's first account. He started studying the drug in 1955, and his third subject was a painter who pronounced the experience the equal of four years in art school. Janiger began giving LSD to other artists, actors, and members of the Hollywood elite, including diarist Anaïs Nin, actors Jack Nicholson and James Coburn, and conductor André Previn. "All my life I've been searching for peace of mind," said actor Cary Grant, a particularly enthusiastic convert. "Nothing really seemed to give me what I wanted until this treatment."[5]

LSD was starting to spread. "Captain" Al Hubbard was a Kentucky-born raconteur who served during World War II in the OSS, the predecessor to the CIA. In the early '50s, he bought four thousand vials of LSD from Sandoz and began distributing it with religious fervor on the West Coast and in Canada, an activity that earned him the sobriquet the "Johnny Appleseed of acid." Michael Hollingshead, a stylish Englishman with a similar mission, acquired 10,000 doses that he carried about in a mayonnaise jar. This stock launched the first trip by Harvard professor Timothy Leary, who in turn became a devoted proselytizer. ("There is some possibility that my friends and I have illuminated more people than anyone else in history," Hollingshead wrote.[6]) In 1957 LSD from the Sandoz plant in Hanover, New Jersey, began turning up in New York's underground scene of Beat poets, artists, and folk musicians. At the same time, curious artists such as novelist Ken Kesey lined up to take psychedelic drugs as part of clinical studies at West Coast universities. From there, it was only a short leap to California's burgeoning surf-music scene.

The Gamblers are remembered (when they're remembered at all) as the first rock band to mention LSD on record. "LSD 25" was the B side of "Moon Dawg," an unremarkable single released on the World Pacific label in 1960. The reference was little more than a hip, mysterious title, and there is nothing particularly psychedelic about the instrumental's twangy guitar and barrelhouse piano. The band broke up less than a year later, and drummer Sandy Nelson went on to a successful solo career. In an ironic twist, Gamblers keyboardist Bruce Johnston would replace Brian Wilson in the Beach Boys several years later when Wilson broke down under the pressures of stardom, family, and psychedelic drugs. "I don't even remember the Gamblers," Johnston told me in 1994. "I was also a Hollywood Argyle for one day. I used to back up Ritchie Valens with Sandy Nelson, and Sandy, Phil Spector, and I were in the same band before that. The '60s surf scene was simplistic. It was a lot of people who didn't surf recognizing that there was something out there. As far as the LSD, it's something I've never thought about and I've never done."

In the early '60s, use of LSD was still so limited that it seemed as if everyone who had taken it knew everyone else. "Taking LSD was like being in a secret society," Charles Perry wrote in *The Haight-Ashbury: A History*. "There was no way of knowing how many people might be messing with psychedelics. If you thought about it, you might conclude the only people taking LSD were Leary and the Harvard crowd, some Beats, and a few others, not many more than your own circle of insane friends."[7] Or, as Byrds producer Jim Dickson put it, "Everybody who got high knew each other then."[8] More musical references popped up, often in the form of a wink and a nod between people in the know. New York folk musician Peter Stampfel claims to be the first person to use the word "psychedelic" in a song lyric, 1963's "Hesitation Blues." In 1964 Bob Dylan sang in "Mr. Tambourine Man" about what may or may not have been a psychedelic trip ("Take me for a trip upon your magic swirling ship . . . "). The next year, Dickson and the Byrds electrified the

Author Ken Kesey poses by the Merry Pranksters' bus in 1990. (Photo by Roy Sebern.)

Opening the Doors of Perception: The Road to Psychedelic Rock

1794
Mystic-poet William Blake publishes *Songs of Innocence.*

1808
Physician John Stearns publishes the first modern account of medicinal uses for ergot.

1816
English poet Samuel Taylor Coleridge publishes the image-filled "Kubla Khan."

1816–1819
Romantic poets Lord Byron and Percy Bysshe Shelley cavort like rock stars.

1821
Thomas De Quincey publishes *Confessions of an English Opium-Eater.*

1839
Opium enthusiast Edgar Allan Poe publishes *Tales of the Grotesque and Arabesque.*

song; a former Chicago cop opened a rock club called The Trip on Sunset Strip, and Dylan sang about "Johnny in the basement mixing up the medicine" in "Subterranean Homesick Blues."

Meanwhile, a thirty-year-old chemist named Augustus Owsley Stanley was running the first major underground acid factory in the bathroom of a house in Berkeley. Stanley's potent LSD powered the Acid Tests hosted by Kesey and his band of Merry Pranksters. Flush from the success of *One Flew Over the Cuckoo's Nest,* Kesey sponsored nightlong multimedia "happenings" that featured films, strobe lights, taped messages, weird skits, and anything else that the Pranksters could come up with to jumpstart the psychedelic experience. "It started off as a party, with movies flashed on the walls, and lights, and tapes, and the Pranksters providing the music themselves, not to mention the LSD," journalist Tom Wolfe wrote, describing the first Acid Test in 1965 in *The Electric Kool-Aid Acid Test.* "The Pranksters' strange atonal Chinese music broadcast on all frequencies, à la John Cage."[9]

Rechristened "Bear," Stanley became the sound wizard and resident chemist with the Grateful Dead, the house band at the Acid Tests. The group made its recorded debut in March 1967, after the major record companies descended on San Francisco in a rush to sign what were now regularly called "psychedelic" or "acid"-rock bands. But to the extent that it can be pinned down at all, the birthdate of psychedelic rock is best listed as 1966.

Inspired by the soul-searching that followed Brian Wilson's first encounter with LSD, the Beach Boys' *Pet Sounds* was released in May 1966. Their competitors in studio innovations, the Beatles, followed in August with *Revolver,* which included "Tomorrow Never Knows," a song inspired by John Lennon's first profound acid trip. In Austin, Texas (of all places), a group called the 13th Floor Elevators was winning sometimes unwelcomed attention for strange songs with lyrics that openly addressed the experience of taking psychedelic drugs. Although they maintained that it was about jet flight, the Byrds' otherworldly "Eight Miles High" was blacklisted by radio programmers because of its psychedelic subtext. The Rolling Stones scored a hit with the mysterious,

Eastern-tinged "Paint It, Black," and New York's Velvet Underground brought happenings to the heartland, touring the country with a sensory assault of swirling lights, underground films, whip-cracking dancers, and white-noise drones called Andy Warhol's Exploding Plastic Inevitable.

The psychedelic influence seemed to be everywhere. Columnist Walter Winchell warned users that LSD would make them go blind. Some headlines claimed that the drug killed the sex drive forever, while others claimed it turned people into sex maniacs. (One rumor held that the initials stood for "Let's Strip Down.") Prompted by lurid stories of acid excess and mounting public pressure to protect their nations' youth, politicians in the United States and England started outlawing LSD at the end of 1966, but it was too late. The drug that Hofmann came to call his "problem child" continued to increase in popularity. It peaked during 1967's Summer of Love, but following a brief lull in the mid-'70s, LSD use by young people has been consistent ever since. From 1977 to 1992, 7 to 10 percent of every high school senior class surveyed by the federal government reported trying LSD at least once.[10]

Equally significant, LSD captured the popular imagination by 1966 to the point where people who had never had a psychedelic experience thought they had a fairly good idea of what one was like. The drug became inextricably intertwined in the crazy quilt of social, political, sexual, and racial issues raised by children of the Baby Boom in what is now inevitably referred to in cultural shorthand as The Sixties. As with most psychoactive drugs, a subculture developed around the use of psychedelics, and it was brought to mainstream attention by the fresh media outlets of FM radio, hip new magazines such as *Esquire, Rolling Stone,* and *Crawdaddy!,* and hip young writers working for older outlets (including Tom Wolfe, who would write the definitive chronicle in *The Electric Kool-Aid Acid Test*). This subculture differed from others (say, heroin or methamphetamine users) in that the idea of "mind expansion" had spiritual and intellectual connotations beyond the usual druggie goal of "getting wasted" (though those didn't always translate to the mass audience). Psychedelics users were dubbed "hippies" in a snotty derivation of the Beat "hipsters," but even before that, the subculture's slang, fashions, and mannerisms were filtering into popular culture, and key players such as Leary and Kesey became celebrities. Many of the bands that recorded psychedelic-rock songs in the wake of the groundbreaking efforts of 1966 had never taken psychedelic drugs, but the subculture told them everything they needed to know to sound authentic or, as Kesey's Pranksters

Opening the Doors of Perception: The Road to Psychedelic Rock

1844
Writer Théophile Gautier opens Le Club des Haschischins in Paris, attracting regulars Charles Baudelaire, Honoré de Balzac, Alexandre Dumas, Gerard de Nerval, and Victor Hugo.

1855
Von Bibra's *Die Narkotischen Genussmitteel unde der Mensch* identifies seventeen types of mind-altering plants.

1857
Baudelaire publishes *Les Fleurs du Mal.*

1865
English author Lewis Carroll publishes *Alice's Adventures in Wonderland.*

1871
Arthur Rimbaud frequents the absinthe bars of Paris with his lover Paul Verlaine and achieves synaesthesia through "a systematic derangement of all the senses."

1884
Sigmund Freud publishes *Über Coca,* which advocates the medicinal uses of cocaine.

1894
Surrealist Alfred Jarry writes "The Passion Considered as an Uphill Bicycle Race."

1896
Lewis Lewin and Arthur Heffter isolate the alkaloid mescaline from the Mexican cactus *Lophophora williamsii,* a.k.a. peyote.

Opening the Doors of Perception: The Road to Psychedelic Rock

1918
Arthur Stoll isolates ergotamine—the first pure ergot alkaloid—at the Sandoz Company in Basel, Switzerland.

1919
Ernst Späth produces the first synthetic mescaline in Germany.

1924
The Bureau of Surrealist Enquiries opens on the Rue de Grenelle in Paris.

1926
Ergot-contaminated rye causes the last great outbreak of St. Anthony's Fire in southern Russia.

1928
Spanish painter Salvador Dalí visits Paris and meets the French surrealists.

would say, to sound as if they were "on the bus." More important, the word "psychedelic" came to signal a set of sonic clues.

The psychedelic pioneers noted the unique effects of the drugs on music, often referring to *synaesthesia*, or the sense that sounds could be seen as kaleidoscopic bursts of color. During the very first LSD trip, Hofmann noted that "every sound generated a vividly changing image with its own consistent form and color."[11] Psychedelic drugs made inanimate objects seem to buzz with energy as if they were alive. Describing an LSD experience in *The Joyous Cosmology*, Alan Watts wrote, "I am listening to the music of an organ; as leaves seemed to gesture, the organ seems quite literally to speak."[12] The drugs caused a loss of ego (depersonalization) and made users feel as if they were physically connected to everything they were seeing and hearing. "I *became* every musical instrument," Leary wrote.[13] Huxley and Beat poet and novelist William S. Burroughs added that music not only enhanced their psychedelic experiences, but the music they heard while tripping helped them to process and relive them long after the drugs wore off. Musicians couldn't specifically reproduce any of these sensations, but drug users also talked about a transfigured view of the everyday world and a sense that time was elastic. These feelings *could* be evoked—onstage, but even more effectively in the recording studio—with circular, mandala-like song structures; sustained or droning melodies; altered and effected instrumental sounds; reverb, echoes, and tape delays that created a sense of space, and layered mixes that rewarded repeated listening by revealing new and mysterious elements. The presence of all or any one of these sounds is enough to earn a piece of music the label "psychedelic."

Of course, the recording studio had been used before the onslaught of psychedelia to create rock 'n' roll with distinctive moods or atmospheres. Brian Eno, one of rock's most imaginative producers, said that as a young boy, he was fascinated by Elvis Presley's "Heartbreak Hotel" because of the way the echo created a feeling of loneliness. "Nobody in my family could tell me what that was," he said.[14] In the late '50s, record producers made extensive use of reverb and other studio effects to create feelings of creepiness, distance, or strange spaces—as

Screamin' Jay Hawkins is the '50s singer whose methods in the studio best predicted psychedelic rock.

on instrumental hits like Link Wray's "Rumble" (1958), Santo and Johnny's "Sleep Walk" (1959), Dick Dale's "Let's Go Trippin'" (1961), and the Tornadoes' "Telstar"—or to produce a larger-than-life, multi-layered effect, as on Phil Spector's fabled Wall of Sound productions, including "Then He Kissed Me" (1963), "Be My Baby" (1963), "Walkin' in the Rain" (1964), and "River Deep—Mountain High" (1966). Outside the realm of rock 'n' roll, the "space-age bachelor pad music" made from the mid-'50s through the early '60s made maximum use of stereo gimmickry and studio effects. But the song that best predicted psychedelic rock was "I Put a Spell on You," recorded in 1956 by a twenty-seven-year-old singer from Cleveland. Over a slow and sinister R&B groove, Screamin' Jay Hawkins created a manic voodoo vibe by singing, shouting, and screaming like a man possessed, raging at the girl who walked out on him and at other demons too sinister to name. "Arnold Matson, who was the head of Columbia at the time, felt that we had to do something different in regards to the song," Hawkins said. "So he brought in a case of Italian Swiss Colony muscatel, and we all got our heads bent! Ten days later, the record came out. I listened to it and I heard all those drunken screams and groans and yells, and I thought, 'Oh, my God!'"[15] The record made bluenoses rail, charging that it evoked everything from devil worship to anal rape, but it was also a major hit.

Evoking the experience of becoming one with the universe through psychedelic drugs was considerably more difficult than duplicating a muscatel bender, but by 1966 musicians had more tools at their disposal. Like all of the '50s rockers, Hawkins and his band recorded live. The Beatles and the Beach Boys were among the first groups to utilize multitrack recording, allowing them to overdub instruments one at a time without performing everything in one take. What's more, their phenomenal success earlier in the decade gave them license and the means to explore the new technology at length over entire albums. On *Pet Sounds* and *Revolver*, they created worlds that existed only on tape and which couldn't necessarily be duplicated onstage, even with the help of an orchestra. In addition to familiar instruments such as organ, bass, and piano, "Tomorrow Never Knows" utilized radically compressed drums, backward guitars, voices fed through a rotating Leslie speaker, double-speed guitar, tape loops, and percussive sounds played on wine glasses.

Because of its emphasis on sounds that fire the imagination, psychedelic rock has often been the first genre to embrace technological advances in music making. The recording studio itself has been its most effective

Opening the Doors of Perception: The Road to Psychedelic Rock

1929
Chemists at the Rockefeller Institute in New York isolate the nucleus common to all ergot alkaloids and name it lysergic acid.

1932
English novelist Aldous Huxley publishes *Brave New World*.

1935
Albert Hofmann resumes the study of ergot alkaloids at Sandoz.

1937
Harry Ainslinger, commissioner of the U.S. Bureau of Narcotics, signals the start of the war on drugs with a harrowing article entitled "Marijuana: Assassin of Youth."

1938
Hofmann produces his twenty-fifth synthesis, lysergic acid diethylamide.
French poet Antonin Artaud travels to Mexico to participate in the peyote ritual with the Tarahumara Indians, the basis of his 1955 book *Peyote Dance*.

1942
The U.S. Office of Strategic Services (OSS) experiments with various truth drugs, hitting on a potent extract of marijuana.

1943
Scientists achieve nuclear fission at the University of Chicago.
Hofmann takes the first acid trip.

**Opening the Doors of
Perception:
The Road to
Psychedelic Rock**

1944

Mayor Fiorello LaGuardia asks
the New York Academy of Medicine to study the pros and
cons of marijuana. The academy contradicts almost all of
Harry Ainslinger's alarmist
warnings.

1947

Psychiatrist Werner Stoll publishes a study on LSD, and
Sandoz issues a prospectus to
researchers.

The U.S. Navy experiments
with mescaline as a truth
serum, drawing on the results
of tests conducted by the Nazis
on prisoners at the Dachau
concentration camp.

1951

The CIA, successor to the OSS,
begins to experiment with LSD.
OSS veteran Al Hubbard takes
LSD and has a visionary experience.

1952

Humphry Osmond studies the
effect of mescaline and LSD on
alcoholics in Canada.

1953

Under Osmond's supervision,
Huxley tries mescaline and
writes *The Doors of Perception*.

1955

Oscar Janiger gives LSD to the
Hollywood elite, including Cary
Grant.

Hofmann and his Sandoz colleagues isolate and synthesize
the key compounds of psilocybin and psilocin from psychedelic mushrooms.

instrument, and psychedelic rockers were at the forefront as the technology went from four tracks, to eight, to sixteen, to twenty-four and more. Starting in the late '60s, synthesizers offered musicians access to sound at its most basic physical level, allowing them to shape the actual wave forms. The instruments' potential was illustrated by Eno, Pink Floyd, Hawkwind, and a wave of adventurous bands in Germany in the early '70s. In the mid-'80s, digital samplers made it possible to record virtually any sound— a clap of thunder, a chirping cricket, or a rushing subway train—and turn it into a musical instrument. Groups such as De La Soul, PM Dawn, and the Orb did just that. But in all of these cases, the technology itself was less important than the imagination of its users and the music's listeners.

David Thomas of Pere Ubu calls psychedelic rock "the cinematic music of the imagination." Comparing the psychedelic experience to the poetic vision, scholar R. A. Durr wrote that every aspect of the drug experience really entails "the single fact of imaginative being: In imagination the Real Man knows ecstatically that he is That eternally. . . . or, otherwise worded, to be awake in the present moment is to be in union with life, which is the Self, which is ecstasy."[16] The quest to seize the moment is common to the psychedelic subculture, the Beat movement, and romanticism, while ecstasy—literally, "standing outside" routine ways of feeling, perceiving, and acting—is an experience fostered in many religions. Drugs can be a means to reaching these ends, but they aren't the only one, and as many psychedelic rockers say that they've taken them as say that they haven't. Psychedelic rock doesn't mean "drug rock," but rock that is inspired by a philosophical approach implied by the literal meanings of "psychedelic" as "mind-revealing" and "soul-manifesting."

Psychedelic rock offers something for the intellect as well as the body. Drug users are often called "heads," and the genre could just as easily be called "head rock." The early psychedelic rockers brought the lyrical sophistication of Dylan to rock 'n' roll, and, through him, they connected with the Beats and the romantics. They gave birth to the concept album, the musical equivalent of a novel or at least a collection of short stories. But psychedelic lyrics are less political than those in folk rock, more playful than those in progressive rock, and more open-ended than either. Listeners are allowed to determine meaning for themselves, choosing between different interpretations—as in the case of the Byrds' "Eight Miles High" or the Beatles' "I Am the Walrus"— or searching for clues as if solving a puzzle. Witness the veiled reference to the psychedelic drug

DMT in the 13th Floor Elevators' "Fire Engine," or the (perhaps unintentional) initials LSD in Lennon's "Lucy in the Sky With Diamonds."

The overwhelming majority of early psychedelic rockers were middle- to upper-middle-class college students, and many of them were art-school students. (This remained true into the '70s, though by the time the psychedelic punks appeared, it was no longer so easy to generalize.) They looked at rock 'n' roll as a romantic art form because it emphasized energy, originality, spontaneity, and emotional truth. Psychedelic rock became its most romantic genre because it was most devoted to shaking off emotional and intellectual repression. The romantics lionize children and madmen because they aren't bound by society's rules, hence they are, theoretically, the most open to creativity. Psychedelic rockers approach the recording studio with a spirit of playfulness and an open-minded attitude that isn't restricted by rules about the "right" or "sane" way to do things. "Since psychedelic drugs expose us to different levels of perception and experience, use of them is ultimately a philosophic enterprise, compelling us to confront the nature of reality and the nature of our fragile, subjective belief systems," Leary wrote. "The contrast is what triggers the laughter, the terror. We discover abruptly that we have been programmed all these years, that everything we accept as reality is just social fabrication."[17]

Living a psychedelic lifestyle or creating psychedelic art means rejecting rules, breaking down boundaries, and opening doors wherever possible. In their study of gender and sexuality in rock 'n' roll, *The Sex Revolts,* critics Simon Reynolds and Joy Press characterized male psychedelic rockers as mothers' boys longing to return to the womb. But a case can be made that male artists such as Lennon, Eno, and Kevin Shields of My Bloody Valentine are models of a more enlightened male sexuality, one that is in touch with the feminine (especially in terms of emotions) and open to sexual experimentation. Years before the '70s glam movement, the English psychedelic scene reached out to homosexuals and bisexuals. The invitation to a famous happening called the Spontaneous Underground read, "Who will be there? Poets, pop singers, hoods, Americans, homosexuals (because they make up 10 percent of the population), 20 clowns, jazz musicians, one murderer, sculptors, politicians, and some girls who defy description."

Psychedelia has also been at the forefront of breaking down gender roles. Women were accepted early on, not just as lead singers (the Jef-

---

Opening the Doors of Perception: The Road to Psychedelic Rock

1956
Beat poet Allen Ginsberg publishes his booklength poem, *Howl.*

1957
Jack Kerouac publishes *On the Road.*
R. Gordon Wasson writes a seventeen-page article on psychedelic mushrooms for *Life* magazine.

1960
Timothy Leary and Richard Alpert begin researching psilocybin at Harvard University. Ginsberg takes psilocybin at Leary's house, calls Kerouac, and identifies himself as God. Kerouac hangs up.
Ken Kesey is paid seventy-five dollars to take psilocybin at Stanford University.

1962
Leary and Alpert drop acid with Michael Hollingshead and add LSD to their research.

1963
Leary and Alpert are expelled from Harvard.
On that day that President John F. Kennedy is assasinated, Huxley dies at age seventy after his wife grants his last request: an intravenous injection of LSD.

1964
Kesey and his Merry Pranksters visit Leary and his researchers at Millbrook, New York.

Opening the Doors of Perception: The Road to Psychedelic Rock

1964

Leary, Alpert, and Ralph Metzner publish *The Psychedelic Experience: A Manual Based on the Tibetan Book of the Dead,* a guide for taking LSD.

1965

Large batches of acid start to appear on big-city streets.

Between March and December, psychiatrists at New York's Bellevue Hospital treat sixty-five people admitted during bad acid trips.

Kesey holds the first Acid Test.

1966

Bill Graham opens the Fillmore in San Francisco. The city of San Francisco estimates that fifteen thousand "hippies" are living in the Haight.

Sandoz terminates all research contracts and stops manufacturing LSD.

A Texas court sentences Leary to thirty years and a $30,000 fine for possession of marijuana.

Marshall McLuhan advises Leary to fight in the court of public opinion.

Leary holds a press conference at the New York Advertising Club to announce the formation of the League for Spiritual Discovery (LSD). "Like every great religion of the past, we seek to find the divinity within and to express this revelation in a life of glorification and the worship of God," he says. "These ancient goals we define in the metaphor of the present—turn on, tune in, drop out."

Timothy Leary continued preaching self-discovery through psychedelics into the mid-'90s.

ferson Airplane's Grace Slick), but as instrumentalists, such as the Velvet Underground's drummer Maureen Tucker, Sly and the Family Stone trumpeter Cynthia Robinson, or Christina "Licorice" McKechnie and Rose Simpson of the Incredible String Band. When riot grrrls were making "women in rock" an issue in the '90s, psychedelic guitar bands such as the Feelies, My Bloody Valentine, Spiritualized, Stereolab, Lush, and others had already gotten past the point where it was considered an issue. The women in these bands were equal, creative members—not "female rockers," but rockers, period.

Psychedelic drugs open people up to exploring other ways of living, and psychedelic rock circled the globe to incorporate the sounds of other cultures, including instruments such as the sitar, the gamelan, and the didgeridoo, which all produce tones that are considered to be conducive to meditating. Rhythmically, rock reconnected back through the blues to its African roots, and drummers turned to patterns that were more repetitive and trance-inducing. Since they were often part of religious rituals, these sounds could imply a mysterious spiritual dimension. "The modal progressions, the drone, the use of open tuning on guitars, and the improvising off one chord—those sounds became associated in people's minds with 'nonlinear' and 'non-Western,'" said Joe Boyd, who produced records by Pink Floyd and the Incredible String Band. "In a way, that was what the drugs were accomplishing, getting out of that 'knocking back a scotch and soda' mentality to a more contemplative and agape mentality."

Peter Stafford, author of the *Psychedelics Encyclopedia,* suggested that psychedelia's second meaning as soul-manifesting is best understood in terms of contrast. "Just as 'empty' implies 'full,' so 'soul-manifesting' implies an enlargement or actualization of consciousness," he wrote.[18] The impulse is not to escape the everyday but to transcend it. Psychedelic rock is open to spirituality, whether it's in the form of Eastern religions, nature worship, or Christianity. "The major conceptual breakthrough of the '60s was its romantic movement back toward nature, the awesome, star-studded panorama dwarfing social conventions and forms," scholar Camille Paglia wrote.[19] The psychedelic reconnection with the natural world spawned the environmental activism that flourished in the '70s and continues today. But while psychedelic rock is full of images celebrating the beauty of nature, there are just as many cautionary tales about its power, which can't be harnessed or controlled. The list of psychedelic rockers who tempted fate and damaged their natural facilities by overindulging in chemicals is a long one—including Brian Wilson, Roky Erickson, Syd Barrett, Skip Spence, and Robert Calvert—and their plight is often romanticized. Their abuse of drugs didn't make them visionaries, it killed their visionary talents and removed them from the land of the living.

Many others who turned on and dropped out never came back, but their stories are less dramatic. "After a serious immersion in LSD, one couldn't go back to the 9-to-5 world of sales managers and upward moblity," Jay Stevens wrote in his definitive history of LSD, *Storming Heaven.* "Better to work for yourself, doing something simple and useful, which was why so many hippies became entrepreneurs, farmers, craftspeople."[20] The quest to fill a spiritual void led some people astray, as in the case of Charles Manson's followers. Others went searching through the crystals and quackery of the New Age movement, or the cryptic conspiracies of cults like the Illuminati. Some returned to the Christian church. Christianity's emphasis on peace and love and the notion that being godlike is remembering what it is to be childlike neatly fit the psychedelic mind-set. The early '70s witnessed the flowering of Christian rock in the form of vaguely psychedelic musicals such as *Jesus Christ Superstar* and *Godspell.* But unlike Christian rock, psychedelic rock doesn't preach, and its spiritual invocations are left open to interpretation. The references in Brian Wilson's "God Only Knows" and the Velvet Undeground's "Jesus" are nonspecific in that the sentiments could be addressed to *any* higher force, including one within ourselves.

Psychedelic rock is by definition polytheistic. When Lennon said in 1966 that the Beatles were more popular than Jesus, he was stating the obvious. Rock 'n' roll *is* a religion. Music is its sacrament, and the musicians are its god and saints. "Rock 'n' roll provides what the church provided for in other generations," Grateful Dead guitarist Jerry Garcia said. (Having been raised a Roman Catholic, he was certainly in the position to know.) To many people, it is just as important as any other form of organized worship and celebration, and just as life affirming. Like Lou Reed, psychedelic rockers believe in the possibility of a life that's saved by rock 'n' roll. Of course, the music isn't always capable of achieving this lofty goal.

There is no denying that the genre has resulted in some pointless indulgence. "*Sgt. Pepper's* was the thing that did it," psychedelic punk Julian Cope said. "That was the kiss of death, with people taking themselves way too seriously. I could sit down and say, 'Look, man, you've got to understand where I'm coming from, 'cause it's deadly important!' But the greatest artists have to accept that it has to be top entertainment. There's got to be that side to it, otherwise it's not rock 'n' roll."

A school of thought voiced by the Grateful Dead's Phil Lesh holds that psychedelic music is any music that's heard while tripping. But the best psychedelic *rock* never forgets the second half of the equation. It works first and foremost as rock 'n' roll, retaining the power, immediacy, and honesty of the music at its best. In Dionysian fashion, it celebrates the vital forces of life through all forms of ecstasy. But it also attempts the Apollonian goal of transcending the everyday and creating something pure, beautiful, artistic, and spiritual. These two drives can't be squared, but they aren't necessarily opposed. If God, however you define it, can indeed be found everywhere, why not in three chords and a backbeat?

Why Don't We Sing This Song All Together? The Psychedelic Beach Boys, Beatles, and Rolling Stones

Albert Hofmann's "problem child" had a profound impact on the three most influential bands of the 1960s. Like many of their smart, wealthy, curious, and slightly hedonistic peers, the members of the Beach Boys, the Beatles, and the Rolling Stones were game to try just about anything once. They were first exposed to LSD between 1964 and 1965. A few years later, the Beatles were particularly vocal in their endorsement, and their comments were quickly condemned as irresponsible. "When George Harrison once capriciously said he liked jelly beans, the Beatles spent three years performing in a perpetual hailstorm of them," Beatles biographers Peter Brown and Steven Gaines wrote. "If every jelly bean equaled a tab of LSD, there were going to be a lot of psychedelicized children around."[1]

The charge was exaggerated, but it underscored the band's influential position, and the Beach Boys and the Stones were only a little less powerful. The psychedelic experience inspired radical changes in each band's music, and the music inspired fans and other musicians to follow in their psychedelic footsteps.

Let's Go Away for Awhile

When Marilyn saw Brian the day after his first trip, he looked drained and exhausted. "I'll never do it again," he swore. "But what happened?" she asked him. "What was it like?" Tears welled in his eyes, and suddenly he was crying and hugging her. "I saw God," Brian told her. "I saw God and it just blew my mind."
— Steven Gaines, *Heroes and Villains: The True Story of the Beach Boys*[2]

Still wearing their matching striped shirts and neat, new cardigans, the happy harmonizers from Hawthorne, California, started 1965 with their last great albums about cars, girls, and fun in the sun. *Beach Boys Today* and *Summer Days (And Summer Nights!!)* yielded the hits "Help Me, Rhonda" and "California Girls." But the band members—especially songwriter Brian Wilson—were changing, and their Chuck Berry–style rock 'n' roll was about to be replaced by sounds that were much more complex, disturbing, and psychedelic.

Brian toured with his brothers and the rest of the band for the last time in December 1964. He was twenty-two and newly married, but he was still under the thumb of his abusive father and manager, Murry. Brian was feeling the strain of a relentless schedule of writing, recording, and performing. He broke down in public during a flight from Los Angeles to Houston, screaming hysterically that his new wife was falling

The mid-'60s Beach Boys, pre-psychedelic drugs; Brian Wilson, center.

for his cousin, singer Mike Love. Later, during tense meetings with the group and his father, he insisted that he wanted to stay home and concentrate on making albums. Murry and the band weren't happy, but in early 1965, they had no choice but to replace Brian in the touring group, first with guitarist Glen Campbell, then with former Gambler Bruce Johnston. (The Beach Boys had covered the A side of the Gamblers' "Moon Dawg" b/w "LSD-25" single and knew Johnston socially.)

Brian took LSD for the first time with his friend Loren Schwartz in mid-1965, dropping acid that came from the lab of Augustus Owsley Stanley. The experience had a profound impact on the way he heard music. "As I had been promised, music had never sounded so full and tangible, and it was denser and heavier than any music I'd ever heard," he said. "I imagined wading through it like a river, until I felt consumed by it."[3] Wilson wrote that he tripped only twice after that, but the LSD contributed to an unraveling mental state that he called "psychedelicate." "My trips took me to the gates of consciousness, and then on to the other side," he wrote. "On acid, I saw myself stretched out from conception to death, the beginning to the end. Acid was everything I could ever be and anything I wouldn't be, and I had to come to grips with that. . . . I opened the Pandora's box in my mind and saw things that scared the fucking daylights out of me, and I decided to hide."[4]

Brian believed that the Beach Boys were in an intense competition with the Beatles, and each group was spurring the other on to better work. He first heard *Rubber Soul* while he was stoned on pot. "It flipped me out so much I said, 'I'm gonna try that, where a whole album becomes a gas!'" he recalled.[5] The Beach Boys' last album in 1965 was a live disc that included three Beatles covers. It spawned a hit with surf-style throwback "Barbara Ann," and its success bought Brian some time with Capitol Records. He was standing at the edge of a frightening precipice. The years of stress and his LSD experiences had prompted an emotional crisis, and his marriage and family problems were coming to a head, but he was determined to make an album that bettered *Rubber Soul*. Sitting at the piano, he began writing bits of music that he called "feelings," each evoking a specific mood. Lyrics were written later in collaboration with Tony Asher, an advertising copy writer who had the ability to convey, simply and eloquently, Brian's feelings.

The resulting album, *Pet Sounds*, is a touching and tender plea for love and understanding. While psychedelic drugs inspired the Beatles to look at the problems in the world around them, they made Brian turn his attention inward and probe his emotional longings (as on "Caroline No" and "Wouldn't It Be Nice," a song of unrequited love for his sister-in-law) and his deep-seated self-doubts ("You Still Believe in Me" and "That's Not Me"). He yearned to escape to someplace safe and peaceful, a theme reflected in the instrumental "Let's Go Away for Awhile," a cover of the folk standard "Sloop John B" (with the key line, "This is the worst trip I've ever been on"), and "Caroline No," which ends with the sounds of a departing train. ("Can't you just see me on the back of that train?" Wilson asked his wife. "I can. Just going away.") Despite their intensely personal nature, the songs touch a nerve with anyone facing difficult challenges, whether they're the standard trials of adolescence or something much more serious. (In the early '90s, "Doonesbury" cartoonist Garry Trudeau wrote a series of strips in which the album helps a character with AIDS find the strength to face his impending death.)

Although the Wilsons were raised as Christians, theirs wasn't a particularly religious household, so it's ironic that Brian is one of the first rock musicians to use the word "God" in a single (a fact that originally worried Capitol execs). "God Only Knows" is less of a prayer than a sensitive meditation about moving forward in the face of loss. In the midst of emotional turmoil, Brian was aware that there are no easy answers, either in religion or in drugs. In "I Know There's an Answer," he expresses pity for the uptight people who "trip through the day and waste all their thoughts at night," but he doesn't try to tell them how to live. "I know there's an answer, but I had to find out by myself," he sings. While the lyrics are full of questions, the music itself is optimistic, and its beauty suggests that somehow everything is going to work out.

Working with orchestra musicians and session players, Brian created a sonic tapestry of organs, strings, acoustic guitars, banjos, grand pianos, sleigh bells, and percussion so complex it's often hard to trace an individual instrumental line through an entire song. Every tune is full of haunting and beautiful melodies that continue to reveal themselves after dozens of listens, just as previously unnoticed corners of the world reveal themselves during the psychedelic experience. But when the Beach Boys came off the road to add the vocal parts that Brian carefully prescribed, not everyone was impressed. "When we left the country, we were just a surfing group," Al Jardine said. "This was a whole new thing."[6] Mike Love called the new sounds "Brian's ego music" and said he found the lyrics "offensive" and "nauseating" in their psychedelic suggestiveness.[7]

When it was released in May 1966, *Pet Sounds* sold half a million copies, but it was a commercial disappointment compared to the previous albums. Love felt vindicated by what he considered to be Brian's failure, and he began an effort to seize control of the band so that it could stick to the proven formula of the early hits. Brian held onto the reins only long enough to complete one more single.

"Good Vibrations" is a three-and-a-half-minute "pocket symphony" that took six months to record, and its many melodic changes and complex vocal arrangements were worked out over ninety hours of tape. The distinctive swooping hook comes from a theremin, an early synthesizer played by moving your hand over an antenna. (Jimmy Page later used one on Led Zeppelin's "Dazed and Confused," but before "Good Vibrations," it was most often featured on the soundtracks to '50s science-fiction movies.) Capitol executives were worried that the song was "too modern" and that the lyrics had sensual, druggy overtones. But while Brian said the production was inspired by LSD, the lyrics came from an offhand remark by his mother. "My mom told me dogs discriminate between people," he said. "They like some people because the people give off good vibrations. . . . I have a feeling that this is a very spiritual song, and I want it to give off good vibrations."[8]

"Good Vibrations" turned out to be one of the Beach Boys' biggest hits—and the beginning of the end. In late 1966, Brian began his ill-fated collaboration with enigmatic songwriter-producer Van Dyke Parks on *Smile*. The album was originally called *Dumb Angel*, and Brian described it as a "teenage symphony to God," adding a spiritual element to Phil Spector's earlier description of his hit singles. The sessions are legendary for their indulgence. Brian was taking speed and smoking marijuana constantly, and he suffered bouts of depression and paranoia. He built the infamous sandbox in his living room, and he refused to leave his bed for long periods of time. The nadir came when he tried to destroy the tapes of a track called "Fire" because he was convinced that the song caused several blazes around Los Angeles. In May 1967 Capitol announced that *Smile* had been abandoned. The group canceled a headlining appearance at the Monterey Pop Festival, and Jimi Hendrix told the crowd it had heard the last of surf music. Brian withdrew further and further from music, his family, and the world, until, finally, he wasn't there at all.

The songs from *Smile* that were salvaged for 1967's *Smiley Smile* and subsequent albums and those that appeared on a 1993 box set show flashes of inspiration, especially "Surf's Up" and "Heroes and Villains."

Brian Wilson, surviving in the '90s.

But after "Good Vibrations," Brian was unable to realize his ambitious visions, and the Beach Boys ceased to be more than a nostalgia act. People close to Brian dispute his being characterized as an acid, or mental, casualty, but there's no denying that his creative output was effectively curtailed for nearly two decades. He resurfaced in 1977 to reunite with the Beach Boys on the underwhelming *Beach Boys Love You* album, and again in 1988, when he produced a pleasant but slight solo effort with help from the controversial psychiatrist Eugene Landy. It was another seven years before he followed that with a burst of activity in 1995, including a new collaboration with Parks, *Orange Crate Art*, and the Don Was–produced album and film *I Just Wasn't Made for These Times*.

Interviewed on camera by Was, Brian comes across as a vulnerable and frightened man with a childlike openness. He has survived a confrontation with his demons, but is still struggling to come to terms with his life and art. Critic Greil Marcus wrote that, since *Smile*, the Beach Boys' artistic reputation has been based on music that no one ever really heard, since it was never really finished. But focusing on what may or may not have been an aborted masterpiece—or whether or not Brian can pick up where he left off three decades ago—detracts from the brilliance of *Pet Sounds* and the real accomplishments of the Beach Boys' psychedelic era.

Into the Void

When the Beatles' work as a whole is viewed in retrospect, *Rubber Soul* and *Revolver* will stand as their major contributions. When the slicks and tricks of production on this new album no longer seem unusual, and the compositions are stripped to their musical and lyrical essentials, *Sgt. Pepper's* will be Beatles baroque—an elaboration without improvement.

—Richard Goldstein, 1967[9]

The Fab Four are remembered as the Acid Apostles of the New Age, among other things, but the Beatles' earliest personal psychedelic experiences were unfulfilling. John Lennon and George Harrison first tripped in 1964 after they were unknowingly dosed by their dentist during dinner at his flat. (The LSD came from Michael Hollingshead's notorious mayonnaise jar.) Though the dentist begged them to stay, the two Beatles were angry and stormed out. They made the mistake of speeding around London in Harrison's Aston Martin, landing at several nightclubs where the crowds and the noise only unnerved them further. They finally escaped to Harrison's house and unwound by playing music and drawing. Their second trip wasn't much better. In August 1965 they took LSD with members of the Byrds and others while they were staying in L.A. to perform at the Hollywood Bowl. This time, actor Peter Fonda wouldn't stop babbling about how he almost died on the operating table, until a freaked-out Lennon finally screamed at him to shut up.

Like the Beach Boys, the Beatles were struggling to meet a ridiculous schedule imposed by their label, EMI. *Help!*, the group's eighth U.S. album since early 1964, was released in August 1965, and a new album was expected by December. The band didn't start working on *Rubber Soul* until mid-October, but the musicians finished writing and recording in little more than a month. They had started to escape the pressures of their relentless pace by smoking marijuana, and their carefully constructed image as lovable moptops was disintegrating. In its place was a cross between the wiseass rockers who played speed-crazed sets in Hamburg and the second-generation Beats who sat around in coffee shops dissecting Bob Dylan's electric turnarounds, *Bringing It All Back Home* and *Highway 61 Revisited*.

Rubber Soul is an album about change. The Beatles' worldview is expanding, their music is maturing, and the title and lyrics hint at concerns that are more spiritual than chasing and being chased by female fans. "It was the first album to present a new, growing Beatles to the world," producer George Martin said. "For the first time, we began to think of albums as art on their own, as complete entities."[10] Biographer Nicholas Schaffner described *Rubber Soul* as the moment in *The Wizard of Oz* when Dorothy's world goes from black and white to Technicolor. The relaxed rhythms are a surprising change, and Ringo is as likely to play finger cymbals, tambourine, or maracas as drums. The instrumental textures are more elaborate, and Harrison plays sitar for the first time. (The guitarist was exposed to the twenty-one-stringed instrument on the set of *Help!* by Indian musicians who played during one of the chase scenes.) The lyrics bear an obvious Dylan influence. "In My Life" finds

Lennon looking back wistfully at the people and places he's left behind, while "Girl," "I'm Looking Through You," and "Norwegian Wood" are cynical songs about relationships that are much more complicated than the one in "I Want to Hold Your Hand."

Like a lot of Baby Boomers in the mid-'60s, the Beatles were beginning to question authority and search for a way of living that was richer and fuller than what straight society offered. The A sides of the two singles that followed *Rubber Soul*—"Day Tripper" and "Paperback Writer"—both take a harsh view of people caught in the rat race. Lennon said the former was a critique of "weekend hippies" (though clearly it also works as an angry rant about a relationship gone bad), while the latter features a marijuana-inspired fascination with droning melody and lyrics that can be heard as sneering at the unbridled ambition of the young protagonist who so badly needs a job (though many note that McCartney himself displayed such ambition). But it's the B side of "Paperback Writer" that is the Beatles' first great psychedelic-rock song. "Rain" uses a stuttering rhythm and an expanding and contracting melody to evoke the sense of timelessness created by LSD, while the lyrics are inspired by Lennon's reading of philosopher Alan Watts, whose LSD experiences prompted him to question such basic assumptions as whether we can really say if it is raining or the sun is shining.

Lennon had had his first profound psychedelic experience in December 1965, a month after the release of *Rubber Soul*. Sitting alone in his attic, armed with Timothy Leary and crew's how-to manual, *The Psychedelic Experience*, he traveled toward the "white light" described by Aldous Huxley. Three months later he started work at Abbey Road on a song he called "The Void." The tune was eventually retitled "Tomorrow Never Knows," after one of Ringo's pet phrases. Inspired by Lennon's acid trip, it featured several lines lifted directly from *The Psychedelic Experience*, which in turn had been adapted from *The Tibetan Book of the Dead,* ancient advice to a dying soul on how to reach heaven. "Turn off your mind, relax, and float downstream," Lennon sings. His voice is both intimate and distant, as if he's whispering in your ear from somewhere over the horizon. An insistent drumbeat folds in on itself again and again—a tribal trance groove—while an ominous organ drones in the background and strange birdcalls of backward guitars mock the monotone vocals, which Lennon intended to evoke the sound of a thousand chanting Tibetan monks.

Although it closes the album, "Tomorrow Never Knows" was the first song recorded for *Revolver*. It set the tone for an album that is pregnant with possibilities. Released the month the Beatles played their last scheduled live concert, the album calls attention to the fact that it is a studio creation. It opens with a voice counting off the intro to "Taxman," as if the Beatles are inviting the listener inside the recording process. The title is an in-joke referring to the revolving slab of vinyl that carried these new sounds in the days before CDs, while the cover art evokes the creative process with a collage of images flowing out of the musicians' heads. After his third LSD trip, Lennon began taking the drug almost every day. McCartney, a swinging young bachelor, immersed himself in the London underground, while Harrison and Starr

Mop Tops no more: The Fab Four go psychedelic

struggled to grow beyond the caricatures drawn at the height of Beatlemania. The four were starting to pull apart, but they still functioned as a group in the studio, and the joy they felt while working together is transmitted in their recordings.

Revolver shows each of the Beatles in his best light (especially the original British LP, which was cannibalized in America but restored to the original running order on CD reissues, which I'm referring to here). McCartney's "Here, There and Everywhere" is sweet and romantic without being saccharin, and his "Eleanor Rigby" makes a sharp social comment on isolation in the midst of community. (The lives of its subjects are centered around the church, where people gather to pray, but this religious community does nothing to quell their loneliness.) On "Taxman" Harrison whines about the bite from his paycheck, but he also questions governmental authority for the first time in a Beatles song. ("Don't ask me what I want it for" is the bureaucratic reply.) "Love You To" is the best of Harrison's Eastern ragas because it's the most frantic, with the sitar chasing the vocals through the song. A dreamy tune about floating upstream, Lennon's "I'm Only Sleeping" foreshadows the full-blown psychedelic voyage of "Tomorrow Never Knows." With its underwater sound effects and singalong chorus, "Yellow Submarine" is a whimsical children's ditty with a touch of perversity (at least if you believe biographer Albert Goldman's contention that it's about yellow, sub-shaped Nembutals). The soaring guitar, rolling drums, and flowing bass of "She Said She Said" carry on a spirited exchange that recalls the nonstop babble of the L.A. acid trip, with lyrics inspired by Fonda's monologue. ("He said, 'I know what it's like to be dead.'")

While critics such as the *Village Voice*'s Goldstein recognized the importance of *Revolver* when it was released, many fans didn't really catch up with the Beatles until the next album, ten months later. *Sgt. Pepper's Lonely Hearts Club Band* is remembered because of its timing. It's the album that was on the turntable during the Summer of Love, when psychedelic drugs went from being part of a subculture to a media phenomenon. "The closest Western Civilization has come to unity since the Congress of Vienna in 1815 was the week *Sgt. Pepper's* was released," critic Langdon Winner wrote. "In every city in Europe and America the stereo systems and the radio played . . . and everyone listened."[11] But what they heard was not the Beatles' best. "Like an over-attended child, this album is spoiled," Goldstein wrote. The language he used would be repeated countless times in years to come whenever a punk attacked an art-rock album thick with pretensions: "It reeks of horns and harps, harmonica quartets, assorted animal noises, and a forty-one-piece orchestra."[12]

The conceptual conceit is that the group is portraying a sentimental, old-time, Salvation Army–type band (as depicted on the cover) in an effort to free itself from the expectations of making "Beatles music." But the psychedelic rock on *Revolver* wasn't bound by any constrictions, and only three songs on *Sgt. Pepper's* transcend the boundaries the musicians set for themselves. "Lucy in the Sky With Diamonds" is a catchy but slight piece of escapism. McCartney drew hostile criticism for talking to the press about psychedelics—"LSD opened my eyes," he said. "It made me a better, more honest, more tolerant member of society, brought closer to God."[13]—and Lennon's denial that the title was an acronym for L-S-D seemed coy and motivated by commercial concerns. "Being for the Benefit of Mr. Kite!" is notable only for the tape montage of calliope sounds that Martin created to realize Lennon's vision of a sinister circus. "A Day in the Life" succeeds in grafting half a McCartney song onto half a Lennon song, evoking an unexpected trip from the workaday to the cosmos, but its positioning at the end of *Sgt. Pepper's*—the slot held by "Tomorrow Never Knows" on *Revolver*—isn't enough to redeem the rest of the album.

Imaginative and influential psychedelic rock songs are scattered through the rest of the Beatles' releases. "Strawberry Fields Forever," one of the Beatles' greatest studio accomplishments, looks at some familiar terrain (the Liverpool orphanage near Lennon's childhood home) through the idealistic and impressionistic eyes of a child. "I Am the Walrus" features Lennon flirting with the madness that is the flipside of the psychedelic ideal, something attempted less successfully by McCartney on "Maxwell's Silver Hammer," though the lyrical nod to surrealist Alfred Jarry is amusing. The rollicking "Magical Mystery Tour" was inspired by Ken Kesey, the Merry Pranksters, and their psychedelic bus, and "Baby You're a Rich Man" commented on the English underground's first big happening, the 14-Hour Technicolour Dream, which was billed as a gathering of "beautiful people." Written while he was fogbound in L.A., Harrison's "Blue Jay Way" captures an uneasy sense of dislocation, and Lennon's "Across the Universe" evokes the drained but optimistic feeling that comes with the dawn after a nightlong acid trip.

By the time the latter was recorded in 1968, the Beatles were in the process of shifting to a more stripped-down approach in the studio, though psychedelic touches still decorated otherwise straightforward rock songs such as "Glass Onion," "Everybody's Got Something to Hide, Except Me and My Monkey," and "Dear Prudence." The search for spiritual enlightenment sparked by psychedelic adventures had led to the group's dalliance with the Maharishi Mahesh Yogi, and in recoiling from the charlatan guru, the band members more or less abandoned cosmic concerns. After the Beatles split, Lennon, the group's biggest user of psychedelic drugs, turned to heroin and distanced himself furthest from psychedelia with cathartic and intensely personal songs that probed his inner turmoil instead of transcending it. (Though the chaotic guitars of *Live Peace in Toronto 1969* hinted at the "better living through noise" approach of psychedelic guitar bands in the '80s and '90s.) McCartney perfected his consummate pop craftsmanship, and a belated return to mid-'60s experimentation with the 1993 ambient-house project, the fireman, fell flat. Unable to sustain entire rock albums, Harrison produced his best solo effort with the instrumental soundscapes on *Wonderwall Music*. Ringo was Ringo. The pieces were never as strong as the whole, and the whole was never stronger than during the recording of *Revolver* in the heady spring of 1966.

Something Happened to Me Yesterday

I don't know how Mick and Ronnie and little Mick moved so fast, but they disappeared, leaving me with Jo and Charlie Watts, the world's politest man. I tried to move him through the sea of sleeping bags, wine bottles, dogs, bodies, and hair. . . . We were pushing through the crowd, stumbling, trying to avoid the big dogs. People were tossing us joints and things. Looking at a yellow-green LSD tab, Charlie asked, "D'you want it?" "I ain't too sure about this street acid," I said. "Maybe Keith will want it."

—Stanley Booth at Altamont[14]

The notorious bad boys of '60s rock came late to the psychedelic party, and with the exception of their blond, sleepy-eyed founder Brian Jones, they never truly joined the festivities. During the frantic days of the Rolling Stones' early tours, former economics student Mick Jagger and art-school dropout Keith Richards were known to have people thrown out of their dressing rooms for smoking pot. This embarrassed bassist Bill Wyman and drummer Charlie Watts, who, regardless of their own proclivities, were used to marijuana as part of the jazz scene. But by 1965, the Stones' attitudes were changing.

The band started smoking a lot of pot while touring America, and Jones and Richards dropped acid at a party thrown by Kesey. By the end of the year, Jones and manager Andrew Loog Oldham were tripping regularly. Wyman wrote that "the effect of marijuana and LSD brought about a sea-change in the outlooks, attitudes, and aspirations of thousands of musicians around the world," not the least of whom were the Stones.[15] Thanks largely to Jones, the band's music was growing more elaborate. In 1966 *Aftermath* added exotic textures such as dulcimer, sitar, and marimba. Though he remained loyal to the blues that inspired him to start the band, Jones's musical curiosity was insatiable, and he was drawn to new electronic synthesizers, ancient Eastern percussion, and the master musicians of Joujouka, who drummed for hours in a drug-induced trance. The guitarist could pick up any instrument and find the perfect way to incorporate it into the Stones' music. "Charlie would recall how Brian sat for hours learning to play sitar, put it on 'Paint It, Black,' and never played it again," Booth wrote.[16]

The drug influence was obvious in the titles and themes of the band's mid-'60s singles. The frantic "19th Nervous Breakdown" includes the line, "On our first trip I tried so hard to rearrange your mind." "Paint

Rock's notorious bad boys the Stones, pre-LSD.

It, Black" has mysterious Eastern overtones, and "Mother's Little Helper" pokes fun at suburban moms on speed. The title of the 1966 best-of compilation, *Big Hits (High Tide and Green Grass)*, winks at fellow pot-heads, but the psychedelic influence really comes to the forefront on 1967's *Between the Buttons*. The Stones peer at fans from the cover's blurry haze, and the songs include the swirling "Ruby Tuesday" and the jugband ditty "Something Happened to Me Yesterday," which critic Robert Christgau called "the most accurate LSD song ever."[17] "He don't know if it's right of wrong / Maybe he should tell someone," Jagger and Richards sing. "He don't know just what it was / Or if it's against the law."

The Beatles were openly embracing LSD in 1967, but it was the Stones who were tagged as druggie outlaws. On February 5 the *News of the World* published a story charging that Jagger had attended an acid party at a house shared by members of the Moody Blues. (The reporters fingered the wrong Stone; it had really been Jones.) In private, Jagger praised the effects of LSD. He told photographer Cecil Beaton, "You see yourself aglow. You see yourself beautiful and ugly, and other people as if for the first time."[18] But the singer wanted to keep the public guessing about his drug habits, and he filed a libel suit against the tabloid. A week later, Jagger and Richards were busted during a raid on Redlands, Richards's country estate, that was generally considered a setup. The weekend's guests included Jagger's girlfriend, Marianne Faithfull; gallery owner Robert Fraser; George and Pattie Harrison (who ducked out before the bust), and a mysterious American nicknamed Acid King David, who dispensed LSD with the morning tea. Everyone was coming down from a day of tripping when the police arrived at 8:00 P.M.

To the delight of the tabloids, the officers found Faithfull nude except for a bearskin rug, and they collected marijuana residue and a vial of pills. As the property owner, Richards was charged with allowing marijuana to be smoked on the premises. Jagger took the rap for the vial of speed, though it actually belonged to Faithfull. The band's troubles continued mounting through the year. Jones's lover Anita Pallenberg left him for Richards, and Jones was devastated by the loss. He had been busted as well, and he was facing trial for possession of pot, methedrine, and cocaine. The group was in the process of an ugly split with its manager, Oldham, and it was coming under the influence of the American pitbull-manager Allen Klein. It was under these gray clouds that the band began to record its eleventh album, *Their Satanic Majesties Request*, a record that Jagger said was made "under the influence of bail."[19]

The title was the first time the Stones toyed with satanic imagery, and it reflects a shift in Jagger's reading habits from the Beats to stranger fare (including *The Master and Margarita*, the Russian novel that was one of the inspirations for "Sympathy for the Devil"). The album opens with "Sing This All Together," a singalong that wouldn't sound out of place at one of Kesey's Acid Tests. Over soundscapes that include theremins, synthesizers, shortwave radio static, and distinctive string arrangements by future Led Zeppelin bassist John Paul Jones, the Stones invite listeners to open their minds and "let the pictures come." The most colorful images include "Citadel," a candy-coated tune with a cheery Mellotron hook; "2000 Man," a song about alienation in familiar surroundings; "2000 Light Years From Home," which is just the opposite, a sort of space-age version of "Sloop John B"; the symbolic "Lantern"; and the the beautiful "She's a Rainbow." But even at their spaciest, the Stones can't get away from their central obsession: sex. "She comes in colors everywhere," Jagger sings leeringly.

Wary of psychedelic drugs, Wyman parodied the band's current interest with "In Another Land," his first songwriting contribution. Originally titled "Acid in the Grass," the simple love song is decorated with such psychedelic clichés as tremeloed vocals and lyrics about "blue flowers." The chorus—"Then I awoke / Is this some kind of joke?"—predicts the return to basics that soon followed. The Stones' particular journey toward the white light was never too far removed from earthly concerns, and this may be the reason that *Satanic Majesties* was written off by critics. Consensus held it as a failed attempt to copy *Sgt. Pepper's*, a facile charge as deep as the observation that the 3-D cover was designed by the same artist, Peter Blake. "Despite moments of unquestionable brilliance, it puts the status of the Rolling Stones in jeopardy," Jon Landau wrote.[20] *Rolling Stone* publisher Jann Wenner added that it was "the prototype of junk masquerading as meaningful" (and he should certainly know).[21]

The Stones themselves were soon dissing the album—even the unfailingly loyal roadie Ian Stewart called it "that damn *Satanic Majesties*"—but Christgau maintained that "the tunes prove remarkably solid and the concept is legitimate in its tongue-in-cheekness."[22] *Satanic Majesties* is one of the first psychedelic-rock albums to satirize the prevailing optimism about LSD and to hint that there could be a dark side to the psychedelic experience. The perception was that, like the brutish Hell's Angels at Kesey's Acid Tests, the Stones didn't understand the drug. But the reality was that they knew that it didn't guarantee peace and ecstasy, and it was foolish to pretend that it did. When the band followed *Satanic Majesties* with *Beggars Banquet* a year later, the songs were more sinister and streetwise ("Sympathy for the Devil," "Street Fighting Man"). "The short psychedelic dream had withered," Wyman wrote.[23] The stripped-down sound took a turn toward country blues—the music of factory girls and other salt of the earth—but there was a mysterious dimension that was later amplified by Jones's death by drowning and the chaos at Altamont in late 1969. After *Satanic Majesties*, the Stones rarely made music that recalled its specific psychedelic sounds, as on the brilliant single "Child of the Moon" and the dreamy break in "Rocks Off." But they carried the lantern along with all the other baggage they picked up. It could be glimpsed through the murk of their decadent masterpiece, 1972's *Exile on Main Street*, as they groped for spiritual salvation amid the insanity that they'd created. But with every passing year, the spark grew dimmer. "The group is still strong and together," critic Lillian Roxon wrote in 1969. "But nothing is the same. How could it be?"[24]

CHAPTER THREE

Drugs, Dementia, and Amplified Jugs:
Psychedelic Punk

I began to realize that it was all the same—my teenage-dissolution lifestyle and the music of groups like the Troggs, Shadows of Knight, Music Machine, Seeds, Question Mark, Count Five. They were all full of shit and so was I. And none of us cared. We had all heard the Yardbirds' brilliant innovations, but since almost none of the above listed groups really knew how to play their instruments, all they could do was bang away in rackety imitation. Which was when I first realized that *quality* and *musicianship* and *taste* actually had nothing whatsoever to do with rock 'n' roll; in fact might be its worst enemies.

—Lester Bangs[1]

In the early '60s, garages across America were filled with teenagers living out their rock-'n'-roll fantasies on cheap Sears, Roebuck instruments. At first, these acne-plagued legions imitated the surf bands, playing endless variations of "Wipe Out" that always fell apart during the drum solos. Later they pushed aside Dad's lawnmower and the folding chairs to bash through songs by the Byrds and the British Invasion bands. By late 1965, there was a new element in the mix. Some of these rock-star wannabes discovered psychedelic drugs, but most wrote about what they *imagined* the psychedelic experience to be. They were aided in their quest to freak out listeners by technical innovations such as fuzztone, electric twelve-string guitar, echo, and tape delay—tools that, as punk connoisseur Bangs noted, "put truly awesome sonic possibilities within the reach of the most limited musicians."[2] At the same time, they were conscious of complying with the demands of AM radio for singles that were short, catchy, and devoid of instrumental displays that detracted from the tune at hand. The result was some of rock's most inventive and enduring one-hit wonders.

In 1972, barely five years after the trends shifted to more ponderous sounds, Lenny Kaye rounded up some of the best psychedelic punks on *Nuggets: Original Artyfacts From the First Psychedelic Era, 1965–1968*. A rock fan and writer, Kaye was working as a talent scout for Elektra Records when he compiled the album. (It was reissued in the more familiar version on Sire in 1976.) "These bands were more intoxicated by the Gibson fuzztone, the first fuzztone that came out, than by any drugs," Kaye said. "Unless you lived in New York or San Francisco, I doubt you'd seen any LSD. A lot of it was just desire. That's what made these bands wonderful—there were millions of them, and if they were heard five blocks away, it kind of spoiled what they were doing." *Nuggets* spawned a legion of archeological imitators—*Pebbles*, *Boulders*, *Rubble*, and the like—but it remains the definitive compilation. "What strikes me about *Nuggets* now is how unified it is, when at the time, it seemed to cover a lot of stylistic ground," Kaye said.

In sharp contrast to the whimsical psychedelia that became the rage in England, the sounds and visions of the American *Nuggets* bands were dark and ominous. "This was 'bad trip' psychedelia as opposed to the predominantly dreamy, optimistic feel of the U.K.," wrote Larry Grogan, editor of the psychedelic fanzine *The Evil Eye*. "This might be due to extreme antidrug paranoia in the U.S., or to real-world experiences with cheap street drugs (glue sniffing, bad acid, and/or speed)." Stories about people driven over the edge by marijuana use had been circulating since 1937, when U.S. narcotics commissioner Harry Ainslinger published a harrowing article entitled "Marijuana: Assassin of Youth." A wave of media hysteria and government propaganda followed, including the classic camp film *Reefer Madness*, until pot was firmly stereotyped as the drug of choice for lowlifes and loonies. Hysteria about psychedelic drugs built in similar fashion, fanned by some accurate but even more anecdotal accounts of LSD users going crazy, losing their eyesight, destroying their chromosomes, or jumping out of windows in doomed attempts to fly. There were also tales of horror from army veterans who learned that they had been used as human guinea pigs in psychedelic experiments by government agencies, including the CIA. Then, too, there was the longstanding association by white, middle-class America of illegal drugs with African Americans and "lower class" lifestyles.

In early 1966, Dr. Huston Smith of MIT told an LSD conference that confusion about the drug was so great and genuine knowledge so small "that there is no hope of telling the truth about it at this point."[3] By 1967, LSD was outlawed across the United States. The flood of media attention fixated on the idea that the drug caused psychosis in otherwise sane individuals. This notion convinced some initiates to fear that they were losing their minds. "In any society whose culture contains notions of sanity and insanity, the person who finds his subjective state altered may think he has become insane," sociologist Howard Becker wrote in 1967. "We learn at a young age that a person who 'acts funny,' 'sees things,' 'hears things,' or has other bizarre and unusual experiences may have become 'crazy.' The drug experience, perhaps viewed originally as a momentary entertainment, now looms as a momentous event which will disrupt one's life, possibly permanently. Faced with this conclusion, the person develops a full-blown anxiety attack, but it is an anxiety caused by his *reaction* to the drug experience rather than a direct consequence of the drug use itself."[4]

Nineteenth-century romantics had equated the creative process with madness. As a romantic art form, rock 'n' roll was considered best when it was truly "out of control." Given all of these factors, it's not surprising that losing your mind became the topic of many psychedelic singles, including the Electric Prunes' rollicking "I Had Too Much to Dream (Last Night)," a cautionary tale of a psychedelic hangover, and the Count Five's "Psychotic Reaction," a shameless rip-off of the Yardbirds' "I'm a Man" with one of the most demented vocals since Screamin' Jay Hawkins's "I Put a Spell on You." Both songs were Top Ten hits, but most of the *Nuggets* bands settled for short-lived regional fame, and their marginality was part of their charm. The bands that stuck around inevitably showed their shortcomings—the Electric Prunes went on to record a pompous rock Mass sung in Latin—but the bands that disappeared enabled fans to project their own fantasies on them. The Count Five was never heard from again, but Bangs invented a long career for the group in his epic article "Psychotic Reactions and Carburetor Dung." Like the Count Five, the

Chocolate Watchband hailed from San Jose, but it mixed Rolling Stones–style R&B with heavy-handed sitar playing. The Strawberry Alarm Clock scored a hit with the idyllic "Incense and Peppermints," though the song was a bit cloying even in 1967. The members of the Music Machine each wore one black glove, and they recorded the endearingly snotty "Talk Talk." ? and the Mysterians set a new standard for cheesy organ on "96 Tears," while the Standells sang about the River Charles and Boston University's frustrating curfew (despite the fact that they lived in L.A.) on "Dirty Water." The Seeds were another L.A. band that talked a lot about flower power, but it was always clear exactly what kind of seeds their name referred to. "Pushin' Too Hard" was a minor hit that featured singer Sky Saxon railing against the forces that would keep him down (or bust him for smoking pot), while the band's second album included songs called "Tripmaker" and "Mr. Farmer," a tribute to marijuana growers.

How many of these bands took any drug stronger than marijuana is open to debate. "By 1965 or '66, LSD was available in certain big-city communities, like Detroit, Chicago, L.A., and New York," said Amboy Dukes singer John Drake. "But the suburbanite kids had no idea what it was. They were just singing about something that was in the air. And even later, you had to know somebody who knew somebody to get into it. The somebody *I* knew was John Sinclair." Fueled by acid provided by radical journalist and White Panther Party leader Sinclair, Drake and guitarist Steve Farmer helped craft a 1968 hit called "Journey to the Center of the Mind" that urged psychedelic experimentation over a riff adapted from the theme to the television Western series *Bonanza*. The album of the same name was released with a cover showing an impressive array of pot pipes, but the band's third key member was opposed to drug use of any kind. "I didn't have the faintest idea what those pipes were all about," said firebrand guitarist Ted Nugent, who eventually became a gun-toting conservative poster boy. "Everybody else was getting stoned and trying every drug known to mankind. I was meeting women, playing rock 'n' roll, and meeting girls. I didn't know anything about this 'cosmic inner probe.' I thought 'Journey to the Center of the Mind' meant look inside yourself, use your head, and move forward in life."[5]

The most enduring of America's psychedelic-punk bands left no doubt about their positive stance on drugs. And unlike most of the *Nuggets* groups, their influence reaches far beyond a few scattered tracks on archival compilations.

Step Inside This House

"Who's the head of this band?"—Dick Clark to the 13th Floor Elevators
"We're all heads."—Roky Erickson
                    —The 13th Floor Elevators on *American Bandstand*, 1966

Every March since 1986, the music industry descends on Austin, Texas, for the annual South by Southwest music and media conference. Each year, a sizable contingent hopes to catch a glimpse of one of the city's most renowned residents. Sometimes Roky Erickson complies, but it is always anticlimactic. In 1994 the singer shuffled onstage at the Austin Music Awards to deliver "Starry Eyes," but with his arms folded and his eyes fixed to the floor, it seemed as if he would have preferred being anywhere else. The following year, he was slated to autograph a new album and a volume of his poems and lyrics, his first offerings to the public in nine years, but he wasn't exactly making a comeback. "I have always been here before," he sang in one of his many memorable songs. It's just that his definition of "here" is a little different from everybody else's.

Kicked out of Austin's Travis High School in his junior year for growing his hair like the Rolling Stones, Erickson started his musical career at age eighteen. He'd already written "You're Gonna Miss Me," a minor hit for garage rockers the Spades, when he was approached in 1965 to join a sort of Texas supergroup called the 13th Floor Elevators. Guitarist Stacy Sutherland, bassist Benny Thurman, and drummer John Ike Walton had progressed from playing bluegrass to raunchy garage rock with Port Arthur's Lingsmen. They were introduced to Erickson by University of Texas undergrad Tommy Hall, who played the jug in another band called the Conqueroo. The new band's very name declared a desire to be different: The thirteenth floor doesn't exist in many high-rises, and the band was fond of pointing out that *m* (for marijuana) is the thirteenth letter of the alphabet.

Several years older than his band mates, Hall was a self-styled Beat poet already acquainted with psychedelic drugs and the writings of Timothy Leary and Aldous Huxley. Peyote had been widely available in Austin since 1961, and LSD started to circulate in 1965. The Elevators dropped acid together and set out to evoke the psychedelic experience in both music and lyrics. "When rock 'n' roll was happening and the music was coming on, it would piss you off that people would write really dumb lyrics," Hall said. "You had Leary and the psychedelic concept, the beginning of that, and people didn't follow it. They'd just come out with the same old type of songs, so you'd think, 'Hey, you guys, talk about this. This is what we want to hear about.' It was really more of a brother-to-brother type of thing."[6]

Some of Erickson's friends charge that Hall manipulated the band and used drugs for control. But Erickson enthusiastically embraced psychedelics, describing tripping as an art. "I've always had the quest and want for something that would raise my consciousness up," he said. "People need to say more about what they're afraid to say, because that's how man discovers. That's science—being able to accept that there's something beyond."[7] While Hall gave the band a philosophical backdrop, Erickson provided its musical focus. Roger Kynard Erickson had been born into a musical family. His mother sang at church and with a local opera group, and his younger brother, Sumner, would become a world-class symphonic tuba player. Roky favored different sounds, especially the powerful screaming of Little Richard and James Brown. "This is meant as a compliment," he said. "[Rock 'n' roll] just *horrified* me."[8] His own voice combined that kind of intensity with the plaintive emotion of another influence, Buddy Holly.

The Elevators built a reputation on powerful live shows and an independent single featuring a new version of "You're Gonna Miss Me," its sinister tone sharply contrasting with the prevailing sentiments of "I Want to Hold Your Hand" and "She Loves You." Erickson's snarled warning to an errant lover is delivered over Sutherland's churning, Duane Eddy-gone-bad guitar and a classic E–D–A–G chord progression second only to "Louie Louie" in garage-rock history. Through it all runs the high-pitched burbling of Hall's "electric" jug. The jug had been a staple of the folk and bluegrass combos of the early '60s. Hall amplified his by holding a microphone close to the opening, but it's likely that as much of the sound came from his voice as the jug. According to Elevators lore, the jug was filled with Hall's pot stash, and Hall drew inspiration for his playing from John Coltrane. In retrospect, his random noises foreshadow the chaotic synthesizers of Roxy Music, the krautrock bands, and Pere Ubu.

The Elevators were signed to Houston's International Artists label by Lelan Rogers, the brother of rocker-turned-country-crooner Kenny Rogers. Kenny's first big hit was in 1968 with a clearly insincere psychedelic ditty, "Just Dropped in (To See What Condition My Condition Was in)." By the end of the '60s, International Artists had a remarkable psychedelic roster including Lost and Found, the Golden Dawn, Bubble

Puppy, and the Red Crayola, which debuted with an extraordinary effort called *The Parable of Arable Land* featuring a guest appearance by Erickson. One of the only things these bands had in common was a long list of complaints about the label and Lelan Rogers, whose business practices doomed most of them to obscurity. Rogers's level of involvement in the Elevators' recordings was marginal. "I didn't produce them, I baby-sat them," he claimed.[9] But despite the fact that it was recorded quickly on three tracks, *The Psychedelic Sounds of the 13th Floor Elevators* is one of rock's most powerful debuts, with sounds that viscerally evoke the lyrical topics at hand.

"The music makes you see things if you want to," Erickson said.[10] Indeed, "Roller Coaster" careers like the amusement park ride. The chorus of "Reverberation (Doubt)" echoes as if bouncing off the walls of a dark cavern; "Splash 1" creates waves of sound like the ripples on a still pond; and "Fire Engine" is propelled by urgent, wailing sirens. These sounds didn't connect with a mass audience, but they did attract the attention of the band's peers. The Rolling Stones later rewrote the Elevators' "Monkey Island" as "Monkey Man," and Pink Floyd lifted the main theme for the *More* soundtrack from "Roller Coaster."

The Elevators' open attitude toward psychedelic drug use was also inspiring. "Recently it has become possible for man to chemically alter his mental state," their liner notes announced. "Kingdom of Heaven" advances the notion that "the kingdom of heaven is within us," waiting to be accessed through psychedelic drugs, while "Fire Engine" pays tribute to DMT, a powerful drug that, when smoked, prompts an intense fifteen-minute trip. "'Let make take you to DMT place,'" Erickson said, quoting the lyrics. "It was like a fire engine without the calamity of a fire."[11]

Not surprisingly, the band attracted the attention of Texas law enforcement. "It was sort of like being in Jesse James's gang," said bassist Danny Galindo, who joined the group in 1967. "We had the cops after us wherever we went."[12] The harassment began to take its toll, but the band recorded a second brilliant release before fracturing. *Easter Everywhere* opens with the eight-minute "Slip Inside This House." Unlike similar efforts by the San Francisco bands, the rhythm and melody never flag as the epic lyric unfolds. "If your limbs begin dissolving / In the water that you tread / All surroundings are evolving / In the stream that clears your head / Find yourself a caravan / Like Noah must have led / And slip inside this house as you pass by," Erickson sings. As on the first album, the psychedelic sounds of songs such as "Slide Machine," "Levitation," and

"Earthquake" perfectly match the lyrics, but there is also a strong soul influence, and the album includes a cover of Bob Dylan's "It's All Over Now, Baby Blue" that's as impressive as any of the Byrds' reworkings.

Shortly after the second album's release, Erickson was busted for pot for the second time. In court, his lawyers called a psychiatrist who said that the singer had taken three hundred LSD trips that had "messed up" his mind, but the strategy backfired. Erickson was acquitted of possession, but the jury declared him insane and the judge sentenced him to Rusk State Mental Hospital, where he was prodded by shock therapy and kept fully stoked on mood-altering drugs. "I was going to jail and so I said, 'Hey, man, I'm seeing things on the wall and I'm hearing voices. I'm crazy, put me away.' So they said, 'Alright, he's crazy,'" Erickson said. "I was such a good actor. When you put your mind to it, you can really convince people, but you gotta be careful. 'Cause at the end of three years, I'm sitting there and they said, 'Hmm, so you're still hearing voices.' And I said, 'No, man, I lied.' And they said, 'Yeah, sure, you lied.'"[13]

Without Erickson, the band fell apart, but that didn't stop International Artists from releasing two more albums. *Bull of the Woods* is comprised of unremarkable Sutherland tunes and three old Erickson songs, while *The 13th Floor Elevators Live* is made up of studio outtakes with crowd noise dubbed in. Sutherland kept playing, but he was shot to death by his wife during a fight in 1978. Hall moved to San Francisco, and when Elevators fan Bill Bentley tracked him down in 1990, he was still taking LSD weekly.

Bearded, bulkier, and no longer the teenaged rock star, Erickson emerged from Rusk in 1972 after a jury declared him legally sane. In 1975 he reappeared on record with the single "Starry Eyes," a touching, romantic piece of Holly-style pop, and "Red Temple Prayer (Two-Headed Dog)," which pairs driving guitar rock with vivid horror-movie imagery. Erickson was now obsessed with monster movies. "The horror of Rusk sort of made fantasy easier to deal with," said his mom, Evelyn.[14]

From the mid-'70s through the mid-'80s, Erickson shuffled between Austin and San Francisco. At one point, he declared himself an alien and had his statement legally notarized. On the cover of his first book, *Openers*, he appointed himself a reverend and presented poems such as "Jesus Is Not a Hallucinogenic Mushroom." Through it all, he played with a succession of bands that appear on a lengthy list of bootlegs and independent releases. The best of these, *Roky Erickson and the Aliens*, was produced by former Creedence Clearwater Revival bassist Stu Cook and released in 1980

Roky Erickson, collecting mail in the '90s. (Photo by Scott Newton.)

by CBS International after the label's U.S. branch passed. The intensity of Erickson's vocals on tunes such as "I Think of Demons," "Don't Shake Me Lucifer," "Bloody Hammer," and "If You Have Ghosts" contrasts with the campiness of the lyrics. "When you're working with Roky, you're basically living B-grade horror movies all day," Cook said. But the fact is, Roky *believed.* "In his fashion, he had come to know the devil the way that Robert Johnson knew the devil, by carrying on daily conversations with him," critic John Morthland wrote.[15]

By 1986 Erickson was reluctant to talk about "the real world" at all. When I spoke to him by phone shortly after the release of *Don't Slander Me*, which was supposed to have been his second release for CBS International, Erickson chatted amiably about horror films such as *Halloween, The Evil Dead,* and *Friday the 13th,* but he dodged every question about music. At one point, he said that "his lady" had just been hit by a car and wanted to say hello. He disappeared, leaving a long stretch of silence before he returned. "Lady just said 'hi,'" he said. It dawned on me that Lady was Roky's dog. Trying to sound nonplussed, I asked what kind of canine she was. "Black," he said. (Of course.) Finally he thanked me for calling, invited me to visit anytime, and indicated that he shared Brian Wilson's belief about dogs picking up good vibrations. "You're a really nice guy," he said. "And Lady liked you."

A short time later, Erickson moved into federally subsidized housing outside Austin and officially retired from the music scene. These days, he surrounds himself with TVs turned up full volume, sometimes with nothing on but static, and waits enthusiastically for each day's mail. In late 1989 he got a little too enthusiastic and was arrested for collecting his neighbors' mail. He was found unfit to stand trial and briefly hospitalized with a diagnosis of organic brain damage and schizophrenia. For years, a large circle in Austin's tight-knit music community has provided Erickson with support and companionship. After the mail trouble, Warner Bros. Records executive Bill Bentley put together a strong tribute album, *Where the Pyramid Meets the Eye: A Tribute to Roky Erickson,* with contributions from fans such as R.E.M., the Jesus and Mary Chain, and Julian Cope. In 1995 Texas music booster Casey

Monahan and Sumner Erickson compiled the book *Openers II* for punk poet Henry Rollins's 2.13.61 imprint, and Monahan and Speedy Sparks midwifed *All That May Do My Rhyme* for the Butthole Surfers' Trance Syndicate label. Half of the songs date from aborted sessions a decade earlier, and all of them were written before the early '80s.

Erickson has lost either the ability or the desire to write new material. As with Syd Barrett and Brian Wilson, the words "acid casualty" precede his name in most rock histories, but this angers people who know him. His art speaks for itself, they say in Austin, and it's wrong for any fan to hang expectations on him. On the other hand, Erickson clearly isn't what anyone would call a productive member of society. "Roky's crazy, but he's also smart enough to kind of use the craziness," said friend and journalist Rob Patterson. "It's a real chicken-or-the-egg thing. He works with it, and he's been able to use it in a way where he just gets to sit around and relax and watch TV." "Roky is one of the funniest—and the laziest—people you ever want to meet," Monahan added. "He doesn't talk about music, but he knows what he's doing."

"I couldn't really care less what people think, and that puts them in a place where they don't have any kind of say-so or control over anything I do," Erickson wrote in 1984.[16] But nothing he ever says or does could be enough to stop fans from wanting a part of him. At South by Southwest in 1995, one hundred fifty people filled the funky Iron Works barbecue next door to the Austin Convention Center to get Erickson's signature on a copy of his new book or album. After a handful of big childlike scrawls, first name only, he quit and headed out to the parking lot. There he signed a few more books, but the scene clearly made him nervous, and finally he left and went home. It was certainly his right, and most of the fans wished him well as he shuffled off. "If you fear I'll lose my spirit / Like a drunkard's wasted wine / Don't you even think about it," he once sang. "I'm feeling fine." And who are we to second-guess him?

And Then My Mind Split Open

Coming here on a trip is bound to make a tremendous difference. But we're here to stimulate a different kind of intoxication. The sounds, the visual stuff—all this bombarding of the senses—it can be very heady in itself, if you're geared to it.

—John Cale, 1966[17]

The band's influence has been cited so many times that it seems to be part of the name: the Seminal Velvet Underground. "There was a direct line from the *Nuggets* groups to the Stooges, the Dolls, and the glitter bands," Lenny Kaye said. "There was an alternative recognized music scene, but the Velvet Underground was certainly the most important band."[18] Producer Brian Eno noted that although the group didn't sell a lot of records in its lifetime, it seemed as if everyone who bought one went out and started a band. In his typically hyperbolic fashion, Lester Bangs went even further. "Modern music begins with the Velvets," he wrote, "and the implications and influence of what they did seem to go on forever."[19] But many of the groups that draw from the Velvets seize upon only one of many elements: the New York street reportage of some of Lou Reed's lyrics or the unedited stream of consciousness of others; the concise, churning rhythm guitars or the startling blasts of feedback and white noise; the desperate, primal aggression or the quiet, painful introspection. The Velvet Underground was a schizophrenic band, and from its most schizophrenic moments come its psychedelic legacy.

The Velvets' best work resulted from the collision of two radically different sensibilities. Reed grew up in a middle-class family on Long Island, and he fell in love with rock 'n' roll as a teenager. Concerned about his fondness for the devil's music and his homosexual tendencies, his parents subjected him to electroshock therapy at age seventeen. At Syracuse University, Reed studied poetry, imitated the excessive ways of his mentor Delmore Schwartz, and cultivated a snotty punk persona. When he was finally kicked out, he wound up back at home, commuting into Manhattan to work as a staff writer at Pickwick Records and churning out imitation Motown and surf singles. In contrast, John Cale was born in Wales and became a child prodigy on the piano. He studied music in London in the early '60s, but instead of the blues that captivated so many of his peers, he was fascinated with the electronic experiments of Karlheinz Stockhausen and John Cage. (The German composer Stockhausen would be an especially significant influence on many psychedelic rockers, who related to the intuitive and often very noisy approach to synthesizers and recording technology in his early '60s work.) In 1963, Cale moved to New York to work with Cage and wound up playing with avant garde musicians and composers Tony Conrad and La Monte Young in the Dream Syndicate, a group whose use of long, trance-inducing drones predated any rock band's embrace of Eastern sounds.

Reed met Cale and Conrad at a party, and he recruited them to play a few gigs as the Primitives, the *nom de rock* behind a quickie Pickwick single called "The Ostrich." The record flopped, but a friendship grew. "It seemed like a very powerful encounter in a sense, each of them moving in a direction which was daring and audacious for the other as well as themselves," Conrad said. "John was moving at a very, very fast pace away from a classical training background through the avant-garde and into performance art and then rock. It was phenomenal for Lou, considering his interest in what would be referred to today as punk— somebody who is really living rock and is interested in an extremely aggressive, assertive position—to discover that classical musicians and avant-garde artists were also engaged in that."[20]

The group slowly came together in an apartment on the Lower East Side. Sterling Morrison was a guitarist that Reed knew from Syracuse. Original drummer Angus MacLise brought Eastern percussion into the mix, but he disliked demands such as having to show up at gigs on time. Maureen Tucker, the sister of another Syracuse buddy, was a last-minute replacement whose powerful backbeat became a key element in the band's sound. (Her tom-heavy approach came from fave raves Bo Diddley and African drummer Olatunji.) The band name was borrowed from the title of a paperback about sadomasochism.

The Velvet Underground was already playing much of what would become its first album when it linked up with Andy Warhol. The pop artist was at the height of his popularity, and expanding into music seemed like a natural move. "The pop idea, after all, was that anybody could do anything, so naturally we were all trying to do it all," he said. "Nobody wanted to stay in one category, we all wanted to branch out into every creative thing we could."[21] Warhol convinced the band to add the platinum-blonde ice princess Nico, and the Velvets began to perform as part of Andy Warhol, Up-Tight, a multimedia show that featured lights, films, and dancing by Factory regulars Gerard Malanga and Edie Sedgwick. The show went on tour as Andy Warhol's Exploding Plastic Inevitable, a swirling psychedelic circus much like Ken Kesey's Acid Tests or the disorienting shows that were starting to be held in the San Francisco ballrooms.

With the exception of the Byrds—whom Reed praised for "Eight Miles High"—the Velvets despised the California rock scene. "People like the Jefferson Airplane and the Grateful Dead are the most untalented bores that ever came up," Reed said.[22] "San Francisco was rigged," Morrison added. "It was like shooting fish in a barrel, the fish being the innocent heads prowling around Haight-Ashbury."[23] As part of Warhol's inner circle, the Velvets certainly had access to LSD, but perhaps because they associated the drug with the West Coast, the musicians distanced themselves from psychedelics even as the Exploding Plastic Inevitable played off people's curiosity about tripping. While the members of the Velvets may have personally preferred recreational use of other drugs (including speed and heroin), rumor held that the peelable Warhol banana on covers of the group's first album were steeped in acid.

By all accounts, Warhol did little to earn his producer's credit on the band's first album, but the connection brought notoriety, the blessing of unhampered creative freedom, and a sense that what the band was doing was *art*. Released in March 1967, almost a year after it was completed, *The Velvet Underground and Nico* was like *Pet Sounds* or *Revolver* in that it used the studio to transport listeners to worlds that they had never visited. The Velvets frequented a much darker world than the Beatles or the Beach Boys: a drug dealer's street corner in Harlem ("I'm Waiting for the Man"); the inner sanctum of a sadomasochistic couple ("Venus in Furs"); the crime-ridden New York subway ("Run, Run, Run"), and the decadent scene of the rich and bored ("All Tomorrow's Parties"). Melodically, the songs are divided between short, catchy "pop" songs and noisy, experimental "art" songs. Contrary to their image as defiant anticommercial revolutionaries, the Velvets were aware of AM radio and tailored the "pop" songs to its specifications, though usually with some twist. The calm and quiet of "Sunday Morning" begs questions about the excesses of Saturday night. Nico's vocals add mystery to "Femme Fatale" and "I'll Be Your Mirror," fragile songs that she sings "in perfect mellow ovals, like a cello getting up in the morning," in the words of Richard Goldstein. On the surface, "There She Goes Again" is a simple rock rewrite of Marvin Gaye's "Hitchhike," but Reed portrays a brutal misogynist whose response to his lover's actions is "better hit her."

The art songs are even more explicit in their depiction of the dark side. Upping the ante on the Byrds and even the 13th Floor Elevators, "Heroin" addresses the experience of shooting up in language that is crystal clear as surging waves of sound evoke the opiate high. Punctuated by Cale's droning viola, "The Black Angel's Death Song" is a powerful evocation of the ultimate bad trip, while the waves of feedback and explosions of noise in "European Son" convey the sheer exhilaration of tearing things down. At one point, Cale scrapes a chair across the floor and shatters a glass. To fathom hell or soar angelic, indeed.

The first album contains the roots of all of the Velvets' future innovations, and the group equaled but never topped it. The first post-Warhol effort, *White Light/White Heat*, extends the noisy experimentation of "The Black Angel's Death Song" and "European Son" to its logical conclusion with the epic cataclysm of "Sister Ray" and the controlled fury of "I Heard Her Call My Name," which features Reed screaming about his mind splitting open before launching into one of rock's most explosive guitar solos. (When it was released, the album title was widely believed to refer to an acid trip instead of the amphetamine rush that Reed intended.) After the album's release, Reed was no longer willing to share the creative reins, and he pushed Cale out of the band. The Velvets' self-titled third album further explored the quiet intimacy of "Sunday Morning," including a touching plea for redemption in "Jesus," while the fourth delivered more straightforward rock in the style of "There She Goes Again." The title was *Loaded* because the band hoped it was loaded with hits, but it was also a dope pun, and the cover art showed a cloud of smoke wafting up from a subway entrance.

The Velvets' greatest talent was striking a balance between the polished beauty of great art and the raw spontaneity of great rock 'n' roll, between the Apollonian and the Dionysian. That balance is something that Reed never really got right again, though his lengthy discography boasts such game attempts as the dramatic 1973 concept album *Berlin;*

The Velvets liked to dress in black. A lot. (Photo by Gerard Malanga.)

the extreme white-noise fuck-you *Metal Machine Music* (1975), and the driven collaboration with Robert Quine, *The Blue Mask* (1982). Cale came closer on grand, stylized efforts such as *Paris 1919;* a trio of albums for Island in the mid-'70s (*Fear, Slow Dazzle,* and *Helen of Troy*), and groundbreaking productions for the Modern Lovers, Patti Smith, and the Stooges. Nico's efforts hold up as spectacularly curious footnotes, though the Cale-Reed contributions to her *Chelsea Girl* (1968) explore some of the terrain left behind after parting with Warhol, and *The Marble Index* (1969) is a masterpiece of purged misery. "Everybody assumes that mind and body are opposed," Bangs wrote in one of his many attempts at the ultimate Velvets eulogy/tribute. "The trog vs. the cerebrite. How boring. But we still buy it, all of us. The Velvet Underground were the greatest band that ever existed because they began to suggest that such was not so."[24]

CHAPTER FOUR

Eight Miles High: Folk Rock Turns Psychedelic

Bob Dylan's enormous influence on mid-'60s rock not only led directly to the birth of folk rock but also inspired the psychedelic rockers who followed. "For all that he had effectively renounced conventional politics, the notion that Dylan embodied—that what he and his expanding coterie believed, what they did, what they *were*, was immeasurably superior to the orthodox culture surrounding them—was a profoundly political and prescient idea," critic Geoffrey Stokes wrote. "It informed the Buffalo Springfield's seminal 'For What It's Worth' and would be at the core of virtually all the important San Francisco music."[1] But while Dylan was in turn inspired to go electric, and some of his lyrics might have shown the influence, his music never went psychedelic. Nor did the sounds from the rest of New York's folk scene. The Lovin' Spoonful was an insipid jug band, and though the Fugs eventually recorded acid-inspired odes to poets William Blake and Algernon Swinburne, they are best remembered as latter-day Beats howling about sex and speed on primitive master-

Dylan never went psychedelic.

pieces such as "Coca-Cola Douche" and "New Amphetamine Shriek." The merger of folk rock and psychedelia made its most lasting impact elsewhere—in Los Angeles, San Francisco, and London.

I'd Be Safe and Warm If I Was in L.A.

The sound of the airplane in the '40s was a 'Roaaah!' sound, and Sinatra and other people sang like that with those sorts of overtones. Now we've got the 'Krishhh' jet sound, and all the kids are singing up in there now. It's the mechanical sounds of the era: The sounds are different and so the music is different.

—James (Roger) McGuinn, 1965[2]

Like a lot of groups in the '60s, the Byrds could pinpoint the exact moment that changed their musical styles, careers, and lives. As a teenager in his native Chicago, McGuinn studied at the Old Town School of Folk Music. After touring with the Limelighters and the Chad Mitchell Trio, he moved to the folk capital of the world, Greenwich Village, but he soon found the New York folk scene too rigid. In late 1963 he moved to Los Angeles and started playing at the Troubadour folk club, where he met Gene Clark and David Crosby. A native of rural Missouri, Clark had been a member of the New Christy Minstrels. Crosby belonged to a Hollywood film family—his father was the cinematographer on *High Noon*—and he had done time in Les Baxter's Balladeers. On an off night, the three went to see *A Hard Day's Night*, and the staid folk world suddenly seemed a lot less appealing.

Sharp and cynical, McGuinn has always admitted that the Byrds were formed to ape the Beatles and achieve rock stardom, in that order. "The Beatles came out and changed the whole game for me," he said. "I saw a definite niche where the folk sensibility and rock-'n'-roll energy blended together. If you took John Lennon and Bob Dylan and mixed them together, that was something that hadn't been done before."[3] The group was completed by Chris Hillman, a bluegrass guitarist and mandolin player who bought his first bass for thirty-five dollars, and Crosby's friend, conga player Michael Clarke. Clarke had never even sat behind a real drum set, but he did have a shaggy blond haircut that mirrored Brian Jones's, and that was enough.

The Byrds spent much of 1964 woodshedding at World Pacific Studios with producer and benefactor Jim Dickson, best known for his work with the bluegrass group the Dillards. "We were rehearsing eight hours a day for months and months in this old Hollywood studio, and we just developed that sound and style from nothing," Hillman said.[4] But he wasn't entirely correct: McGuinn acquired an electric twelve-string Rickenbacker because George Harrison used one in *A Hard Day's Night.* (Played with a combination of finger- and flat-picking, the strings he *didn't* play resonated in sympathy, adding the distinctive harmonic drone or "jangle.") Crosby crafted the band's vocal harmonies, reaching back past the Beatles to one of their inspirations, the Everly Brothers. And the song that became the Byrds' first hit came not from the group's three songwriters but from Dylan.

The Byrds weren't thrilled by the idea of covering Dylan's "Mr. Tambourine Man." McGuinn had known Dylan in the Village and was turned off by what he called his "mind games." But Dickson had stirred interest at Columbia Records; he insisted that the band needed a strong single, and the fact that Dylan was signed to Columbia couldn't hurt. The group was beginning to get a taste of stardom courtesy of a regular gig at Ciro's, and they weren't about to derail Dickson's plans. They didn't even complain when most of them were replaced in the studio by session musicians, a common practice at the time. In the hands of the studio Byrds, Dylan's sarcasm disappears and "Mr. Tambourine Man" becomes an invitation to a party. "On the heels of his 'don't follow leaders' message, the song assumes an ironic glow: Dylan is himself the 'Mr. Tambourine Man' whom people are looking to follow," wrote critic Tim Riley. "Like a Day-Glo painting dipped in glitter, the Byrds' version seduces you into the Tambourine Man's con and misses the art of the con in the process."[5]

Dickson was replaced by Columbia staff producer Terry Melcher on the Byrds' first two albums, *Mr. Tambourine Man* and *Turn! Turn! Turn!* "They remain the definitive folk-rock albums, charged with a giddy effervescence," critic David Fricke wrote.[6] They also remain faithful to the formula of the Byrds' first hit. More chart successes followed, but in their rapid ascent, the Byrds were starting to fly too high. They were using speed to keep up with their schedule and marijuana to chill out in the off moments. "A connoisseur of grass, Crosby was the first man in anyone's experience who could hold forth on weed the way oenophiles go on about wine," wrote biographer Carl Gottlieb.[7]

Always the Beatest Byrd, Crosby was the first to try LSD, and he shared his enthusiasm with his band mates. Crosby was also fascinated with Indian culture, an interest that may have started when he played with Les Baxter, an ethnomusicologist who wrote some of Martin Denny's best cocktail-lounge exotica. Dickson later introduced Crosby to sitar master Ravi Shankar, and Crosby came to consider Shankar and free-jazz saxophonist John Coltrane "the finest musicians on the planet." Crosby bombarded his fellow Byrds with Shankar and Coltrane music as the group toured the south in a van in late 1965, and the influences are obvious on the band's fifth single. "Eight miles high, and when you touch down / You'll find that it's stranger than known," the group sings. McGuinn maintained that the tune wasn't about drugs, but about a 1965 flight to London on which Clark nearly had a nervous breakdown because of his acute fear of flying. (McGuinn, a devoted fan of jets and airplanes, couldn't have been less sympathetic.) The song was banned by radio regardless. The lyrics may be ambiguous, but there is no denying the psychedelic sound. After the ominous opening bass line, McGuinn launches into an explosive free-form solo while Clarke plays fast and loose with the beat. The song's only anchor is the reassuring three-part harmony, but the friendly naïveté of earlier Byrds singles is replaced with a sarcastic sneer. On "Eight Miles High" the Byrds finally capture the tone of Dylan's original "Mr. Tambourine Man."

The group continued exploring varied psychedelic sounds. Ornate and orchestrated, 1966's *Fifth Dimension* includes the enchanting ballad "I See You" and McGuinn's country-flavored science-fiction novelty "Mr. Spaceman." Released in 1967, *Younger Than Yesterday* is a sparer effort noteworthy for the driving raga "Why?", Hillman's mysterious "Thoughts and Words," and McGuinn's effects-laden "CTA-102," another tale of life on other planets. But the creative forces in the Byrds were pulling apart. Gene Clark left the group in 1966. The tension between songwriters continued, and Crosby was fired after *Younger Than Yesterday*. The Byrds shifted gears as the group fell firmly into the control of Roger McGuinn. (In late 1966 McGuinn joined the Moslem subsect of Subud and changed his first name. He converted again to Christianity in 1969 but kept the name Roger.)

Many critics perceived the jangly but bitter "So You Want to Be a Rock 'n' Roll Star" as McGuinn's farewell to rock. Released in 1968 and 1969, *The Notorious Byrd Brothers*, *Sweetheart of the Rodeo*, *Dr. Byrds and Mr. Hyde*, and *The Ballad of Easy Rider* paved the way for the country-rock explosion of the early '70s. "The Byrds were the first acid rockers, the first head rockers, the first message rockers, and, of course, the first outer-space rockers," critic Lillian Roxon wrote. "It's no wonder that by the time everyone else caught up with it all, they lapsed happily back into the country sound that had been in their music all along."[8]

McGuinn finally disbanded the Byrds in 1973. After several uneven solo releases, he was on the verge of becoming an oldies act, but he returned to form in 1991 after a fourteen-year break from recording. *Back From Rio* is the most Byrdsy of any Byrds solo effort, but it was generally ignored. "You still need the hair, you still need the pants, and you still need the guitar," McGuinn said, paraphrasing his recipe for stardom. "Just different hair, different pants, and a different guitar."[9]

The Byrds' early success prompted a wave of folk rock on the L.A. scene, including Sonny and Cher, the Turtles, and the Left Banke. Barry McGuire had played with Clark in the New Christy Minstrels, and he copied Dylan's lyrics and the Byrds' sound on his "Eve of Destruction." The Mamas and the Papas released the cheerfully transcendent "California Dreamin'." After relocating from Portland, Paul Revere and the Raiders scored a hit with the anti-drug tune "Kicks." The members of the American Kaleidoscope were genuine folkies and talented multi-instrumentalists who pioneered an early blend of psychedelia and world beat, and the Peanut Butter Conspiracy debuted in 1967 with a sound that was similar to the San Francisco bands' but more focused and melodic. Tim Buckley remained in the folk realm, though his image-filled excursions were clearly influenced by the burgeoning psychedelic sub-culture (as well as his heroin addiction). The Buffalo Springfield came closest to psyche-delic rock on Stephen Stills's eerie "For What It's Worth," which was inspired by a police riot on the Sunset Strip, and Neil Young's fuzz-driven "Mr. Soul." But after McGuinn, Crosby, and Co., L.A.'s most important psy-chedelic rock band was Love.

Love thrived on the combination of two mismatched songwriters. Born in Memphis, singer Arthur Lee was raised in L.A.'s tough Crenshaw neighborhood. Strongly influenced by Mick Jagger, he presented what Lillian Roxon called "an amusing paradox," an African American singing like a white Englishman singing like an old African Ameri-

Cooler than you'll ever be: Love; Arthur Lee, second from left.

can. His partner Bryan MacLean was the son of a Hollywood architect who swam in Elizabeth Taylor's pool. His first girlfriend was Liza Minnelli, and he was raised on classical music and Broadway standards. "You hear more of my influence on Arthur than his influence on me," MacLean said. "What you have [in Love] is a black guy from L.A. writing show tunes."[10] There were also heaping doses of the Beatles circa *Rubber Soul* and folk rock via the Byrds. (Lee originally linked up with MacLean because MacLean was a Byrds roadie and Lee thought he was likely to draw their crowd.)

Love debuted in 1966 with a self-titled album that opens with a snarling, speed-freak version of "My Little Red Book," a Burt Bacharach–Hal David tune from the soundtrack to *What's New Pussycat?* Several songs are steeped in drug imagery, including "Signed D.C.," a warning against heroin use, the foreboding "Mushroom Clouds," and the expansive "Colored Balls Falling." The album also boasts a cover of "Hey Joe" inspired by the Byrds' rendition but much punkier. (The Leaves later copied Love's version and scored a major hit.) Like the Byrds, Love worked hard to present a hipper-than-thou image, and the album cover features the quintet scowling like angry young poets posing before a broken-down chimney in a fire-gutted mansion that was said to have belonged to Hollywood's Dracula, Bela Lugosi.

The cover of *Da Capo*, released in 1967, shows the expanded sextet back at the same site, but the baroque sounds are a major leap forward. "7 and 7 Is" builds on an even more rollicking version of the beat that propelled "My Little Red Book." MacLean contributes the timeless "Orange Skies," and Lee delivers his best vocal. The title of the ballad "She Comes in Colors" was borrowed by the Stones in "She's a Rainbow," but Lee wasn't being metaphoric. (He said the tune is about making love to a woman who has her period.) Lee's raunchy side also comes through on the epic "Revelation," which was produced by an uncredited Neil Young. At the time, the bluesy, nineteen-minute jam was the longest rock track ever released. "I believe we did that long tune out of laziness," MacLean said. "But Arthur claims it was an innovation."[11]

Hip to the streets, Lee never fully bought into the hippie ideal. MacLean said that Lee made taking LSD a religious experience, but while the band was making gentle, idyllic music, Lee's impressionistic lyrics were often lampooning psychedelic culture. ("The snot has caked against my pants," is a memorable line from the band's third album.) Lee managed the group himself, but his tactics were far from egalitarian. "He was the tough guy from the neighborhood; that was the only reason he was the leader," MacLean said. Lee's decisions not to tour or play certain gigs cost the band dearly. "When we didn't do Monterey Pop, that was when we missed the train."[12]

By 1968, Love was starting to suffer from drug problems. Lee contends that prejudice also kept the band from the heights achieved by some of its label mates. "I wasn't gonna go eat garbage like the Doors did," Lee said. "And then, too, I wasn't white. The cold fact of the matter is birds of a feather flock together."[13] When Love recorded *Forever Changes*, Lee was convinced that his life and his career were coming to an end. (The back cover shows the singer standing with a cracked vase full of dead flowers.) But although the album is the last collaboration between Lee and MacLean, it's their most cohesive effort. The group recorded acoustically, sitting in a circle as if jamming in the living room, and the tracks were augmented later with tasteful orchestrations. MacLean presents two quiet and beautiful tunes, "Alone Again Or" and "Old Man," and Lee explores his psyche on "The Red Telephone," which builds from a quiet ballad to a paranoid nursery rhyme. "They're locking him up today / They're throwing away the key / I wonder who it will be tomorrow / You or me?" he chants. "We're all normal and we want our freedom," another voice responds.

Lee's failure to produce much worthwhile music after 1968 has prompted some critics to put him in a class with Syd Barrett, Brian Wilson, and Roky Erickson. After MacLean left the band, Love made one more album for Elektra, 1969's *Four Sail*, but Lee was the only band member left. *False Start* was noteworthy only for a guest appearance by Lee's friend Jimi Hendrix. With the exception of occasional reunion shows, Lee dropped out of sight after 1972's *Vindicator*. (He and MacLean both became born-again Christians, but that didn't bring them closer.) MacLean continues to write, and his songs have been covered by Debby Boone, Patty Loveless, and his sister, Maria McKee. Lee resurfaced in 1992 with an album on the French New Rose label, and he toured the United States in 1994. Fans listened politely to his new tunes but saved their enthusiasm for the older material, especially songs from *Forever Changes*.

"*Forever Changes* were my last words of Love," Lee said in 1981. "My last words to the world, only I've been here ever since. Just like a guy saying goodbye, and you look out your front door and he's still there fifteen years later."[14]

If You're Going to San Francisco, Be Sure to Wear Flowers in Your Hair

You who stand, sit, and crawl around and about the floor, about you and above you, on the ceiling—that madness that's running in color is your brain!
                                    —Ken Kesey at the San Francisco State Trips Festival, 1966[15]

Like the musicians in L.A., the players who drew national attention to San Francisco in 1966 and 1967 all had roots in the folk scene. Jerome Garcia played bluegrass banjo in Palo Alto coffeehouses, Paul Kantner sang at hootenannies, and Marty Balin owned the Matrix, a Fillmore Street folk club. The Jefferson Airplane's first manager tried to coin the word "fojazz" from "folk" and "jazz" to describe their sound. "Most of the rock musicians in San Francisco were basically folkies learning how to play electrified instruments," Charles Perry wrote in his definitive history *The Haight-Ashbury*. "They had a tentative sound at first and played a lot of solemn, chiming chords on the beat. When it came time for the guitarist to take a solo break, he often noodled up and down the notes of the scale in a way that might owe as much to inexperience in improvisation as it did to the influence of Indian ragas."[16]

The musicians were quick to emphasize the distinctions between the bands, but the San Francisco groups did have some common traits. One was the absence of driving rock beats. Bill Kreutzmann of the Grateful Dead was one of the few genuine drummers—most of the other groups had former folk guitarists in the percussion seat—and the rhythms tended to shuffle or percolate rather than propel. The bands shared a fondness for Chicago blues via the Rolling Stones, and they embraced the Paul Butterfield Blues Band when it came to town for a three-night stand in March 1966. (Many drew inspiration from that group's epic "East-West," a raga-inspired piece that guitarist Mike Bloomfield wrote while listening to Ravi Shankar during an LSD trip.) Of course, there was also a common fascination with LSD, which flooded the scene courtesy of Augustus Owsley Stanley. "The San Francisco 'sound' was less a musical phenomenon than a manner," Perry wrote. "It was premised on the simple and straightforward assumption that this was trip music being played by dopers for other dopers."[17]

These dopers were essentially a new class of rich Beatniks. The first-generation Beats coined the word "hippies" as a derisive term to describe kids who were living on their parents' money or cash from dealing pot.

"Dealing wasn't work, really, and by doing what came naturally to them, hippies found money raining down upon them," Perry wrote. "They spent it on mod or antique or handmade clothes, or on toys or Navajo jewelry or Persian rugs."[18] They backed a new class of stores on Haight Street—*their* stores—but mostly they supported the bands at dances in old ballrooms such as the Avalon and the Fillmore. By 1967, these places were as famous as any of the bands, and so were some of the characters behind the scenes. Bill Graham was the prototype for the frantic, bullying promoter who was also obsessed with good sound and great music. Chet Helms and the Family Dog sponsored dances with fanciful names such as "A Tribute to Dr. Strange," and Ken Kesey and the Merry Pranksters moved the Acid Tests down from the hills into the city. Stanley Mouse, Rick Griffin, Victor Moscoso, and others defined a style of psychedelic poster art, and by 1968, there were five hundred people working with psychedelic light shows such as Bill Ham's, Roy's Audioptics, and the Holy See.

"The important thing about San Francisco rock 'n' roll is that the bands here all sing and play live and not for recordings," said Ralph Gleason, the jazz-turned-rock critic for the *San Francisco Chronicle*. "You get a different sound at a dance; it's harder and more direct."[19] In other words, you really had to be there. The recorded legacy simply doesn't support the scene's vaunted psychedelic-rock reputation.

Most musical histories start with the Charlatans, a group whose stretched-out blues tunes were as old-timey as their Western costumes. Though they were the first band on the scene, they didn't release their self-titled debut until 1969, and by then, founder George Hunter and much of the spirit were gone. The first band to make an impact *outside* San Francisco was Sopwith Camel, a campy folk outfit that scored a hit in 1967 with "Hello Hello," but the band was quickly and justly forgotten.

The Jefferson Airplane made its debut in 1966 with an album of Balin's simple ballads tarted up by the dexterous playing of bassist Jack Cassady and guitarist Jorma Kaukonen. Great Society vocalist Grace Slick replaced Signe Anderson on 1967's *Surrealistic Pillow*, and the album's best songs came from Slick's old band. "Somebody to Love" was written by Slick's brother-in-law during a depressing LSD trip while he waited for his girlfriend to come home, and "White Rabbit" was a tribute to Lewis Carroll's *Alice's Adventures in Wonderland*. Both succeed because of Slick's soaring vocals. The Airplane followed with two albums of failed experiments. *After Bathing at Baxter's* (1967) is a pastiche of song fragments and long, unfocused "suites," including the tedious "Ballad of You and Me and Pooneil." *Crown of Creation* (1968) introduces Kantner's thematic obsession with science fiction, but the only standout is Slick's version of David Crosby's homage to threesomes, "Triad." More noteworthy is 1969's *Volunteers.* Critic Paul Evans described it as "a summing up of psychedelia," a rousing call to political activism in the face of failed utopianism. Balin left after *Volunteers,* and the feuding factions—Kantner and Slick versus Cassady and Kaukonen—fought for control. In time, the Airplane became the Starship, a group committed only to commercialism. Cynics pointed out the seeds were there ever since the Airplane recorded a commercial for Levi's jeans in 1967.

The Grateful Dead had been a fixture on the scene since it performed under its earlier guise as the Warlocks at Kesey's Acid Tests. By the time the group made its recorded debut in 1967, many Haight residents were sporting buttons that read, "Good Ol' Grateful Dead." Recorded in a three-day amphetamine blur, *The Grateful Dead* is a bluesy folk effort that tries unsuccessfully to impose structure on the band's live improvisations. "They didn't, as might be expected, play what we now call acid or psychedelic rock, but instead produced fine, strong, straightforward traditional blues," Roxon wrote.[20] The band expanded in 1968 with the addition of second drummer Mickey Hart, a player well versed in ethnic rhythms, and keyboardist Tom Constanten, an avant-garde musician inspired by John Cage and Karlheinz Stockhausen. Owsley knew as much about sound as chemistry, and he and Dan Healy recorded the band at every stop on a Northwest tour. The result was *Anthem of the Sun,* an album compiled with hundreds of edits from fourteen different performances. The sprawling, improvised collage has moments of hypnotic beauty, but it's ultimately a compromise, neither a spontaneous live document nor a consistent studio creation.

Aoxomoxoa (1969) returned to more familiar song structures and marked the Dead's first collaboration with Beat poet and lyricist Robert Hunter, a friend of Garcia's from the folkie days in Palo Alto. "St. Stephen" is a shuffling hippie anthem with a pretty psychedelic bridge, and "Rosemary" is a delicate ballad with a creepy phased vocal. But the Dead didn't really come into its own on album until a trio of 1970 releases. *Live Dead* introduced the moody jazz excursion "Dark Star," while *Workingman's Dead* and *American Beauty* are melodic, stripped-down efforts with harmonies crafted by David Crosby and lyrics that try to find common ground between the reality of life in America and the fantasies of the psychedelic ideal. The albums boast some of the Dead's best tunes— "Sugar Magnolia," "Uncle John's Band," "Casey Jones," and "Truckin'"— but they are modern folk music, not psychedelic rock.

Of the other San Francisco bands, Big Brother and the Holding Company played clunky blues elevated by the soulful voice of Texan Janis Joplin. (Joplin moved to San Francisco after an offer to join the 13th Floor Elevators as second vocalist fell through.) Downing Southern Comfort, she fashioned herself after blues belters like Bessie Smith and Willie Mae Thornton, and she joked that her music was "alkydelic." Country Joe and the Fish were a jug band best remembered for their antiwar songs ("Feel-Like-I'm-Fixin'-to-Die Rag") and the "F-U-C-K" cheer. Quicksilver Messenger Service was long on meandering jams featuring fluid lead guitarist John Cipollina, but it was short on solid rhythmic drive and strong songwriting; its most impressive numbers, live and on record, were borrowed from Bo Diddley ("Mona" and "Who Do You Love") and Buffy Sainte-Marie (the addict's lament, "Codine"). Santana merged South American rhythms and psychedelic jamming, distancing itself early on from its initial garage-rock edge. And the Steve Miller Band used psychedelic sound effects to decorate its blues before shifting toward a slicker and sleaker sound.

With tight harmonies, a layered three-guitar sound, and an exuberant spirit, Moby Grape rocked harder than its peers, but the band members were victims of too much hype, overindulgence, bad management, and bad luck. The quintet's self-titled debut might have scored a hit with the rollicking "Omaha" if Columbia Records hadn't seized on the gimmick of releasing five singles at once. Rock fans resented this and other crass promotional stunts, and the company started resenting the band after three members were busted with underage girls the morning after their record-release party. The band's second album, *Wow*, was recorded in New York using strings and horns to mask a lack of inspiration and a deteriorating situation. Guitarist-vocalist Skip Spence was living with a practicing witch and ingesting too much acid, and he was committed to Bellevue Hospital after attacking drummer Don Stevenson with an ax. "He was a visionary," Stevenson said. "And what happened was he broke through."[21]

The group stumbled on without its best songwriter until splitting up in 1969. Spence went on to make a weird psychedelic country record in Nashville, 1969's *Oar*, before dropping out of sight. When Johnny Angel tracked him down for the *L.A. Weekly* in 1994, he was a diagnosed schizophrenic living in a residential care facility in San Jose, scraping by on an allowance of a dollar a day provided by Santa Clara County.

After a visit in 1967, New York critic Richard Goldstein wrote that it would "be interesting to visit the Bay Area when the breadmen have gutted every artery, to watch the Fillmore become the Radio City Music Hall of pop music, to take a Greyhound sightseeing tour through the Haight."[22] All of these things came to pass, but even more problematic was the flood of heroin and an increase in violent crime that started shortly after the Summer of Love. Like the residents of Seattle in the early '90s, San Franciscans blamed the media and big business for ruining their scene, but the roots of its undoing were there from the beginning. Novelist Bill Craddock joked that the unspoken conclusion of Timothy Leary's "Turn on, tune in, drop out" was "Freak out, fuck up, crawl back." The same week in December 1969 that a free concert at the Altamont Raceway ended in murder, a grand jury in L.A. was investigating former Haight resident Charles Manson for a series of ritualistic murders committed by the young followers whom he brainwashed with psychedelic drugs and messianic preaching. "The real dead end," Perry wrote, "was the dream that this was a blessed generation, immune to the darkness of the heart that has always caused violence and oppression."[23]

Minotaur Songs in the Season of the Witch

Earth water fire and air / Met together in a garden fair / Put in a basket bound with skin / If you answer this riddle, you'll never begin.
> —The Incredible String Band, "Koeeoaddi There"

In Britain, Bert Jansch and John Renbourn were the urban folkies who paved the way for the first wave of English folk rock. Like Dylan, they provided a link between folk, the Beats, and the blues, and they eventually went electric with the jazzy quintet Pentangle. But there was an added dimension in their music, a whimsical style of storytelling and a timelessness in the gentle melodies. America had musical traditions that went back generations, but the folklore of the British Isles was measured in centuries.

Born in Glasgow, Donovan Leitch was raised in Hatfield, England, but he had an abiding fascination with his Celtic heritage. When he first won attention in 1965 with appearances on the TV show *Ready Steady Go,* he was positioned as the British Dylan. Dylan laid waste to that idea when the two met, a moment captured in D. A. Pennebaker's film *Don't Look Back,* but it was never a fair match. Dylan was sharp, cynical, and serious where Donovan was carefree, naive, and happy to deliver jolly psychedelic melodies. Initially a straight arrow, Donovan sampled some of Michael Hollingshead's LSD in 1966, an experience that inspired his most lovable work. The single "Sunshine Superman" is a jazzed-up skiffle tune that captures the teenage tripper's sense of indomitablity ("Superman and Green Lantern ain't got nothing on me"). Crafted by new producer Mickie Most, the album that followed later in 1966 contains the cheerfully creepy "Season of the Witch" and a tribute to Jansch called "Bert's Blues."

Donovan's next hit was the brassy 1967 single "Mellow Yellow," which features horns arranged by John Paul Jones and a whispered chorus by Paul McCartney. The tune was inspired by the rumor that you could get high smoking dried banana peels. (Around the same time, Donovan wrote "Super Lungs My Supergirl," a tune that was shelved because of the controversial connotations of the line "She's only fourteen but she knows how to draw.") In addition to Jones, soon-to-be Zeppelinites Jimmy Page and John Bonham contributed to 1968's "Hurdy Gurdy Man," Donovan's wonderful, rhythmically shifting answer to "Mr. Tambourine Man." Almost as good is "Atlantis," a hypnotic, circular tribute to the lost continent with an unintentionally hilarious spoken-word intro. But Donovan started to lose it in 1969 when he released *Barabajagal,* a flaccid collaboration with the Jeff Beck Group. The singer took up with the Maharishi, moved to the Irish countryside, ran out of memorable melodies, and, in the words of critic Paul Nelson, "floated away into the lilac mist."

More influential were the folk-rock sounds recorded by transplanted American Joe Boyd. A talent scout for Elektra Records and the promoter of the psychedelic rock club UFO, Boyd came to England from Harvard University, where he knew acid acolyte Richard Alpert and followed the work of Timothy Leary. "It's important to remember that both in the early '60s and in the '80s, taking acid did not necessarily mean that you liked things in Day-Glo and paisley," Boyd said. "It was an awareness of a social context more than anything else, and it linked you to certain types of people who were interested in certain types of things." Boyd produced Fairport Convention's 1968 debut after he saw guitarist

Richard Thompson deliver a mindblowing version of "East-West" at the UFO Club. Drawing heavily on the Byrds, Fairport added a Scottish-Irish accent and Sandy Denny's voice, a powerful instrument that surpassed even Grace Slick's. But the band never fully embraced psychedelia, and Boyd described the musicians as "seventeen-year-old kids from Muswell Hill who had hardly ever seen a cigarette."

The otherworldly vibe in the music of Nick Drake came from deep within the artist himself. An awkward, lonely college student, Drake expressed himself freely only when he was playing his songs around Cambridge. His first album, *Five Leaves Left* (1969), is the tentative work of a twenty-year-old musician, but Boyd called 1970's *Bryter Layter* the one perfect album he's produced. The songs feature a jazzy, R&B feel similar to *Astral Weeks,* Van Morrison's spiritual masterpiece, and they boast fine playing by Thompson, Dave Mattacks, and Dave Pegg of Fairport as well as John Cale, who had recently left the Velvet Underground. Drake sank into a deep depression after *Bryter Layter* and was barely able to speak by the time he recorded *Pink Moon* in 1972, but the latter stands as his best album. The songs offer an intimate look into the soul of a deeply troubled individual struggling to find a reason for living. Shortly after their release, Drake died of a drug overdose.

The most psychedelic of the artists on Boyd's roster or anywhere else in England were the members of the Incredible String Band. The group was formed in 1965 by three Scottish musicians, guitarist-vocalists Clive Palmer, Robin Williamson, and Mike Heron. Their self-titled 1966 debut hints at the promise of things to come, but it's hesitant in embracing the ethnic sounds that later became a staple of the band's mix. "I started off doing Scottish and Irish music," Williamson said. "But I also liked the visionary writing of Americans like Walt Whitman and Jack Kerouac, and those two opposites caused me to go and search for a common root to world music. I went to North Africa in 1963 to learn more about the music there, and I got interested in Indian music from the tremendous wave of immigrants entering Britain at that time. The notion of fusion music wasn't a word used in 1963 when we started doing it. We just thought it would be a good idea."[24]

Williamson was the folkie and Heron the rocker. The two forces were balanced by Palmer, but between the first and second albums, Palmer went off to Morocco and didn't return. "Mike and Robin were each friends of Clive but not of each other," Boyd said. "It was like they'd both come to Clive's party and he'd left. There they were with each other, and they didn't like each other. They hated each other." The rivalry wasn't even quelled by a shared enthusiasm for LSD, but somehow the pair produced beautiful, pastoral music. Williamson's distinctive, wide-ranging vocals take some getting used to—they slither and slide around a melody like an eel swimming through the reeds—but the duo's over-dubbed orchestrations are truly impressive. (Together Williamson and Heron played some forty instruments.) Their tunes sink into your subconscious, and the whimsy of the lyrics approaches Whitman's sunny optimism without being laughable.

Robin Williamson plays harp.

Released in 1967, *The 5000 Spirits or the Layers of the Onion* features a psychedelic cover painted by The Fool—the artists who decorated John Lennon's psychedelic Rolls-Royce—and a lusher, more mysterious sound than the debut. But *The Hangman's Beautiful Daughter* is the band's finest moment. The lyrics of "The Minotaur's Song" and "Koeeoaddi There" evoke classical myths and pagan rituals, while the mini-symphony "A Very Cellular Song" deals with the acid-trip revelation that all living beings are interconnected. Even more than the lyrics, it's the quality of the strange and exotic sounds that creates what Evans called "a free-form spiritual buzz." "Initially, we were just having fun discovering what you could do with a multitrack machine," Boyd said. "Of course, each one had to impose their personality on the other one's songs. They wouldn't allow a song to join the repertoire unless they could make it their own—Mike playing sitar on Robin's songs, and Robin singing harmonies on Mike's songs."

After *Hangman's*, Williamson and Heron were joined by their girl-friends, Christina "Licorice" McKechnie and Rose Simpson. (This electrified lineup played a little-remembered set at Woodstock.) The two songwriters continued trying to outdo each other with wilder and more elaborate arrangements on the double album, *Wee Tam and the Big Huge,* but over the next few releases, invention gave way to indulgence. "One of the reasons for the decline was that they stopped hating each other," Boyd claimed. "They all became Scientologists, and Scientology taught them to like each other." The band forged ahead through various permutations, outliving Williamson's and Heron's relationships with

McKechnie and Simpson, until calling it quits in 1974. Heron made several solo albums, including *Smiling Men With Bad Reputations*, which features backing by most of the Who. Williamson continues to tour as a folk artist and Celtic storyteller. Both agree that the first four of the String Band's nine years were the best.

"There was an inspired amateurism in those days, a feeling that anybody could play music, that anybody could play a lot of different instruments," Williamson said. "Mike and I were radically different characters, and I think that inspired the creativity of the band. Mike was inspired by rock-'n'-roll music, and I was interested in folk music and poetry. Now we have both reverted to type."[25]

CHAPTER FIVE

Pipers at the Gates of Dawn: The Pink Floyd

Sudden and magnificent, the sun's broad golden disc showed itself over the horizon facing them, and the first rays, shooting across the level water-meadows, took the animals full in the eyes and dazzled them. When they were able to look once more, the Vision had vanished, and the air was full of the carol of birds that hailed the dawn.

—Kenneth Grahame, *The Wind in the Willows*[1]

In 1964 the founding members of the longest-running psychedelic rock band were 4 of the 120,000 middle-class art students in fifty-nine colleges spread across England. Rick Wright, Roger Waters, and Nick Mason met while studying architecture at Regent Street Polytechnic. They played together in a succession of bad R&B bands with awful names (the T-Set, the Meggadeaths, and the Architectural Abdabs) before linking up with Roger "Syd" Barrett, a nineteen-year-old painter who lived in the same apartment building as Waters. Both grew up in Cambridge, where Barrett learned to play guitar with his future replacement, David Gilmour. Barrett named the band after two blues heroes, Pink Anderson and Floyd Council, and the group played its first gig in late 1965.

Pink Floyd biographer Nicholas Schaffner noted that the band members were different from earlier art-students-turned-rockers (including John Lennon, Pete Townshend, and Eric Clapton) because they were members of rock's third generation, "just young enough to have been drawn into rock 'n' roll as much by the Beatles and the Rolling Stones as by first-generation stars like Buddy Holly or Elvis Presley." When the Floyd started, the Byrds had already scored a hit with "Mr. Tambourine Man" and the Beatles were recording *Rubber Soul.* "A new sophistication and self-consciousness was already well established in pop music," Schaffner wrote. "Unlike previous art school rock 'n' rollers, the band Syd made famous conceived their music as *art* virtually from day one."[2]

Like many of the early British psychedelic bands, Pink Floyd started out playing R&B to audiences of drunken college students who wanted to dance. "We were interested in the R&B revival, but we never had the abilities along those lines," Mason said. "In fact, if the Summer of Love and the underground never would have happened, I don't think we would have passed the starting point." The psychedelic rock of the Beatles, the Byrds, and Love inspired the Floyd to expand its horizons. "I was trying to tell Syd about this Arthur Lee song I couldn't remember the title of, so I just hummed the main riff," recalled the group's first manager, Peter Jenner. "Syd picked up his guitar, followed what I was humming, and went on to use the chord pattern he worked out for 'Interstellar Overdrive.' "[3]

Starting in the spring of 1966, the Floyd's outer-space excursions were launched from its slot as house band at Spontaneous Underground, mixed-media events at the Marquee Club that were similar to the happenings in San Francisco. "Initially, I never saw the Floyd as individuals. I saw them as part of an avant-garde movement that was happening in London," said Barry Miles, founder of the underground newspaper *International Times.*[4] Among the movement's catalysts was the now readily available LSD. The psychedelic influence became apparent in the Floyd's music as songs were extended into lengthy explorations of feedback and echoed effects, and the band took up a residency at the UFO, the new psychedelic rock club booked by Joe Boyd. The British psychedelic-rock scene coalesced here around regular performances by Tomorrow, the Crazy World of Arthur Brown, and the Soft Machine, but the Floyd was always the crowd's favorite. Elektra Records passed when Boyd suggested that the company sign the Floyd, but the group secured a contract with EMI, and Boyd produced its first single in early 1967.

Hesitant to tailor the band's onstage jams to fit the singles format, Barrett eventually responded to the opportunity by crafting a brilliant pop song, "Arnold Layne," perhaps the catchiest song ever about transvestism. Over a driving bass and upbeat organ, Barrett's soaring vocals tell the story of a lad with a penchant for stealing women's underwear from Cambridge clotheslines. English bluenoses attacked it as smut, and some rock critics dismiss it as judgmental because it ends with Arnold in jail, admonished not to do it again. But the song's most effective hook is the line "It takes two to know," and Barrett certainly sings with empathy. In colorful finery from the Granny Takes a Trip boutique, the members of the Floyd didn't look much different than Arnold when he was all dolled up. "Arnold Layne just happens to dig dressing up in women's clothing. A lot of people do, so let's face up to reality," is how Barrett addressed the subject.[5] The BBC wasn't appeased, and the song was banned but became a hit anyway. There was just as much controversy over the single's B side, a jaunty throwaway called "Let's Roll Another One," which was retitled "Candy and a Currant Bun" after censors objected to the obvious marijuana reference.

For subsequent projects, EMI insisted that Pink Floyd work with staff producer Norman Smith, an engineer who won the nickname Normal when he was working with George Martin and the Beatles. (He adopted the more flattering "Hurricane" when he later became a pop star in his own right.) The Floyd's second single, "See Emily Play" b/w "Scarecrow," was released shortly after an all-night happening called the 14-Hour Technicolour Dream in June 1967. Though these songs were less provocative lyrically, the dominant instruments of Barrett's voice and Wright's organ are no less effective melodically. Still, the band members considered them a step backward. They believed they had grown beyond three-minute pop novelties, and with the release of *The Piper at the Gates of Dawn* in 1967, they showed that they were right.

The Floyd used Abbey Road studios with the same glee as label mates the Beatles, working with the white-coated technicians to craft new and imaginative sounds. "A lot of the best sounds were developed by some of the dullest people," Mason said. "Some of the engineers at Abbey Road were enormously clever and devised some very weird sounds, and they'd never had more than a glass of beer." (This was also true of the crew that worked with the Beatles, including George Martin.) The Floyd's debut opens with radio noise and a high-pitched electronic signal cueing the start of "Astronomy Dominé," a frightening tour of the cosmos that also evokes the chill of "icy waters underground." "Pow R. Toc H." and "Interstellar Overdrive" are the first of many evocative Floyd instrumentals, and it's hard to hear these tracks without thinking of the swirling light shows and gyrating dancers at UFO. "The Scarecrow" shows that Barrett had listened to the Incredible String Band, while "Chapter 24" is as effective as any of George Harrison's Eastern meditations. (The lyrics were inspired by the *I Ching*, an ancient Chinese system for assessing a situation and divining the best course of action.) But it's the closing track that comes closest to matching the Beatles' studio accomplishments. "Bike" builds in intensity as Barrett tries to impress his heartthrob with an array of fanciful gifts, including a (white?) bicycle, a clan of gingerbread men, and a pet mouse named Gerald. We never know whether or not he gets the girl, since the last gift is a mysterious room of "musical tunes" that swallows the singer whole in an impressive explosion of sound effects.

The Piper at the Gates of Dawn was clearly Barrett's album. He wrote eight of the eleven songs, and he chose the title from a chapter in his favorite book, Kenneth Grahame's *The Wind in the Willows*. The singer had also become the center of attention during live shows, raising his arms in dramatic gestures and wringing increasingly amazing sounds from his Telecaster, which was covered with mirrors to reflect the swirling light show. Considering his importance to the group, it's not hard to imagine his band mates' concern when Barrett started to lose his grip on reality. He was overindulging in the sex and drugs that were so readily available to young rock stars. He had been smoking huge amounts of marijuana since the age of seventeen, and after his first LSD experience at nineteen, he began dropping acid almost daily. The rock-star lifestyle seemed to aggravate a manic-depressive nature, and he could veer instantly from lucid conversation to a blank stare or an evil, mocking laugh.

What Schaffner called "the classic Barrett episode" came during a gig in late 1967 following the Floyd's tour opening for Jimi Hendrix. "While Syd lingered before the dressing room mirror, primping up a luxuriant Afro modeled after the American guitar hero's—'the obligatory Hendrix perm,' as Roger Waters would call it twelve years later in *The Wall*—his exasperated colleagues finally hit the stage without him. This apparently prodded Barrett to take decisive measures. Impulsively crushing the contents of a jar of his beloved Mandrax tablets (a powerful barbiturate marketed until the late '70s in the United States under the brand name Quaalude), he ground the fragments into his hair along with a full tube of Brylcreem. Syd then joined the group onstage, where the heat of the spotlights soon turned his unique beauty treatment into a dribbling mess that left the Pink Floyd's star looking, in the eyes of their dumbstruck lighting director, 'like a guttered candle.'"[6]

The band's response to this deteriorating situation was to recruit Barrett's pal Gilmour as a fifth member to fill in on guitar and vocals. It was thought that Barrett could keep contributing new songs, like Brian Wilson in the Beach Boys. The story goes that the rest of the Floyd decided while en route to a gig that picking Barrett up was more trouble than it was worth. Behind the scenes, tensions with management played into this "spur of the moment" decision. Jenner and Andrew King of Blackhill Enterprises were adamant that Barrett *was* Pink Floyd, and Pink Floyd was eager to prove otherwise. In unguarded moments, the band members still wonder if they did the right thing. "Could we have saved the day? Could we have prevented Syd from going off the rail? I suppose this is the issue exercising me the most," Mason said in 1995. "We are not really talking about four lovable moptops, we are talking about a bunch of poised individuals who were so busy pursuing their own ends that they weren't even capable of looking after each other."

Released a year after *The Piper at the Gates of Dawn*, the Floyd's second album contains guitar work by both Barrett and Gilmour but only one Barrett original. (Two other Barrett-Floyd tunes from this era, "Scream Thy Last Scream" and "Vegetable Man," have been heavily bootlegged but remain officially unreleased.) "Jugband Blues" seems to be Barrett's sarcastic farewell to his band mates: "I'm most obliged to you for making it clear that I'm not here," he sings. Yet his influence weighs heavily throughout *A Saucerful of Secrets*. The ominous "Set the Controls for the Heart of the Sun" is a staple from his time in the band, and two delightfully silly pop songs—Wright's "See Saw" and Waters's "Corporal Clegg"—are clearly in the style of Syd's songbook. Only the instrumental title track points to a new direction. "'A Saucerful of Secrets' was the first thing we'd done without Syd that we thought was any good," Waters said.[7] The psychedelic instrumental summons images of a battle in the heavens between angry Greek gods, moving from an uneasy vamp with fluttering organ chords and layers of weird cymbal overtones to a section titled "Syncopated Pandemonium." The hypnotic Mason drum loop yields to discordant clashing until the song is resolved with the majestic melody and wordless vocals of "Celestial Voices." It's all a bit pretentious, but the song succeeds because of the lush, made-for-headphones production and the powerful hooks.

"The title track strikes me as being the first of a line of ideas that led on into what Pink Floyd later became," Gilmour said. "That sort of half a side of strange sections joined together with sound effects and things. That theme was followed in the four pieces on *Ummagumma*, the title track on *Atom Heart Mother*, and "Echoes" on the *Meddle* album, and it developed into becoming a whole album by the time we got to *The Dark Side of the Moon*."

The Amazing Pudding

I still think most people think of us as a very drug orientated group. [Pause, smile.] Of course, we're not. You can trust us.

—David Gilmour in *Pink Floyd Live at Pompeii*, 1972

Never let it be said that the Floyd didn't stick with a winning formula. The band's midperiod albums are strikingly similar, but each includes a handful of memorable tunes in addition to a lot of pot-smoking background music. Taking its title from a slang phrase for screwing, 1969's *Ummagumma* contains one album of old songs from a prime live set and another of very dismissible solo suites by each of the band members. The title track of 1970's *Atom Heart Mother*—formerly titled "The Amazing Pudding"—is another catchy side-long suite, this one beefed up by Scottish composer Ron Geesin's over-the-top orchestrations and choral arrangements. The central piece on 1971's *Meddle* grows from a single piano note driven through an echo box on its maximum setting. "Echoes" proceeds to add vocals to the mix, with Gilmour and Wright singing hippie-dippy lyrics about a motionless albatross, a dangerous image to evoke.

The Floyd's music was tailor-made for soundtracks, and the group did more than its share. *More* was recorded for the Barbet Schroeder film of the same name and released in 1969. It includes "Cymbaline," which muses on the mundane life of a rock star ("Your manager and agent are both busy on the phone / Selling colored photographs to magazines back home"), and "The Nile Song," a furious stomper that's the closest the Floyd got to heavy metal before "Run Like Hell" from *The Wall*. The band contributed three tracks to Michelangelo Antonioni's *Zabriskie Point*, sharing space on the 1970 soundtrack album with the Grateful Dead, while *Obscured by Clouds* was recorded in 1972 for another Schroeder film, *La Vallée*. The latter is the only sub-par offering, but the band has dismissed all of its soundtracks as "contract work," and they were excluded—along with *Atom Heart Mother*—from the 1992 box set *Shine On*.

One of the best tunes from the period didn't make it onto any of the band's albums. "Point Me at the Sky" was the group's only single between 1968 and "Another Brick in the Wall, Part Two" eleven years later. The song is clearly influenced by the Beatles' "Lucy in the Sky With Diamonds," but it's one of Waters's best science-fiction lyrics, painting an old-fashioned picture of Jules Verne–style space travel. The verses display the bassist's increasingly sharp and nasty wit. "If you survive to 2005 / I hope you're exceedingly thin," he sings. "For if you are stout, you will have to breathe out / While the people around you breathe in."

The rap during the early '70s was that, like the Dead, the Floyd was best experienced live. The 1972 concert film *Pink Floyd Live at Pompeii* has its share of silliness. The group plays in the ancient ruins, traipses over fields of volcanic ash, and says incredibly dopey things in "off-the-cuff" interviews. But the movie is a valuable document of four guys seducing fantastic sounds from a relatively small and primitive collection of instruments, pre-samplers, digital synthesizers, or sequencers. "A Saucerful of Secrets" is especially inspiring as Wright plays the grand piano with his elbows and Gilmour fools with his Strat and an echo box while sitting cross-legged in the dirt. By the late '80s, the Floyd was using a small army onstage and off to duplicate such sounds.

While many fans claimed that midperiod Floyd sonically replicated many of the sensations of an acid trip, the band members claimed that they never took a lot of psychedelic drugs. Waters said he used psychedelics only twice. "None of us were tripping except for Syd," Mason said. "We surfed on the psychedelic movement. We used it more than we played a part in it." "The post-Barrett Floyd inherited that 'acid generation' image almost by default and were often mystified by it," said a longtime friend quoted by Schaffner. "They were a bit too balanced to go the whole way, and seeing Syd so greatly affected by all the chemicals he pumped into himself was a lesson to be learned. Their attitude was, 'Fair

Four bus-stop ratbags in the mid-'70s. From left: Wright, Gilmour, Waters, Mason.

enough—they may *think* we're doing it, and we're very happy they think so, but we'll just carry on in our own normal way.'"[8]

Unlike the progressive-rock bands that they were sometimes wrongly grouped with, the Floyd stayed grounded in rock conventions. Wright's organ and Waters's trademark swooping bass never failed to provide big, beefy hooks, and Gilmour's solos invited you to hum along. Mason's wonderfully ham-fisted drumming kept even the wildest interstellar overdrives from careering out of control. Although tracks were sometimes stretched a bit thin over entire album sides, the Floyd always emphasized the importance of *songs.* "That came from Syd, mostly, because he was a songwriter," Mason said. "Syd was a natural; he was the romantic who spun it off in a stream of consciousness. Whereas Roger had to work to become a songwriter, and he worked at it like mad. Much of what passed for psychedelic rock was blues, because people weren't songwriters and they just had a repertoire of classic blues pieces that they wrote their own versions of."

When the Floyd and Barrett parted ways, Blackhill Enterprises stood by Syd. Jenner produced the first tentative Barrett solo sessions in May 1968, but the recordings soon broke down. When the sessions resumed a year later, production chores fell by default to Malcolm Jones, the new head of EMI's Harvest subsidiary. Gilmour and Waters expressed interest halfway through the project, and Jones was happy to let them finish it. The moonlighting Floyds added a few touches, but most of the backing music was provided by Humble Pie drummer Jerry Shirley, bassist Willie Wilson, and special guests the Soft Machine. They often had to add their contributions to guitar and vocal tracks that Syd had recorded in one take, matching his mistakes and tempo changes. Released in January 1970, *The Madcap Laughs*—with its title the eerie cover art of Barrett crouching in an empty apartment, and an inside photo of a baby lost amid the clouds—would seem to be about alienation and isolation. Yet the disc is often beguiling, upbeat, and carefree—even if unsettling hints of Barrett's mental state *do* creep out. "Terrapin" is a stark acoustic love song that borders on a stalker's obsessiveness. The fuzz-driven "No Man's Land" is a statement about entropy ("When I live I die") that dissolves into babble and a meandering instrumental, and "Dark Globe" features the singer cracking on the telling lines "With Eskimo chain I tattooed my brain all the way / Won't you miss me? / Wouldn't you miss me at all?"

A second Barrett solo album produced by Gilmour and Wright followed less than a year later. Criticism of *Barrett* holds that the songwriter is unraveling on tape, but that's dramatic nonsense. While the acoustic tunes are even sparer and less focused, "Baby Lemonade," "Gigolo Aunt," and "Wined and Dined" are pop songs every bit as strong as "Arnold Layne." The album contains several skiffle throwaways, but "Dominoes" is an idiosyncratic tune that seems to be moving forward and backward at the same time, and "Rats" is a creepy rant that evokes paranoid visions of insects on the walls, the image that Barrett chose for the cover.

Barrett: The madcap poses.

Aside from a short and quickly aborted session in 1974, *Barrett* was the singer's last interaction with the world of rock 'n' roll. (The 1988 collection *Opel* features unreleased material from the Jenner sessions and alternate versions of songs that appear on the albums.) But Barrett wasn't about to be forgotten. "Make your name like a ghost," he sang on "Baby Lemonade," and a cult of celebrity sprang up in his absence. "I'm not really surprised by it. He's a very charismatic figure, and he did write some wonderful songs," Gilmour said. "But you can say this of anyone whose career is cut off in its prime and died young—James Dean or anyone else—they are considered wonderful because they never grew old and showed us all their weaknesses." Rock scholar Deena Weinstein contends that the canonization of the drug-addled madman is in the romantic tradition of worshiping the idiot savant. "In part, it's the whole conflation of creativity and nonrationality," Weinstein said. "And in part it is the far more ancient notion of 'the innocent' and the brain-damaged as speakers of the Truth—Dostoyevsky's *Idiot*, Faulkner's Benjy in *The Sound and the Fury*—a variation on *in vino veritas*."

The only truth Barrett found in LSD was that he couldn't handle a daily dose of it. His recorded output displays an inventive guitar style, an intuitive melodic talent, and a flair for sharp wordplay that owes more to a perceptive reading of James Joyce and William Blake than random stoner babbling. Drugs didn't create these talents, and romanticizing Barrett's abuse of them blunts the tragedy of his decline. "Certainly acid had *something* to do with it," Wright said. "The point is, you don't know whether the acid accelerated this process that was happening in his brain or was the cause of it."[9] The Floyd spent the next four albums partially wondering about "the cause of it"—fame, money, drugs, or plain old lunacy—and asking how they themselves fit into the society that Syd dropped out of.

Money Changes Everything

"He came into the studio," recalls Rick Wright, "And no one recognized this person." Andrew King tried to break the ice by asking his former star client how he'd put on so much weight. "I've got a very large fridge in the kitchen," Syd explained, "and I've been eating a lot of pork chops."

—Barrett visits his old mates during the recording
of *Wish You Were Here*, 1975[10]

Pink Floyd wrote most of its eighth album in late 1971. Unlike previous efforts, *The Dark Side of the Moon* evolved in live performance before recording started. It was premiered as part of the set in February 1972, at London's Rainbow Theatre. The Floyd entered Abbey Road in June, wrapped up in January, and the album was released in March 1973. Ubiquitous on classic-rock radio ever since, it's difficult to listen to *The Dark Side of the Moon* today with fresh ears. Subtly reworking melodies that had been almost-but-not-quite-there on earlier albums, it is the Floyd's catchiest record. The power of the hooks can't be underestimated, as *Dark Side* became one of the best-selling albums of all time. But there are additional reasons for its success. Years of knob-twirling practice, a strong partnership with engineer Alan Parsons (who used his connection with the band to launch his own progressive-rock group, the Alan Parsons Project), and Abbey Road's new twenty-four-track tape machines produced a luxurious psychedelic sound that deserves its vaunted reputation. (Not for nothing is *Dark Side* the favorite of stereo salesmen everywhere.) Gilmour and Wright never sang better than on "Time" and "Us and Them," the guitar and synthesizer solos are extraordinary, and Mason's drumming is musical and creative, especially on "Time" and "Money."

Writing in *Melody Maker*, Chris Charlesworth offered that *Dark Side* is "a *great* record to fuck to," especially side one, which climaxes with Clare Torry's orgasmic vocals on "Great Gig in the Sky." Dick Parry's saxophone and a quartet of backing singers give the album a stronger and more sensual R&B feel than anything the Floyd recorded earlier. *Dark Side* also betters earlier concept albums because it is much more intriguing and open-ended. Shifting into the role of the band's primary lyricist,

Waters reveals himself as a romantic *and* a pessimist. He believes that the need to care for and be cared for by others is what makes life meaningful, but it is difficult if not impossible to attain authentic interpersonal communications. The songs explore the factors that drive people apart, resulting in isolation and ultimately madness. Rather than contrived lyrical bridges, thematic links are provided by sound effects and snippets of interviews in which people respond to questions such as, "When was the last time you were violent?" and "What do you think of death?" (Abbey Road doorman Jerry Driscoll provides the memorable closing, "There is no dark side of the moon, really. Matter of fact, it's all dark.")

In an interview with me nineteen years after *Dark Side*'s release, Gilmour reflected on the album's success. "All the things we'd been doing before had been pointing toward it, but it was the first time all the elements came together really well," he said. "The words were brilliant, it had a lovely cover, and it was just at that point in our career where we were moving to becoming quite popular. There was something to appeal to everyone in the world in at least one of the songs, and everything gelled perfectly at that one moment." The problem with perfection is that it's hard to top. "At that point," Waters said, "all our ambitions were realized."[11] The group had become a money-making megalith, enabling the musicians to buy holiday villas in the Greek Islands and indulge passions for collecting guitars (Gilmour), antiques (Wright), cars (Mason), and French Impressionist paintings (Waters). The cocoon of creature comforts slowly smothered their creativity, but in the mid-'70s, the musicians hadn't yet lost that playful psychedelic spirit.

In the autumn of 1973, the Floyd started work on the aborted *Household Objects* album. The group spent several months recording the sounds of stretched rubber bands, cardboard boxes, and an assortment of wine glasses filled with different amounts of water. "We tried to make all the sounds without using real instruments," Gilmour recalled. "Of course, it's a dead easy thing to do today with samplers, but then we abandoned it without having made any real tracks. It just got too difficult—and pointless. I mean, in the end, after you've spent weeks trying to make cardboard boxes sound like bass drums and snare drums, you think, 'Well, why the fuck don't I use a bass drum and snare drum?'"

When the band finally went back to using real instruments, there were three originals that had been tightened, like the songs on *Dark Side*, through live performances. Gilmour wanted to put "Shine On" on one side of an album and "Raving and Drooling" and "You Gotta Be Crazy" on the other and be done with it. But touring commitments kept interrupting the sessions, and the musicians succumbed to a general ennui as the recording grew labored and torturous. Waters felt that the only way the Floyd could rise above its artistic malaise was to cut "Shine On" in two and complete the album with new material that drew on the emotions the band was experiencing at the moment. It's revealing that the new songs include two that are superficially about the evils of the music business while in a broader sense addressing false promises and a failure to communicate.

Released in September 1975, *Wish You Were Here* stands as the best of the Floyd's four "classic-rock" efforts. The title track is a touching and tender acoustic folk song, and the subject of distance and longing is underscored by the sound of the introduction, which is mixed to create the effect of tuning in on a crappy transistor radio. (Waters commented that the song could just as well have been called "Wish *We* Were Here.") "Welcome to the Machine" is a state-of-the-art exposition of what could be done with a synthesizer, and the repetitive throb perfectly evokes the machine in the title. "Have a Cigar" is a funky throwaway, the sort of tune that used to serve as filler on Floyd soundtracks, but its very ordinariness compliments the sarcastic lyrics. Guest vocalist Roy Harper plays a smug but clueless music executive who utters the immortal line, "Oh, by the way, which one's Pink?" (Another Jenner-King client, Harper was a ubiquitous figure on the English underground.) The album's crowning achievement is "Shine On You Crazy Diamond," a tribute to that "painter, piper, prisoner, and martyr" Barrett. More gripping and graceful than any of the Floyd's other long suites, it has a symphonic elegance while retaining a rock 'n' roll grit, thanks in part once again to Mason, master of the slow-motion drum fill. The tension between the plodding rhythm and the soaring keyboards and guitar evoke an injured bird struggling to fly. The music perfectly complements Waters's lyrics—the idea that Barrett "wore out his welcome with random precision" is a thoughtful assessment of his decline—but the fact that Waters thought the long instrumentals distracted from the lyrical concept is evidence of the rift that would eventually divide the band.

Seven months after the release of *Wish You Were Here*, the Floyd returned to the studio. "Raving and Drooling" became "Sheep," and "You Gotta Be Crazy" became "Dogs" as the band got downright nasty with the allegorical *Animals.* "It was the moment of high punk over here in England, where everyone sort of hated everything," Gilmour said. "I'm sure that had an influence on us making a bit of a tougher, starker, more aggressive album—as close as we ever got to a punk album, if you like." There's still the matter of Floydian tempos and song lengths, but the album *is* full of jagged edges and harsh instrumental textures. Lyrically, Waters takes dead aim at the mind-numbing constraints of society, attacking the pigs (which include the "bus-stop ratbag" lumpenprole-tariat, the "house-proud town mouse" bourgeoisie, and the "well-heeled big wheel" wealthy); the sheep who unthinkingly accept religion as panacea, and the ruthless yuppie dogs who prey upon them.[12] This cynical vision was very much in line with the punks', even as Johnny Rotten was making headlines for sporting a Pink Floyd T-shirt with the words "I Hate" scrawled on it.

In many ways the Floyd had fallen into the trap that Waters despised. Wright said that *Animals* was "the beginning of where Roger wanted to do everything."[13] Despite his pleas for interpersonal communications, Waters didn't really want to hear from his musical partners anymore, even though the band's best moments had always been the result of four individuals working together. The solo suites on *Ummagumma* were flops; the Gilmour, Mason, and Wright solo albums released between *Animals* and *The Wall* were interesting primarily for the way they illuminated the individual players' strengths and weaknesses, and Waters's solo collaboration with Geesin, *Music from The Body,* was a way-too-clever novelty. The bassist's new self-image as the Floyd's primary auteur simply wasn't based in fact, and *The Wall* suffers from its creator's delusion and the exclusion of his band mates.

Released in November 1979, *The Wall* mixes elements from Waters's and Barrett's life stories, but its primary themes had all been covered before with more subtlety and artistry. Waters wrote about the tragedy of war in "Corporal Clegg" and "Us and Them"; the cruelness of society in *Dark Side* and *Animals*; the machinations of the music business in "Cymbaline," "Have a Cigar," and "Welcome to the Machine," and the self-constructed wall of insanity in "If," "Brain Damage," and "Shine On You Crazy Diamond." Some of the instrumental settings are familiar—"Mother" recalls the the idyllic vibe of *More,* and "Comfortably Numb" has a patented Gilmour guitar solo—but there's no evidence of the Floyd playing as a band. *The Wall* could have been recorded by anybody, and in fact, the roster of unlikely session contributors includes lounge chanteuse Toni Tennille, Beach Boy Bruce Johnston, and Toto drummer Jeff Porcaro.

The Floyd's subsequent output nosedives quicker than the spitfire

Three well-heeled big wheels in the mid '90s. (Photo by Albert Watson.)

that crashed into the wall during the bands's overwrought stage shows. Nobody but Waters showed up for *The Final Cut,* a relatively tune-free album released in 1983 and inspired by the war in the Falklands. Afterward, Waters and the rest of the band parted ways in an ugly burst of lawsuits and bitter slurs. It was a tawdry end for a group that had previously avoided public rock-star embarassments. Gilmour, Wright, and Mason continued as a Floyd devoid of intellectual structure (*A Momentary Lapse of Reason, The Division Bell*), while Waters continued as a songwriter devoid of musical inspiration (*The Pros and Cons of Hitchhiking, Radio KAOS,* and *Amused to Death*). Even if the remaining members of the Floyd settle their differences with Waters (which those in the know say is unlikely), the band will probably never recapture the "no-rules" psychedelic spirit of its best work.

"In the beginning, you think that you can do anything you like, but as time goes by, it narrows down," Mason told me with welcomed frankness in 1995. "So your breadth of vision in 1967 is like one-hundred feet, but thirty years later, you have learned so much that you have found the areas where you operate best. It's not laziness, but now you operate within three feet. One has to make a very concious effort to break those boundaries. I think, also, that when you get more successful, it gives you increased responsibility. You carry the baggage of your history, and every record is judged against all the other things that you have done, and that can be quite onerous. You feel like you are limited to what you can do."

Barrett has avoided this dilemma by simply doing nothing at all. Gilmour said he checks in with his former mate's family from time to time to make sure that he's getting his royalty checks (which are considerable in the age of CD reissues), but the band hasn't seen Syd since he showed up unexpectedly at Gilmour's wedding during a break in the recording of *Wish You Were Here* in 1975. "Syd Barrett, or Roger as everyone now calls him, is today the antithesis of the colorful '60s rock star that so many fans remember," wrote biographers Mike Watkinson and Pete Anderson. "A balding, rather heavyset figure who lives alone in his Cambridge flat, he seldom ventures into the center of town. His brother-in-law, Paul Breen, says of his current lifestyle: 'He's improving with age, like good wine, and is happy to get on with his life. He doesn't really see anyone, apart from his sister, and clearly enjoys his own company. He does not really show much emotion but certainly gives the impression that he is comfortably settled into his way of life.'"[14]

It's tempting to think of the madcap sitting at home and laughing—about the cost of opening the doors of perception, about the way his life has been romanticized, and about how he still figures in the story of his former band after a quarter of a century. (The Floyd's 1994 tour featured a film of a group of men struggling to carry an enormous bust of someone who looked very much like Syd, though not at all like Roger.) But it's more likely that Barrett concentrates on his favorite diversions—TV, painting, and the occasional bike ride through town—and in that way, he's not much different from Gilmour, Mason, Waters, Wright, or many of the rest of us.

CHAPTER 6

The 14-Hour Technicolour Dream and the Art-Rock Nightmare

On April 29, 1967, an all-night happening called the 14-Hour Technicolour Dream overran London's stately Alexandra Palace, a Victorian exhibition hall atop Muswell Hill. Ostensibly a benefit to raise cash for the *International Times*, an underground newspaper whose offices had been raided by the police, the event became a coming-out party for England's psychedelic underground. Some ten thousand people, clad in brightly colored caftans, long lace scarves, and flowing robes and beads, roamed the grounds. They were entertained by mimes, underground films, a full-sized fairground helter-skelter, a giant jelly mold, an igloo dispensing free but ineffectual banana-peel joints, and poetry and performance art by Ron Geesin, Yoko Ono, and her husband at the time, Tony Cox. But the main attraction was the music.

Tomorrow took the stage just as the party was starting to swing. Twink, the group's lunatic drummer, bashed his set in an anarchic flurry while his band mates fiddled with their effects boxes and amplifiers. Wearing a red velvet suit from Granny Takes a Trip, a young guitar prodigy named Steve Howe played a droning raga that was just on the verge of feeding back. (He had customized one of the pickups on his Japanese Guyatone so that the D string fed back automatically whenever he stepped on his volume pedal.) As usual, bassist John "Junior" Wood was clad only in a loincloth. He and Twink fell into a quick eight-beat rhythm that rushed past like the posts on a picket fence during a brisk bike ride through the country. Singer Keith West held the microphone stand as if to steady himself. "The lamppost hangs his head in disgrace / Shines no light upon my face," he sang. "Through the darkness we still see / My white bicycle and me." Most of the lyrics were a blur, but three words leaped out of the mix, repeated in the choruses and echoed by the other band members: *"My white bicycle."*

Twenty-seven years later Howe told me that he and the other members of Tomorrow hadn't been aware of Albert Hofmann's famous acid-powered bike ride. He recalled "My White Bicycle" as a song about the Provos, a sect of anarchist hippies in Holland who shared communal bicycles. "It was, on the other hand, a pretty druggy kind of song," he added with a chuckle. "This was definitely a record that challenged the establishment to ride the white bicycle." Tomorrow certainly wasn't alone in issuing such a challenge. The bill at the 14-Hour Technicolour Dream was indicative of the diversity of English psychedelia in the wake of *Rubber Soul* and *Revolver*, and in addition to Tomorrow and the Pink Floyd, the Crazy World of Arthur Brown, the Soft Machine, the Pretty Things, and the Creation all delivered transcendent sets.

Arthur Brown was an operatic singer with a flair for the dramatic. He went on to score a hit in 1968 with "Fire," an overwrought tune that he performed while wearing a flaming crown. Produced by Pete Townshend, the Crazy World's debut album went gold and the band appeared on the popular British music show *Top of the Pops*. But Brown was suspicious of the star-making machine and decided to release future recordings independently. "We represented a different sort of music and a different approach altogether to what the [pop] music thing was about," he said.[1] Relocating to a communal farm, the group recorded a more ethereal album called *Strange Lands* that wasn't released until two decades later in 1988. The Crazy World ended when organist Vincent Crane and drummer Carl Palmer left to form Atomic Rooster. Brown subsequently recorded three albums of Hawkwind-style space rock with Kingdom Come; painted houses with former Mothers of Invention guitarist Jimmy Carl Black in his new hometown of Austin, Texas; released two techno albums, and formed a new version of his old band for odd gigs in England and the United States.

Leaders of the active scene in Canterbury, the Soft Machine took its name from a novel by William S. Burroughs. The group was formed by bassist-vocalist Kevin Ayers, drummer-vocalist Robert Wyatt, organist Mike Ratledge, and guitarist Daevid Allen, but Allen quit before the first album. (He later moved to France and formed the indulgent space-rock ensemble Gong.) Produced by Chas Chandler of the Animals and released in 1968, *The Soft Machine* attempts to cross the Beatles' psychedelic rock and Ornette Coleman's harmolodic jams. On tracks such as the joyful "Hope for Happiness" and "Why Are We Sleeping?" (a political call to arms), it nearly succeeds. Ayers left and went on to craft a strong solo album, *Joy of a Toy*, while the Soft Machine moved toward a more peculiar and less rocking brand of jazz fusion. Wyatt later collaborated with David Sinclair of the jam-happy Canterbury bands Caravan and Camel in the tuneful Matching Mole, but in 1973 he was paralyzed from the waist down after falling out of a third-story window while partying a bit too enthusiastically. He mined the depths of his painful experience to produce the most beautiful and enduring album by any member of the Canterbury mafia, 1974's *Rock Bottom*, produced by Nick Mason of Pink Floyd.

Inspired by psychedelic drugs, the Pretty Things were one of the many bands that shifted from R&B to more expansive sounds, starting with the heavily orchestrated *Emotions* in 1967. Like Brian Wilson, Phil May and his band mates tried to evoke a different emotion on each song, but the result was much less successful than *Pet Sounds*. The group fared better with a pair of 1968 concept albums recorded by Pink Floyd producer Norman Smith, the cult favorites *S.F. Sorrow* and *Parachute*. The stories are convoluted and a bit silly—*S.F. Sorrow* climaxes with disaster aboard a dirigible—but the albums succeed on the strength of the melodies and the inventiveness of the soundscapes. Unfortunately, the band soon devolved into a proto-grunge hard-rock parody.

Declaring that its music was "red with purple flashes," the Creation came together in 1966 from the remains of a mod combo called the Mark Four. Signed to a label started by Shel Talmy, the producer of the Who and the Kinks, the quartet made its recorded debut with a noisy three-minute epiphany called "Making Time" that featured guitarist Eddie Phillips soloing with a violin bow. (Led Zeppelin's Jimmy Page was a fan and later borrowed the trick on "Dazed and Confused.") The group's second single, "Painter Man," was a humorous tale of art-school pretensions that predicted the course that many psychedelic-pop bands would soon take. A hit in Germany, the Creation spent much of its time touring there at the expense of building a following in England or the United States. Its only album included trippy pop gems such as "How Does It Feel to Feel?" and "The Girls Are Naked," but by the time it was released in February 1968, the group had disbanded. Singer Kenny Pickett landed a job on Zeppelin's road crew, and he and Phillips later wrote "Teacher Teacher" for Rockpile. The band reunited in 1993 for a surprisingly vital live album called *Lay the Ghost*, but it's probably best remembered for giving a name to Alan McGee's Creation Records—the home of many of the best psychedelic-rock bands in the '90s.

Steve Howe in the '90s: If you can remember the '60s. . . .

As for Tomorrow, "My White Bicycle" became a hit when it appeared on the group's only album in 1968. The self-titled disc boasts such highlights as "Real Life Permanent Dream" and "Revolution," a scary tune commemorating the night police raided a Pink Floyd gig at UFO and turned their dogs on a crowd of stoned freaks. But it also includes such slight, whimsical ditties as "Three Jolly Little Dwarfs" and "Auntie Mary's Dress Shop" (like "Arnold Layne," a song that looked kindly on transvestites). *Tomorrow* is awfully derivative of the Beatles, right down to the unremarkable cover of "Strawberry Fields Forever." But the band's story is worth telling because it's so typical of the first wave of English psychedelia.

Howe and West first came together in 1965 in a group called the In Crowd. The band wore modish striped polo shirts and tapered jeans and played revved-up soul and R&B, but by 1966, things were starting to change. "We were starting to 'psychedelic' things up," Howe recalled. "It came from the Byrds, really. We were looking at more obscure music than the Beatles, but of course, they were in there, too." The change was partly due to the London social scene—the exchange of ideas as musicians gathered in the clubs—but LSD also played a role. "The idea that you could go beyond normality was somehow so incredibly irresistible," Howe said. "Humanity had gone through two world wars and one needed—I don't think you can avoid the word—*escape*, whether it was a blind, useless escape or actually a very therapeutic and beautiful experience. Although it was against mainstream thinking, in a way, it became a mainstream of people who were on to something, and it became very fashionable and trendy to be part of that thing."

Among those who followed the trend were Apple, the Koobas, the Open Mind, and the English Kaleidoscope—slight, opportunistic groups that were quickly forgotten—but other bands deserve at least a footnote. The Birds (not to be confused with that American group) played overamped R&B and featured a young guitarist named Ron Wood. Hailing from Birmingham, the Move one-upped the Who's instrument-smashing by wrecking TV sets and pianos while recording gentle psychedelic-pop songs such as "Fire Brigade" and "Flowers in the Rain." Status Quo had a hit single with "Pictures of Matchstick Men," and John's Children featured a pre–Tyrannosaurus Rex Marc Bolan on the infamous *Legendary Orgasm Album*, a "live" record with crowd noise dubbed from other recordings. As with the American *Nuggets* groups, many of these bands copied psychedelic rock as a style without ever having had a psychedelic experience. "There were English working-class guys, as opposed to the Pink Floyd, the Incredible String Band, and the Soft Machine, who were all very middle-class," said promoter and record producer Joe Boyd. "Twink and the guys from the Move would have been on a building site if they hadn't been working in a band. The Move learned psychedelia while drinking beer. They copied the musical ethos, and they copied it almost better than the people who invented it."

Other groups that took a sharp left turn into psychedelia are better known. The Yardbirds formed in late 1963 from the remains of the Metropolis Blues Quartet, and they followed the Stones into the Crawdaddy Club as house band. By 1965 they had progressed from relatively straight covers of Bo Diddley, the Isley Brothers, and Muddy Waters to extended blues-based raveups, improvisations that allowed guitarist Eric Clapton to jam for as long as thirty minutes. Clapton quit in disgust when the group moved into the pop mainstream with the 1965 hit "For Your Love." He was replaced by Jeff Beck, who started to experiment with fuzzboxes, sitarlike drones, and other exotic colors on captivating singles such as "Heart Full of Soul," "Shapes of Things," and "Train Kept a-Rollin.'" Beck also presided over the Yardbirds' most psychedelic album, *Over Under Sideways Down*, which featured a high point he'd never match again with the title track. Jimmy Page joined the group as a bassist and eventually replaced Beck on lead guitar before the band finally split in 1968.

Steve Marriott, Ronnie Lane, Kenney Jones, and Ian McLagan were fresh-faced young mods ("faces") who came together as the Small Faces in 1965. The band members maintained their R&B influence and a

Cockney sense of humor while coloring their sound with flower-power lyrics (as on the early single "Itchycoo Park") and trippy, ever-shifting productions (as on their second and last album, *Ogden's Nut Gone Flake*, a post–*Sgt. Pepper's* conceptual curiosity that came packaged in a round album cover). Marriott left in 1969 for Humble Pie, and Ron Wood and Rod Stewart joined. The band became the Faces, and the substance of favor turned from psychedelic drugs to lager.

The first incarnation of Traffic was strongly influenced by the psychedelic sounds of 1967, as evidenced on the singles "Paper Sun" and "Hole in My Shoe" and the debut album *Mr. Fantasy*, but the band soon shifted into a less cosmic merger of jazz, rock, and folk. After the original R&B Animals split, singer Eric Burdon relocated to San Francisco, put together the New Animals, and recorded an acid-tinged testament to the times called *Winds of Change*. (Burdon also wrote a tune paying homage to the original manufacturers of LSD, "A Girl Named Sandoz," and effectively captured a drunk and trippy vibe on "Spill the Wine.") The less substantive British Invasion bands were mostly history by 1967, but two groups from that earlier era tried to reinvent themselves by drawing on psychedelic sounds. With their swirling organ, the Zombies already had a spooky undertone on singles such as "She's Not There," but 1968's inspired *Odyssey and Oracle* is a moody concept album featuring musings on World War I and faded love, and it ends with the haunting "Time of the Season," a song that captures the underlying tensions of the day almost as well as "For What It's Worth." The Hollies were less successful. They had emerged in 1963 with a string of simple harmony-driven pop hits such as "Bus Stop," but they explored more elaborate instrumental backings and orchestration on the 1967 album *Dear Eloise/King Midas in Reverse*, a spectacular flop. (Graham Nash eventually left to link up with David Crosby and Stephen Stills and form the supergroup of Crosby, Stills and Nash.)

Grounded: The Birth of Art Rock

Jon Pareles argues that if we honor high school punks we should also honor high school poets. I say we stick to high school punk poets.
—Robert Christgau on Van Der Graaf Generator[2]

While the Zombies and the Hollies symbolize the shift of one era of

British rock into another—the beat groups of the British Invasion to psychedelic rock—Procol Harum, the Moody Blues, the Nice, and King Crimson herald the move from psychedelia to art rock. As the name for a genre of music, "art rock" is misleading. Great rock is art, but there isn't much great art rock. What art rock, or "progressive rock," really signifies is music that self-consciously tries to elevate rock 'n' roll to high culture by embracing high-culture values such as technical virtuosity and conceptual density. Many musicians in the first wave of British psychedelia were upper-middle-class kids who discovered rock, drugs, and the London nightlife and dropped out of college or art school. *Sgt. Pepper's* convinced them that they could make music that was just as serious as the art they'd been studying before they tuned in, turned on, and dropped out—and maybe it could even be respectable enough to please Mum and Dad.

"Why British bands feel compelled to quote the classics, however tongue-in-cheek, leads into the murky waters of class and nation analysis," critic John Rockwell wrote. "In comparison with the British, Americans tend to be happy apes. Most American rockers wouldn't know a Beethoven symphony if they were run down by one in the middle of a freeway. One result of such ignorance is that American art (music, painting, poetry, films, etc.) can develop untroubled by lame affectations of a cultured sensibility. In Britain, the lower classes enjoy no such isolation. The class divisions and the crushing weight of high culture flourish essentially untrammeled. Rockers seem far more eager to 'dignify' their work, to make it acceptable for upper-class approbation."[3]

Procol Harum took its name from the Latin phrase for "beyond these things" and scored its biggest hit by paraphrasing a Bach cantata, Suite no. 3 in D Major. The pretensions are thick even without hallucinatory lyrics about vestal virgins, flying ceilings, and light fandangos, but nevertheless, "A Whiter Shade of Pale" remains a hauntingly effective single. The band plays as if it is barely restraining an emotional outburst: The group could be a hippie version of the dance orchestra on the *Titanic*, dutifully playing as the ship sinks into the icy depths. The quintet's first three albums explored increasingly less interesting variations of this theme until the band finally lapsed into a fatal coma in 1970 after the departure of guitarist Robin Trower.

The Moody Blues first surfaced as a modish second-tier British Invasion band, scoring a 1965 hit with "Go Now." The group fell apart in 1966 when singer Denny Laine quit, but keyboardist Mike Pinder recruited new members and moved everyone to Belgium so that they could "find themselves." They reappeared in 1968 with *Days of Future Passed*. The Moodies recorded some catchy if melodramatic tunes, including "Nights in White Satin," "Forever Afternoon (Tuesday)," and "Legend of a Mind," which paid tribute to Timothy Leary. But their albums bogged down with long, snooze-inducing instrumentals and dramatic poetry readings, and like many in the art-rock class of 1968, they never learned when to call it quits. After a brief lull in the mid-'70s, they came back commercially reinvigorated but softer and more bloated than ever.

Managed by the post-Stones Andrew Loog Oldham, the Nice certainly knew how to get attention. "At their New York debut at Steve Paul's Scene in 1968, they stripped to the waist and whipped each other," Lillian Roxon wrote. "In England, they stabbed an American flag with knives, stomped on it, and burned it onstage, and organ player Keith Emerson has been known to tap-dance on the keys with remarkably musical results."[4] Unfortunately, the group's albums are flaccid and awful. As the titles indicate, 1968's *The Thoughts of Emerlist Davjack* and 1969's *Ars Longa Vita Brevis* are clumsy beasts that stomp with equal disdain on jazz, blues, Tchaikovsky, Sibelius, and *West Side Story*.

King Crimson's stew was a lot tastier. Mutton-headed lyrics and instrumental fat are still part of the recipe, but the group's 1969 debut, *In the Court of the Crimson King*, is liberally seasoned with pop hooks. "21st Century Schizoid Man" is driven by a killer riff, sinister vocals, and Beat-poetic lyrics that evoke the panic of a bad acid trip. But nearly every tune is flogged to death. (The 7:21 "21st Century Schizoid Man" bears the subtitle, "including Mirrors." Presumably, that's the chaotic, long-winded instrumental that does little but drag the song down.)

The best improvisational breaks by the Yardbirds are hypnotizing, while those by the Velvets or the 13th Floor Elevators are cathartic. King Crimson's are just pointlessly busy. Nevertheless, *Crimson King* influenced a flood of art rock that followed. It signaled that there was free rein to stretch one humble hook over twelve minutes; that lyrics didn't have to mean anything as long as they had a few enigmatic catchphrases ("the wall on which the prophets wrote" or "the rusted chains of prison moons"); and that rock's basic drive could be sacrificed to jazzy meters and jerky syncopations as long as the group had a good drummer. (Michael Giles added control and chops to Keith Moon–style chaos, inspiring Phil Collins, Bill Bruford, and others.) "Confusion will be my epitaph," Greg Lake sings, and he could be talking about the genre he helped usher in.

With unlimited studio time, plentiful drugs, and high-art pretensions destroying everyone's bullshit detectors, the naive, whimsical, and sweetly melodic psychedelic pop of 1967 gave way to the plodding, ponderous art rock of 1970. In 1967 a psychedelic-pop band called the Syn scored a hit with a catchy single, "Grounded," which rewrote the Beatles' "Rain" and added lyrics about a truly awful trip ("I'm high and I'm dry and I'm grounded"). In 1968 Syn bassist Chris Squire formed Yes with vocalist Jon Anderson to play overblown arrangements of tunes such as the Fifth Dimension's "Paper Cup." Tomorrow broke up in 1968 when Keith West quit to concentrate on a concept album called *Teenage Opera*, and in 1970 Howe joined Yes. From the ashes of the Move came the Electric Light Orchestra, and from the Nice, King Crimson, and the Crazy World of Arthur Brown came Emerson, Lake and Palmer. Through the early '70s, these bands were joined by kindred spirits such as Renaissance, Gentle Giant, Jethro Tull, Lindisfarne, and Van Der Graaf Generator, and, later, by American and Canadian pretenders such as Kansas, Styx, and Rush.

Psychedelic rock and psychedelic drugs have to take some of the blame. "Yes couldn't have played the kind of music it made without having the experience of developing the freedom and total nonconformist approach that came from the psychedelic bands," Howe said. But what was lost between Tomorrow's "My White Bicycle" and Yes's impenetrable *Tales From Topographic Oceans* was the second half of the equation. The indulgence and pretensions might have been tolerable if the music still *rocked*, but most of the art rockers checked their pomposity only when they tried to score a hit single. ("Hit" being relative, since only so-called album-rock stations played them, catering to late-night audiences huddled around their bongs and stereo FM receivers.)

ELP's "Lucky Man" is a pretty if melodramatic folk tune that visits the Twilight Zone when Emerson's weird synthesizer tears through like a rampaging elephant. It's hard to deny the hooky riffs and turnaround rhythms of Yes's "Starship Trooper" or "Long Distance Runaround," and Holland made a rare contribution to rock via Focus's "Hocus Pocus," a silly tune driven by a catchy melody and some over-the-top yodeling. But a handful of enduring songs doesn't justify careers that span three decades, and art rock's legacy as a bad trip is ultimately well deserved—with two notable exceptions.

Plus . . . Tubular . . . Bells!

The closest rock music has got to the classical symphony.
—Review of *Hergest Ridge*, 1974[5]

Sometimes wrongly lumped into the New Age genre, Mike Oldfield's music is more like instrumental surf rock given a psychedelic twist and taken to its ultimate conclusion via symphonic instrumentation and studio wizardry. An introspective child subject to fits of depression, Oldfield turned to the guitar for solace from a troubled family life. He was influenced by the baroque folk of John Renbourn and Bert Jansch, and he started his career in 1967 as part of a folk duo with his sister Sally. In 1970, at age seventeen, he linked up with former Soft Machine bassist Kevin Ayers in a group called the Whole World, and he started to turn heads as a soloist. "I would do an electric guitar solo and, depending on how pissed I was, I used to let it feed back and do somersaults all over the floor," he said.[6]

Oldfield lived with members of the band, and he recorded the demos for what would become *Tubular Bells* in his bedroom. Using a tape recorder borrowed from Ayers, he found that he could overdub more than one instrument if he masked the erase head with a piece of cardboard. Virgin Records founders Simon Draper and Richard Branson heard Oldfield's tape and agreed to front him studio time. Over the next nine months, the guitarist recorded some twenty-eight instrumental parts—including everything from Spanish guitar to Lowrey organ to glockenspiel—saturating the master tape with some two-thousand overdubs. The result was *Tubular Bells*, a sprawling, psychedelic instrumental full of hum-along melodies that serves as a sort of a soundtrack for an imaginary film. (Four minutes of the piece would later be used on the soundtrack of *The Exorcist*.) This is classical music for people who wouldn't otherwise touch the stuff, or rock 'n' roll that rejects conventional song structure, vocals, and instrumentation. (And who ever said you couldn't rock out with a glockenspiel?) A masterpiece of headphone rock, the lulling tour of Oldfield's bedroom world is interrupted only when Vivian Stanshall of the Bonzo Dog Doo-Dah Band makes his grand entrance to introduce each of the instruments: "Double-speed guitar . . . one slightly distorted guitar . . . plus . . . tubular . . . bells!" The dramatic voiceover caused more than a few tranced-out potheads to jerk awake and spill the bongwater.

Released in 1973, *Tubular Bells* sold sixteen million copies. Virgin was established as a major record company, and Oldfield was signed to a lengthy contract, a situation he came to regret. ("It was a horrible situation to be in, just like serving a prison sentence," he said.) Oldfield followed *Tubular Bells* with two more albums that adhered to the formula of one long instrumental per vinyl album side, and *Hergest Ridge* and *Ommadawn* are only slightly less engaging than the debut. The first live performance of *Tubular Bells* drew together an all-star ensemble featuring Ayers, Mick Taylor of the Rolling Stones, Steve Hillage and Pierre Moerlen of Gong, and Fred Frith of Henry Cow. Oldfield also popped up alongside Ayers, Nico, John Cale, and Brian Eno in the ultimate art-rock supergroup, recorded on the album *June 1, 1974*. Later, he toured with a fifty-member band captured on an excellent 1979 live album *Mike Oldfield Exposed*. But the rest of Oldfield's discography is spottier.

In the early '80s the guitarist formed the Mike Oldfield Group, a sextet featuring powerful vocalist Maggie Reilly. The group recorded *QE2* (1980), which introduced shorter, poppier songs, and *Five Miles Out* (1982), which scored two European hits with the title track and "Family Man," which later became a massive hit for Daryl Hall and John Oates. But Oldfield said he found writing pop songs "limiting and boring." In 1984 he returned to instrumental soundtracks, recording the moving score to *The Killing Fields*. Finally freed from his original label, Oldfield recorded a sequel to *Tubular Bells* for Warner Bros. in 1992, working with producer Trevor Horn. "All these years I've avoided sounding like *Tubular Bells* while a lot of people have been doing the opposite," he said. "You hear it on adverts and film soundtracks. Apparently the film soundtrack world will say, 'I want a piece of *Tubular Bells*–type music here.' It's become integrated into the culture. So I was talking to this guy from the record company and I said, 'Maybe I should start sounding like myself.'" A slicker, digital version of the original, *Tubular Bells 2* is still full of hooks, unencumbered by dumb lyrics, and fueled by a healthy sense of humor. (The straitlaced announcer this time is everyone's favorite screen villain, Alan Rickman. "We did try and get Viv Stanshall to do this new one, but the day that we turned up to pick him up for the session, he was asleep in the bath covered by a pot plant and wouldn't respond to proddings to get up," Oldfield said.)

While his instrumental visions aren't nearly as unique as they once were, Oldfield's work stands with Brian Eno's ambient albums as psychedelic rock's version of respectable background music. "I think my music is what rock 'n' roll would have become if it hadn't been for punk rock and it hadn't been for sampling," he said. "But I suppose if punk and sampling hadn't happened, it would have been rather pompous. You just have to listen to it and watch the performance to see that when people play *Tubular Bells 2*, there's a lot of fun in there, a lot of laughs, and a lot of enjoyment. It's not like 'I'm a genius' stuff. You'll find *that* if you look at the Guns n' Roses video with the orchestra. Now *that's* pompous."

Watchers of the Skies

The visual sense, the kind of landscape of another world—it's definitely a secret world on *Us* where there are a lot of psychedelic references. Psychedelia is definitely a period that interests me. It was one of the few periods where experimentation *was* the style.

—Peter Gabriel, 1993

In the beginning, there was Genesis the art-rock band, the oh-so-serious quintet of polite, proper, upper-middle-class boys' school students. Tony Banks and Peter Gabriel met as teens attending the Charterhouse school near Godalming, Surrey, and they struck up a friendship based on playing songs by the Beatles, Otis Redding, and Screamin' Jay Hawkins. Their music-room jams attracted several classmates, including Mike Rutherford. In late 1968 this loose-knit group recorded a demo that Gabriel slipped to Charterhouse graduate Jonathan King. King had scored a sub-Donovan novelty hit in 1965 with "Everyone's Gone to the Moon" and went on to build a career as a minor mogul. He liked the band's gentle, Beatles-inspired melodies, and he produced its first album, *From Genesis to Revelation*, released in Britain on Decca in March 1969. The album sold only six hundred copies and the band was dropped, but the eighteen-year-old musicians weren't easily discouraged.

Genesis moved into an isolated cottage in Dorking. The musicians set up in a circle and jammed for hours every day for six months, forging the flowing, pastoral sound that would characterize their best early work. Former Creation manager Tony Stratton-Smith heard one of their rare gigs and signed them to his new label, Charisma Records, fostering their development on 1970's *Trespass* and 1971's *Nursery Cryme*. On the latter, Gabriel, Banks, and Rutherford were joined by two new members, guitarist Steve Hackett and drummer Phil Collins. "Genesis was full of charm and weakness," Hackett said. "Feminine, you know. Very pastel shades. 'Stagnation' is a very impressionist sort of thing, very evocative of branches and leaves. It conjures up feelings of scenery to me."[6]

The romantic sound that attracted Hackett gelled for the first time on record on 1972's *Foxtrot*. Unlike Yes or ELP, Genesis was more interested in sounds and textures than virtuosic solos, and its long, ever-shifting songs keep the focus on melody and storytelling. Banks's regal organ introduces "Watcher of the Skies," which includes a bravura Gabriel vocal about aliens and the end of the world. Twelve-string guitars create a folkie backdrop for "Time Table," a dramatic tune that couches antiwar sentiments in a medieval setting, and Gabriel plays several different roles in "Get 'Em Out by Friday," a tune that satirizes greedy slumlords. But the album's centerpiece is the side-long, hook-filled psychedelic epic "Supper's Ready," a song disguised as a screenplay (or vice versa). The tune deals with no less than the balance between good and evil and man's place in the universe, and it was inspired by an odd experience that Gabriel had with his first wife, Jill, at her parents' house in Kensington. "We just stared at each other, and strange things began to happen," the singer recalled. "We saw other faces in each other, and I was very frightened. It was almost as if something had come into us and was using us as a meeting point. It was late at night, and we were tired and all the rest, so it was quite easy for us to hallucinate, [though] we hadn't been drinking or drugging."[7]

After *Foxtrot*, Gabriel's performances started to get more theatrical. He donned masks, robes, and giant bat wings to act out the characters in different songs, and he became the center of attention (not surprising, considering that the other members played sitting down and staring at their feet). The band followed with 1973's *Selling England by the Pound*, but its most effective merger of theater and musical invention is *The Lamb Lies Down on Broadway*. The double album was written in 1974, at a time when Gabriel and the band were pulling apart. The singer argued for the opportunity to write the lyrics alone as part of a unified story, and he added his vocals to music that the band had already recorded. *The Lamb* sounds a bit disjointed at points, and the science-fiction tale of a Puerto Rican graffiti artist swept into a hallucinatory underworld of Lamia and Slippermen is a bit hard to fathom. But the album is full of twisted but memorable melodies and unique sounds, including Banks's synthesizer textures and Hackett's conversational guitar lines.

The Lamb inspired Genesis's most elaborate stage show yet, and the group performed the album in its entirety 102 times. Midway through, Gabriel announced he was leaving at the end of the tour, and the band didn't try to dissuade him. "They didn't like what I was becoming," he said. "I felt that my hands were beginning to feel tied within the group because the publicity thing was getting worse rather than better; the jealousy."[8]

Gabriel launched his solo career in 1976 with the first of three self-titled solo albums. (He wanted fans to view each of his albums like new issues of a magazine.) Produced by Bob Ezrin, the high point of the first album is the celebratory single, "Solsbury Hill," a messianic fantasy with an indelible melody. The 1978 follow-up was produced by Robert Fripp, and it's a darker, sparer effort that pays tribute to the punk aesthetic on the tune "D.I.Y." But the singer's best post-Genesis album is the third *Peter Gabriel*, produced by Steve Lillywhite and released in 1980. Working with Kate Bush, XTC's Dave Gregory, Fripp, Tony Levin, and others, Gabriel focused on the rhythm and his vocals, using the other instruments to add color or the odd instrumental hook. Over tribal, cymbal-less rhythms, he delivers ten vignettes that explore the minds of a presidential assassin ("Family Snapshot"), a prowler ("Intruder"), and an imprisoned mental patient ("Lead a Normal Life"). In "Biko," he pays heartfelt tribute to slain South African activist Steven Biko, and in "Games Without Frontiers," he creates one of the catchiest singles ever about the stupidity of war.

Gabriel's subsequent efforts all offer variations on these formulas, incorporating ethnic instruments and more elaborate beats, or streamlining the production for MTV-friendly dance tunes. Hits such as "Sledgehammer" and "Steam" have permanently changed his status from art rocker to pop celebrity, but he continues to experiment with more ethereal sounds on soundtracks such as *Birdy* and *The Last Temptation of Christ*, and his live shows consistently set new standards for what's possible in enormodomes. In contrast, Genesis followed a slow but steady decline into

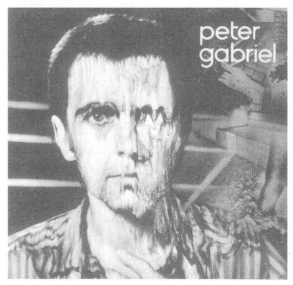

Gabriel goes it alone: the singer's third solo album.

They can't dance: Genesis in the '90s.

stultifying mediocrity, even as it became one of rock's bestselling bands. Collins came out from behind the drum set and flaunted a hammy nature that had long been stifled, and it wasn't long before Hackett left, too. Although only four albums of new material followed in the '80s, each was a platinum seller that yielded such easy-listening hits as "Misunderstanding," "Mama," "Invisible Touch," and "Land of Confusion."

Sitting in the presidential suite at New York's ritzy Peninsula Hotel in 1991, I talked with the three remaining members of Genesis about their seventeenth album, a declaration of pride in dinosaurdom called *We Can't Dance*. Did they ever wish they could record under a different name, I asked, lock themselves in their studio, get really stoned, and cut loose to make another album as willfully weird as *The Lamb Lies Down on Broadway*? "I suppose if one was doing that, one would probably try to be more off the wall," Banks said wistfully, transformed for a moment into the teenage musician jamming in the cottage in Dorking. "I think the sheer reason for doing it would surely be to try to do a few things that might be disastrous."

"At the same time, it might be nice to do something like we've just done and call it a different name and see how it's received," Collins added with more than a touch of annoyance. "By saying that, you're playing into—what's your name?—Jim's hands, because you're admitting that, because we're going in and calling it a different band, we actually have confines within Genesis that we want to stick to."

"Well, that's a fair enough comment to make," Banks replied, scowling at his partner. "Because there's probably some truth in it."

CHAPTER 7

Just Say Yes: Psychedelia Stretches Out

Jimi Hendrix was the flower generation's electric nigger dandy—its king stud and golden calf, its maker of mighty dope music, its most outrageously visible force—superspade, in the argot of the day. Though his music still sounds resonant today—even his most faddish stuff, somehow—his image remains a troubling one. For Hendrix was a revolutionary musician—perhaps the only one, in the end, to come out of the whole mid-'60s psychedelic explosion. Yet this has often been obscured, both by the rather degrading image and by the freakishly flamboyant veneer that helped make his art so popular.

—John Morthland[1]

Starting in the late '60s and continuing into the '70s, the influence of psychedelic drugs and the rock 'n' roll they inspired could clearly be heard in other musical genres, including soul, jazz, and blues. The most influential artists synthesized sounds in ways that hadn't been heard before, and the first and most influential synthesist was a guitarist from Seattle.

Critic John Morthland wrote the words quoted above in the mid-'70s. Through the '80s, yuppie nostalgia for the halcyon '60s obscured Hendrix's contributions even more, at least in the minds of post-Baby

Boomers. Today, record store bins are filled with dozens of pieces of Hendrix product, despite the fact that he sanctioned the release of only three studio albums and one live disc in his lifetime. It's difficult if not impossible for new listeners to assess his legacy when the meaningless notion that he was "the greatest electric guitarist who ever lived" is carved in granite on the base of his statue in the rock pantheon. "The 'authorized version' of the Jimi Hendrix experience [*sic*] is that Hendrix was a crazy black man who did funny things with a guitar, had thousands of women, and eventually died of drugs, which was a shame because he was a really good guitarist, and he could play it with his teeth, too," Charles Shaar Murray wrote in *Crosstown Traffic*, the best guide to appreciating Hendrix's music.[2] The problem with the "authorized version" is that it doesn't tally with the facts.

He was born John Allen Hendrix in Seattle in 1942 (when he was three, his father legally changed his name to James Marshall Hendrix), and he turned to the guitar at age thirteen as refuge from a troubled home life. He dropped out of high school, joined the 101st Airborne, and was discharged in 1962 when he injured his back. For the next three years, Hendrix worked as a freelance R&B sideman on the Southern chitlin' circuit, playing with Little Richard, the Isley Brothers, and Curtis Knight, among others. In 1966 he struck out on his own, leading Jimmy James and the Blue Flames in an extended run at the Cafe Wha? in Greenwich Village. If Hendrix hadn't been exposed to LSD before—and the biographies are sketchy on this point—he certainly sampled it when he began hanging out with Ed Sanders and the Fugs. By this time, he'd become a devotee of John Coltrane, Ornette Coleman, and Roland Kirk, and echoes of free jazz could be heard in his extended onstage jams. These soon attracted the rock cognoscenti. Animals bassist Chas Chandler presented himself as manager and brought Hendrix to London in September 1966. The guitarist was immersed in the nascent psychedelic-rock scene, and he was paired with the Experience: Englishmen Noel Redding, a guitarist turned bassist, and Mitch Mitchell, a jazzy drummer heavily influenced by Elvin Jones.

Over the next four years—until he choked on his own vomit in September 1970—Hendrix produced four albums. *Are You Experienced?* (1967) and the singles that preceded it are raw, focused psychedelic rock that wouldn't sound out of place on *Nuggets*. Much of *Axis: Bold as Love* was recorded at the same Chandler-produced sessions, but it's looser, jazzier, and more expansive. *Electric Ladyland* (1968) is the only album

Hendrix produced himself, and it's a sprawling exploration of the studio as a place to create what he called "sound paintings." Finally, there's *Band of Gypsys*, recorded live at New York's Fillmore East with army buddy Billy Cox and drummer Buddy Miles on New Year's Eve, 1969. With the exception of "Machine Gun," it's a sloppy throwaway released to pay off the claims of an earlier manager.

Jimi Hendrix registers the joy of playing electric guitar, 1968.

Those who worked with Hendrix talk about his high standards in the studio, but those standards were trashed soon after his death. *The Cry of Love* and *Soundtrack From Rainbow Bridge* (1971) cannibalized the double album in progress when he died at age twenty-seven. In the years that followed, jams, demos, and studio experiments were packaged and sold with the justification that every note played by the greatest guitarist who ever lived was something to be cherished. But the albums that Hendrix himself sanctioned show that his accomplishment was crafting songs, sounds, and stylistic syntheses—not solos. "Hendrix was a composer and lyricist of considerable gifts, but his songwriting talents have been largely overshadowed by his achievements as a showman and an instrumentalist," Murray wrote.[3] His three studio albums succeed because of the emotions conveyed by the melodies and lyrics on songs such as "Manic Depression," "Purple Haze," "Spanish Castle Magic," "Rainy Day, Dream Away," and "1983 . . . (a Merman I Should Turn to Be)." These songs didn't exist just so Hendrix could solo over them. On all of these tracks, Hendrix is more interested in creating moods with the sound of his guitar than impressing people with the notes that he's playing.

Hendrix's time as an R&B sideman taught him that rhythm guitar was as important as lead. His style was based on playing both at once, as well as employing the psychedelic rocker's arsenal of effects (feedback, wah-wah, fuzz and distortion, variable tape speed, and the rotating Leslie speaker). "It's the most psychedelic experience I ever had, going to see Hendrix play," Pete Townshend said. "When he started to play, something changed: colors changed, everything changed."[4] In a famous dis of his appearance at the Monterey Pop Festival, Robert Christgau called Hendrix "a psychedelic Uncle Tom." Unlike the songs of many of his peers, Hendrix's didn't directly address political issues. But as Murray and others pointed out, Hendrix's whole public life was a political act—a challenge to conformity among both whites and blacks—and he did have a political vision, albeit a utopian one. Hendrix was fascinated with science fiction (the exploration of outer space) and psychedelic drugs (the exploration of inner space), not because he wanted to escape but because he wanted to create an ideal world. He had a dream, and he called it the Electric or Sky Church. Murray described it as "a context for participatory worship, learning and communion without regard for denomination or demeanor."[5]

Hendrix himself rejected the label "psychedelic" for his music. "It's a mixture of rock, blues, and jazz, a music that's still developing, that's just now coming, a music of the future," he said. "We just happened to be playing freak-outs and psychedelic things, but it does bother us because 'psychedelic' only means mind expansion anyway. There's so many other types of music."[6] "Third Stone From the Sun" and "Manic Depression" synthesize free jazz and psychedelic rock. "Red House" and "Voodoo Chile" fuse psychedelic rock and blues, complete with the ancient black-magic mysteries. ("Hendrix played Delta blues for sure— only the Delta may have been on Mars," bluesman Tony Glover wrote.[7]) As for soul, it was there in the rhythms and in the way that Hendrix arranged tunes for his bands. "Jimi Hendrix's music could not have existed without soul music, and modern soul music would have been inconceivable without his," Murray wrote.[8]

One of the saddest aspects of Hendrix's legacy is that the syntheses he created were never extended in jazz or blues. The jazz fusion that followed was arid and vapid, full of indulgent instrumental displays and devoid of rock 'n' roll grit or punch. (Miles Davis hinted at what his aborted collaboration with Hendrix could have sounded like on 1976's *Agharta*, but it was only an approximation.) Plenty of blues musicians invoke Hendrix's tones and notes while remaining hopelessly earthbound in their vision. But things were different in the realm of soul and funk.

Cosmic Contrivances and Psychedelic Soul

"Mommy, what's a Funkadelic?"
"Someone from Carolina who encountered eternity on LSD and vowed to contain it in a groove."

—"Mommy, What's a Funkadelic?" 1970

The Experience followed Sly and the Family Stone at Woodstock, but it was the other way around on the pop charts. Hendrix's success paved the way for Texas-born Sylvester Stewart, a former Bay Area record producer and deejay whose radio show mixed Bob Dylan, the psychedelic Beatles, and R&B. Stewart/Stone took the same approach with his own band, adding a slippery bass and snappy backbeat that took prominence over everything else in the mix.

Like Hendrix, Stone had a vision of a psychedelic utopia. His band was a microcosm of this ideal world: men and women, blacks and whites, working together, shifting roles, and sharing the spotlight. He urged the rest of America to do the same on songs such as "Everyday People," "Everybody Is a Star," and "I Want to Take You Higher." But like many idealists, his optimism was drained by the end of the '60s. Critic Dave Marsh called 1971's foreboding *There's a Riot Goin' On* the aural equivalent of William Burroughs's *Naked Lunch.* "Sly's utopia had revealed its other face: hell," Marsh wrote.[9] As the '70s progressed, Stone was increasingly lost in a druggy haze and his albums turned to uninspired disco, until he finally withdrew from music completely.

Others picked up where he left off. Curtis Mayfield and War blended elements of Hendrix's guitar sound and Stone's rhythms into soul and pop classics. Hendrix pals the Chambers Brothers created a brilliant psychedelic single with 1968's "Time Has Come Today." Stevie Wonder adopted psychedelia's open-ended approach to synthesizers and the recording studio, using it to talk with God, deride superstition, and rail against living in the city. Working with producer Norman Whitfield, Wonder's Motown label mates the Temptations produced a string of uplifting psychedelic singles, including "I Can't Get Next to You," "Cloud Nine," and "Psychedelic Shack." Comedian Bill Cosby parodied this outbreak of psychedelic soul on a 1968 single called "Hooray for the Salvation Army Band." Like many members of his generation, he dismissed the music as escapism, but this was before he or anyone else had heard Parliament-Funkadelic.

George Clinton was born in Kannapolis, North Carolina, in 1941, and he likes to say his momma delivered him in an outhouse. In 1952 his family moved north to Newark, New Jersey. He found escape from the spiritless urban sprawl in doo-wop music, and he formed his first group at age fourteen, taking the name from a brand of cigarettes. The Parliaments recorded for two small labels based in Detroit, and Clinton was intrigued by groups such as the Amboy Dukes, the Stooges, and the

MC5. He was also a fan of the Beatles and Sly Stone, and he was impressed by what they had accomplished in the studio. Taking the PATH train from Newark to Manhattan after a day's work at the Uptown Tonsorial Parlor, the young barber and musician immersed himself in the psychedelic subculture and he soon convinced his group to adopt its colorful fashions.

The band traveled regularly to Boston and indulged in LSD courtesy of the test program at Harvard University. "We weren't even supposed to be there, but the kids were giving it to us," Clinton told me. "We met Tim Leary, but we didn't know who the hell he was and he didn't know who we were. We were older, so we thought they were all crazy. We were just having a ball with the free love, and we just thought we were getting over. But it just kind of changed us. The LSD thing and traveling around really opened us up and got us out of the whole ghetto thing."

Another turning point came when the Parliaments opened for the sludge-metal group, the Vanilla Fudge and used that band's massive Marshall stacks. "Now we knew what that sound was about," Clinton said. The band dropped the "s" from its name and started honing a new and weirder sound, extending soul, R&B, and psychedelic rock into a new brand of funk. Motown passed, but another Detroit label called Westbound was interested. For a while, it wasn't clear that Clinton had rights to the name, so the same band started recording as the Funkadelics. When Clinton recovered the Parliament moniker, the group started using that to record for Casablanca. Thus Clinton pulled off the rare feat of signing the same band to two labels at once.

The ParliaFunkadelicment family came to include several veterans of James Brown's band—Fred Wesley, Maceo Parker, Rick Gardner, and William "Bootsy" Collins—as well as Hendrix-inspired guitarists Eddie Hazel, Glenn Goins, and Dewayne "Blackbird" McKnight. Parliament was the more focused, accessible, horn-driven group; Funkadelic, the trippier, guitar-happy, experimental outfit. Albums were released at the frantic pace of two or three a year into the early '80s, when the bands fell apart amid mounting financial and drug problems. (Funkadelic's swansong was 1981's pioneering electronic effort, *The Electric Spanking of War Babies*, for which Clinton briefly coaxed Sly Stone out of retirement.)

Most Clinton albums are equal parts brilliance and bullshit, but the music is bearable even at its most indulgent because the emphasis is always on the hypnotic groove. The bands were never really about songs, so they are ill served by "greatest hits" collections. (Listeners tend to wind up owning either all or none of the thirty-odd releases, not counting offshoots such as Bootsy's Rubber Band, a side project that spun out of the bassist's ability to improvise long cosmic monologues in the style of Hendrix.) At the core of every effort is the rhythm section, harmony group vocals, and trademark chanting, but at any given time, these can be augmented by bagpipes, steel guitars, synthesizers, early drum machines, cartoony Alvin-and-the-Chipmunks vocals, and countless other weird overdubs, most of them done on the fly.

George Clinton in all his psychedelic splendor.

One of the best of the early albums, 1970's acid-drenched *Free Your Mind and Your Ass Will Follow*, was recorded and mixed in one day. "I had just learned about panning," Clinton said. "I still don't know about the board. I don't wanna know nothin' about the board. . . . Sly said, 'Hey, man, don't learn no better.' I said, 'What do you mean?' He said, 'If you knew better, you wouldn't do that!' It takes you a long time to think about what that means: If you knew better, you wouldn't make those *nice mistakes.*"[10]

Clinton's lyrics can be scatological or nonsensical, but a central message emerges loud and clear on every album. Robert Christgau described this recurring theme as "the forces of life—autonomous intelligence, a childlike openness, sexual energy, and humor—defeat those of death: by seduction if possible, by force if necessary."[11] In the mid-'70s Clinton began couching this idea in elaborate outer-space fantasies in concept albums modeled after *Tommy* and *Sgt. Pepper's*. In 1977 Parliament toured with an outrageous spaceship stage set. "The idea was putting blacks in places where you weren't supposed to see them," Clinton said. "I thought, 'Space!' The only black person you saw in space was Uhura on *Star Trek*. A nigger on a spaceship was probably a real cool dude, especially if it was leaving."

In his fascinating essay "Brothers From Another Planet," critic John Corbett linked Clinton's "Afronauts" and "space madness" to the work of two other influential black musicians: jazz composer Sun Ra and reggae producer Lee "Scratch" Perry. All three men were innovators. Clinton's use of drum machines and raps paved the way for hip-hop, Sun

Ra was among the first musicians to use synthesizers, and Perry pioneered the production technique known as dub by "dubbing out," or stripping away, the vocals in effects-laden instrumental remixes. All three worked under various aliases; sported outlandish, colorful costumes, and favored wild and sometimes incomprehensible wordplay. And all three were dismissed as loony after claiming to be aliens.

"While this E.T. metaphor—if it can be considered a metaphor—may indicate the insanity of its maker, it also cuts back the other direction, suggesting the fundamental unreality of existence for people imported into New World servitude and then disenfranchised into poverty," Corbett wrote.[12] He included Sun Ra's *Sonic Tones for Mental Therapy*, Funkadelic's "Back in Our Minds," and Perry's "I Am a Madman" in a long line of African-American songs that talk about "madness" not only in terms of the intoxicating effect of drugs, but as a way of shaking off inhibitions and escaping social oppression. These artists weren't trying to run away to outer space. Like Hendrix, they were hoping to build a new society there. "Tradition = earth; innovation = outer space," Corbett wrote. "In the language of black music, madness and extraterrestriality go hand in hand."[13] Of course, space wasn't restricted only to the funky.

Psychedelic Warlords

Originally, we just wanted to freak people out. We used to portray different trips, and because of our own experiences, we knew exactly how to get through to people.

—Dave Brock[14]

While many groups in the initial wave of psychedelic rock proceeded to hone a more genteel brand of art rock, a mixture of radical politics, psychedelic drugs, and rock 'n' roll prompted music with a much harder edge from several likeminded camps in England and the United States. The same Detroit scene that spawned the Amboy Dukes produced punk and metal forebearers the Motor City (MC) 5 and the Psychedelic Stooges. The members of the MC5 combined John Sinclair's White Panther politics with ferocious two-guitar assaults that drew inspiration from Ornette Coleman, John Coltrane, and Sun Ra, whose "Starship" they covered. The Stooges eventually shortened their name and alternated droning ragas with raw rock on their 1969 debut, then offered their own take on free jazz on 1970's *Fun House*.

San Francisco's Blue Cheer mangled Eddie Cochran and Mose Allison with gleeful, noisy abandon. The band was managed by Augustus Owsley Stanley, who was still pursuing his primary career as a master chemist, and he brewed up a special batch of his finest in honor of the group. Iron Butterfly will be forever cursed for ushering in the endless drum solo with "In-a-Gadda-Da-Vida." In London, singer and writer Mick Farren led a group called the Social Deviants that urged anti-authoritarian action over raw, bluesy rock. In 1969 the Deviants mutated into the Pink Fairies, and they continued mining the same guitar-heavy vein through shifting lineups that included Pretty Things drummer Twink and guitarist Larry Wallis of UFO, a band that took its name from the psychedelic-rock club.

Now considered heavy-metal pioneers, UFO, Judas Priest, and Black Sabbath started as bluesy psychedelic-rock bands complete with trippy effects and lighting. "Acid rock was aimed not at one's legs or crotch, but at one's head," Deena Weinstein wrote in her definitive book, *Heavy Metal: A Cultural Sociology*. "It wasn't dance music. Getting lost in the music was 'getting' the music. This ecstatic use of music was taken up by heavy metal in a Dionysian key, for heavy metal revels in the powers of life."[15] Metal was born when these bands shifted modes from mind-bending to head-banging, but one group managed both at once.

Guitarist Dave Brock, free-jazz saxophonist Nik Turner, and electronics wizard Dikmik first came together as Group X in London's Ladbroke Grove hippie community, which was also home to the Pink Fairies. In late 1969 Group X became Hawkwind, and in 1970 it signed to Liberty/United Artists, which was also home to several adventurous German bands. Hawkwind built its early reputation by playing long jams at free shows and festivals such as the Glastonbury Fayre. Produced by the Pretty Things' Dick Taylor, its 1970 debut is typical, bluesy proto-metal with occasional nods to Pink Floyd.

Before returning to the studio, the group added several key ingredients: the more elaborate synthesizers of Del Dettmar (perhaps the only dwarf to ever play in a rock band), a more assertive style of bass playing courtesy of Dave Anderson from the German group Amon Düül II, and imaginative lyrics penned by Robert Calvert, a talented South African poet and science-fiction writer. Pink Floyd and Hendrix had flirted with science fiction on tunes such as "Interstellar Overdrive" and

"Third Stone From the Sun," but 1971's *In Search of Space* was an album-length voyage into the cosmos, and Hawkwind never really returned. Not coincidentally, the album arrived in the middle of the United States' six lunar expeditions. "There was the exploration of the moon and all of that, and we seem to have caught the public's attention by doing that sort of stuff at the same time," Brock said.[16]

Like many Hawkwind albums, *In Search of Space* was recorded live in the studio without the benefit of overdubs or retakes. "We were taking a lot of LSD at the time," Turner said. "It helped."[17] The random synthesizer sounds and saxophone bleats verge on the chaotic, and the lyrics can be laughable to anyone who doesn't appreciate science fiction. But the group is saved from pointless indulgence by a love of pounding backbeats and catchy riffs—hallmarks of the best heavy metal. Not for nothing was Hawkwind adopted by bikers on both sides of the Atlantic.

The pinnacle of Hawkwind's psychedelic-metal-science fiction synthesis is the anthemic single "Silver Machine." The song features a driving bass line and vocals courtesy of former Hendrix roadie Lemmy Kilmister, who spent five years with the band before he was kicked out for taking too much of the wrong drug. (The speed-happy Lemmy went on to form the punk-metal Motörhead, which took its name from a Hawkwind song.) A bona fide hit, "Silver Machine" funded the band's ambitious Space Ritual tour in 1973. The traveling group consisted of seven band members, six roadies, five lighting technicians, three go-go dancers (including the legendary Stacia), and DJ Andy Dunkley, who spun records backward before and during the set in a primitive precursor to scratching and sampling. "It was a very communal thing," Turner said, but members joined and left the community at a dizzying pace. Calvert had started performing with the group in 1972, singing, reading poetry, and acting out characters in the songs by swinging a giant broadsword or donning an aviator's helmet and goggles. He quit in 1974 and was replaced by his friend, science fiction writer Michael Moorcock. "Periodically, [Calvert] would have to be carted off by the men in white coats," Moorcock said. "He was certifiably crazy, whatever that means."[18] On

Space pirate Robert Calvert, pre-freak-out.

his own, Calvert made two extraordinary concept albums with Brian Eno, *Captain Lockheed and the Starfighters* (1974) and *Lucky Lief and the Longships* (1975). He rejoined Hawkwind in 1976 as the group switched labels from United Artists to Charisma, quit again a few years later, and was reportedly considering another return when he died of a heart attack in 1988.

Turner left the group following *Astounding Sounds Amazing Music* in 1976, and by this time, the group's "all-aboard" collaborative spirit was long gone. "Throughout the history of Hawkwind, Dave is the guy who hired and fired everybody," Turner told me. "Everybody thought it was their band until they suddenly got the sack." Reenergized by interest from the ambient and techno communities, Brock is the sole original member leading Hawkwind into the '90s. Turner is going strong as well, and in 1994 he toured with Dettmar

Nik Turner, still tripping in the '90s. (Photo by Iggy Vamp.)

and San Francisco guitarist Helios Creed as Nik Turner's Space Ritual. Both camps still provide wonderful live experiences.

"Personally, I'm surprised we've got so far," Turner said in 1971. "I never thought our music would appeal to anybody, simply because we've never pandered to public taste, never compromised, and just played exactly what we wanted. By a happy accident, people seem to dig it."[19] His words still ring true twenty-five years later.

Tits! Tits! The Blimp! The Blimp!

I had the rare good fortune to talk to the Captain recently about his music, and noted that I hadn't really understood *Trout Mask Replica*. "That's okay," he said, "just put it on and then go back to doing whatever it was you were doing and it'll come to you." Well, what I was doing was sweeping the floor, so I had my doubts, but I did it anyhow. Damned if it didn't push the broom.

—Ed Ward, 1970[20]

Though few serious contenders emerged to extend the specific fusions that Hendrix pioneered, some bands did incorporate elements of jazz, blues, and psychedelic rock in other distinctive syntheses. England's Soft Machine toured with Hendrix and readily swapped free-jazz influences, while Georgia's Allman Brothers honed a merger of bluesy vocals, jazzy polyrythms, and intricate twin-guitar parts that recalled a more structured Grateful Dead. The Allmans also incorporated psychedelic mushrooms into their mythology the same way the Dead incorporated Owsley's acid.

A more focused and melodic version of Southern-fried psychedelia was explored by the Memphis band Big Star on its third album. The band's first two efforts combined a love of British pop with soulful Stax/Volt roots. Much of the magic came from the interplay between former teen sensation Alex Chilton, a veteran of the Box Tops, and band founder Chris Bell, who quit early into the making of 1974's *Radio City*. Bell went on to craft a transcendent album called *I Am the Cosmos* with strings, marimbas, synthesizers, and backward guitars floating in and out of the mix, but it was not released until long after his death in 1978. Burned out, bitter, and abusing drugs and alcohol, Chilton purged his demons on *Third* (a.k.a. *Sister Lovers*), a haunting, soul-searching disc that contorts the band's influences into strange and often psychedelic shapes. Chilton never matched its power again.

The other heavies of psychedelic synthesis were two teenage buddies from the Mojave Desert town of Lancaster, California. Frank Zappa and Don Van Vliet attended Antelope Valley High School together in the late '50s. They shared a fondness for raw blues, R&B, and doo-wop, and they played in a number of unrecorded bands before drifting apart. Zappa moved to Los Angeles in the early '60s and linked up with a five-piece R&B band called the Soul Giants, which became the Mothers of Invention. Under Zappa's direction, the Mothers progressed from standard bar-band fare such as "Louie Louie" and "Gloria" to compositions that combined modern classical music, jazz, R&B, and rock.

The Mothers were signed to MGM/Verve by producer Tom Wilson, who also worked with the Velvet Underground. Four times more expensive to record than most rock albums at the time, *Freak Out!* was released in 1966 and featured the Mothers plus a seventeen-piece orchestra. While some of the songs allude to modern composers Igor Stravinsky, Edgard Varèse, and Karlheinz Stockhausen, much of the album is raw, fuzz-driven, *Nuggets*-style rock. At the time, it was perceived as a druggy, scatological effort in the style of the Fugs, but in fact, Zappa was positioning freaks (genuinely weird and creative people) against hippies (whom he considered sheep), and he was strongly antidrug. "We are here to turn you loose, not turn you on," he wrote. "Turn *yourself* on."[21]

The band continued railing against conformity in similar fashion on 1967's *Absolutely Free*. Later the same year, Zappa took a detour along with some of the Mothers and a fifty-piece orchestra to experiment with electronics and *musique concrète* on *Lumpy Gravy* before gearing up for his ultimate assault on plastic people, psychedelia, and idealism. The cover of 1968's *We're Only in It for the Money* parodied *Sgt. Pepper's Lonely Hearts Club Band*; its lyrics mercilessly lampooned the hippies, and its music was the most intricate from Zappa or rock in general to date. "Whether it is the *best* is a moot point—how would you compare it with, for instance, Otis Redding?" wrote *Rolling Stone* reviewer Barret Hansen.[22] Actually, it wasn't a moot point, and comparisons show that—regardless of his accomplishments in the unique genre best described as Zappa music—Uncle Frank was never an especially great *rocker*. "In the end, the most pertinent thing to be said about Frank Zappa is probably that for all he knows about music, he lacks the talent to write a song like 'Louie Louie,'" Lester Bangs wrote. While Zappa was conning rock audiences into thinking that his arrogance and condescension were warranted by his horizon-broadening sounds, Bangs contended, Captain Beefheart was making statements that were much more far-reaching.[23]

Rechristened by his old pal Zappa, Van Vliet/Beefheart had a much harder time getting his musical career off the ground. In the mid-'60s, he won a Vox battle of the bands contest and got to record two singles for A&M Records. The first, a garagey version of "Diddy Wah Diddy," was a regional hit, but A&M rejected a debut album as "too negative." Beefheart formed a new band and recorded *Safe As Milk* for Kama Sutra in 1967. It was straightforward garage-band blues distinguished by Beefheart's remarkable vocals, which were strongly influenced by Howlin' Wolf and Little Richard. When the music took a turn for the weirder on tour, guitarist Ry Cooder quit just in time to force the cancellation of an appearance at the Monterey Pop Festival.

Released in 1968, *Strictly Personal* started to focus on Beefheart's new sound, a music that was as carefully planned and orchestrated as Zappa's but as raw as the rawest Delta blues and as unrestricted as the most adventurous free jazz. Unfortunately, the album was mixed without Beefheart's participation, and the Captain was disgusted by the addition of

The Captain gives orders.

superfluous psychedelic effects. (The music was strange enough as it was.) Beefheart was beginning to think he'd never get it right on tape when Zappa reappeared and offered him the chance to record for his new label, Straight Records. Zappa gave Beefheart the same sort of freedom that Andy Warhol gave the Velvet Underground. "When we did the album with him, Frank said, 'Hey, let's go into the studio and you rehearse the group and we'll put down exactly what you want,'" said Zappa's manager, Herb Cohen. "It was the first album he ever made where he had total control of everything that went down."[24] Zappa's level of involvement is hard to pin down; Beefheart later complained that he just fell asleep at the console, but Zappa biographer Ben Watson believes that Frank gave Beefheart the necessary grounding so that his brand of surrealism wouldn't dissolve into irrationality. Zappa's bitter cynicism balanced Beefheart's childlike charm.

The mix on 1970's *Trout Mask Replica* highlights the recording in progress, including false beginnings, shouted cues, and flubbed vocal lines. The feeling of inspired improvisation contrasts with the knowledge that Beefheart obsessed over every note, carefully prescribing the intertwining guitar parts and preparing the drums by muting them with bits of cardboard to make the polyrhythms even harder to get a grip on. The influence of Delta blues and free-jazzer Albert Ayler are clear, but the album retains an essential rock-'n'-roll drive, and the Magic Band plays with a deliberate, primitive force. The music may or may not have been influenced by psychedelic drugs—"I can paint better than that," Beefheart said of LSD—but the swirl of guitars, drums, clarinets, and saxophones creates its own reality, and it's as disorienting as a sudden hallucination. The lyrics prompted Bangs to call Beefheart "the only true dadaist in rock," and they are a delight for anyone who savors the way words *sound.* "Children stop yer nursin' unless yer renderin' fun / The mother ship the mother ship / The mother ship's the one / The blimp the blimp / The tape's uh trip it's uh trailin' tail / It's traipse'n along behind the blimp the blimp," goes one memorable passage from "The Blimp (mousetrapreplica)."

Trout Mask Replica stands as Beefheart's masterpiece, but that's not to slight the albums that followed. *Lick My Decals Off, Baby* (1970) hones the sound of its predecessor, adds marimba, and reflects the influence of African music. *The Spotlight Kid* (1971) is simpler and bluesier, while *Clear Spot* (1972) has a harder rock edge. *Unconditionally Guaranteed* (1974) and *Bluejeans and Moonbeams* (1974) are both watered-down attempts to penetrate the mainstream, but Beefheart returns to his own idiosyncratic backwaters on *Shiny Beast (Bat Chain Puller)* (1978), *Doc at the Radar Station* (1980), and *Ice Cream for Crow* (1982). Always at odds with the business of making music and sensing that he had stopped breaking ground, Beefheart retired in 1983 to concentrate on sculpture and painting. His artwork now sells in the range of $40,000 per piece, and he rarely discusses his earlier adventures, making him one of the very few rockers who actually shut up once he said what he'd had to say.

CHAPTER 8

Broken Head
(Quiet, Super Genius at Work)

Use "unqualified" people . . . Give way to your worst impulse . . . A line has two sides . . . Do we need holes? . . . Is it finished?

—Oblique Strategies[1]

Standing in the shadows, just out of view but always part of the action, Brian Eno has been present at the back-alley births of some of the most adventurous musical movements since the early 1970s. Through the different phases of his career—from synthesizer player in Roxy Music, to solo artist, to producer and artistic instigator—the sounds he has made and the ideas he has expressed have inspired others in such diverse subgenres as as punk, noise rock, and ambient music. The common thread in all of his work has been an extremely psychedelic approach to the recording studio. Eno has never been at a loss to explain his methodology, and while some of his music ranks with the best psychedelic rock ever made, in the end, he earns a place of honor in this book as psychedelic rock's great philosopher.

Given his reputation as the ultimate "ideas man," it's ironic that Eno first gained attention as a supporting player in a project planned to the last detail by another artist. Eno and Bryan Ferry both attended art school in the mid-'60s, but they emerged with radically different philosophies. The son of a miner from County Durham, Ferry studied at Newcastle University with the pop artist Richard Hamilton. "Both the surrealists and the dada people were interesting to me because they shook things up so much without being so serious," Ferry told me. "But with pop art and Richard, suddenly there was a whole new world that was relevant, and that was sexier and more potent because it had to do with everyday life."

Born in 1948 to upper-middle-class parents in Woodbridge, Suffolk, Eno enrolled in Ipswich Art School in 1964. The school was run by Roy Ascott, a visionary teacher who had earlier taught Pete Townshend at Ealing Art College. After lunch one day, Ascott and the other teachers directed Eno and his classmates to assemble in the courtyard. The teachers locked them in and left them there for an hour, looking down at them from a rooftop but refusing to answer their questions. "All kinds of odd things began to happen," Eno recalled. "Guys tried to scale the walls, others banded together into ad hoc revolutionary committees, some said this was the last straw, others cried or formed conga chains and walked round chanting abuse at the staff." Finally, a taped voice announced, "You are worse than chickens . . . You have drawn with your own hands the formula, and now you look at it instead of reality."[2] Eno came away with an object lesson in creative thinking and the tension that can arise from being plunged into a novel situation.

While he was in college, Ferry gigged with a horn-driven R&B band called the Gas Board, singing songs by Otis Redding, Sam and Dave, Screamin' Jay Hawkins, and Wilson Pickett. After graduation, he moved to London and taught ceramics at a girls' school in Hammersmith, but his interest in music remained. "When I started writing music, I found it was like pop art," he said. "I was using images—like in the lyrics— throwaway clichés and amusing phrases that you found in magazines or used in everyday speech."[3] By late 1970, he was talking with former Gas Board mate Graham Simpson about forming a band that would be a total pop-art concept expressed in music. Ferry wanted a synthesizer player, and he heard that Andy Mackay was his man. Mackay was actually a classically trained woodwinds player, but he was interested, and he knew someone who *did* play synthesizer.

Mackay and Eno had been drawn together in college by a mutual interest in John Cage, Karlheinz Stockhausen, and electronic music pioneer Morton Subotnick. Eno had fooled around with tape recorders, signal generators, and synthesizers in two improvisational bands, Merchant Taylor's Simultaneous Cabinet and Maxwell's Demon. The notion of mixing things up in a rock band appealed to him. "I'd been working with avant-garde music but had just become interested in the many sides of rock music—not least the audience-performer relationship," Eno said. "There's a whole lot of physical excitement in it, which appealed to me."[4] Eno called this physical excitement "idiot energy." Growing up in the shadows of two American air bases, he had become addicted to it while listening to Armed Forces Radio. The psychedelic rock of the '60s— especially the Beatles, Jimi Hendrix, and the Velvet Underground—convinced him that the music was unlimited and could even be expanded to include more "serious" ideas from the electronic avant-garde.

Electronic music making had evolved from early, primitive instruments such as the theremin, through the limited and enormous synthesizers of the mid-'60s (including the one that transsexual Walter/Wendy Carlos used on the celebrated *Switched On Bach*), to relatively portable and reliable "performance" models such as the Moogs favored by most rockers. Synthesizers crept into rock slowly through the late '60s and early '70s, and snatches of Moog could be heard on the Beatles' *Abbey Road*. More significant and psychedelic was synthesizers' use on the self-titled 1968 debut by the United States of America; 1968 and 1969 albums by the strange New York duo, Silver Apples; the 1968 bow by Colorado's electronic garage rockers, Lothar and the Hand People, and *In a Wild Sanctuary* and *Gandharva*, environmental soundscapes crafted by San Franciscans Paul Beaver and Bernard Krause.

By the early '70s, every progressive-rock band had to have a synthesizer, but classically trained keyboardists such as Yes's Rick Wakeman and ELP's Keith Emerson treated them like souped-up organs. Eno prized them as purely electronic instruments, and he favored sounds that didn't mimic the instruments of the orchestra. He used them to throw an element of alien noise and random chaos into rock, the way psychedelic guitarists used feedback and the 13th Floor Elevators used their amplified jug. Twirling any one of the dozens of knobs and dials on a Mini-Moog could produce fantastic results that no one could predict, least of all Eno, and he further heightened the unpredictability of his keyboards by refusing to have them serviced when they developed glitches.

Ferry had already chosen a name for his group when Eno and Mackay joined. A press release noted that Roxy Music "was intended to convey a slightly old-style glamour with a pun on rock." Ferry had also designed

Retro-futuristic chic: The center spread of Roxy Music's debut album; Eno left; Ferry, center.

the look as a cross between '50s greaser and futuristic glitz. The band was completed by two final recruits, drummer Paul Thompson and guitarist Phil Manzanera. (Originally the band's soundman, Manzanera replaced Ferry's first choice on guitar, Davey O'List of the Nice.) Ferry knew that pop art is half marketing and half art. A well-orchestrated campaign spread the word about Roxy through the *Melody Maker* and a session with BBC DJ John Peel recorded while O'List was still in the group. The band's popularity exploded almost overnight, and with only half a dozen gigs to its credit, the group was signed to Island Records.

Roxy Music was recorded in March 1972. King Crimson guitarist Robert Fripp had been pegged as producer, but he had scheduling conflicts, so the band settled for former Crimson lyricist Peter Sinfield. Naturally, Ferry designed the art. The nostalgic Vargas-style pinup on the front cover fit perfectly, but the inside shots of the band in their retro/futuristic outfits backfired. More than one reviewer dismissed the group as "Sha Na Na with a synthesizer," which was a horrible injustice. *Roxy Music* draws on rock's past and twists it thoroughly, as evidenced by the crazy-quilt construction of "Re-make/Re-model." The tune could be a love song to a girl, a car, or both. (Its driving beat builds to a shouted chorus based on the English license plate number CPL 593A.) The band's four lead instruments—Mackay's '50s-style sax, Manzanera's fluid guitar, Eno's synthesizer, and Ferry's sexy, theatrical singing—fight a constant battle for dominance. At one point, each player is given a solo spot, and the musicians draw attention to the influences at work. Simpson plays the bass lick from the Beatles' "Day Tripper," Eno wooshes and bleeps like a passing UFO, Mackay quotes Wagner's "The Ride of the

Valkyries," Manzanera churns through some classic garage-band chords, and Ferry pounds his piano in Cage-style discord.

The rest of the album is equally inventive. The first wave of psychedelic rock had been adventurous in embracing different musical genres and world beats, but Roxy was going even further, and—in pop-art fashion—it was drawing attention to the creative process. As publicist Simon Puxley wrote in the album's Beat-poetic liner notes, "Fantasising: phantomising: echoes of magic-golden moments become real presences . . . dreamworld & realworld loaded with images." Onstage, Ferry was a captivating frontman with matinee idol looks and a voice to match, but Eno was just as hard to ignore. Blond hair flying and ostrich feathers flapping, he played the role of mad scientist, coaxing strange noises from his Mini-Moog and warping the sounds being made by Manzanera and Mackay by feeding them through an EMS modular synthesizer. Much was made in the early '70s of Eno's status as a "nonmusician." He never had any formal musical training and he couldn't read music, but he certainly had an ear for melody, harmonizing with Ferry, and later layering vocals on his own albums. Eventually, he learned to play chords on keyboard, guitar, and bass, but the instrument he loved best was the studio itself. With childlike naïveté, Eno simply refused to believe that there were things that *couldn't* be done.

Rock was primed for such fresh thinking in 1972. Along with David Bowie and Marc Bolan of T. Rex, Roxy was fighting boring pub rock on one front and pompous art rock on the other. The glam movement's weapons of choice were sex, drugs, and good old-fashioned rock-'n'-roll energy, but in Roxy, the sex and energy were always more evident than the drugs. Eno in particular thought that the "view of the musician or artist as an impulsive, drug-taking romantic" had become a cliché.[5] He challenged convention in other ways, proudly proclaiming his love for women's clothing. "I don't like masculine clothing," he said. "The Western version of masculinity opposes rational man against intuitive woman. The part of my being that interests me has always been my intuition."[6]

Before its second album, Roxy underwent a series of personnel changes. Ferry fired his old chum Simpson for missing rehearsals. He was replaced by Rik Kenton, who in turn was canned for thinking that the group should record some of *his* songs. The cover of *For Your Pleasure* reminded everyone who was boss. Ferry is the only band member pictured, posing as a limo driver waiting to chauffeur a glamorous model who is walking a black panther on a chain. The album polishes formulas established on the debut. It was even more successful critically and commercially, but tensions in the band erupted during the group's first headlining tour. "Basically, the problems stemmed from the fact that we're too similar," Eno said of Ferry. "We're both from almost identical backgrounds, with a very similar approach to music in the sense that we're both non-musicians, working from an ideas angle rather than musical material."[7] Eno was derailing Ferry's concepts simply by being Eno. "I was cramping Eno's style," Ferry said in the official press statement. "Two nonmusicians in a band is one too many. I think he'll do very well by himself."[8]

Ferry didn't do badly, either. He replaced Eno with violinist Eddie Jobson of progressive rockers Curved Air, and the other band members were only temporarily peeved that they weren't consulted. The group took a break while Ferry recorded his first solo album, *These Foolish Things*, but it returned with *Stranded* in 1973, *Country Life* in 1974, and *Siren* in 1975. The rough edges of Ferry's increasingly romantic pop songs gradually smoothed out, but Manzanera and Mackay powered occasional tunes such as "Amazona," "Street Life," and "The Thrill of It All" with bursts of psychedelic energy. Roxy Music took a four-year hiatus after *Siren* but returned at the height of the new wave with *Manifesto*. Where before Ferry's suave crooning was one of several elements in a unique mix, it was now the focus. The band continued until 1982, disbanding after the pleasant background music of *Avalon*, its biggest U.S. hit.

Since the mid-'80s, Ferry has been at his best recording other people's songs (from "Eight Miles High" to John Lennon's "Jealous Guy" to "I Put a Spell on You"). In the spirit of surrealist artist Marcel Duchamp, he prefers the term "readymades" to "covers." "A lot of people have this strange prejudice against singers doing other people's songs," Ferry said. "But Elvis and Sinatra, the biggest singers of our century, they weren't songwriters. I think there's room for an interpretative role." Unlike Eno, Ferry chose his role and settled into it.

The Pop Albums

Repetition is a form of change . . . Honor thy error as a hidden intention . . . Ask people to work against their better judgement . . . Turn it upside down.

—Oblique Strategies[9]

Freed from Roxy Music but left with idiot energy to spare, Eno embarked on his solo career. Between 1973 and 1977, he produced four extraordinary efforts that are often referred to as his "pop albums." Rock 'n' roll continued to fascinate him, and now he was free to tackle it on his own terms. "What [*Stranded*] lacks for me is one of the most important elements of my musical life, which is insanity," he said. "I'm interested in things being absurd."[10]

One of Eno's central ideas was juxtaposing styles that were normally at odds. He provided a diverse group of musicians with a "central issue"—a basic groove, a melody, or a chord progression—then directed them through body language and the use of visual images. They often took his skeletal tunes in directions he'd never anticipated. The idea of "happy accidents" in the studio has a Zen beauty: You accept whatever fate has in store. But it also acknowledges the immediacy and spontaneity of all great rock 'n' roll. "Early rock music was, in a lot of cases, the product of incompetence, not competence," Eno said. "There's a misconception that these people were brilliant musicians, and they weren't. They had terrific ideas and a lot of balls."[11]

Eno recorded *Here Come the Warm Jets* during twelve days at London's Majestic Studios. He played "simplistic keyboards, snake guitar, electric larynx, and synthesizer" and electronically "treated" the other musicians' parts by feeding them through his synthesizers and racks of effects. The ten tunes are rock songs with identifiable verses, choruses, and solos, but everything is a bit left of center. Sometimes the drums provide the hook, the solos are deliberate "nonevents," or the vocals are buried in the mix. In many cases, all of the instruments are used in rhythmic roles.

During his college fascination with the avant-garde, Eno performed a piece by avant-garde composer La Monte Young that required him to hit the same cluster of notes on the piano at one-second intervals for an hour. This exercise taught him that repetition is a form of change, with slight variations in a repeating pattern taking on tremendous importance. In rock, he found similar ideas in Sly and the Family Stone—who placed the snare drum and bass guitar as the dominant instruments in the mix—and the Velvets. "The Velvet Underground used all of their instruments in the rhythm role and the singing in a deliberate monotone, which is a deliberate nonsurprise," Eno said. "When you listen to the music, your focus is shifting all the time because there's no ranking."[12]

Here Come the Warm Jets opens with the prominent, pounding rhythms of "Needles in the Camel's Eye." The title was inspired by the discordant "needlelike" guitar sound, which Eno achieved by rhythmically "playing" the tremelo bar on Phil Manzanera's guitar. Equally inventive are "Driving Me Backwards," a tune with an unwavering 4/4 rhythm that creates the feeling of swimming against a strong current; "Blank Frank," a song based on an Ipswich gangster who spoke only in the "incomprehensible proverbs" of a benzedrine head; "Baby's On Fire," which climaxes with one of the most frightening psychedelic guitar solos ever, and the title track, which recalls Mike Oldfield's regal instrumentals. (Eno said the phrase refers to urinating, but the feel of the song has more in common with the tides rolling in.) The singing that begins late in the song never becomes fully audible, and one of the only lines that can be made out is about "words that mean nothing to me."

At Ipswich, Eno was impressed with the phonetic recordings of dadaist poets Hugo Ball and Kurt Schwitters. In the studio, he often added his vocals after the instruments were recorded, developing melodies by scat-singing nonsense syllables. Eno was more interested in letting sounds rather than lyrics dictate what a song was "about." "I don't want to hear [lyrics] most of the time," he said. "They always impose something that is so unmysterious compared to the sound of the music that they debase the music for me."[13] Nevertheless, Eno could be a smart and funny lyricist. His tunes are full of evocative, poetic images. As biographer Eric Tamm noted, "Eno's lyrics stand directly in the tradition of painting with words in rock music that begins with Dylan and runs through the psychedelic songwriters of the late 1960s and early 1970s."[14] ("Send for an ambulance or an accident investigator / He's breathing like a furnace / So I'll see you later, alligator / He'll set the sheets on fire / Mmm, quite a burning lover," Eno sings in "The Paw Paw Negro Blowtorch," a song inspired by a Michigan man whose breath supposedly caused things to ignite.)

On his second album, Eno worked with a core band of Manzanera, Brian Turrington, and Freddie Smith (the rhythm section of the Winkies), and former Soft Machine vocalist Robert Wyatt. He found the title on a set of postcards depicting scenes from a Chinese opera. Some journalists probed the implications of *Taking Tiger Mountain (By Strategy)*—Was Eno a Maoist?—but as always, Eno shied away from politics. "To require of art that it gives political direction strikes me as rather like asking Albert Einstein to tell you the four-times table," he said.[15] It's likely that Eno meant the phrase as an obscure reference to his own creative process and a set of cards called Oblique Strategies. The origins of Oblique Strategies can be traced to index cards that Eno left lying around the studio to challenge his band mates in Roxy Music. By *Tiger Mountain*, he had formalized sixty-four "worthwhile dilemmas" in collaboration with his painter friend Peter Schmidt. The dilemmas were in the spirit of the *I Ching*. Their purpose, Eno said, was to bring the consciousness of an objective listener to one's consciousness as a composer. In 1975 Eno and Schmidt published Oblique Strategies as a deck of one hundred cards. They advised artists to choose a card and follow its advice absolutely whenever a problem arose in a creative endeavor.

It's impossible to say exactly how Oblique Strategies were used on *Tiger Mountain*, but the disc is full of abrupt left turns. Overall, it's bouncier and more upbeat than Eno's first effort, but the rollicking rhythms and strong melodies mask sinister subject matter. Behind the cheerful doo-wop vocals of "Burning Airlines Give You So Much More" is a lyric inspired by the 1974 explosion of a Turkish DC-10, at the time the worst air disaster in history. "The Fat Lady of Limbourg" is one of several of what Eno calls "Burroughs-type" songs. It could be the soundtrack to a spy film set in the Interzone, but it's actually about a town in Belgium where the inmates of a famous asylum outnumber the townfolk. As with slightly older peers such as Roger Waters, World War II loomed large during Eno's childhood, and a distinctly British wartime spirit is echoed in "Back in Judy's Jungle" and "Mother Whale Eyeless." But the most striking tune—and the one that predicts Eno's next move—is "The Great Pretender." The song depicts "the rape of a suburban housewife by a crazed machine," and it fades into an electronic chorus of chirping crickets that evoke natural forces as evil as the unnatural acts in the lyrics.

The "crickets" were evidence of Eno's growing interest in the texture of sounds. "To a great extent, Eno's music is concerned with the sheer color of sound, rather than with the linear, horizontal growth of melodies," Tamm wrote.[16] Eno began to think song structure was irrelevant. He wanted it to seem as if his songs existed before he turned on the tape recorder and continued after he stopped. Lyrics were becoming less important than ever, and nine of the fourteen pieces on *Another Green World* are instrumentals. Using a Hammond organ, synthetic percussion, and "electric elements and unnatural sounds," Eno conjures dinosaurs dancing on the edge of the tar pit on "Sombre Reptiles." "Little Fishes" takes the listener inside Eno's aquarium; the title track paints a picture of a womblike Garden of Eden, and "In Dark Trees" is full of lurking menace.

Less forceful than its predecessors, *Another Green World* stands as the best of Eno's pop albums. He was aware that he had reached a pinnacle, and the pressure of crafting a follow-up weighed heavily. He spent nearly three years recording some one hundred pieces, and after months of indecision, he finally settled on ten tracks that were released as *Before and After Science*. In keeping with the futuristic themes of several songs, the album is the coldest and most clinical of Eno's pop efforts. "Energy Fools the Magician" could be a sample of the Muzak playing in Dr. Frankenstein's lab. Several songs are in a similar mold, and only "King's Lead Hat" and "Kurt's Rejoinder" rock out. (The former is a tribute to Talking Heads—the title is an anagram—and the latter samples Eno's old hero Kurt Schwitters.)

After leaving Roxy Music, Eno played live on only a few occasions. In 1974 he taped a session for the BBC backed by the Winkies, playing a set that climaxed in a psychotic version of "Fever." With Manzanera and bassist Bill MacCormick, he was a member of the "all-star" band 801, which was captured on a live album released in 1976. An earlier live effort, *June 1, 1974*, features former Velvets John Cale and Nico, Kevin Ayers of the Soft Machine, and Mike Oldfield. The standouts on both albums are songs from the first psychedelic era. 801 covers the Beatles' "Tomorrow Never Knows," and the *June 1* group takes on "The End" by the Doors.

Eno wasn't interested in touring, and he didn't care about recording hits. With *Before and After Science*, he concluded that he had accomplished as much as he could in the rock idiom. "Effectively, what I've done is abandoned rock music," he said. "For me, rock isn't capable of producing that spiritual quality anymore. . . . Despite all the criticism that's been made of psychedelic music, it certainly was committed to the production of an expanded awareness."[17]

Ambient Albums and Productions

Take a break . . . Listen in total darkness, or in a very large room, very quietly . . . Ghost echoes . . . Give the game away.

—Oblique Strategies[18]

Eno abandoned rock, but he didn't abandon the psychedelic goal of transporting listeners to unexplored (and sometimes nonexistent) places. He began a series of albums that lacked vocals and obvious rhythmic drive and which boasted only simple, minimal hooks (when there were any at all). What Eno called his "ambient" efforts were albums that were designed to subliminally enhance the thousand tasks of everyday life; he said they rewarded close listening but didn't demand it. Something similar would be claimed by another genre that started gaining popularity at roughly the same time in the late '70s and early '80s. New Age music is the soundtrack to what *The New Rolling Stone Encyclopedia of Rock & Roll* called a "loosely defined metaphysical movement that incorporates Jungian psychology, ecological concern, and nontraditional spirituality." But while New Age music appeals to some veterans of psychedelic exploration, diverse practitioners such as synthesizer players Vangelis and Jean-Michel Jarre, harpist Andres Vollenweider, guitarist Kitaro, and virtually the entire Windham Hill roster are obsessed with such decidedly nonrock musical values as virtuosity and good taste. They have as their antecedent the impressionistic composer Claude Debussy, who tried to find musical equivalents for natural sounds. In contrast, ambient music is rather "punk" in its technical demands (there are none), and its techniques come from psychedelic rock (via its approach to the studio) and *musique concrète* (which used natural sounds themselves as music).

Eno's methods on his ambient albums were similar to the ones on his rock albums. Still no virtuoso, he simply set up systems that allowed the recordings to generate themselves. "I tend towards the roles of planner and programmer and then become an audience to the results," he said.[19] Anyone who had a digital synthesizer (the Yamaha DX7 was Eno's new weapon of choice), an echo unit, and two tape recorders could make similar pieces at home. Eno's albums were available for those who didn't want to bother. Recorded in September 1975, the thirty-minute title track on *Discreet Music* was intended to serve as the background for a live performance by frequent collaborator Robert Fripp (they had also recorded 1973's *No Pussyfooting* together). "Perhaps in the spirit of Satie, who wanted to make music that could mingle with the sound of the knives and forks at dinner," Eno said.[20] "Discreet Music" is perfect for writing, reading, drifting off to sleep, gentle afternoon lovemaking—or giving birth. "There are maternity hospitals that have this record around to play in the background because pregnant mothers like it a lot," Eno said. "That's one of the nicest things to me, to think that I've made something that people actually can use and like to have in their lives."

Music for Films followed in 1978. A compilation of eighteen instrumentals recorded during the sessions for the pop albums, it features regular contributors such as Fripp, Collins, MacCormick, Cale, and Fred Frith. The uninspired quality of many of the fragments makes it clear why they originally wound up as outtakes. *Music for Airports* was released in 1979, and to Eno's joy, it was actually pumped into New York's LaGuardia Airport. Unfortunately, the music is less evocative of flight than of

Eno chills out. (Photo by Michiro Ikeda.)

waiting around in a sterile public place. *The Plateaux of Mirror* and *Days of Radiance* are unremarkable collaborations with, respectively, composer-pianist Harold Budd and the hammer-dulcimer player Laraaji. *On Land* (1982) is more involving; in addition to recording frogs and insects, Eno reworked sounds from some of his earlier albums. "Some earlier pieces I worked on became digested by later ones," he wrote. "This technique is like composting: converting what would otherwise have been waste into nourishment."[21]

These and other ambient albums were recorded at the same time that he was becoming known as a producer. At first, his production work resulted from personal relationships with other musicians. Later, artists began seeking him out because of his novel and well-publicized ideas. In the studio Eno was part guru, part guilty conscience, and part child-hood troublemaker prodding the other kids to misbehave. "I often take extreme positions in the studio," he said. "I try to push opinions as far as I can, even to the point of saying, 'This is potentially the best piece of music I've ever heard in my life! And here, next to it, is possibly the worst.' It gets people's blood going, gets them fighting to defend something."[22] Eno's early productions included John Cale's *Fear*, Robert Calvert's *Lucky Lief and the Longships*, and the debut by a beguiling instrumental group called the Penguin Cafe Orchestra. Eno made two albums with the German group Cluster, and he contributed soundscapes and songs to projects by Manzanera, Genesis (*The Lamb Lies Down on*

Bowie in Berlin.

Broadway), and Wyatt. (Cluster's *Old Land* includes the Eno tune "Broken Head," a throwback to the pop albums and a song that Eno considers autobiographical. "I was just a broken head / I stole the world that others punctured," he sings. "Now I stumble through the garbage / Slide and tumble, slide and tumble.")

A year older than Eno, David Bowie had a similar background and many of the same interests, but his personal style was in sharp contrast. Bowie was fascinated with playing the star, and he had an obsessive desire to continually reinvent his public persona. He had flirted with psychedelic rock on "Space Oddity" and a cover of Pink Floyd's "See Emily Play," but by the mid-'70s, he had also played at being a mod, a Dylanesque troubadour, an ambisexual glam-rock alien, and a Philadelphia soul man. His biggest talent was orchestrating these strange ch-ch-ch-changes at precisely the right times. But with *Station to Station* in 1976, he began to distance himself from his various poses by embracing new technology and deconstructing some of his earlier sounds. Bowie had been impressed with *Another Green World,* and he saw in Eno a bottomless well of new ideas. Eno had admired *Station to Station* and saw in the Bowie a willing vehicle for taking some of his ideas into the pop mainstream. Their three collaborations—*Low,* "*Heroes,*" and *Lodger*—gave Eno a new notoriety and Bowie the most psychedelic albums of his career, mixing ambient instrumentals with rock songs turned inside-out and upside-down.

By the '80s, Bowie was back to his old tricks, spinning off into vapid dance pop and fake grunge. "Artistically, 1977–81 were absolutely dynamic," he concluded from the safe distance of the '90s. "Brian Eno treats studios the way no other person has. He works with it like an instrument, which is actually quite the thing now, especially in dance music, but at the particular time, there was no one else doing that, except for a couple of Germans. He really hipped me to the potential of arranging musical accidents."[23]

Eno did the same for many others. He was at the controls as Talking Heads expanded their sound far beyond their early minimalism by embracing African and Funkadelic-style rhythms and mandalalike melodies. Eno also recorded *My Life in the Bush of Ghosts* with head Head David Byrne, taking the title from Nigerian novelist Amos Tutuola and snippets of sound from talk radio, chanting Algerian moslems, and Egyptian pop music, thereby prompting an early controversy over what would later be called sampling. "Like most 'found' art, *My Life in the Bush of Ghosts* raises stubborn questions about context, manipulation, and cultural imperialism," critic Jon Pareles wrote.[24] Even more notorious was Eno's work with U2. After helping the echo-happy Irish rockers strike a balance between ambiance and earnestness on *The Unforgettable Fire* and *The Joshua Tree*, he prodded the group into crafting a distinctly '90s brand of psychedelic rock on *Achtung Baby* and *Zooropa*—the perfect soundtracks for slipping on the virtual reality helmet or flipping through three hundred channels of satellite TV while waiting for the Ecstasy to kick in. Eno accomplished this by dropping in on the *Achtung Baby* sessions every few weeks and erasing anything that sounded too much like U2. "It's much easier to encourage something that you recognize, so people from the company and the people they work with will come along and say, 'That sounds great,' because it sounds like the U2 they know and love," he said. "I'm part of the small contingent that redress that by coming along and hearing things that I don't recognize and saying, 'Wow, now that sounds really exciting. Let's follow that for a while.' "

The Perfect Circle

Trust in the you of now . . . Don't be frightened to display your talents . . . Use an old idea . . . Just carry on.

—Oblique Strategies[25]

In the fall of 1990, Eno and I sat in a suite in Minneapolis's most luxurious hotel as he prepared to give a lecture at the Walker Art Institute on high art versus low art. Perhaps because he has always straddled that line himself, he was in the rare mood to reflect. "*The Joshua Tree* sold more copies in the first morning than all of the records I've made put together, but I don't mind that," he said. "I think you can see certain things as a kind of research, things that are made for other artists in a way. It's what other artists take and use, like a single strong spice that then forms part of their work."

A few months later, Eno made the surprising move of singing again on a new pop album with John Cale. His only vocal appearance between *Before and After Science* and *Wrong Way Up* was a moving rendition of the blues "You Don't Miss Your Water" on the soundtrack to Jonathan Demme's 1988 film *Married to the Mob*. The following year, he went to Moscow to record *Words for the Dying*, an album of Cale compositions performed by the Orchestra of Symphonic and Popular Music of Gosteleradio. Almost as an afterthought, Cale and Eno tacked on a catchy singalong called "The Soul of Carmen Miranda," and that prompted them to record a full album.

Wrong Way Up was not an easy album to make. Evidence of the tension is seen in cover art of the two exchanging daggers. Eno would say only that he and Cale weren't likely to work together again. Cale offered that Eno had attempted to do too much, acting as producer, writer, engineer, and host at his home studio in Woodbridge, England. He added that Eno has a nasty habit of erasing his partners' work. Despite these problems, *Wrong Way Up* is an optimistic album full of catchy, upbeat rock songs built around newly streamlined computer rhythms and Cale and Eno's familiar keyboard styles. The two clearly enjoyed trading lead vocals and building "harmonic stacks" of backing vocals, but Eno seemed surprised by the positive reaction. "I like the way I sing, but I never really expected anyone else to like it," he said.

Eno continued to incorporate vocals on 1992's *Nerve Net*, which was recorded with a variety of musicians as he crossed the United States on his 1990 lecture tour. He had become convinced that the most innovative work in the studio was being done in the dance genre, and he was impressed by techno musicians such as Moby and the Orb, who were incorporating some of his ambient ideas. *Nerve Net* and *The Shutov Assembly* (a collection of "robot instrumentals" recorded during the *Nerve Net* sessions) pay tribute to the dance musicians who paid tribute to Eno, but they aren't nearly as inspired as *Wrong Way Up*.

After decades of trailblazing, Eno seems to finally be repeating himself. The 1993 ambient effort, *Neroli* (subtitled *Thinking Music Part IV*), was inspired by his new hobby of crafting his own perfumes, but the music isn't anything he didn't do better before. In 1994 he contributed unremarkable synthesizer playing to *Mamouna*, a solo album by Ferry, and in 1995, he worked with another figure from his past, Bowie, on an embarrassingly bad concept album called *Outside*. He also crafted another mediocre volume of music for films with members of U2 under the *nom de disque* Passengers. Eno claims he is becoming increasingly less interested in music because it is increasingly less important as a cultural force, but it could just as well be said that his music is increasingly less vital because making music is increasingly less important to him. Nevertheless, his ideas remain inspirational.

"For me, it's all about passion," he said. "One of the challenges of being alive and staying alive is knowing how to use these different styles: to be sometimes passionate, sometimes analytical, and sometimes a gardener around the house. People are sometimes disappointed to hear that. They say, 'Fuck, he's just like me.' Either that, or sometimes they're very pleased, because they realize the potential is there for them as well."

CHAPTER 9

Yoo Doo Right: The Krautrock Invasion

Some skeezix from one of the local dailies was up here the other day to do a "human interest" story, and naturally our beneficent publisher hauled me into his office to answer this fish's edition of the perennial: "Where is rock going?" "It's being taken over by the Germans and the machines," I unhesitatingly answered. And this I believe to my funky soul.

—Lester Bangs, 1975[1]

The psychedelic rock made in England and the United States in 1966 and 1967 didn't go unheard in mainland Europe, but with few exceptions, contemporary European bands were content to play covers or thinly veiled rewrites of songs by British and American groups. "Perhaps because of the lack of musical role models, the European student movements took on serious political overtones," critic Pascal Bussy wrote. "They were unwilling to merely sit around with flowers in their hair, listening to rock music, thus avoiding the hedonistic excesses produced by the London, San Francisco, and New York hippie 'scenes.'"[2] European student activism climaxed with the Paris riots of 1968, in which left-wing students nearly toppled the French government.

This anarchic energy was also felt in West Germany, where a generation of young people was searching for an identity amid the cold war tensions, the lingering consciousness of Nazism and World War II, and the same experimentation with alternative lifestyles, sex, and psychedelic drugs that was happening in the West. From this milieu came a generation of artists dedicated to challenging the mainstream and establishing a new German cultural identity, including filmmakers Rainer Werner Fassbinder and Wim Wenders and the bands that the English music press dubbed krautrock. (The Germans themselves initially preferred the far more psychedelic *kosmische musick*, or cosmic music, though they came to embrace the term krautrock with several song and album titles.)

The krautrock/cosmic music bands occasionally shared the same stage or producer—notably Conrad (Conny) Plank or Dieter Dierks—or recorded for the same label, especially the adventurous independents Brain and Ohr. But most prided themselves on their self-sufficiency, funding their own recordings and building their own home studios. "Krautrock wasn't a movement, but a moment, a final thrust of the psychedelic project to gobble up every kind of music—and every kind of nonmusical noise, too—in order to excrete the outermost sound conceivable," critic Simon Reynolds wrote.[3] The press release for Faust's 1971 debut described the goals in even grander terms: "Unlike rock musicians in other countries, this new breed of German musicians is not interested in imitating what's gone before them. They're looking for new sounds and new forms of expression. Their music is no hand-me-down Beatles or Stones or the white man's idea of R&B. It's their own, building as much on the immense tradition of German music as on the Anglo-Saxon-dominated traditions of current pop."[4]

Like the psychedelic bands in England and America, the German groups never believed that rock had to be limited to tidy three-minute packages. They embraced long Eastern drones and hypnotic percussion. The work of Terry Riley and La Monte Young taught them the power of repeating simple melodic patterns. From *musique concrète* and avant-garde composer Karlheinz Stockhausen they got the idea of music based on the sounds of industry, and from the Velvet Underground came the raw rock aggression of "Sister Ray." These influences were combined with a Teutonic fascination with technology, especially synthesizers and the recording studio, itself. "In a studio, you make a concert for machines," said Can's Holger Czukay. "And machines really like to listen."[5]

That Can, Kraftwerk, and Neu! were the most important krautrock

Amon Düül II, post-commune, pre-cabaret

bands is evidenced to some degree by their commercial success, but even more by their enduring influence. Can's world-beat experiments inspired Public Image and the Talking Heads of *Remain in Light*, while their earlier, noisier sounds influenced the bands on England's Too Pure label in the '90s. Time has revealed the members of Kraftwerk to be forefathers of synthesizer groups such as Depeche Mode, Gary Numan, and the Human League, as well as pioneers in a new way of making music based on rhythms and samples. Neu!'s rhythmic trance rock was echoed in the '80s in the Feelies and Sonic Youth (whose alter egos Ciccone Youth paid tribute with a song called "Two Cool Rock Chicks Listening to Neu!"), and in the '90s by Stereolab, LaBradford, and the ever-tasteful Julian Cope. But this isn't to say that the other krautrock bands aren't interesting footnotes.

"If Can and Neu!'s sometimes minimalist approach was indicative of a harsh, spare German outlook, then Amon Düül may represent all that was grand and eloquent," krautrock chronicler Armstrong Whitworth wrote.[6] The group was the musical arm of an anarchist-libertarian commune formed in 1968 near Munich. The band and its would-be utopia shared the same name, taking the "Amon" from the Egyptian sun god Amen-Ra and the "Düül" from the Turkish god of music. But it wasn't always fun and games in the ideal community, and the group splintered after performing with the Fugs and the Mothers of Invention at Essen's Song Days Festival in late 1968. The best musicians left to form Amon Düül II, while Amon Düül I made a joyous cacophony in the style of the free-form sounds at Ken Kesey's Acid Tests. Its first three albums all date from one twenty-four-hour recording session/freak-out.

Amon Düül II mixed spacey, free-flowing jams with expressionist lyrics, the classical violin of Chris Karrer, and the sensual vocals of Bavarian earth mother Renate Knaup-Krötenschwanz. Englishman Dave Anderson played bass on the band's best efforts, 1969's *Phallus Dei* ("God's Cock") and 1970's *Yeti*, a double album featuring a tribute to the original manufacturer of LSD called "Sandoz in the Rain." The surreal cover of *Yeti* featured sound man and commune member Wolfgang Krischke portraying Der Sensenmann, or the Grim Reaper; a few months after the photo was taken, he was found frozen to death near a lake, and some said he had taken acid and fallen asleep in the snow. Anderson left in 1970 to join Hawkwind, but the group continued to make wonderfully trippy rock on *Dance of the Lemmings* (1971) and *Wolf City* (1972) before starting a long, slow decline into shlocky, sub-cabaret jazz.

With a name inspired by John Lennon's vision of "tangerine trees and marmalade skies," Tangerine Dream progressed from imitating Pink Floyd to delivering snooze-inducing synthesized instrumentals. The band was formed in 1967 by Edgar Froese, a sculptor who studied under Salvador Dalí. Its first album, *Electronic Meditation*, was released on Ohr in 1970. Featuring Froese on guitar, Klaus Schulze on drums, and Konrad Schnitzler ("the mad genius from Berlin") on organ, it borrows liberally from Pink Floyd's *A Saucerful of Secrets*. Schulze and Schnitzler departed the next year, and the faint but distinctive rock heartbeat went with them. Leading a new, three-synthesizer lineup, Froese recorded several mildly engaging albums, including *Atem Alpha Centauri*, dedicated to "all people who feel obliged to space," and 1975's *Rubycon*. But it was all downhill into bland New Age music after that, a depressing fact when you consider that the group's discography contains some forty more albums including the soundtrack to *Risky Business*.

Schulze did a brief stint with Ash Ra Tempel before striking out on his own. The band members were the most overt acidheads of any of the krautrockers. The cover of their self-titled debut features a portrait of a psychedelicized Egyptian pharaoh, and nuggets of Eastern philosophy are sprinkled among the exotic electronic drones. Timothy Leary can be heard howling horny improvised blues lyrics under the psychedelic cacophony of the the band's sophomore effort, *Seven Up*. Recorded live in Switzerland when Leary was on the lam after escaping from an American prison, it was named after the brand of soda pop that the good doctor spiked with LSD before the show. The band's driving force, guitarist Matt Gottsching, eventually abandoned his freakier impulses and went on to record genteel New Age instrumentals under the trimmed-down name of Ashra.

Synthesists Dieter Moebius and Hans Joachim Roedelius of Cluster did their best work in collaboration with others, either with Brian Eno or as part of Harmonia. On their own, they produced pleasant but unmemorable ambient drones. Revolving around the Gothic-sounding, minor-chord moodiness of synthesist and primary auteur Florian Fricke, Popol Vuh (named after the Mayan *Book of the Dead*) is best remembered for crafting the Pink Floyd–style soundtracks to most of Werner Herzog's films, including *Nosferatu the Vampyre, Fitzcarraldo*, and *Aguirre: The Wrath of God*. But the group's first two albums, 1971's *Affenstunde* ("Ape Hour") and 1972's *In Den Garten Pharoas* ("In the Garden of Pharo") include some of the best—and most psychedelic—krautrock. "We have an old expression in Germany, " Fricke said. "'To have one's feet in the sky.' Isn't that what it's all about?"[7]

The krautrock list goes on. Floh De Cologne recorded a rock opera called *Profitgeier* as a sarcastic response to the Who's *Tommy*. Guru Guru started out as a trio recording hard-rock instrumentals such as "Der LSD-Marsch" and wound up making bad cabaret music. But the only other band with anywhere near the influence of Can, Kraftwerk, and Neu! is Faust. Formed in 1971 at the instigation of producer and former journalist Uwe Nettlebeck, the quintet lived in a converted schoolhouse in Wümme in the countryside between Hamburg and Bremen. "Devoted to the spirit of the May 1968 revolts," to quote their press release, they believed that each musician should make his own instruments. Clanging metal, tumbling bricks, and resounding sledgehammers powered Faust's music a decade before industrial pioneers Throbbing Gristle or Einstürzende Neubauten used such techniques. The quintet was determined to tear down rock 'n' roll and romp in the debris, a point driven home by snippets of the Beatles' "All You Need Is Love" and the Stones' "Satisfaction" buried in the first album's murky mix.

"We were naive and arrogant," Jean-Hervé Peron recalled. "We took some drugs, took a few trips, but we never played on trips. We would stand on the rooftop of the farm, staring out at the stars, and shout until we were empty. That would be a high. Or we would dig a hole for hours in the yard. We were our own drugs. . . . We wanted to break everything, not just the rules."[8] Like Can, the members of Faust simply let the tapes roll while they experimented, and albums were compiled later from the diverse results. *Faust* (1971) featured three long suites that Reynolds described as a mix of "acid-rock hoo-ha, zany chorale, found sounds, synth-gibberish, free-form jazz, nonsense incantations, mock-Muzak, [and] animal noises (genuine and falsified)."[9] The follow-up, 1972's *So Far*, was more accessible and featured several genuine songs, including the Velvets-style stomper "It's a Rainy Day, Sunshine Girl."

After two albums on Polydor, Faust followed many of its Krautrock contemporaries to Virgin, releasing *Faust IV* and *The Faust Tapes* before disbanding in 1974. The former is a scattered collage of twenty-six pieces recorded between 1971 and 1973. The band members considered it their best effort, but Virgin disagreed and started to pressure the group. "They wanted us to sell records and to tour," Peron said. "That was not the situation we wanted to be in, so we split."[10] (Though not before a final incarnation that included Peter Blegvad and other members of the experimental English pop group Slapp Happy.) Cult appreciation prompted Peron and fellow veteran Werner Diermeier to form a new version of the group in 1990. Faust picked up where it left off, scrounging instruments from the junkyard and incorporating a bleating goat in its sets.

Looking back in 1993, Peron offered what may be the most succinct summation of the krautrock philosophy. "We're German, we're not afraid of it, we're not ashamed of it, and we make different music," he said.[11] That he meant "German" in a new cultural sense rather than the old nationalistic sense was underscored by the fact that, in 1993 as in 1970, he was a French national transplanted in the Fatherland, "living naked and growing dope and tomatoes."

Then I Saw Mushroom Head

Any music without energy I throw to my tape machine's starving eraser heads.
—Holger Czukay[12]

When they came together in Cologne in 1968, the members of Can had little experience with rock 'n' roll. Czukay played the French horn and studied composition under Stockhausen. His goal in forming a band was to merge free jazz, contemporary classical music, and "ethnic music"/world beat. His first recruit, Irmin Schmidt, studied classical piano and composition, and Jaki Liebezeit was an accomplished jazz drummer. Only

Can, at home in the studio. From left: Czukay, Liebezeit, Schmidt, Karoli.

Czukay's student, guitarist Michael Karoli, was a full-blown rock fan. It was Karoli who suggested that the Beatles were more interesting than Stockhausen. "I Am the Walrus" indicated that he might be right, but the Velvets proved even more inspirational.

The musicians jammed in a castle called Schloss Norvenich, and improvisation was key from the beginning. "We began without any concept," Schmidt said. "Our only idea was to find a concept in making music all together spontaneously, in a collective way without any leader."[13] Can's method of reworking songs at each performance came to be called "instant composition," and the group's fans frequently used the word "telepathic" to characterize the members' playing. What set Can's improvisations apart from free jazz, the space jams of the Grateful Dead, or the virtuousic meanderings of Cream was a devotion to rock simplicity. Czukay was the master of one- and two-note bass lines. Karoli played in what's been described as a spidery, chip-chop style, and Schmidt attacked his keyboards with rapid-fire karate chops. "Inability is often the mother of restriction, and restriction is the great mother of inventive performance," Czukay said.[14] As for Liebezeit, even when he played in unusual time signatures, he had a way of locking into a powerful and hypnotic pulse. It was rumored that he learned several "forbidden rhythms" from a Cuban musician who practiced Santeria. Supposedly, the Cuban was executed onstage because he had dared to play the rhythms outside sacred ceremonies. "It is something that I heard, I did not witness the actual execution," is all Liebezeit would say.[15]

Two months after their initial jams, the members of Can were joined by vocalist Malcolm Mooney, an eccentric African-American sculptor from New York who was bumming around Europe. Mooney had never played music, but he was a jazz and blues fan who dreamed of being a singer. The Germans were drawn to his manic energy, and he was soon improvising rhythmic torrents of words over the band's churning music. The rehearsal room at Schloss Norvenich was converted into a studio with the addition of a two-track recorder and some old U.S. Army mattresses, and there Can recorded its first album. *Monster Movie* was initially released in a batch of five hundred copies on a small Munich label, but United Artists signed the band and rereleased the album in August 1969. The album was credited to "the Can," but the article was dropped a short time later. In the spirit of 1968, Schmidt told journalists that the letters stood for "Communism, Anarchism, and Nihilism." The original liner notes introduced the musicians as "talented young people who want to stay in line but can't."

As the title indicates, *Monster Movie* is a cinematic album whose ominous tones summon images of lurking predators. It opens with "Father Cannot Yell," recorded in the second take of Mooney's first session with the band. The keyboard, the bass, the frantic rhythm, and the insistent guitar combine to create a feeling of panic as Mooney free-associates in a desperate rap, but the album's most impressive track takes up all of side two. "Yoo Doo Right" is some three minutes longer than the Velvets' "Sister Ray," which was clearly its inspiration. Recorded live during a concert at the castle, one of the band's two amps blew up in the middle of the piece, but the group kept right on playing. Over a primal drumbeat, Mooney rants about a love letter from a girlfriend in America. The tension builds throughout the song and it is never resolved, leaving the listener wondering exactly what action the letter prompted.

Even before the release of *Monster Movie*, Mooney's growing psychological problems had undermined his position in the band. During one concert at the castle, he had an episode similar to one of Syd Barrett's onstage freak-outs when he fixated on audience members moving between Can's show and an art exhibit upstairs. He screamed, "Upstairs, downstairs!" for two hours until he finally collapsed. "Malcolm lost his head, which happened sometimes," Karoli explained.[16] When a mystic friend told Mooney he was taking the wrong path in life, the singer grew paranoid. On the advice of a psychiatrist, he quit the band in late 1969 and went back to America.

Can spent some time recording music for art films and porno movies (compiled on *Soundtracks*) before recording its third album in 1971. *Tago Mago* introduced a new vocalist, Damo Suzuki, a twenty-one-year-old Japanese singer whom Liebezeit and Czukay saw busking outside a cafe in Munich. "I saw Damo from far away, and he was screaming and sort of adoring the sun," Czukay recalled. "I said to Jaki, 'Here comes our vocalist!' and Jaki said, 'No, no, it can't be true!'"[17]

Suzuki was invited to that night's performance. He began screaming at the audience and cleared the room in record time, thereby assuring his position in the band.

The group considered *Tago Mago* its "magic record." Named after a site that figured in the legend of black magician Aleister Crowley, the standout tracks have an air of mystery and forbidden secrets. "Aumgn" features Schmidt chanting ritualistically over a creepy Eastern instrumental, and Suzuki's ranting on the tom-heavy "Hallelujah" is even weirder than Mooney's on "Yoo Doo Right." The trance-inducing "Mushroom" is clearly a tribute to those of the psychedelic variety, and the memorable lines, "When I saw mushroom head / I was born and I was dead" neatly encapsulate a psychedelic experience.

In late 1971, Can moved out of Schloss Norvenich and into an old cinema outside Cologne. The new studio was called Inner Space, and it became the band's permanent home. The group was still recording with a simple two-track tape machine, but its live performances were becoming more elaborate. Concerts often featured a juggler and a fire eater as added attractions while the group played for up to four hours for as many as ten thousand German fans. Can's fourth album, *Ege Bamyasi*, took its name and cover art from a can of vegetables found in a Turkish restaurant. The music offers more of the same dark grooves, but it doesn't improve on the first two albums. *Future Days* is another story, expanding the band's sound in an almost symphonic style. "Moonshake" is meant to evoke tugboats chugging down the Rhine, and the side-long "Bel Air" uses echoes and tape loops to create an impressionistic portrait of the windswept cliffs on the Portuguese coast.

Suzuki left the group in September 1973 after marrying a German girl and becoming a Jehovah's Witness. This time, Can abandoned the idea of an outside singer, and Karoli and Schmidt divided the vocals. Subsequent albums suffer from this decision, but they have their moments. "Dizzy Dizzy" from 1974's *Soon Over Babaluma* incorporates a reggae beat, and "Chain Reaction" is flavored with African percussion. In 1975 Can signed with Virgin Records, and its Virgin albums mix pieces from the "ethnological forgery" series with warped pop tunes such as "Hunters and Collectors" from 1975's *Landed* and "I Want More" from 1976's *Flow Motion*. In 1977 Czukay quit after first retiring to a behind-the-scenes role of mixing and "playing" shortwave radio and telephone. By 1977 the band included two veterans of Traffic, bassist Rosko Gee and percussionist Reebop Kwaku Baah. The early experimentation was replaced by rote European dance sounds, and the band offered up a lame disco version of the "Can-Can." A short time later, the group wisely called it a day.

Can reunited in 1986. Mooney, now a remedial reading teacher in New York, flew in to sing, but the resulting album, *Rite Time*, was anti-climactic. The musicians had grown too much during their solo projects, their egos had gotten too big to accept musical accidents, and the lure of fancy technology had become irresistible. The group disbanded again and the members went their separate ways. Mooney offered the best epitaph: "It's like they used to have manual can openers. Now they have these automatic ones."[18]

The Man-Machine

We are playing the machines, the machines play us, it is really the exchange and the friendship we have with the musical machines.

—Ralf Hütter[19]

While the musicians in Can were happy to play for their machines, the members of Kraftwerk fantasized about *becoming* machines themselves. Primary auteurs Ralf Hütter and Florian Schneider often talked about the group as if it were a device that generated music at the touch of a button. How many of these statements were for effect and how many were part of a genuine philosophy is open to debate. What can't be disputed is that Hütter and Schneider created a perfect pop group, one in which presentation, subject matter, and sound combined to create a timeless archetype. Not for nothing were they called the Beach Boys of Düsseldorf.

Hütter and Schneider would prefer people to think that they surfaced in 1974 as fully formed electronic-pop pioneers, but in fact, the two met at the Düsseldorf Conservatory in the late '60s. They were from similar upper-middle-class backgrounds—Hütter's father was a doctor and Schneider's, an architect—and they were drawn together by an interest in electronic avant-garde music. (They talked about seeing a Stockhausen concert as students while tripping on LSD.) In 1968 the two formed a group called Organisation to play improvised music with organ, flute, and electronics at art galleries and happenings. At one of these gigs, they met Conny Plank, a jazz musician and recording engineer who had started his career doing sound for Marlene Dietrich and

Duke Ellington. In the late '60s, he became fascinated with the the Velvets, Jimi Hendrix, and Jamaican dub producer Lee "Scratch" Perry. He was intrigued by the possibility of working with a rock group that had a distinctive European sound and identity.

Plank recorded Organisation's first album, 1970's *Tone Float*, in a studio set up in a former oil refinery. He released the album on his own Rainbow label in Germany and secured a deal with RCA in England, but the meandering electronic sounds were a flop. Hütter and Schneider regrouped. Inspired by Can, they set up their own studio, located then as now in a rented loft in the center of Düsseldorf. Rather than the cosmic monikers of many krautrock groups, the two wanted a name that evoked images of industry to compliment a new industrial edge in their music, and they chose as a name the German word for "power plant." Once again recorded by Plank, the self-titled *Kraftwerk* is starker and more rhythmic than the Organisation album, thanks in part to drummers Andreas Hohman and Klaus Dinger. The album received favorable reviews, but the group's progress was soon interrupted by a series of personnel shifts. At one point, Hütter quit. The lineup of Schneider, Dinger, and guitarist Michael Rother recorded thirty-five minutes of music at Plank's studio, including an eleven-minute piece called "Truckstop Gondolero." Before it could be released, Hütter rejoined and Dinger and Rother left due to what Rother called "a question of temperament, of character."[20] Dinger and Rother started a new project called, quite literally, Neu!, and Hütter and Schneider released the quickly produced *Kraftwerk 2*.

Kraftwerk 2 is strikingly similar to the debut, and since the cover is almost identical, many listeners thought it was just a repackaging. Released in 1973, *Ralf and Florian* is more distinctive visually and musically. The cover shows the duo in the midst of a growing collection of electronic instruments at their studio, which had been christened Kling Klang after the central seventeen-minute composition on *Kraftwerk 2*. The sound is cleaner and less cluttered on melodic pieces such as "Elektrisches Roulette" ("Electric Roulette") and "Tanzmusik" ("Dance Music"), and for the first time, Kraftwerk displays a sense of humor. The album ends with "Ananas Symphonie" ("Pineapple Symphony"), a goofy track that sounds like *South Pacific* on acid. Hütter and Schneider generally dismiss all of these efforts, and they have yet to sanction their release on CD. Considering the radical turn their music took with *Autobahn*, it's easy to understand why.

In 1974 the duo turned away from the insular world of the avant-garde and made a calculated attempt to go pop. In their new friend, visual artist Emil Schult, they found a guru with a talent for conceptualizing their music and presenting a unified multimedia image. And in the new Mini-Moog synthesizer, they found an electronic instrument that was perfectly suited for rock 'n' roll. It was as if Chuck Berry had just discovered the electric guitar. *Autobahn* was conceived as an aural version of driving on the German-Austrian superhighway. Neu! had made music evocative of this experience in 1971, but Hütter and Schneider made it even more obvious—adding lyrics for the first time—and they did it by using electronic instruments exclusively. The title track starts with the sound of a car revving up, then the pulsating percussion kicks into gear. The song is propelled by an ultra-hummable riff repeated in the rich harmonic overtones of the Moog. The monotone vocals echo the main riff, and it isn't clear whether Hütter is singing in German or English. The lyrics could be "Fahr'n, fahr'n, fahr'n on der autobahn"—"Riding, riding, riding on the the autobahn"—or a very Beach Boys–like "Fun, fun, fun on the autobahn."

The album caught on slowly in Germany, but it was a big success in America. Producer Robin McBride edited the title track into a three-and-a-half-minute single, and it spread from Chicago radio throughout the States. The group's image and sound were exotic. Before making *Autobahn*, Hütter and Schneider expanded to a quartet featuring percussionist Wolfgang Flur and violinist Klaus Roeder (Roeder was soon replaced by a second percussionist, Karl Bartos). These musicians were hired hands, and Hütter and Schneider never shared composing credits, but they helped present a distinctive image of Kraftwerk as a new kind of all-electronic band: Ladies and gentlemen, the robotic Beatles.

After *Autobahn*, Kraftwerk split with Plank. (The engineer went on to work with Eno, Killing Joke, Eurythmics, DAF, and Devo before dying from cancer in 1987, but he never forgave Kraftwerk for abandoning him after what he considered to be key contributions.) Kraftwerk recorded the follow-up, *Radio-Activity*, on its own at Kling Klang. The title was a play on the central theme of invisible forces that could be positive (radio waves) or negative (nuclear fallout). Schult and Hütter drove across Germany in search of the right radio for the cover, finally settling on a short-range model that had been was used during the war for Nazi propaganda (a swastika between the dials was judiciously removed). Only the title track boasted a strong melody, but the album

Kraftwerk trades places with its machines.

continued to win fans, including director Rainer Werner Fassbinder, who included passages on the soundtracks to *Chinese Roulette* and *Berlin Alexanderplatz*. The cinematic nature of Kraftwerk's music was growing more pronounced, and the band's ability to make movies for the mind kept it in the psychedelic tradition even as the musicians adopted the lifestyles of Buddhist monks. "We had certain rules, like we wouldn't get drunk at parties or drunk onstage," Bartos said. "It is not so easy to turn the knobs of a synthesizer if you are drunk or full of drugs."[21] The musicians referred to themselves as workers, and they followed a very workmanlike routine. "I wake up in the morning, I brush my teeth, I go to the studio, I work, I go back home, I eat, I sleep," is how Hütter described the daily ritual.[22]

Released in 1977, *Trans-Europe Express* was the natural successor to *Autobahn*. While the former duplicates a car trip, the latter conjures the sounds of traveling by rail. It was named after the elegant and now-discontinued rail line that once passed through Düsseldorf Station not far from Kling Klang. Kraftwerk was using the most modern technology—including increasingly sophisticated sequencers—to evoke a bygone era. The outdated fashions and stylized tinting of the cover photo only heightened the dichotomy. In addition to several memorable hooks and Kraftwerk's strongest rhythm track yet, the title cut boasts funny lyrics recounting a meeting with Iggy Pop and David Bowie. (Bowie hoped to collaborate with Hütter and Schneider, but he had to settle for dedicating a song to the duo, *"V-2 Schneider,"* on *"Heroes."*)

By 1978 the musical landscape had changed. When punk and new wave arrived, Kraftwerk was recognized as an important influence. Hütter and Schneider had long subscribed to the punk philosophies that less is more and training is overrated. "Our music is rather minimalist," Hütter said. "If we can convey an idea with one or two notes, it is better to do this than to play a hundred or so notes. With our musical machines, there is no question of playing with a kind of virtuosity, there is all the virtuosity we need in the machines."[23] In turn, Hütter and Schneider drew inspiration from the new bands' energy and simplicity to produce their minimalist masterpiece. The songs on *The Man-*

Machine (1978) are built with streamlined precision from simple repetitive melodies that interconnect like the gears on mechanical rotors. "The Robots" plays with the band's image and pays tribute to its new alter egos. (At press junkets, specially constructed robots filled in for the absent band members.) Rereleased a few years later as a single B side, "The Model" became Kraftwerk's biggest hit; its unbearably catchy riff is perfect accompaniment for a stroll down the runway, while the lyrics satirize the mechanical nature of "too-perfect" high-fashion queens. The album ends with the elliptical title track, and the word "machine" is echoed by a mechanical voice. The tune suggests the Man-Machine being switched off until it is time to make music again tomorrow.

Kraftwerk spent three years holed up at Kling Klang crafting the next album. The themes and melodies on 1981's *Computer World* are stretched thin, and there isn't much behind the concept that the modern world is run by computers (though "Computer Love" has taken on added meaning since the advent of cybersex). In the early '80s, Hütter and Schneider were more interested in pursuing their new passion for bicycling than making new music. This was reflected in 1983 on a single called "Tour de France," notable for a rhythm track based on a bike racer's heavy breathing. Plans to release an album called *Technopop* later in the year were scrapped after Hütter was hurt in a cycling accident. But there were rumors that the band realized that, for the first time, its new music was sounding outdated. Starting in 1982 with Afrika Bambaataa's "Planet Rock," rappers began sampling Kraftwerk to forge some of hip-hop's freshest grooves. A few years later, Detroit house DJs did the same to craft high-energy dance music.

Kraftwerk finally released a song called "Technopop" on 1986's *Electric Cafe*, and it can be heard as the group passing the baton to a new generation of musicians. Kraftwerk biographer Pascal Bussy noted that *Electric Cafe* predicted the move of in house and techno away from songs and toward the groove as the be-all and end-all, and it brought Hütter and Schneider "full circle back to where they had started—building up atmospheric pieces of music rather than writing conventional songs."[24] The band hasn't released any new material since. After *Electric Cafe*, Hütter and Schneider launched what would become a five-year project called *The Mix*, reconstructing their old material using new digital technology. Bartos, Flur, and Schult were unhappy after spending four years on the thirty-five minutes of music on *Electric Cafe*, and *The Mix* was the last straw. "Would Leonardo da Vinci have taken the Mona Lisa back and painted her over?" Schult asked.[25] One by one, the two percussionists and the conceptual guru defected. In 1991 Bartos and Lothar Manteuffel of the German duo Rheingold formed Elektric Music. Working in collaboration with Schult, who added lyrics and design, they released an album of short, catchy electronic-pop songs. Like Kraftwerk's best albums, *Esperanto* is united by a theme: The tools of modern communications are actually driving people apart.

When it was finally issued, *The Mix* was neither a satisfying best-of—too many important tunes were missing—nor a step forward. "How can we change now?" Hütter asked in a rare interview in 1991. "We've put twenty years into this kind of thing."[26] The Man-Machine has stalled, unable to move forward and unable to go back.

Riding Through the Night

Theirs is music for the present—alive, urgent, bursting with energy, and demanding to be played. Neu! are as relevant today as they were a decade ago.
—David Elliott, 1982[27]

In Germany there is no speed limit on the autobahn. The most culturally deprived American knows this and so tends to envision futuristic superhighways criss-crossing the country. In fact, the autobahns were built by Hitler to provide a system for quick and easy troop transport, and they have only two lanes running in either direction. They are simple but efficient blacktops cutting through the countryside, unobtrusive intrusions of modernity in the rolling green hillsides. Neu! is the sound of driving late at night on these quiet, empty roads. The white lines sweep toward the headlights with mechanical regularity, in time to the steady speed of the car. They are the only thing you see, but the Fatherland is out there in the darkness. You can feel it.

Rother and Dinger emerged from Kraftwerk frustrated and unfulfilled. One suspects that they had been "too rock" for Hütter, or Hütter had been too staid for them. In any event, they were determined to make improvised electronic music that retained the rhythmic drive and harsh edge of the best rock 'n' roll. They recorded with Plank, who had just moved his studio to a farmhouse near Hamburg. The recording room was in the old pigsty, and the mixing desk was in a former stable. The trio finished Neu!'s self-titled debut in just four days. Dinger handled drums, synthesizers, some guitar, and the album's one vocal, while Rother was responsible for the majority of guitar, piano, bass, and tape manipulations. The two played with a rare empathy, and their improvisations were uncommonly structured and immediate. The key track on Neu!'s first album is the psychedelic opener, "Hallogallo" ("Hullabaloo"). The long, hypnotic instrumental is built around Rother's backward, echoplexed, or heavily reverbed guitars; simple five- or six-note keyboard patterns, and Dinger's metronomic drumming. The 4/4 rhythm is Neu!'s secret. Dubbed *motorik*, the beat is unrelenting, straightforward, and entrancing—the sound of the white line. Even the fills are dedicated to propelling the song rather than decorating the spartan beat.

The rest of the album—and, indeed, Neu!'s career—offers subtle variations on this entrancing hullabaloo. Released in late 1971 on Brain, *Neu!* was a respectable hit in Germany, selling more than thirty-five thousand copies. It was issued in the United States on the Chicago label Billingsgate, but aside from influencing a few pockets of freaky music fans—including a fellow in Cleveland named David Thomas—its impact was minimal. "The record is only the beginning," Dinger said. "We are looking for a third member of the group to dig deeper into the trends we introduced in our first album."[28] Neu! recruited Uli Trepte of Guru Guru on bass and played a handful of unsatisfying gigs. The group's true home, it seemed, was the recording studio. The band returned to Plank's barn, but this time, the musicians spent way too much time obsessing over the characteristically Neu! instrumentals on side one. "Für Immer," "Spitzenqualität," and the other songs on the first half of the album are as strong as anything on the first *Neu!*, but with the budget exhausted, Dinger and Rother simply took both sides of their earlier single, "Super" b/w "Neuschnee," and filled side two with versions at 33, 45, and 78 r.p.m. (With a similarly perverse sense of humor, the covers and titles of all three albums were identical, featuring the word "Neu!" scrawled against different colored backgrounds.)

A few months later, the band was temporarily shelved as Rother joined Moebius and Roedelius of Cluster to record as Harmonia, while Dinger worked with his brother, Thomas, and Hans Lampe. Only Harmonia produced vinyl. The debut, *Musik Von Harmonia*, and a follow-up, *Deluxe*, were both released on Brain. Harmonia's music is more expansive and much less direct than Neu!'s, and it lacks the driving beat. The group disbanded in 1975 because of poor album sales, and Rother rejoined Dinger in Neu!. The pair recorded the first half of their third

Neu! auteur No. 1: Michael Rother. (Photo by Ann W.)

Neu! auteur No. 2: Klaus Dinger. (Photo by Dieter Eickelpoth.)

and final album as a duo, while side two was done as a quartet featuring Lampe and Thomas Dinger. The 1975 version of *Neu!* predated the punk explosion by a year, but its most exciting tracks have the raw, primal power of the Sex Pistols or the Ramones. "Hero" features the basic Neu! instrumental augmented by Klaus Dinger's frantic shouted vocals. Obscured by the mix, bad diction, or both, the words and even the language are unintelligible, though the English phrase "riding through the night" seems to jump out. Given the intensity of "Hero" and "After Eight," you might assume that Dinger intended the stoned moaning on the lulling "Leb' Wohl" as a joke. Pictured on the album's inner sleeve wearing black clothes, white boots, sunglasses, spiked hair, and a sneer, he could pass for Sid Vicious. In sharp contrast, the bearded, ponytailed Rother is depicted against a fluffy white background, the model of hippie tranquillity.

Perhaps the clash in styles finally proved to be too much. Neu! broke up for good shortly after the release of its third album. The Dinger brothers and Lampe formed La Düsseldorf, and Rother went the solo route, frequently working with Can drummer Jaki Liebezeit. Their subsequent efforts have moments of inspiration, but the further you get from Neu!, the less you hear the rock-'n'-roll edge. The distinctive beat is overpowered by more formal European harmonies and melodies, the guitars and synthesizers grow more symphonic, and the grit of the highway is replaced by the gentle sounds of the idyllic countryside. Late at night on the empty highway, they don't hold a candle to Neu! But then not much does.

CHAPTER 10

An Evening of Fun in the Metropolis of Your Dreams: Psychedelic Punk Return

Hopefully, there's going to be a second psychedelic era. People misunderstand what it's all about, because psychedelic music wasn't drug music. . . . It makes you experience different things, and that's essentially where we're at.

—David Thomas, 1976[1]

The punk explosion of 1975 and 1976 is often portrayed as a direct reaction to the self-satisfied, pretentious, boring, and bloated groups that had come to dominate rock, especially groups like the Eagles and Fleetwood Mac, but also including art rockers like Yes and Genesis. Many of the most important punks realized that psychedelic rock had lost its way. They were dedicated not only to reassessing rock's musical and philosophical values, but to placing a different set of heroes in the rock pantheon. *Nuggets* compiler Lenny Kaye started a new career as guitarist for the Patti Smith Group. The flowery, extended solos of Television guitarist Tom Verlaine were compared to Jerry Garcia; the band covered "Fire Engine" by the 13th Floor Elevators and "Psychotic Reaction" by the Count Five, and it worked with Brian Eno on a set of legendary demos. It may not have been obvious when they surfaced, but the Ramones shined a light on some of their psychedelic influences years later with their 1994 covers album *Acid Eaters.* The Damned were devoted fans of the early Pink Floyd and tried to get Syd Barrett to produce their second album. (They had to settle for Nick Mason.) But Pere Ubu was the most vocal in calling its sounds part of the psychedelic tradition.

To Ubu and its peers, psychedelic rock's legacy was an imaginative approach to the recording studio more than it was music inspired by psychedelic drugs. "Pere Ubu has always been concerned with creating a cinema of the imagination," singer David Thomas said. "If you call that psychedelic, then I suppose so. But we never would endorse the use of drugs as a necessary part of that. There is a basic idea of music as sound having a visual element, and that goes back to the 1800s. We discuss sound visually. When we put together songs, we always see them being in the context of sound as opposed to a melody or a rhythm or something. We see them as being *inside* of something else."

The founding members of the band met in their hometown of Cleveland in 1974. Thomas was a frizzy-haired singer fronting a jokey garage band called Rocket from the Tombs, and Peter Laughner was a leather-jacketed guitarist who dreamed of being in a band. Both men were part-time rock critics who enjoyed discussing music almost as much as they enjoyed playing it. "This was a generation that was interested in seeing rock 'n' roll as a serious musical form—as true art," Thomas recalled. "This was the time that Soft Machine with Kevin Ayers had its greatest day; Can, all that German stuff, the early Eno, *Warm Jets, Tiger Mountain,* the Roxy Music stuff."[2]

Laughner joined the Rockets on guitar. Although the incarnation lasted barely a year, it produced three of what critic Clinton Heylin called "American punk's most potent anthems"—"Sonic Reducer," "Final Solution," and "30 Seconds Over Tokyo"—before splitting into the hell-bent-for-leather Dead Boys (Cheetah Chrome and Johnny Blitz) and the artier Pere Ubu. Ubu was originally intended as a one-off studio project so Laughner and Thomas could record the Rockets' best originals. The band's name referred to a monstrous character in Alfred Jarry's surrealist play *Ubu Roi;* uncomfortable with his substantial girth and odd, high-pitched singing, Thomas portrayed the character of Father Ubu, losing himself in a lurking, menacing alter ego that he named Crocus Behemoth. The rest of the band included several residents of an apartment building called the Plaza—guitarist Tom Herman, drummer R. Scott Krauss, and Allen Ravenstine, who coached strange sounds out of a homemade synthesizer—as well as bassist and guitarist Tim Wright.

It was Wright who came up with the riff for what would become "Heart of Darkness," and as the band jammed on the sinister, rumbling progression, it became clear that Pere Ubu would have a life beyond one recording.

The 1985 compilation *Terminal Tower: An Archival Collection* (named for the structure that provides the central focus of the Cleveland skyline), offers a compelling overview of early Ubu, tracing the band's development from psychedelic punks wallowing in postadolescent angst to rock visionaries rejoicing in the power of music. It opens with the group's first single, released on Thomas's own Hearthan Records. "Heart of Darkness" builds in intensity over a monolithic drumbeat just as Joseph Conrad's novel builds up to the moment when the reader meets Kurtz, the personification of evil. The song climaxes with Thomas's frantic screams in the face of the abyss as the band loses itself in a swirling, chaotic din. Pere Ubu threw Laughner out after its second single, in part because of his drug and alcohol abuse. (He died in June 1977, leaving a legacy of scattered recordings.) The second half of *Terminal Tower* finds Pere Ubu moving out of its Laughner-dominated "dark period" and creating more optimistic soundscapes, as on the positively giddy 1977 single "Heaven." Crocus Behemoth has been replaced by the affable frontman of later years, a lovable eccentric who bears more than a passing resemblance to Oliver Hardy.

Despite its influence on England's postpunk dance bands (especially Joy Division), Pere Ubu's 1978 debut album, *The Modern Dance*, has aged more quickly than the singles collected on *Terminal Tower*. Released only a few months later, Ubu's second album, *Dub Housing*, stands as the best from the first half of the band's career. Dense and dissonant, it is also filled with undeniably catchy melodies. Hooks are crafted from such unlikely sources as eerie, jagged guitar noise, Ravenstine's unmusical synthesizer squeals and saxophone bleats, and Thomas's adenoidal vocals. The album was inspired by an upbeat period during which Ubu was the house band at a bar on Cleveland's Flats, the industrial wasteland on the banks of the Cuyahoga River. Thomas's lyrics examine the odd juxtapositions of the modern world ("I saw secret scenes in the cracks of the cities / Secret scenes in the seams of the world!"), while upholding the punk ideal of celebrating your individuality, even if you *are* one of the most unlikely frontmen in rock history. ("I've got these arms and legs that flip-flop! / Flip-flop! / I have desire / Freedom!")

Subsequent albums are less consistent. *New Picnic Time* (1979)

Pere Ubu returns in the '80s; David Thomas, center.

brings the Beefheart influence to the fore-front, while the lyrics reflect more of Thomas's religious beliefs. (Raised as a Jehovah's Witness, he left the religion during his early punk days but later returned.) Following *The Art of Walking* (1980) and *The Song of the Bailing Man* (1982), both less focused ambient efforts, the group disbanded for what would become a six-year layoff. (One of the last incarnations before the split featured former Red Krayola guitarist Mayo Thompson—the first generation of psychedelic rock linking up with the third.) Reinvigorated by the break, Pere Ubu relaunched its career in 1988 with *The Tenement Year*. This time, the band's heavy rhythms, gurgling synthesizers, and noisy guitars were incorporated into songs that recalled the '60s psychedelic garage bands that the musicians grew up with. "Something's Gotta Give," "George Had a Hat," and "We Have the Technology," are pop tunes—weird, upside-down, and inside-out pop tunes, but pop tunes nonetheless.

The group continued to explore a more accessible direction on 1989's *Cloudland*, which yielded an MTV hit with the wonderful trouble-in-clubland video "Waiting for Mary." *Worlds in Collision* (1991) is more polished and less effective, but 1993's *Story of My Life* features some of Ubu's best songs ever. The opening track, "Wasted," begins as a lulling sea chantey, with Thomas playing melodeon and musing about "throwing time away." It sounds like a melancholy tone poem about wasted youth, until Thomas croaks, "Rock!" and the band kicks in with a chaotic assault that leaves the listener dizzy. The song makes it clear that Pere Ubu continues to uphold the psychedelic ideals of living in the moment and fashioning a personal utopia in the music.

"In the end, we're doomed people," Thomas told me. "We were young and came to manhood musically in a time when music was still considered by most people to be important, and when it was the poetry and language of the human experience. It was the idea of it being art, and we happen to believe all that stuff. We're like the people who became communists in the '30s. They had a powerful vision of the way things should be in an ideal world. And as the years went by, one thing after another, their vision of the world became more and more detached from the reality of the world around them. And it was a tragic, tragic experience."

I Feel Mysterious Today

Sometimes they sound like several species of small furry animals grooving with a Pict, if you get my drift, if not I will come right out and say it: Syd Barrett. Early Pink Floyd, to be sure. . . . The crucial difference is that whereas Pink Floyd wanted (pretended?) to take you into *outer* space (big deal, so go watch Buck Rogers), Wire's saucerful of secrets is headed in the opposite direction, down your esophagus like a stray carcinogen. Wire wanna isolate and dissect leucocytes. They're into the micro rather than macrocosm.

—Lester Bangs[3]

Energized by the music and the D.I.Y. spirit that surrounded them, the members of Wire came together in London in the summer of 1976, but they were always more than a little different than the others in England's class of freshman punks. For one thing, they were older: Bruce Gilbert had already passed thirty. They had no musical training, but like many of the English rockers in the '60s, they had all attended art school. Their idea of subversion was more humorous and less direct than shouting, "Anarchy!" Rather than tearing down rock 'n' roll and starting over, they were fascinated with what could be built up in the recording studio, and they drew inspiration from Roxy Music, the Velvet Underground, and Captain Beefheart.

After garnering some attention for two tracks on the live compilation, *The Roxy, London WC2*, Wire was signed to Harvest/EMI by Nick Mobbs, the man who had signed Pink Floyd years earlier. "What's interesting is that I hadn't really heard any Syd Barrett before people made the comparison," singer Colin Newman said. "I then started listening to his albums, and I quite liked them."[4] As part of its overall aim to thwart expectations and be as perverse as possible, the band members embraced the comparison because it made them stand out. "Any form of misinformation was useful," Gilbert said.[5] Originally a quintet featuring Newman, Gilbert, bassist Graham Lewis, drummer Robert Gotobed, and lead guitarist and songwriter George Gill, the band lurched through angry-young-Englishman tunes such as "I Just Don't Care" and "Mary

Is a Dyke." When Gill was sidelined with a broken ankle, Newman and Lewis figured that they could do better without him. "Graham said, 'Well, I can write lyrics,' and I said, 'Well, I'll write tunes,'" Newman recalled. "So it was, 'There, let's do it!'"

Wire's 1977 debut, *Pink Flag*, is a dense and carefully constructed twenty-one-song suite that intentionally "cocks a snoot at the history of rock 'n' roll." "If the first Ramones album was like Phil Spector, then *Pink Flag* was like all the history of rock mashed up," Newman said.[6] But the vibe was considerably darker; as Robert Christgau wrote, "Wire would sooner revamp 'The Fat Lady of Limbourg' or 'Some Kinda Love' than 'Let's Dance' or 'Surfin' Bird.'"[7] Having said all they wanted to say about rock history, the band members were ready to move forward. Released in 1978, their second album, *Chairs Missing*, takes a sharp turn toward more imaginative and psychedelic sounds. "There was a tremendous sense of excitement, of doing things for the first time," producer Mike Thorne said. "The synthesizer was very new to us, and it was, 'Let's plug it into a distortion box and see what it does!' On one level, we still didn't know what we were doing, but the results were brilliant."

Undercurrents of isolation and madness run through *Chairs Missing*, starting with the title. "My father-in-law seemed to have a whole bank of phrases about people who weren't all quite there," Gilbert said. "One was, 'So-and-so's got a few plums short,' and 'He's got a few chairs missing in his front room.' It was like a musical joke, and one that stuck."[8] In "Another the Letter," the drums, rhythm guitar, and synthesizer move at a frantic pace that evokes a messenger rushing to his destination. The surreal punch line is that the letter carrier bears the message "I took my own life." "Mercy" is an ominous guitar epic with impressionistic nightmare lyrics; "Outdoor Miner" and "I Am the Fly" are deceptively catchy pop songs about insects, and "I Feel Mysterious Today" is about an out-of-body experience. It ends abruptly after posing the psychedelic question "Did you ever perceive that you too could leave exactly when you like?"

Although they were praised by critics, *Pink Flag* and *Chairs Missing* didn't really win an audience until the early '80s, when groups as diverse as the Minutemen, Big Black, R.E.M., and Minor Threat extended Wire's ideas in several postpunk directions. Despite the band's good reviews, EMI was unhappy with Wire's sales at the time, and the company wasn't sure whether it had signed art rockers or punks. After an unpleasant tour supporting *Manifesto*-era Roxy Music, Wire was just as unhappy with EMI and the promotional merry-go-round. The band recorded one more album for the label before the relationship fell apart.

Released in 1980, *154*, which was issued on Warner Bros. in the States, was named for the number of gigs that Wire had played to date. The band continued to show its mastery of the sonic vignette, exploring colorful landscapes over longer songs and an even lusher production, but strains were beginning to show. *154* divided Wire into a "pop" camp—with Newman, Gotobed, and Thorne favoring catchy, well-crafted songs such as "The 15th"—and a "noise camp," with Gilbert and Lewis pushing for more unstructured experimentation. The battle resulted in failed experiments such as "The Other Window" and "40 Versions," as well as highlights such as "Map Ref. 41° N 93° W," a sweeping, cinematic tune inspired by Lewis's first flight across the United States, and "On Returning," a Newman song that ends with the singer in the role of a travel broker promising a somewhat foreboding "evening of fun in the metropolis of your dreams."

After splitting with EMI, Wire recorded a single, "Our Swimmer," and the fractured live album, *Document and Eyewitness*, both for Rough Trade. Shortly thereafter, the group went on hiatus. An avalanche of solo releases followed, with Newman's being the most enjoyable. Several of the songs on *A-Z* (1980) and *Not to* (1982) were performed during Wire's final tours, and a few feature lyrics by Lewis. Both albums continue in the cinematic, psychedelic style of *Chairs Missing* and *154*. Newman also recorded an Eno-inspired ambient album called *provisionally entitled the singing fish* (1981), and he combined the pop and ambient approaches on *Commercial Suicide* (1986) and *It Seems* (1988) before moving into ambient house music in the '90s.

The activities of Gilbert and Lewis were more scattered and diverse. Working together as Dome, they released four albums of industrial experimentation, works-in-progress, and occasional pop epiphanies ("Rolling Upon My Day"). Duet Emmo was an industrial dance effort with Daniel Miller, the founder of Mute Records; Cupol and 3R4 were Gilbert and Lewis mixing things up under different names, and Mzui featured Gilbert, Lewis, and artist Russell Mills. In the years since, Gilbert has released several albums on his own of randomly interesting noise, and Lewis has recorded electronic dance music as He Said and H.A.L.O.

It's no coincidence that the three most influential psychedelic punk bands all reunited a few years after their initial breakups. Several years after Wire, Pere Ubu, and the Feelies called it quits the first time, a new

Comeback in two halves: Wire in the '80s. From Colin Newman, Bruce Gilbert, Robert Gotobed, and Graham Lewis.

network of college radio stations, fanzines, independent record labels, and rock clubs emerged. In the late '80s that network was happy to hear from the groups that had originally inspired it. Wire initially came together for a three-day trial run in 1985. "If that hadn't worked out, it would have been over, because after that it would have been a bloody weak excuse to do anything," Lewis said. "But it worked, and 'Drill' and 'Serious of Snakes' came out of that."

Both songs appeared in 1986 on the *Snakedrill* EP, which features a stripped-down sound based on rhythmic repetition and noise. *The Ideal Copy* followed in 1987, continuing the rhythmic approach with a sound that owed more than a passing nod to New Order. The group proceeded to explore electronic dance music with diminishing results on *A Bell Is a Cup Until It Is Struck* (1988), *It's Beginning To and Back Again* (1989), *Manscape* (1990), and *The Drill* (1991). By *The First Letter* in 1992, Gotobed had quit, the band was now calling itself Wir, and Newman, Gilbert, and Lewis were all playing guitars hooked up via MIDI (musical instrument digital interface) to a computer controller. Each member added to a continuously evolving digital loop, a system not unlike Kraftwerk's vision of the Man-Machine. Unfortunately, the results were less interesting than the working methods, and the group split up for good.

By reuniting, Wire blew its legendary status, and as the band progressed through its second incarnation, it alienated even its cult following. But if the remaining members were concerned, they never let on. "When we did *Pink Flag* and came out with *Chairs Missing*, there were a lot of people who just went, 'You guys, you've let us down,'" Lewis told me. "The same thing happened with *154*, and I think that's an inevitability. If you're changing what you're doing and you're committed to that, then that's what happens."

"Some people would regard that as pure self-indulgence and tell us to go straight to hell," Gilbert added. "But it's a very spurious, moralistic view, the self-indulgent thing. *I* think it's extremely healthy."

The Boys With the Perpetual Nervousness

"Going to the Feelies this evening, Henry?" enquired the Assistant Predestinator. "I hear the new one at the Alhambra is first-rate. There's a love scene on a bearskin rug; they say it's marvellous. Every hair of the beast reproduced. The most amazing tactual effects."

—Aldous Huxley, Brave New World[9]

Like a drop of water shattering the still surface of a pond, the Feelies' first album starts with the ringing sound of rosewood claves: *click, click.* Then silence, until again—*click, click*—this time higher in pitch and richer in reverb. The scattered drops turn into a gentle rain as a needle-thin electric guitar repeats a two-note pattern. The song picks up speed, building in intensity, and then a second guitar echoes the first. The guitars combine on the downbeat to form a chord, but there's no relief in the melody. The raspy sound of a sandblock adds a sharp counterrhythm, cuing the uneasy vocals. "There's a boy I know but not too well / He hasn't got a lot to say / Well this boy lives right next door and he / Has nothing to say." Without ever visiting Haledon, New Jersey, a quiet, hilly suburb of blue-collar Patterson, you know the place that the Feelies are singing about: chipped white paint on the shingles, a slightly overgrown lawn, a tree-lined street filled with mounds of autumn leaves. But the Feelies never felt stifled by surburbia. Like the hero in the tune "The Boy With the Perpetual Nervousness," they were into "better things"—namely the music of their imaginations.

The Feelies first came together in Haledon in 1972. Guitarist-vocalist Glenn Mercer was playing with drummer Dave Weckerman when Bill Million decided to check them out. In those days, a common affinity for the Stooges and the Velvets was all that was needed to forge a friendship and a musical bond. Mercer and Million started writing songs and Million suggested the name for the group from a favorite diversion in Huxley's *Brave New World.*

After several years spent honing a sound in the basement, the Feelies started driving east on New Jersey's Route 3 through the Lincoln Tunnel to play at CBGB and Max's Kansas City. Mercer and Million were perfectionists, and they were unhappy when they couldn't duplicate the sounds in their heads onstage. Their button-down persona was partly a cultivated image like Talking Heads'—they were fond of telling journalists that they hated to play in New York because driving through the tunnel gave them headaches—but they were also genuinely obsessive, refusing to compromise their ideas about what the Feelies *should* sound like. Their five-hour soundchecks became legendary, and drummer Vinny DeNunzio eventually quit when Mercer and Million told him he couldn't use his cymbals because the frequencies clashed with the guitars. He was replaced by Anton Fier, who moved to New York from Cleveland after playing with the Electric Eels and Pere Ubu.

Although they had similar influences, the Feelies were never really part of New York's punk scene, and they were overlooked in the initial major-label feeding frenzy. But as punk became new wave, several labels started to show interest. The English independent Stiff was the most persistent, and the Feelies became the unlikely label mates of Lene Lovich, Ian Dury, and Wreckless Eric. *Crazy Rhythms* was recorded over four weeks in 1980, a record amount of time for a Stiff band. Former CBGB soundman Mark Abel was credited as producer, but Mercer and Million seized control early in the project. "They are the most obstinate people I've ever met," Abel said. "They had real set ideas of what they wanted. That record was the culmination of four years of fantasizing about how they were going to record those songs."[10]

"The Boy With the Perpetual Nervousness" and the other tracks on *Crazy Rhythms* display a distinctive vision and a unique set of sonic hallmarks, including layered rhythm guitars that frantically strum simple two- and three-chord progressions; simple gestures such as handclaps and cymbal crashes that become dramatic pop hooks; elaborate fade-ins and fade-outs that lend the songs a sense of endlessness; harmonic, overdriven solos that erupt from the mix, and deceptively banal lyrics that are half spoken and half sung in a Lou Reed monotone. But the most important element is the beat—the Feelies' own crazy rhythm—a kinetic, tom-heavy groove that can be traced through the Velvet Underground, back to Bo Diddley and the polyrhythms of tribal Africa.

Crazy Rhythms stands as a brilliant album with its own inimitable ambience. These are after-hours party tunes for the gang down at the mad scientist's lab, and even after hundreds of listens, the mix reveals new surprises. The band's small but devoted following was originally disappointed because the album didn't capture the frantic energy of the Feelies' live shows. (Mercer and Million used to down several cups of coffee laced with chlorophyll and shave with electric razors just before going onstage so that they'd literally be bouncing up and down.) But while the drug of choice at Feelies concerts may have been speed, *Crazy Rhythms* is a much more psychedelic experience. Mercer and Million's approach to the studio came from *Revolver*, *Their Satanic Majesties Request*, *Another Green World*, and the Velvets' first album, and they went on to pay homage to all of those discs with cover songs.

Sluggish sales and the Feelies' refusal to take part in a Son of Stiff package tour soured relations with the label, and by 1982 the band was free from its five-album contract. Mercer and Million never considered the Feelies to be officially broken up. They collaborated on the soundtrack to the punk film *Smithereens* and concentrated on playing with other groups, covering the psychedelic Beatles in a band called Dr. Robert and the Velvets in Foggy Notion; joining some high school friends in the Trypes, and backing Weckerman as he sang his own songs with Yung Wu. The main outlet for all of these bands was a Sunday-night series dubbed "Music for Neighbors" at a Haledon bar called the Peanut Gallery, and the Trypes were always the most interesting band on the bill. Their sound drew inspiration from George Harrison's Indian drones, avant-garde composer Phillip Glass, and Brian Eno, as evidenced on their 1984 EP *The Explorers Hold*. When the Feelies were reactivated in 1986, the core members of the Trypes continued as Speed the Plough, releasing four strong albums in a similar vein.

The Feelies played a handful of gigs between 1982 and 1986, almost always on holiday weekends. (Mercer and Million wanted them to be events.) Some of these shows featured two drummers—Fier and Stanley Demeski—as well as Weckerman on percussion. The Feelies played only old material, but Mercer and Million had begun working on new songs with the Willies, a group they formed with Demeski, Weckerman, and bassist Brenda Sauter. Initially, the Willies played textured instrumental drones that recalled Eno's ambient albums; when the band performed, it played completely in the dark. By 1985, the group had turned on the lights and started playing new songs, as well as material from *Crazy Rhythms*. The Willies were becoming the Feelies. The old brute physical force was gone—the classically trained Demeski was a much more mannered and precise drummer than Fier—and the emphasis shifted from crazy rhythms to Million's gorgeous chord progressions and Mercer's dynamic and hummable solos.

The Feelies reemerged just as R.E.M.-inspired jangle-mania took

Night of the living Feelies, part deux. From left, Brenda Sauter, Stanley Demeski, Bill Million, Glenn Mercer, Dave Weckerman. **(Photo by Marty Perez.)**

hold. When the band agreed to record for the Hoboken-based Coyote Records, R.E.M. guitarist Peter Buck was tapped to produce. Not surprisingly, Mercer and Million again grabbed control. Buck spent most of his time sleeping with his feet up on the mixing console (though he did contribute a chorus setting that made the guitars on "Slow Down" sound like bagpipes). All shimmering textures and heartland images inspired by the Feelies' first cross-country tour, the album was a critical and college-radio hit that convinced A&M to sign the band. The albums that followed offered subtle variations on the formula, with the polished *Only Life* addressing the topic of maturing and coming to terms with life, and the rawer *Time for a Witness* making a nostalgic return to the garage (including a cover of the Stooges' "Real Cool Time," one of the first songs Million and Mercer learned together).

The band members' perfectionistic tendencies always made for uneasy relationships, and the group's lack of commercial acceptance contributed to the strain. The Feelies were a major influence on many of the alternative bands that struck it rich in the '90s, but A&M never had a clue about how to promote them. The group was always ahead of its time, and its time finally ran out in late 1991. Mercer and Weckerman kept playing in a basement in Haledon, forming a new band called Wake Ooloo and continuing the return to the garage started on *Time for a Witness.* Demeski joined former Galaxie 500 leader Dean Wareham in Luna, and Sauter played with Speed the Plough and formed her own band, Wild Carnation.

The Feelies have taken lengthy breaks before. This one seems to be for good, but you never know. "Being in the Feelies is kinda like living in this great pyramid," Weckerman said. "Nothing ever changes, and no one ever grows old."[11]

Passionate Friends:
The English Psychedelic Eccentrics

In the wake of punk, the English music scene was up for grabs, with minimalist art bands, synthesized-pop groups, and glam creations all vying for attention. Some of the most interesting groups took punk's energy and reexamined the psychedelic sounds of the '60s and '70s. One band reclaimed the word as part of its name: Revolving around brothers Richard and Tim Butler and wall-of-sound guitarist John Ashton, the Psychedelic Furs debuted in 1980 with a droning self-titled album derived in part from David Bowie and Brian Eno's Berlin collaborations. *Talk Talk Talk* (1981) boasted stronger songs and more of a Velvet Underground and Bob Dylan influence, while *Forever Now* (1982) expanded the sound in orchestral fashion courtesy of producer Todd Rundgren.

Sneering at punks for whom the movement had simply become fashion, the Television Personalities drew heavily from the Byrds and the Creation on albums such as . . . *And Don't the Kids Just Love It* (1980) and *The Painted Word* (1984). But the group will always be best remembered for the single, "I Know Where Syd Barrett Lives" and the fact that bandleader Daniel Treacy announced the madcap's address onstage while opening a show for Pink Floyd.

The driving forces of The Teardrop Explodes, the Soft Boys, and XTC also displayed an abiding fascination with Barrett, and they suffered the inevitable comparisons, partly because they flirted with psychedelic excess or mental breakdown themselves, and partly because they shared similar whimsical styles. But the tradition of fanciful storytelling is as old as the British Isles, and eccentricity has long been celebrated in England, as evidenced by novelist P. G. Wodehouse. Over the course of long and productive careers, Julian Cope, Robyn Hitchcock, and Andy Partridge each perfected their own unique brands of wigginess, in addition to crafting some of the best psychedelic rock of the '80s and '90s.

An Elegant Chaos

If you betray one aspect of yourself, you betray all the others. I'd always rather fall on my ass going for it than be scared to.

—Julian Cope

Waiting in the wings at London's Hammersmith Palais for one of his first solo performances in 1984, Cope seethed in anger as he watched the Woodentops mimic his act. When he finally took to the boards himself, he snapped the mike stand during a frantic version of the story song "Reynard the Fox" and cut himself repeatedly in the stomach. "Infamy, infamy, they've all got it in for me!" he shouted. Two months later, he appeared naked on the cover of *Fried*, crouching under a giant turtle shell. "Namdam am I, I'm a madman," he wrote in the liner notes.

Few figures in rock history have embodied both the psychedelic and punk impulses as thoroughly as Cope. He is equal parts Barrett and Iggy Pop. But although he has survived his self-destructive urges to hone his own distinctive method of working, he maintains that "mad," spontaneous, and sometimes dangerous acts are a vital part of creating rock 'n' roll. "I have no desire to sound sensible," he told me. "I don't think wisdom and sensibleness are particularly combined. When you start sounding sensible, that's when you start sounding like Genesis."

Born in 1957 to a middle-class family in Wales, Cope soon moved to Tamworth, a small mining town midway between Liverpool and London. Doing his best to thwart his parents' high expectations, he ignored his studies in favor of krautrock, Captain Beefheart, and Pink Floyd, and he was lucky to be accepted by C. F. Mott, a small college outside Liverpool. Like countless other young musicians, Cope embraced the first wave of punk, but he saw connections between the new sounds and older groups such as the 13th Floor Elevators, the Seeds, and the Doors. Working in a group called the Crucial Three with his mate, Ian McCulloch, he shamelessly recycled riffs from the psychedelic punks of the past. "I just went through all those songs, ripping off as many as I could," he said. "But the only people who recognized that were people like you who were thought of as madmen."[1]

Distracted by love, McCulloch lost interest in the band and was given the boot in the summer of 1978. Cope regrouped, choosing the name The Teardrop Explodes from an issue of Marvel Comics' *Daredevil.* (The long moniker was intended as an homage to the 13th Floor Elevators.) Although he had never sung before, Cope insisted on being the singer, and he eventually developed an impressive baritone. By the time the Teardrops were ready to perform, McCulloch had a new band of his own—Echo and the Bunnymen—whom Cope asked to open.

As the bands began to build their respective followings, the music press dubbed their sound "bubblegum trance," and a harsh rivalry developed. Both groups recorded for the small independent Zoo Records, which was run by Bill Drummond and David Balfe, who eventually joined The Teardrops as keyboardist. Cope maintains that the Bunnymen were careerist and happy to be manipulated by Zoo, and that they stole The Teardrops' trademark organ and horn sounds and mopey paramilitary look. He addressed McCulloch in one of the Teardrops' best singles, the acerbic "Treason." McCulloch wasn't hurt by his old friend's derision, and he proceeded to explore chiming guitars and existential crises on over a half-dozen albums through the late '80s.

The Teardrops' first two albums outpower all of the Bunnymen's efforts with more melody and diversity. Drummond mortgaged his house to fund the recording of *Kilimanjaro.* He was repaid with the appropriately titled hit "Reward" and a bright, upbeat effort in which Cope liberally applied *Magical Mystery Tour* horns and marimbalike keyboards to emphasize the big new-wave hooks in tunes such as "When I Dream." The second album was a different affair. Before 1980, Cope was a straightedge punk who avoided drugs of any kind, but during the frantic rush of touring before the release of *Kilimanjaro,* his band mates persuaded him to try marijuana and LSD. He quickly became as extreme in his excess as he had been in his nonindulgence. "In two short months, I moved from Drug Puritan to Acid King," he wrote.[2] Released at the end of 1981, *Wilder* is a transitional effort that trumpets his expanded worldview. "Celebrate the great escape from lunacy dividing / Celebrate the great escape, and carry my soul away," he sings over the kicking horn sec-tion, raga guitar, and massive tambourine of "Passionate Friend."

Despite an ever-changing cast of personnel, the Teardrops had made few wrongs moves, but the balance of power was shifting from Cope to Balfe. The keyboardist insisted on sculpting the third album, and he locked Cope and drummer Gary Dwyer out of the studio. They amused themselves by speeding through the countryside, one of them driving and the other clinging spread-eagled to the roof of the car. Convinced that Balfe's album was shit, Cope broke up the group. (The aborted disc was issued in 1990 as *Everybody Wants to Shag . . . The Teardrop Explodes*, and Cope finally admitted that it "wasn't as crap as it seemed in September '82.") Striking out on his own, he announced, "I regard what I want to do next as an opportunity for gross self-indulgence."

The singer holed up in Tamworth, in need of recovery from the end of his group and his first marriage. Cope purged himself with one of his most productive periods. In 1983, he released both *World Shut Your Mouth*, which continued mining the same vein as late-era Teardrops, and the more introspective *Fried*. Between the two releases, he played his infamous concert at the Hammersmith Palais, providing graphic evi-dence of his fragile state of mind. But thanks to the influence of his second wife, Dorian, he began to come to terms with his stardom, drug use, and life in general. By 1987 Cope was healthy enough to poke fun at his position as a cult rock star with the messianic character in the title of *Saint Julian*, but he refused to preach about his earlier behavior. "I always hated people who were considered to be weirdos straightening their act out. I don't apologize for the way I was," he said.[3] In another interview, he added, "I awoke from a Rip Van Winkle acid haze and, unlike everybody else who awakens from an acid haze, I realized that all those days were not a waste of time. The problem you get with reformed lunatics is that suddenly their albums are really boring. But my albums are even weirder."[4]

Saint Julian produced two of Cope's biggest hits, the giddy "Tram-poline" and the "losers' anthem" and MTV hit "World Shut Your Mouth." ("I always rip songs off, and most of the songs that I rip off are my old songs," he said. "When I did the album *World Shut Your Mouth*, it never occurred to me that it was a song title."[5]) The album was followed by an equally straightforward effort, *My Nation Underground*, that included more comments on pop-star pomposity ("Charlotte Anne," a pun on "charlatan") and a tribute to old favorites the 13th Floor Elevators

A madman am I: St. Julian in 1994. (Photo by Ed Sirrs.)

("Easter Everywhere"). But his masterpiece of pop-rock weirdness came in 1991.

As concept albums go, *Peggy Suicide* makes a lot more sense than the story of a deaf, dumb, and blind pinball wizard. "I had a vision of the world," Cope wrote in the liner notes. "This enormous Mother Earth was standing at the very edge of the highest cliff of Infinity and was about to leap off. . . . I had to make this record about the crazy situation." The plight of Mother Earth/Peggy Suicide is explored in songs about the destructive power of automobiles ("East Easy Rider," "Drive, She Said"), apathy in the face of growing conservatism ("Soldier Blue," "Leperskin"), and life in the age of AIDS ("Safesurfer"). The insistent stomp of earlier work is replaced by a seductive, relaxed groove derived from Sly Stone and Funkadelic, and the sonic canvas is full of bubbling synthesizers, echoed guitar, and tambourine. The instrumental passages carry you along like a pleasant daydream, but the double album is punctuated by sly hooks, and every one of the eighteen songs is strong enough to stand on its own.

Most of the songs were recorded in one or two takes by Cope and his core collaborators, bassist Donald Ross Skinner and drummer Rooster Cosby. "I think you can make a great pot album and it won't be long and indulgent," Cope said. "I don't want to bore people. The way I see it, rock 'n' roll must have what Lester Bangs used to call that *yorp.* That moment where the four musicians in the studio are looking at each other and they all go, 'Well, fucking hell,' and they all play this kind of like sonic *klang!* I could sit down and say to people, 'Look man, you've got to understand where I'm coming from, 'cause it's deadly important.' The greatest artists have to accept that it's deadly important, but it's also got to be top entertainment."

Cope has returned to the model of *Peggy Suicide* twice. Released in 1992, *Jehovah Kill* ponders the meaning of ancient formations such as

Stonehenge and the long tradition of pagan symbols being suppressed by the church. (The subtitle is *That'll Be the Deicide*—like *Peggy Suicide*, a pun on a Buddy Holly song—but Island Records mangled it in the cover art as *That'll Be the Decide*.) He left Island and moved to Rick Rubin's American Recordings for 1994's *Autogeddon*. Inspired by the freak accident of his car exploding in the driveway on Christmas night 1992, the album further explores the anti-auto tirades of *Peggy Suicide* while (ironically) paying tribute to the *motorik* beat and highway sounds of Neu! and krautrock.

Partly because of their density, and partly because he was reluctant to tour to promote them, Cope's concept efforts didn't win the audience they deserved in the States. (The most American-influenced of England's psychedelic postpunks, Cope has always been more popular at home, while the very English Robyn Hitchcock and Andy Partridge have bigger followings in the United States.) Unfazed, he busied himself with other projects, including his autobiography, a book about the ancient stones, a history of krautrock, and the self-released instrumental albums *Rite* (Neu!-like meditations) and *Queen Elizabeth* (ambient/electronic krautrock). In 1995 he made a partial return to the more conventional albums of his early solo career with the strong, twenty-song collection, *20 Mothers*.

Like his peers, Cope is firmly pigeonholed as a cult figure, but he vows to keep making records for the next thirty years and expanding his cult one listener at a time. "I lost this desire to impress everybody with what I wanted to say in one album or two albums," he said. "I realized that the best way to really make people believe that I was truthful and that I meant it was to instill some kind of trust. It might need another five albums for the skeptics to believe what I'm saying. They might disagree, but it's a reality, you know."

The Man Who Invented Himself

If you call my music psychedelic, it is. If you say that coffee cups that have a certain amount of grind on the inside are psychedelic, people will say they are not. But if you go on saying it, eventually they will be. Because people will say, "The mugs were very psychedelic when we came down for breakfast today," meaning they were full of old coffee grind.

—Robyn Hitchcock

"The funny thing about interviews is that people always expect me to define myself," Robyn Hitchcock said the first time I interviewed him, proceeding to launch into the sort of absurdist monologue that would become very familiar in the coming years. "It's like saying, 'Good evening, my name is Marsha Lynn. I'm eighteen and I come from Connecticut. I hope to be a goldfish. My hobbies are cycling, tennis, and peeling the skin off old people.'" Hitchcock had come to Maxwell's in Hoboken, New Jersey, in 1985 on his first tour with the Egyptians, but he was known primarily as leader of the late, lamented Soft Boys, a group that was influential in launching the psychedelic revival in the States. While the so-called Paisley Underground bands were so anxious to be linked to the past that they even dressed the part, Hitchcock was reluctant to be pigeonholed—unless it was in a role of his own invention.

Hitchcock was born in London in 1953 to upper-middle-class parents, including a father who was a well-known cartoonist and painter. He attended an all-male boarding school and arrived in art college in the early '70s, "indistinguishable from the general posthippie flotsam." His interests soon shifted to music via a school band called the Beetles, and when they broke up, he decided to move to Cambridge in search of new accomplices. At first, he played solo shows at the Portland Arms or busked on the street, singing "Hey Jude" and a handful of originals such as "Wey Wey Hep Uh Hole." He also goofed around with some friends as Maureen and the Meatpackers. "It took about two years for the real musos to unfreeze themselves enough to come sliding up to see what I was doing," he said.[6] When they did, they included bassist Andy Metcalfe and drummer Morris Windsor, who were playing in a band called Dennis and the Experts.

Hitchcock borrowed this rhythm section and never returned it. The new group was completed in early 1977 by the addition of guitarist Wang Bo, a.k.a. Alan Davies. A deliberately unrocking name was chosen from the titles of two books by William S. Burroughs, *The Soft Machine* and *The Wild Boys*. From the start, the Soft Boys were out of touch with the prevailing trends. "The Soft Boys were accused of being retrospective or psychedelic or all sorts of words that were unacceptable to the new-wave critical elite because we used guitar solos and harmonies," Hitchcock said. "Wire covered their tracks better by having short hair; they were basically a psychedelic group in drag. Andy Partridge and XTC managed to get away with it. But we just didn't fit in."

Nevertheless, the group built enough of a following to release an independent EP called *Give It to the Soft Boys*. Hitchcock has said it's his favorite Soft Boys record, and traces of the group's later sound—including the dueling guitar lines, twisted rhythms, and absurdist lyrics—can be heard on "The Yodeling Hoover" and "Hear My Brane." But Hitchcock was ambitious. Prompted by a desire to be more new wave, he gave Wang Bo the boot and replaced him with the cute and dexterous lead guitarist of another Cambridge band called the Waves. "It was like if the Stones had kicked out Brian Jones and put Jimi Hendrix in," Hitchcock said. "It was sort of greed. We saw this guy Kimberley Rew and thought, 'What a performer. Let's have him!'"

Hitchcock soon regretted the move. He maintains that the Rew group was top-heavy, too loud, and "too Television." The group's first album was never released because Hitchcock claimed it was too bad, though pieces surfaced on later compilations. Recorded in 1978, *A Can of Bees* was the first effort to actually make it to the stores. "A can of bees was just what it was," Hitchcock said. "That music is like a load of insects inside a jar just humming and trying to get out—a load of insects that have been drinking paraffin or something pretty lethal, insects that are on fire because they've been soaked in brandy." But though the arrangements are serpentine, the album is full of what one song calls "Human Music," and even the most experimental tunes boast inviting melodies. The psychedelic influence can be heard in echoes of Captain Beefheart and the Incredible String Band (as well as the more obvious Beatles) and in the lyrical imagery.

Dadaism, surrealism, English folklore, Monty Python, Bob Dylan, and Syd Barrett are all inspirations for Hitchcock's writing, but the biggest factor was and is his fertile imagination. He has only ever had five themes—gender confusion, death, nostalgia, the psychotic side of romance, and sinister doings in the natural world—but he has a thousand metaphors to describe them. Some fans assume that his lyrics and music must be drug inspired, but the Soft Boys were never as enthusiastic about acid as the bands in Liverpool. "I took a few trips, but I didn't trust it," Hitchcock said. "You certainly don't need to take drugs to make creative music." Like Roxy Music, the group approached a rock song as a pastiche. "The Soft Boys' manifesto was one of taking bits and pieces, a bit like a collage," Hitchcock said. "Like if you gummed a tomato to a squirrel's head and then gaffer-taped a pigeon's wings to a cucumber. I would say that the Soft Boys were about arrangements rather than songs."[7]

Give it to the Soft Boys; Robyn Hitchcock, left.
(Photo by Rosalind Kunath.)

This started to change when Metcalfe left and Matthew Seligman joined, shifting the group in a poppier direction and paving the way for its best album. *Underwater Moonlight* (1980) was done primarily on eight tracks, but this time the group and producer Pat Collier indulged in studio amenities such as echo, reverb, and sitar overdubs. A few songs continue in the style of the early Soft Boys, but most are well-crafted updates of the chiming folk-rock sounds of Fairport Convention and the Byrds. Especially effective is the single "I Wanna Destroy You," which is both an antiwar anthem and a jab at punk.

Faced by general indifference at home in England—over half the sales of *Underwater Moonlight* were as American imports—the Soft Boys "just sort of petered out" in early 1980. (*Invisible Hits* followed, but it was a collection of older material recorded between the first and second albums.) While Windsor remained close to Hitchcock, and Metcalfe soon returned, Rew set out on his own, crafting a strong power-pop album called *The Bible of Bop* before returning to the Waves and new singer Katrina Leskanich to score a major hit with "Walking on Sunshine."

Hitchcock's first solo album, *Black Snake Diamond Röle*, features musical contributions from the former Soft Boys, as well as Psychedelic Furs drummer Vince Ely. It opens with "The Man Who Invented Himself," ostensibly a tribute to Barrett, but just as effective as Hitchcock's own theme song. The album continues the upbeat mood of *Underwater Moonlight*, but the sound is expanded with keyboards and more acoustic instruments, shifting the focus closer to the words and melodies. "They're the first set of songs I developed as a songwriter—he said, leaning on the table in a songwriterly fashion—and they're less novelty but no less a freak show," Hitchcock said. "But I'm still not Jackson Browne or anything like that."

One of the few traits that Hitchcock shared with the punk movement was a disdain of rock-star behavior. He lampooned rock excess on several tunes, including the Soft Boys' "Rock 'n' Roll Toilet" and "Trash" from the oddities collection *Invisible Hitchcock*. Nevertheless, he found himself sucked into a disastrous bid at stardom with 1982's *Groovy Decay*, blindly ceding control as he escaped in an alcoholic daze. Producer Steve Hillage buried Hitchcock's songs under obnoxious horns and disco grooves, inadvertently predicting the Manchester psychedelic dance sound that emerged a few years later. Hitchcock had never been a particular fan of Hillage or Gong, and the idea came from his manager at the time. "I think he just thought, 'Oh yeah, psychedelic, alright,'" Hitchcock said. "Hillage had justly got into his sort of 1980's Kings' Row suits and was trying to be anything but psychedelic. He was into club mixes and all that sort of stuff. I was really lost and getting loster in those days."

This spectacular failure prompted Hitchcock to withdraw and reassess. He kept himself afloat by writing lyrics for solo efforts by Captain Sensible of the Damned. But his own songs began to accumulate again, and he finally returned to the studio after a three-year break to craft *I Often Dream of Trains*. The best of his solo albums, it's a quiet, introspective effort driven by acoustic guitar, piano, and vocals. "It's like wanting to see what you're like when you take everything else away," Hitchcock said. It also comes closer than any other album to merging the styles of his two primary heroes. "Bob Dylan showed me what I wanted to do, and Syd Barrett showed me how I could do it," the singer has often said. (Though he always paid tribute to both men in interviews, the Barrett comparison is the one that took root. Not only was the stylistic resemblance more obvious, both artists had ties to Cambridge, and Hitchcock eventually signed with former Barrett and Pink Floyd manager Peter Jenner.)

Reenergized and reunited with Windsor and Metcalfe in the Egyptians, Hitchcock immediately followed *I Often Dream of Trains* with a new electric-pop album, *Fegmania!* During their absence from the scene, the Soft Boys' influence had grown. Peter Buck said the group was more of an inspiration for early R.E.M. than the Byrds. Now the Egyptians were poised to capitalize. Embraced by the American rock underground and college radio, the group graduated from indie labels to A&M Records. Between 1986 and 1993, the Egyptians released a string of albums, including *Element of Light*, *Globe of Frogs*, *Queen Elvis*, *Perspex Island*, and *Respect*. In between, Hitchcock took a break to release another solo acoustic effort called *Eye*. The band's willful quirkiness served as a model for much of the alternative rock that stormed the charts in the '90s, but the Egyptians themselves never expanded beyond a small, loyal cult following. The group's playing grew increasingly polite and predictable, and

Robyn Hitchcock, a surrealist with a guitar in the '90s. (Photo by Greg Allen.)

Hitchcock's lyrical arsenal of dwarves, lobsters, ghosts, and man-eating vegetables started to sound overly familiar. Yet even the least of his albums each has three or four outstanding songs, including brilliant tunes such as "Glass," "Raymond Chandler Evening," "Vibrating," "She Doesn't Exist," and "The Wreck of the Arthur Lee" (a nod to the Love founder as well anyone else who never realized their potential). A&M dropped Hitchcock after *Respect*, making the title especially ironic, and, once again, the band petered out. "There's only so long you can run a six-legged race," Hitchcock said.

Claiming to be burned out on the band format and loud rock in general, Hitchcock determined to forge ahead in the solo mode of *I Often Dream of Trains* and *Eye*, presenting his songs in the most direct manner possible. He has never regretted his more whimsical moments, and he maintains that his "serious" songs and his humorous flights of fancy are both part of his personality. But there's no denying that his songs are sometimes drowned out by the persona he invented. "Hitchcock is the kind of English eccentric who becomes impossible to bear when he's taken up by American Anglophiles," Robert Christgau charged.[8]

"I've set myself up for that, so if I feel trapped, I've only got myself to blame," Hitchcock said. "But both the musicianship angle—working with the others—and the 'Robyn Hitchcock unscrews the top of his head and lets it all spring out all over the floor' angle are secondary to what I am, which is a songwriter. So I'm now concerned with presenting myself as a songwriter."

Senses Working Overtime

Andy's mind was taking him on a terrifying voyage, like a bad acid trip. It was a classic Hollywood horror scenario: The room began to spin as everyone and everything seemed to be drifting further and further away from him. He felt more and more nauseous. Finally he thought, quite literally, he was going to die.
—Andy Partridge freaks out onstage, 1981[9]

There are two major differences between Andy Partridge and his post-punk psychedelic peers. Unlike Cope, he never really shared the punk appreciation for spontaneity and immediacy. And unlike Hitchcock, he came to despise live performance. Chris Twomey's biography, *XTC: Chalkhills and Children*, opens with the central incident in the story of XTC. After years of steady touring, the group was playing in support of its best album to date, 1982's *English Settlement*. Onstage at Le Palais in Paris, Partridge froze only thirty seconds into the set, then ran offstage. In the weeks that followed, he attempted to come to terms with his paranoia and stage fright, but hours before a sold-out show at the Hollywood Palladium, he simply decided that he would never perform live again. After all, the Beatles had done it, and they had proceeded to do some of their best work.

XTC's guitarist-vocalist was born in Malta in 1953 to Vera and John Partridge, who was serving in the Royal Navy. When Andy was three, the family returned to a quiet, working-class life in Swindon, a small farm community seventy miles west of London. Andy was exposed to music from early on—his father was a singer who performed in local skiffle groups—but the interest really took hold when he saw *A Hard Day's Night* at age ten. As he entered his teens, Partridge spent hours listening to psychedelic-rock singles such as the Small Faces' "Itchycoo Park," the Move's "Fire Brigade," and Pink Floyd's "See Emily Play"—"a three-minute thing of a very memorable tune but with a big dollop of magic injected, either some strange effect or totally nonsensical lyrics that painted great brain pictures."[10] He eventually bought a guitar and a used reel-to-reel tape recorder, partly with money that he won in a "Draw Your Favorite Monkee" contest.

Life wasn't always rosy. Reacting badly to his parents' marital problems, Andy was put on Valium to control wild mood swings at age twelve, and he didn't stop taking the drug until thirteen years later. He quit Swindon College in 1971 after a year and a half. By 1973, he was playing in a glam band called Star Park—later the Helium Kidz—with hard-drinking drummer Terry Chambers, quiet bassist Colin Moulding, and Dave Cartner, who was soon to be replaced by keyboardist Barry Andrews. As musical fashions shifted and the group moved away from glam and toward pub rock with science-fiction overtones, a new name was needed. In late 1975, the Dukes of Stratosphear was passed over as too psychedelic, and the band became XTC.

Even though its music had little to do with punk, the group landed a contract with Virgin in the rush of excitement following the Sex Pistols. At Partridge's insistence, early press releases referred to him as a "nuclear-powered Syd Barrett." XTC's first album included a herky-jerk cover of Dylan's "All Along the Watchtower" (a very unpunk choice) and a hyperenergetic declaration that "This Is Pop." Even the title—*White Music*—could be considered a statement against the punks' "white noise." The album and XTC's tense live shows (which many compared to the Talking Heads') began to win an audience, and by August 1978 the band was ready to record a follow-up. XTC considered working with Brian Eno, who was a fan, but Eno said the band didn't need a producer. Virgin disagreed and paired the group with John Leckie. The resulting album, *Go 2*, is more ambitious and experimental. "Battery Brides" is a mechanical pop song that pays tribute to Eno, and Moulding's "X Wires" shows a serious desire to experiment in the studio.

From the start, Partridge wrote most of XTC's material, with occasional contributions from Moulding. Frustrated by this arrangement, Andrews quit and was replaced by Swindon pal Dave Gregory on guitar and keyboards. (Thomas Dolby lobbied for the spot but was rejected, since he was also an ambitious songwriter. Like Gary Numan, he went on to craft low-rent versions of Eno's and Kraftwerk's synthesizer-pop albums.) XTC toured nonstop through this period in what it called "stupidly hard work," and albums (including the wonderfully poppy *Drums and Wires*) were crafted in a rush between commitments. *Black Sea* originally had the protest title *Working Under Pressure*, hence the deep-sea diver suits on the cover. Adding to the edginess, Partridge quit his long-time Valium addiction cold turkey. Ironically, the mounting tensions produced a serene and beautiful double album.

English Settlement was crafted in the summer of 1981, the group's first extended down time in four years. It's a subtle and textured effort that makes extensive use of twelve-string guitar, fretless bass, synthesizer, and tom-heavy drum parts that draw on a variety of global rhythms. "Until *English Settlement*, I'd felt like a child in a sweet shop wanting to try a bit of everything but only being allowed to choose licorice allsorts," Partridge said. "I'd broken from this moral chastity belt that told me it was wrong to put anything on our records that we couldn't reproduce live."[11] Many of the songs feature Partridge reflecting on world issues from the safety of his Swindon home. "I felt more English in the face of traveling the world," the singer said.[12] But the strongest tune is about an inner voyage. If "Senses Working Overtime" wasn't inspired by a pleasurable acid trip—Partridge has never directly addressed the question—its sentiments and expansive sound certainly evoke the feeling. "All the world is biscuit shaped / It's just for me to feed my face," he sings. "I can see, hear, smell, touch, taste / And I've got one, two, three, four, five / Senses working overtime / Trying to take this all in."

The title took on a different connotation in the wake of Partridge's onstage breakdown. Returning to Swindon, Partridge, who was now plagued by agoraphobia, dreaded leaving the house. The band, deeply in debt, was left without a drummer when Chambers quit because of the no-touring edict. The group forged ahead, but the problems contributed to the tentative, stilted sound of *Mummer*, and the album ends with a bitter declaration. "The music business is a hammer to keep you pegs in your holes," Partridge sings in "Funk Pop a Roll." Released in 1984, *The Big Express* has more upbeat moments—including the idyllic "Everyday Story of Smalltown"—but it is often overproduced and leaden. If XTC's earlier albums were limited by time constraints, its work after *English Settlement* suffers from a lack of urgency. The band clearly needed to blow out the cobwebs.

Partridge and Leckie were slated to produce Canadian singer Mary Margaret O'Hara, but she fired them when she discovered they didn't share her strict Roman Catholic beliefs. Virgin owed the pair money, and Leckie convinced the company to give it to XTC for a bit of fun in the studio. The musicians had long been itching to pay tribute to the psychedelic rock that they loved as teenagers. Working at a small studio in Hereford, they recorded six songs in two weeks, forcing themselves to use only vintage '60s equipment. The *25 O'Clock* EP was released on April Fool's Day 1985, under the guise of the Dukes of Stratosphear. XTC's name didn't appear anywhere, but the strong melodies and West Country vocals left little doubt about who the culprits were. Like many of the psychedelic revival bands recording in America at the time, the Dukes' faithfulness to late-'60s sounds, styles, and themes produced a classic rock parody/homage. In a lengthy interview with the XTC fanzine *The Little Express*, the group offered detailed footnotes for each song: "Bike Ride to the Moon" is sung in a sort of "loopy Cambridge" accent over a Move bass line with lyrics that owe "My White Bicycle" and Syd Barrett's "Bike"; "25 O'Clock" is a cross between the Amboy Dukes and the Electric Prunes, and "The Mole from the Ministry" layers Beatles-style Mellotron over a jaunty "I Am the Walrus" singalong.[13]

The Dukes going gray; Andy Partridge, center.
(Photo by Greg Allen.)

While the EP breaks no ground, it's hard not to enjoy the Dukes' spirited musical forgery. On its release, *25 O'Clock* outsold *The Big Express* two-to-one, rekindling enthusiasm at Virgin for what had become a reclusive cult group. The company geared up for another go at making XTC a hit, insisting that the group work with a "name" producer. The band was enthusiastic about the prospect of recording. "With XTC, we'd lost sight of how to enjoy ourselves making a record," Moulding said. "We spent a lot of time and money on our records, and they weren't necessarily any better for it. The Dukes taught us how to have fun again."[14] But Partridge's enthusiasm soon waned as he butted heads with the equally strong-willed producer, Todd Rundgren.

As a member of the Nazz and an innovative solo artist exploring studio wizardy and synthesizers in the '70s, Rundgren had displayed an aesthetic similar to XTC's. He sifted through the group's demos and developed a concept for a song cycle that traced a passing day from dawn to midnight. *Skylarking* returned to the pastoral tranquillity of *English Settlement* while adding a new sophistication that represented influences such as the Beach Boys and the Beatles coming even further to the forefront. Moulding produced two fine pieces of psychedelic rock—"Big Day," which had originally been considered for the Dukes' project, and an homage to making love while lying on and/or high on "Grass"—while Partridge presented an irresistibly catchy three-minute slice of existentialism, "Dear God." The latter became XTC's first major American hit, resurrecting the band's career and securing its future, but its author hadn't even wanted it on the album.

"The band was at a point in their career where if they didn't get some kind of response to their records, they weren't going to be making any more records," Rundgren said. "It had to be a record that people would listen to and enjoy. There were times when I was at loggerheads with Andy's natural propensity for excess."[15] Though Partridge bad-mouthed Rundgren in countless interviews after the album's release, in time even he admitted that the producer had done his job.

XTC followed *Skylarking* with a second Dukes of Stratosphear release, *Psonic Psunspot*. The album fails partly because it lacked the EP's joy and spontaneity, but the biggest problem was that XTC no longer needed its alter egos. *Skylarking* crafted a beautiful marriage of XTC and the Dukes. "I had always wanted to be in a group that made that kind of music," Partridge admitted. "There was a split image, and now they're merged."[16] Unfortunately, Partridge never accepted the lesson of working with Rundgren, which was that the group needed an editor and mediator. When the band was limited by the time constraints of vinyl LPs, extraneous material was relegated to B sides, EPs, and rarities collections. After *Skylarking*, Partridge simply emptied his notebooks onto bloated and overlong albums. He had often eclipsed Moulding in the past, despite the fact that the bassist wrote many of the band's best songs. In the absence of a strong producer, he became even more dominant. *Oranges & Lemons* (1989) and *Nonsuch* (1992) are good albums that could have been great if Partridge had accepted some discipline. Too many of the tunes seem like rewrites of earlier material, and Partridge's propensities for wordiness, cloying cuteness, and fussy baroque arrangements go unchecked.

The band's auteur remains unrepentant. In the grand tradition of English eccentrics, Partridge lives by his own rules. XTC in the '90s is basically "a paying hobby," he said. Between projects, he plays with his armies of toy soldiers, drinks at the pub, and sits up at night reading Jules Verne. From time to time, he produces fellow artists (the Woodentops or Peter Blegvad), or pursues low-key solo projects such as *Through the Hill*, 1994's ambient collaboration with Harold Budd. "People who like XTC like us for precisely the reason we aren't like everyone else," Partridge said. "If you like cheesecake, you don't like it because it reminds you of some other form of cake so you'll put up with the cheese element. You like it because it's cheesecake."[17]

Retrodelic: The American Psychedelic Revival

We belong to the hot generation / Yeah, we belong to the civilization / We have no responsibility / And people just can't see / That we need to be free.

—The Pandoras, "Hot Generation"

On the Sunday night before Labor Day, the crowd was ready to rock into the early-morning hours at the Dive, an aptly named hellhole on New York's West Twenty-ninth Street. Mod haircuts, black turtlenecks, tapered trousers, and Beatles boots were the uniforms of choice for the men, while the women sported long bangs, tight miniskirts, Nancy Sinatra go-go boots, and Mary Quant makeup. Strobe lights bounced off a silvery backdrop as a procession of bands took to the tiny stage to raise money for *99th Floor*, the self-proclaimed "Official Fanzine of Teenage Creeps." The Creeping Pumpkins started off with their raw, grungey garage rock. The Mod Fun had progressed from the roots its name suggested to become an American take on the Creation and the Pretty Things. The Blacklight Chameleons played psychedelicized surf instrumentals; the Tryfles delivered a collection of snotty protopunk anthems, and the Optic Nerve capped things off with a jangly set that did the Byrds proud.

You're forgiven for thinking the year was 1966, but it was 1985, and the benefit was evidence of the American psychedelic and garage revival in full swing. As in England, the American rock underground rediscovered psychedelia as a natural progression from punk. Emerging shortly after the punk scenes that sprang up in Cleveland and New York, Washington, D.C.'s Afrika Korps (later the Slickee Boys) and Boston's DMZ (later the Lyres) were both devoted to faithful reproductions of *Nuggets*-era rock. In the early '80s, these bands were joined by the like-minded Chesterfield Kings from Rochester, New York, the Unclaimed from Los Angeles, and the Fleshtones from New York City. These groups in turn prompted younger musicians to scour the record racks in search of '60s relics to provide a basis for their own sounds.

Greg Shaw of the punk label Bomp! formed the subsidiary Voxx Records in 1979 as home for *Battle of the Garages*, a *Nuggets*-style compilation of modern bands dedicated to "an aesthetic originally formed and perfected in 1966 high school gyms." It took two years and a national competition to round up enough bands for the first volume, but by the time it was released in 1981, Shaw was being besieged with tapes from across the U.S. "Every city in the country has got some kind of band doing this stuff," Unclaimed veteran Sid Griffin said at the peak of the movement in 1986. "Every town has got at least one '60s band."[1]

The revival fascinated editors who had been there the first time, and a host of articles appeared in the national media. Tellingly, *Rolling Stone* covered it as a fashion story. Antifashion had been the rule for punk, but style was a prime concern for the '60s revivalists. Bands were extremely conscious of using only period instruments—Vox and Farfisa organs and Vox and Rickenbacker guitars—and they dressed only in period styles. There was a rigid doctrine, and the rules were spelled out by the albums, films, and magazine articles that documented the original garage and psychedelic movements. By 1986, even Shaw was complaining about the scene's lack of cultural relevance. "It has nothing to do with what's going on today," he said. "I like the sounds, but what made punk important in the '70s was that it was talking about now and handing out answers for now, and that's why it touched so many people."[2]

Defenders of the revival said that its adherents were simply rebelling against boredom. "The garage kids were rejecting the corporate, bland, 'modern' music culture," revival chronicler Timothy Gassen wrote. But unlike the movements in the '60s or the early-'80s punk scene that produced groups such as Hüsker Dü and the Minutemen, the revivalists weren't interested in politics or social change. "Most bands and followers of the '60s sound avoided such personal commitment, many feeling hopelessness in the Reagan and Thatcher years of ever affecting any positive change," Gassen wrote. "Perhaps they didn't equate their rejection of current trends with a return to humanism, or perhaps they couldn't commit themselves to ideas so constantly rejected by their own generation."[3]

Perhaps, like so many people in the '80s, the revivalists were simply searching for escape. The goal at the Dive in New York or the Cavern Club in Los Angeles was to leave with a sexual partner and as few brain cells as possible after a night of loud music, drink, and drugs. While it's debatable how many of the original psychedelic punks ever had psychedelic experiences, LSD and mushrooms were readily available wherever the revivalists were doing their thing. "I remember when [*99th Floor* publisher] Ron Rimsite got up to announce us at that benefit," recalled the Mod Fun's Mick London. "He couldn't even remember the name of the band. He just rambled on about how the world would be so much groovier if Gorbachev and Reagan sat down and took Ecstasy together— and this was years before the rave scene! I'm sure that everybody at the Dive at any given time was on *something*."

Most critics treated releases by the revival groups as novelties or dismissed them as insular and inconsequential—souvenirs that the bands put out for their friends. But as with the original *Nuggets* bands, time has revealed memorable songwriting, musical innovation, and an undeniable spirit. Rochester's Absolute Grey combined chiming guitars and haunting female vocals. Delaware's Plan 9 represented what the Grateful Dead would have sounded like if it hadn't abandoned garage rock. Washington, D.C.'s Velvet Monkeys mixed the disparate influences cited in their name, while Portland's Miracle Workers progressed from hyper R&B to a psychedelic take on '70s Detroit. Hoboken, New Jersey's Tiny Lights combined Sly Stone's psychedelic soul with elaborate, Beatles-inspired productions and gutsy female vocals. The hot desert clime of Tucson nurtured the psychedelic pop of the Marshmallow Overcoat and the raunchy garage punk of Yard Trauma, and the frigid temperatures of Minneapolis produced the barn-burning sounds of the Hypstrz/Mighty Mofos and the enigmatic guitar pop of the 27 Various.

The wave of bands inspired by the psychedelic rock of the '60s wasn't limited to the United States. In Australia, there were the Hoodoo Gurus and the Lime Spiders; in New Zealand, the Chills, the Verlaines, and the Tall Dwarfs; in Germany, the Chud and Yellow Sunshine Explosion, and in Sweden, the Nomads. While several English groups were having chart success with an updated take on psychedelia, a number of underground artists were devoted to "purer" versions of older sounds, including the Barracudas, the Prisoners, Bevis Frond, and Paul Roland. But the hotbeds of the revival were inarguably New York and Los Angeles. In retrospect, fashion was indeed the prime concern on the East Coast, and only a handful of albums are worth seeking out (*Lysergic Emanations* by the Fuzztones, *Outta the Nest* by the Vipers, and *Dorothy's Dream* by the Mod Fun). This is a short list compared to efforts by the L.A. bands, or the entire discography of Milwaukee's remarkable Plasticland.

The Paisley Underground

Like a kaleidoscope / I turn and I'm turning / What I thought was gone / Is now returning / I wonder if it matters / As the pattern shifts and shatters.
—The Rain Parade, "Kaleidoscope"

The term "paisley underground" was coined by Michael Quercio, founder of the Salvation Army and the Three O'Clock, and it would come to be hated by the bands that it described the way that the word "grunge" would be hated by bands in Seattle a few years later. It referred to the paisley fashions that the groups favored, but most of the California bands had some substance beneath the style, at least in the beginning. Many of the groups had roots in suburban Davis, California, but the scene solidified in Los Angeles. "A lot of the friendships started out of the barbecues that Green on Red would have," Dream Syndicate leader Steve Wynn said. "They had this house down in Hollywood in 1982, a little two-story apartment for the whole band and their girlfriends. Every Sunday, we'd get together for a barbecue, bring tons of alcohol and whatever drugs—lots of burgers and chicken—and we'd just sit around, play guitar, and talk. That's how the friendships happened, not in nightclubs or recording studios . . . especially with Green on Red and the Dream Syndicate and the Rain Parade."[4]

Most of the paisley underground musicians were from upper-middle-class backgrounds. They were too young to remember the first wave of psychedelic rock, which they discovered by rummaging through their parents' or older siblings' record collections. They were encouraged to pick up instruments by punk, and they decided to employ them by playing '60s sounds after seeing the Unclaimed. But while the Unclaimed drew its sound almost exclusively from the Seeds and the Music Machine, the younger bands had broader interests and a wider range of emotions, as evidenced by 1983's *Rainy Day* compilation. The album features members of the Rain Parade, the Bangles, the Dream Syndicate, and the Three O'Clock paying tribute to the artists who provided the starting points for their own groups, including Bob Dylan, the Beach Boys, Neil Young, Big Star, the Velvet Underground, and Jimi Hendrix. Like many of the scene's early releases, it was recorded by Ethan James at Radio Tokyo Studios. Other albums were caught on tape by Earle Mankey in his garage, which was outfitted with the console that had been used to record the Beach Boys' *Pet Sounds*.

In addition to using the same studios, the bands often played on each others' records. Unfortunately, they were also united by the fact that they all took turns for the worse when they were signed to major labels. In the days before Nirvana proved that there was money to be made if bands were left to their own "alternative" ways, it's possible that corporate meddling was to blame. The groups may have lost heart as, with the sole exception of R.E.M., American guitar bands were unable to achieve both critical and commercial success. Or perhaps the charges that they were just nostalgic revivalists were too hard to overcome. "The paisley underground tag was simultaneously good and bad," the Rain Parade's Steven Roback told me. "It was good because it helped a lot of serious musicians get some notoriety and make more good music. It was bad because there were a lot of preconceived notions about this psychedelic trip which really were not accurate."

The man who named the scene was born in 1963 in Carson, California, not far from the Beach Boys' hometown of Hawthorne. Quercio formed the Salvation Army as a pop-punk trio in 1981, and he released his first singles on the Minutemen's New Alliance label. But the band really came into its own when he linked up with guitarist Greggory Louis Gutierrez. Shortly thereafter, the group was forced to change its name because of a threat from the real Salvation Army. The Three O'Clock was chosen from a quote by novelist F. Scott Fitzgerald ("In the darkest part of the mind it's always three o'clock in the morning"), and the contention in Tom Wolfe's *The Electric Kool-Aid Acid Test* that people who dropped acid in the early evening would be at the height of their trip at 3:00 A.M.

The influence of the Byrds, the Move, the early Bee Gees, and Syd Barrett's Pink Floyd are obvious on the Three O'Clock's 1982 EP *Baroque*

Hoedown, as well as 1983's *Sixteen Tambourines.* Quercio delivers hook-filled choruses over uplifting rhythms and shifting musical backgrounds based on buzzing keyboards and textured guitar sounds. Like Barrett, the singer projects ambiguity, but one of his most memorable tunes is about being "With Cantaloupe Girlfriend." (Despite the obvious inference, Quercio claimed it was a nonsense phrase for an ideal girl.) The band's decline began with its first release on IRS, *Arrive Without Traveling.* The album boasts two strong tunes in "Her Head's Revolving" and "The Girl With the Guitar" (Quercio penned the latter with Scott Miller, who recorded power pop with a tinge of psychedelia in Northern California's Game Theory), but these moments are overwhelmed by self-parodying schlock like "Simon in the Park (With Tentacles)." Gutierrez left in 1986, and the band signed to Prince's Paisley Park label for the dreadfully slick *Vermillion.* With its original fans alienated and everyone else indifferent, the Three O'Clock finally broke up in 1989.

The Bangles also slid into glossy commercialism after meeting up with Prince, but they started their career as a spare folk-rock quartet with pristine Mamas and Papas–style interval harmonies. The group changed its name from the Bangs and recorded its self-titled debut in 1982. When the band signed to Columbia, it traded mod fashions for Go-Go's–style glamour, but the musicians retained a feisty, independent spirit. *All Over the Place* (1984) succeeds on the strength of guitarist Vicki Peterson's songs, especially "James" and "Hero Takes a Fall," plus an effective cover of former Soft Boy Kimberley Rew's "Going Down to Liverpool." The balance of power shifted after the group scored hits with the Prince-penned "Manic Monday" and the novelty single "Walk Like an Egyptian." By 1988's *Everything,* singer Susanna Hoffs was positioned as the star. The band's original spirit was doused by soggy ballads such as "Eternal Flame," and the group broke up in 1989. Hoffs's solo career crashed and burned after one laughable effort in 1991.

The Rain Parade. Clockwise from bottom left: Eddie Kalwa, Matt Piucci, Steven Roback, Will Glenn, David Roback.

Before the Bangles, Hoffs played in a short-lived group called the Unconscious with brothers David and Steven Roback, who went on to form the Rain Parade with guitarist Matt Piucci. The Rain Parade started with a sound that combined Merseybeat and Rolling Stones–style R&B, but it soon developed a moodier and more complex signature. "We started playing with orchestration, instruments, and different types of guitars," Steven said. "We didn't know what the sound was going to be until we heard it. By the time we got into doing the album itself, all the parts were in place and we went in and did it in a fast, commando sort of thing. There was no money to do it any other way."

Emergency Third Rail Power Trip is not only the best album from any of the paisley underground bands, it ranks with the best psychedelic-rock efforts from any era. Recorded in the winter of 1983, it has a startlingly crisp and clear sound achieved at Radio Tokyo. Songs such as "What's She Done to Your Mind" and "Kaleidoscope" showcase the Robacks' wistful vocals, Eddie Kalwa's precise drumming, Will Glenn's sitar, violin, and keyboard accents, and an intricate two-guitar attack that picks up where "Eight Miles High" left off. But while the melodies are often uplifting, the themes are dark and introspective. "We're psychedelic in a sort of psychoanalytic sense," Piucci said at the time. "I think what psychedelic drugs did to people is that it made them reflect on some very internalized parts of their lives."[5] "The lyrical themes and song content have a sort of punk ethos to them," Steven Roback added. "The state of mind we were all in was pretty dark, and it was like personal therapy for everybody in the band. We were all feeling kind of hopeless and helpless about things, and the band was this sort of idealistic attempt to create some space where we could all feel really great."

Calling the split "a business decision," David Roback quit the Rain Parade in early 1984. "There were just too many cooks, basically," Steven said. "You had three really strong songwriters, and at some point there was just not enough room." The group continued under the direction of Steven and Piucci, recording the even darker *Explosions in the Glass Palace* EP. But while signing to Island Records should have provided the band with the chance to perfect its sound in the studio, *Crashing Dream* was made under hurried, pressured conditions, and the Rain Parade never got another chance. It split up in late 1985. After dabbling with pickup gigs (Piucci played with Crazy Horse between its stints backing Neil Young) and day jobs (Roback had a degree in architecture), the band's driving forces reunited in the '90s in the low-key but pleasant-sounding Viva Saturn.

Once an aspiring rock critic, Wynn formed the Dream Syndicate with bassist Kendra Smith and feedback-happy guitarist Karl Precoda in 1982. The group recorded its self-released EP only three weeks later, following up with a powerful album, *The Days of Wine and Roses*. A raw, energetic effort, the album was strongly influenced by the Velvets, and tunes such as "Tell Me When It's Over" and "Until Lately" have a psychotic edge unique among the paisley underground bands. But Smith left after the first album, the band signed to A&M, and Wynn indulged an embarrassing Bruce Springsteen fixation on later releases. Returning to the model of the Unconscious after leaving the Rain Parade, David Roback formed a series of bands based on gentle, som-

The early Dream Syndicate slumming in Hollywood; Steve Wynn, center. (**Photo by Lynda Burdick.**)

nambulant sounds and wispy female vocals. Smith filled the vocalist roles in Clay Allison and Opal, but she was replaced by Hope Sandoval when Roback formed Mazzy Star in 1990. More successful commercially, Mazzy Star's two albums fail to match the intensity of Opal's *Happy Nightmare Baby* (1987), or Smith's long-awaited solo bow, *Five Ways of Disappearing* (1995).

A native of Louisville, Kentucky, Sid Griffin formed the Long Ryders to explore more expansive sounds after tiring of the Unclaimed's narrow worldview. Debuting with the *10–5–60* EP in 1983, the group brought a garage-punk attitude to the mix of psychedelia and country pioneered by the late-era Byrds. Gene Clark made a guest appearance on the beautiful "Ivory Tower" from 1984's *Native Sons*, but the psychedelic edge disappeared and the group resorted to country corniness after signing to Island in 1985. Griffin moved to England in the early '90s and continues to play with a new combo, the Coal Porters.

Green on Red, the band whose barbecues started it all, are the paisley underground's worst case of arrested development. The group formed in L.A. after three of its members relocated from Tucson, Arizona. Its first two EPs get by on garage-rock energy and a swirling keyboard sound, but the group moved toward drunken Dylan and Young imitations with 1983's *Gravity Talks*, and it spiraled downward after that on seven more albums on four different labels. (Equally forgettable is leader Dan Stuart's 1985 collaboration with Wynn and the Long Ryders, *Danny & Dusty*.) At the fringes of the paisley underground were two other strong guitar bands from Davis: True West (which never delivered on the promise of its 1983 EP) and Thin White Rope (which recorded several albums of ominous psychedelic rock and Can-like repetitive drones), as well as Leaving Trains, a group fronted by celebrated transvestite Falling James. In retrospect, tough-gal psychedelic garage rockers the Pandoras predicted the assertive stance of the riot grrrls. But after the Rain Parade, the best band to emerge from America's psychedelic revival hailed from the blue-collar, beer-loving burg of Milwaukee, Wisconsin.

Color Appreciation

In a moment traveling so far away / Once you're there you'll probably want to stay / Wonder wonderful wonderland.

—Plasticland, "Wonder Wonderful Wonderland"

A few years older than most of their peers, the key players in Plasticland are actually ringers as revivalists, since they were there the first time around. Childhood friends Glenn Rehse and John Frankovic played together in a mid-'60s garage band, and their musical progression followed the development of psychedelic rock. After playing originals in the style of first-wave British psychedelic bands—the Creation, the Pink Floyd, and the Pretty Things particularly fired their imaginations—they moved to progressive rock in a band called Willie the Conqueror, and then to krautrock in a group called Arousing Polaris. "Then we broke up because Glenn and I had a fight," Frankovic said. "My mom would always say that Glenn and I fight like a couple of brothers—'You have a big fight, and then two months later, you're inseparable again.' Being as stubborn as we are, a couple of years later, we got back together, but this time we decided that the band would emphasize recordings rather than live shows."

When Rehse and Frankovic reunited in 1980, they decided to work in the style that inspired them most. The name Plasticland was chosen as what Rehse called "a modernized version of Lewis Carroll's Wonderland." Working with different drummers and second guitarists (including future Violent Femme Brian Ritchie), the duo recorded a series of singles starting with the sensual "Mink Dress," which recalls "Arnold Layne" as the male protagonist sees a lady in a mink dress and decides he needs one himself. The group was usually less obvious in its homages, recalling the spirit of London 1967 without being overly derivative. "We were not out to revive the Creation; we were out to write songs as good as those of the bands we'd fallen in love with years ago," Frankovic told me. "What attracted us to those sounds was the excitement and the cultural ramifications that went with the music. Psychedelia to us

Plasticland auteur No. 1: John Frankovic. (Photo by Ralph Drzewiecki.)

was definitely a state of mind, not a drug. It was an art statement and a fashion statement. Dressing up and not dressing like a slob—pointy shoes, real pants, well-cut Italian-style clothes."

Studying English magazines from the mid-'60s, Frankovic and Rehse put a twist on Carnaby Street fashions by raiding Milwaukee thrift stores, sometimes making their own clothes out of cool fabrics that they found. "This was another thing that Glenn and I had in common: We both loved to dress up," Frankovic said. "We were always in drama club together, and we loved makeup and putting on costumes." Of course, dressing in Edwardian outfits on the streets of Milwaukee could attract unwanted attention. "We ran fast, plus we were punks. We were street-wise, and we knew when it was okay to push people's buttons," Frankovic said. "In high school, I hung out with the burnouts because they never cared. Later, I would hang out in gay bars, because that was where the hippest and coolest people were in Milwaukee. These were people who were kindred spirits, and it didn't matter if you were gay or not."

Plasticland's appearance on *Battle of the Garages* helped spread the word, and after a wiggy, self-released 1982 EP called *Pop! Op Drops*, the French Lolita label fronted the money for a full album. *Color Appreciation* opens with a crazed version of the Pretty Things' "Alexander," creating a frame of reference for the Rehse-Frankovic originals that follow. The songs are filled with unforgettable hooks, inventive playing (includ-

Plasticland auteur No. 2: Glenn Rehse. (Photo by Simon/ Lindemann Photographers.)

ing Rehse's Mellotron parts and Dan Mullen's fuzz-guitar leads), and an absurd sense of humor that finds beauty and drama in such seemingly mundane topics as Rehse's overgrown garden ("The Garden in Pain") and Frankovic's grooming ritual ("Rattail Comb"). The band's enthusiasm virtually flows from the speakers. "It was like, 'It's finally happening, these songs are finally getting recorded,'" Rehse said. "We had a backlog of songs that was knee-deep." "The studio is my playground, and I always have a lot of fun in there," Frankovic added. "That's what having fun is all about: making a lot of noise."

Supportive of the paisley underground bands, California-based Enigma Records signed Plasticland in 1985. Despite the accomplished sound of the first album (which it reissued in the United States as *Plasticland*), the label insisted that the band work with Dream Syndicate guitarist Paul Cutler. (Rehse and Frankovic generally ignored their producer.) An upbeat travelogue of a Carroll-style fantasyland, *Wonder Wonderful Wonderland* is lusher than the debut, with twelve-string guitars, Mellotrons, African percussion, bouzouki, Berimbau, and other textures joining the driving rhythms, fuzz guitar, and Rehse's trademark nasal vocals.

For 1987's *Salon*, the band pared back and emphasized the grooves of new drummer Victor Demichei, revealing roots in Motown and psychedelic soul. "We didn't want to come out like some syrupy, drippy, hippie kind of bullshit," Rehse said. "John and I were always rockers. We came from the Midwest—rhythm & blues and soul music had a hell of a lot to do with our attitude and life." "The whole thing about psychedelia is that it is supposed to take you somewhere," Frankovic said. "Who says that 'Dancing in the Streets' doesn't take you somewhere?" Unfortunately, the album also took the band off the Enigma roster. Enigma wanted the band to tour, but Rehse and Frankovic were too old and too smart for the '80s indie-rock grind of taking a vacation from their day jobs to drive twelve hours in a van every day and sleep on the floor every night. Although they'd started Plasticland as a studio project, it had developed into a strong live act, but the show was an elaborate affair that required hauling lights, go-go dancers, and Rehse's Mellotron. "Enigma said they wanted a band that was going to be touring at least one hundred fifty nights a year, so they opted not to do a last record with us," Frankovic said. When Rehse talks about the period, a bitter diatribe inevitably follows.

Plasticland basically disbanded, though the group came back together for odd reunion shows and one-off recording projects such as a live album backing former Pretty Things–Syd Barrett–Tomorrow drummer Twink. After a tour with Twink fell apart, Rehse and Frankovic were approached by a German label interested in a new recording. Spirits were high as Plasticland started *Dapper Snappings*, but recording dragged on over a two-year period as Repulsion tried to scrape up the money to finish the project. Although it boasts a handful of strong tunes (including "Let's Play Pollyanna" and "When You Get Subliminal, You Really Get Sublime"), the album doesn't sustain a mood like the earlier efforts. By the time it was released in 1994, the group had split up again.

Though they've since pursued a number of solo projects—including the Fabulon Triptometer, the Gothics, and a Frankovic solo album—anyone who knows Rehse and Frankovic says that sooner or later, they'll play together again. "I don't want Plasticland to be a rerun of what we did in the '80s. I have a lot of new ideas," Rehse said, contemplating renewed interest prompted by the 1995 rarities collection *Mink Dress and Other Cats*. "I don't want to have to stop the creative process and become an old fart." Added Frankovic: "Plasticland is a vital part of my life, and it will always be a part of my life. Plasticland lives on, whether the band is playing or not."

Bad Trips and One-Hit Wonders

Okay. You've swallowed the magic cube, downed a cup of "organic" tea with filigree leaves, and placed the diamond needle on the appropriate sounds. Now sit back and wait 20 minutes, until twinges of nausea herald the coming of the hereafter. Meanwhile, ponder this: A discotheque called The World advertises "psychedelic beauty contests." Admen chortle: "Don't blow your cool—blow your mind." . . . Psychedelic shoes. Acid TV commercials. LSD greeting cards. Marijuana brownies. Mandala shopping bags. Tibetan cocktails on the rocks. "Psychedelicize suburbia." Mind-expanding peacock feathers. Buddha himself, gold and grinning, comes embossed on a 100 percent washable cotton sweatshirt in assorted sizes, colors, and cools.

—Richard Goldstein, 1967[1]

As the introduction to a *Village Voice* feature on Timothy Leary's heavily hyped "religion," the League for Spiritual Discovery, Goldstein's giddy laundry list is evidence that psychedelia was well established as a pop-culture phenomenon ripe for free-market exploitation at the same time that psychedelic rock was coming into its own. Many musicians, like other merchants of popular culture, adopted superficial psychedelic trappings; by 1967, bands in search of an instant identity needed only to turn to the plethora of studio production tricks, light shows, and fashions that psychedelia ushered in. Notable examples include the Blues Magoos' "(We Ain't Got) Nothin' Yet" (from their 1967 album, *Psychedelic Lollipop*), the Lemon Pipers' "Green Tambourine" (1967), Richard Harris's original version of "MacArthur Park" (1968), Kenny Rogers and the First Edition's "Just Dropped in (to See What Condition My Condition Was in)" (1968), Tommy James's "Crimson and Clover" (1968), and Zager and Evans' "In the Year 2525 (Exordium & Terminus)" (1969).

This book has generally dealt with less substantial psychedelic rockers by omission, but several camps of bad-trip rockers deserve a closer look, as do some psychedelic rock songs by musicians who weren't really part of the genre.

Jim Morrison is said to have eaten acid like candy during his days at UCLA Graduate School of Film. He formed the Doors

The Lizard King and the flamenco guitarist.

in early 1965 while sitting on the beach and reciting poetry to keyboardist Ray Manzarek. ("Let's swim to the moon / Let's climb through the tide / Penetrate the evening / That the city sleeps to hide.") The group's name came from Aldous Huxley's *The Doors of Perception*, and the singer originally viewed the group as a vehicle to literary immortality à la Rimbaud and Baudelaire. But despite the cult that grew after his death, Morrison's sophomoric lyrics are not in that league. Musically, the jazzy drumming, cocktail-lounge keyboards, and flamenco guitar only rock on rare occasions such as "Break On Through" or "L.A. Woman." "The End," the tune usually held up as the band's psychedelic masterpiece, is in fact a plodding Oedipal melodrama. "It was the first major statement of the Doors' perennial themes: dread, violence, guilt without possibility of redemption, the miscarriages of love, and, most of all, death," Lester Bangs wrote. "Nevertheless, the last time I heard 'The End,' it sounded funny."[2]

Similarly, the indulgent instrumental showcases of Cream, rock's first supergroup, sound like parodies today. "Epic solos were the order of the day, often extended far beyond the bounds of discipline or taste," Dave Marsh wrote. "While the group spawned a seemingly infinite flock of imitators—boogie bands, power trios, heavy-metal groups—it is only as an influence that most of Cream's music, so widely hailed at the time, will last."[3] Ironically, the band's most enduring music is on the truncated psychedelic singles that were considered concessions to commercialism at the time: "Badge," "Sunshine of Your Love," and "White Room."

The shortcomings of some of the progressive rockers of the '70s and the psychedelic revivalists of the '80s have already been examined. Emerging at roughly the same time as Liverpool's postpunk psychedelic rockers, bands in a genre best dubbed "mope rock" embraced some of psychedelia's more obvious stage tricks—enveloping fog, spooky lighting, and a swirling mix—but were generally too self-obsessed to take their listeners anywhere interesting. The Cure, Depeche Mode, and to some extent the Smiths (who went back to guitars instead of synthesizers) are like the guy who takes psychedelic drugs and talks nonstop through the night, trying to convince everyone that they should listen to the Great Truths he's discovered. A '90s alternative-rock update on this theme is offered in the lush, well crafted but annoyingly egocentric soundscapes of Billy Corgan and the Smashing Pumpkins.

Throbbing Gristle/Psychic TV, Ministry and its many offshoots, Nine Inch Nails, and other industrial artists offer elaborate sonic visions that dwell on the dark side, and they often have psychedelic overtones. Genesis P-Orridge and Al Jourgensen have been vocal about their fondness for psychedelic drugs, while Trent Reznor enjoys playing with the acid imagery surrounding the Manson family. But the music is too often cold, mechanical, and unappealingly repetitive, and the poses appear silly in the sunshine. (Dishonorable mention must be made, however, of Coil's coyly titled 1991 album *Love's Secret Domain*—LSD—a merger of industrial and acid house that is one of the most unsettling psychedelic albums ever made.) Jane's Addiction leader and Lollapalooza founder Perry Farrell also talked a lot about psychedelic experiences without his music particularly reflecting the results, at least until he formed his second band, Porno for Pyros, which effectively captures the decadent spirit of a bacchanal with every imaginable variety of drug and sexual fetish thrown into the mix.

Another band with a Manson fixation—as well as myriad other pop-culture obsessions—is New York's long-running noise quartet Sonic Youth. Surfacing in the indie-rock '80s alongside more justifiably influential peers such as Hüsker Dü, the Minutemen, and Big Black, the group merged the high-art pretensions of noise composers such as Glenn Branca and Rhys Chatham with the heavy attitude of hardcore punk bands. Unfortunately, too often they replaced the conviction with cheap sarcasm and campy in-jokes. While it may have been a revelation to young fans such as Nirvana's Kurt Cobain that guitars could be played in different tunings or attacked with drumsticks and screwdrivers, the free-jazz, white-noise experimentation that Sonic Youth attempted was accomplished with more consistently powerful and psychedelic results by the Velvet Underground, the MC5, Can, Spacemen 3, and others.

The transparency of psychedelic poseurs and retro rockers such as Lenny Kravitz and the Black Crowes is so obvious that it's hardly worth pointing out. More curious is the tribe of jam-happy "baby Dead" bands that sprouted in the early '90s, delivering varying degrees of psychedelic nostalgia and LSD imagery. Their styles are similar: blues rock mixed with progressive rock (Phish), blues rock mixed with country rock (the Freddy Jones Band, the Aquarium Rescue Unit), blues rock mixed with pop (Spin Doctors), blues rock mixed with Hawkwind (England's Ozric Tentacles), and just plain old blues rock (Big Head Todd and the Monsters, Blues Traveler). But contrary to what many of these bands's fans

They kept on truckin' . . . and truckin' . . . and truckin' . . .

seem to think, drinking Bud Lite and doing the awkward white person wiggle is not a psychedelic experience.

The Dead itself kept on truckin' until the most efficient and persistent touring corporation in the concert industry was finally stopped by mortality. The mainstream media covered the group's twice-yearly visits with silly features full of tongue-in-cheek '60s drug references, playing into the hands of the stockbroker who traded his tie for a night in a tie-dyed T-shirt. Members of the real Deadhead subculture were impressive in their ability to discern every nuance of the band's rambling mixes of country, blues, folk, and space excursions, but the truth is that the music was secondary to the larger arena crowd. "The phenomenon can partly be understood as a low-risk, low-investment community, almost making community into a commodity," said political philosopher Michael Weinstein. "People could purchase a ticket and be part of a group they felt safe with, that they could express themselves with, and in which they could re-create selective slices of the '60s, like the drugs and the music." "The band is a time capsule from a Camelot-like era of the 1960s," former keyboardist Tom Constanten said after Garcia's death. "It's that magic that people were attracted to."[4] Of course, Camelot never really existed, and the Dead's idealized psychedelic community was sort of like Sixties World at Disneyland.

This isn't to say that the Dead experience wasn't fun; it was. And it's not to say that groups that are simply *acting* like psychedelic rock bands can't make great psychedelic rock; they can and did, as the *Nuggets* bands proved. Many others donned psychedelic trappings for a song or two before returning to their primary styles or moving off in other directions, and the fact that psychedelic rock can be appropriated this way is one of the factors that establishes it as a genre.

One-Hit Wonders

One way to hone in on the genre's distinctive elements is to look at what was borrowed by bands that weren't psychedelic rock but which waded into the genre pool. What follows is a baker's dozen of my favorite "one-hit wonders."

1. The Monkees, "Porpoise Song," *Head* (1968)
Recruited in 1965 as actors to play rockers on TV, the Prefab Four metamorphosed into an actual band by early 1967, though most of their best

songs were still written by pros. The Monkees were drawn to L.A.'s psychedelic subculture, and they were endorsed by
Hollywood hipsters who recognized the
potential for some gentle subversion of
America's youth. A druggy mindset was
firmly in place when they met with Bob
Rafelson the producer and director of their
TV show, and actor Jack Nicholson, who
somehow landed the gig of writing the
Monkees' first feature film, aptly named

The Monkees lose their heads. (Photo by Henry Diltz.)

Head. "We sat around for days smoking, drinking, and generally having
stream-of-consciousness sessions," drummer Mickey Dolenz wrote. "Jack
and Bob took the tapes of the sessions and turned them into one of the
strangest films of all time. . . . Basically, it was the story of the Monkees:
our birth, life, and death, as metaphors for all of Hollywood and its tinsel-
and-fabric manipulations of people, images, and ideas."[5] *Head* opens with
a spectacular vignette featuring the Monkees jumping from a bridge to
frolic with the mermaids in the water below. Taking her cue from *Sgt.
Pepper's*, songwriter Carole King penned the beautiful, undulating "Por-
poise Song" to accompany the scene. A gentle, vaguely Eastern melody is
paired with a full Western orchestra as the Monkees ponder their place
in the universe ("A face, a voice / an overdub has no choice / and it cannot
rejoice"). They also talk to dolphins years before New Age scientist John
Lilly used ketamine, an animal tranquilizer with psychedelic side effects,
to do the same in experiments depicted in *Day of the Dolphin*.

2. The Who, "Armenia City in the Sky," *The Who Sell Out* (1968)

Though some critics charged that the rock opera *Tommy* was psychedelic
excess at its worst, Pete Townshend always went out of his way to distance himself from psychedelic drugs. "I only used acid a few times and
I found it incredibly disturbing," he said. "I have certain psychotic tendencies and found it extremely dangerous for me."[6] Nevertheless, Townshend appreciated the English psychedelic-rock bands, especially the
Creation, whose guitarist he tried to recruit. Elements of psychedelia
creeped into several Who songs (including "I Can See for Miles," which
has the same on-the-verge-of-takeoff rumble as "Eight Miles High"),
but the band's most memorable excursion is the incongruous opening
track from *The Who Sell Out*, the band's paean to rock radio and the pre-

The Psychedelic Influence in Popular Culture

Kathy Acker
A Clockwork Orange
Charles Addams
Altered States
Michelangelo Antonioni
appliquéd tights
Dario Argento
Ralph Bakshi
The Banana Splits
Clive Barker
Batman
Barbarella
Jean-Michel Basquiat
beanbag chairs
Beyond the Valley of the Dolls
birds of paradise
black lights
body paint
Paul Bowles
Roger Brown
Lenny Bruce
bubbles
William S. Burroughs
butterflies
butterfly chairs
candy corn
Carlos Castaneda
channel surfing
chaos theory
Cheech and Chong
Christo and Jeanne-Claude
Arthur C. Clarke
comets
Roger Corman's Edgar Allen
Poe movies
Jacques Cousteau
David Cronenberg
Aleister Crowley
R. Crumb
crystals
curry
daisies
Salvador Dalí
Day-Glo
Philip K. Dick
digital imaging
the Discovery Channel
Doctor Who

hippie lifestyle. The swooping guitars on "Armenia City in the Sky" recall Eddie Phillips's bowed style, Keith Moon's drumming is remarkably restrained and tribal, and Roger Daltrey warbles about his fantasy metropolis with the same endearingly silly sincerity that Donovan brought to "Atlantis."

3. The Kinks, "Wicked Annabella," *(The Kinks Are) The Village Green Preservation Society* (1969)

"When everybody else thought that the hip thing to do was to drop acid, do as many drugs as possible, and listen to music in a coma, the Kinks were singing songs about lost friends, draught beer, motorbike riders, wicked witches, and flying cats," Ray Davies wrote in his "unauthorized autobiography."[7] But like the Who, the band couldn't resist trying out the psychedelic sounds of 1967 at least once. The tale of the wicked witch Annabella unfolds over distorted vocals, disjointed drums, and a snaky guitar line. The effect is like a cartoonish nightmare intruding on a tranquil afternoon daydream. (Honorable mention in this vein goes to the Troggs, who shared a producer-svengali with the Kinks in Larry Page. In an effort to broaden the band's sound beyond the three-chord leer of "Wild Thing," Page crafted "Cousin Jane," a seductive, orchestrated but still leering ballad. Incest never sounded so appealing.)

4. Black Sabbath, "Sweet Leaf," *Master of Reality* (1971)

The best of the English bands that combined blues rock and psychedelic atmosphere to create heavy metal, Black Sabbath created its own comic-book and horror-film realities with the most basic ingredients. Druggy, evocative tunes such as "Tomorrow's Dream," "Am I Going Insane," and "Snowblind" are almost punk in their simple, in-your-face construction and the raw way in which they were recorded. Sabbath earns its place on this list with a touching and heartfelt homage to *cannabis sativa.* Following an absurdly echoed cough and a monolithic guitar riff, Ozzy Osbourne sings: "When I first met you didn't realize / I can't forget you or your surprise / You introduced me to my mind / And left me wanting you and your kind / I love you / Oh you know it." Ah, sweet romance. (Honorable mention for another psychedelic metal anthem: Blue Öyster Cult's Byrds-style "Don't Fear the Reaper.")

5. Led Zeppelin, "Kashmir," *Physical Graffiti* (1975)

Though it wasn't always obvious, the most influential hard-rock band of the '70s derived its approach in part from what the players learned in the psychedelic '60s. As a member of the Yardbirds, Jimmy Page perfected the echo, slide, and Eastern tunings that gave extended guitar jams such as the one in "Dazed and Confused" their otherworldly feel. Page learned the essentials of studio craftsmanship as a session player, and John Paul Jones arranged the impressive psychedelic backings for Donovan's singles and the Rolling Stones' *Their Satanic Majesties Request*. Robert Plant clearly listened to more than a little Incredible String Band. These influences yielded to the bastardized blues of the first two albums and the hippie folk of the third, but they came back strong on the untitled fourth effort (in "The Battle of Evermore" and the psychedelic blues "When the Levee Breaks"), *Houses of the Holy* ("No Quarter"), and "Kashmir," the hashish-scented travelogue that is the centerpiece of *Physical Graffiti*. "I can't say that drugs didn't play a part in those early days, but the eclecticism played a larger part," Jones said. "A lot of the psychedelic thing came from that very early world-music movement; it was just interest in other people's music. . . . I used to take drugs and listen to music and it would actually give dimensions to music that simply didn't have that many dimensions. The best psychedelic music achieves the same effect without drugs."

6. Neil Young, "Cortez the Killer," *Zuma* (1975)

"Everybody gets fucked up sooner or later," Neil Young told rock journalist Cameron Crowe in 1975. "You're just pretending if you don't let your music get just as liquid as you are when you're really high."[8] *Zuma* was the follow-up to the cathartic *Tonight's the Night*, which was inspired by the heroin-induced deaths of Crazy Horse guitarist Danny Whitten and roadie Bruce Berry. Young may have preferred tequila to psychedelics at the time, but the standout track lumbers forward in a peyote daze. The extended guitar workout on "Cortez the Killer" fits the mold of the earlier "Down by the River," but it conjures an even stranger and more sinister place. In addition to revising history and enticing the listener into a hot, humid, and erotic dreamscape, the song posed a metaphorical question for members of the Baby Boom as they moved from the idealistic '60s into the materialistic '80s: Were they going to rape and pillage like Cortez or fight to preserve a doomed lifestyle like Montezuma?

7. Donna Summer, "I Feel Love," *I Remember Yesterday* (1977)

Developed in the gay dance clubs of Manhattan and Fire Island, disco started creeping into the pop mainstream as early as 1974, but it was Donna

The Psychedelic Influence in Popular Culture

Easy Rider
Eraserhead
M. C. Escher
Etch-A-Sketch
Fantasia
Fantastic Voyage
Federico Fellini
fireflies
flying
Forbidden Planet
fractals
Freaks
Fruitopia commercials
geysers
William Gibson
H. R. Giger
Terry Gilliam
Allen Ginsberg
glaciers
gliders
go-go boots
The Golem
Red Grooms
gypsy blouses
gyroscopes
Gumby
Gurdjieff
Keith Haring
Hermann Hesse
Robert Heinlein
hula hoops
the Internet
Jägermeister
Japanese comics
Jell-O
jellyfish
The Jetsons
Betsey Johnson
Chuck Jones
kaleidoscopes
the *Kama Sutra*
kites
Ernie Kovacs
Stanley Kubrick
Akira Kurosawa
ladybugs
Laugh-In
lava lamps
Anton LaVey

Donna Summer: She feels love.

The Psychedelic Influence in Popular Culture

lobsters
Logan's Run
Lost in Space
H. P. Lovecraft
Malcolm Lowry
Lucite
the luge

Magic Eye pictures
René Magritte
Major Matt Mason
Man Ray
Peter Max
Terence McKenna
mescal
Russell Mills
miniskirts
Mister Rogers
mobiles
Mondo 2000
Monty Python's Flying Circus
mood rings
morphing
NASA
Mr. Natural
the northern lights
Claes Oldenburg
opals
Ouija boards
The Outer Limits
Pac-Man
paisleys
peacocks
Pee Wee's Playhouse

Summer's 1975 hit "Love to Love You Baby" that really put it on the map. Born and raised in Boston, Summer made her way to Munich via a touring production of the hippie musical *Hair*. There she linked up with producers and songwriters Giorgio Moroder and Pete Bellotte. The team crafted a bubbly, lighthearted electronic backing track as a demo, and Summer improvised the minimal lyrics and orgasmic moans while lying in the dark on the studio floor (the same way that John Lennon recorded "Tomorrow Never Knows"). The song was a strange but wonderful novelty, the sound of a woman making love to a machine, but Summer's next hit was even better. "I Feel Love" almost beats Kraftwerk at its own game with a phased production that gets trippier the louder it's played and vocals that seem to come from another dimension. It's impossible to imagine the acid house and techno of the '90s without this song. (Honorable mention in a similar vein goes to Madonna's "Justify My Love," especially the *Book of Revelations* remix with Middle Eastern instrumentation and ominous biblical quotes.)

Man love fire? Boy George of Culture Club.

8. Culture Club, "Karma Chameleon," *Colour by Numbers* (1983)

Much maligned by critics in its day and an admittedly lightweight successor to the punk and new wave sounds that preceded it, Culture Club was not without its charms, including the soulful singing and confrontational cross-dressing of frontman Boy George. Its finest moment was its stab at a merger of psychedelic folk and glossy '80s dance pop, an irresistible confection with a sly Moebius strip of a melody and lyrics that are, in great psychedelic fashion, part timeless wisdom and part stoner babble.

9. Prince, "Pop Life," *Around the World In A Day* (1985)

After perfecting his own pop-rock-funk synthesis and following in the tradition of Jimi Hendrix on *1999* and the massively successful *Purple*

Rain, Prince was rumored to be making his version of *Sgt. Pepper's.* It turned out that he was more interested in Lennon and McCartney–level power and celebrity than Beatles-styled sounds. Neither his addled mysticism nor the clichéd orchestrations succeed throughout, but there are two standout tracks on *Around the World in a Day.* In "Raspberry Beret," Prince picks up a girl in '60s thrift store clothing (Bangle Susanna Hoffs?), puts her on the back of his bike, and has his way with her in a barn over a mechanized beat and a sawing string section. Less of a nov-

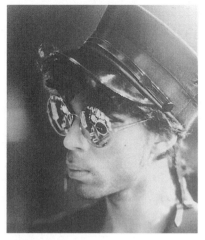

Looking at the world through Prince-colored glasses.

elty, "Pop Life" is stronger musically, more inventive with its shifting production and musical breakdown, and reminiscent of vintage Sly Stone in its lyrics. Aching to be a role model, Prince preaches against cocaine and advises, "U can't get over if u say u just don't care / Show me a boy who stays in school / And I'll show you a boy aware!"

10. R.E.M., "Feeling Gravity's Pull," *Reconstruction of the Fables* (1985)
Peter Buck, the group's resident historian, has long maintained that the favorite sons of Athens, Georgia, were and are a folk-rock band. (He certainly dropped the Byrds' name enough in the early days.) Limiting R.E.M.'s place in this book to a spot on this list may be slighting its contribution: Mitch Easter's layered productions on *Chronic Town* and *Murmur* are certainly inspired by albums like *Revolver;* the discs create a waking dream-state vibe, and Michael Stipe's vocals contribute to feelings of mystery and distance. But thumbing through the group's later output, the psychedelic influences are limited to covers (numerous Velvet Underground B sides, Wire's "Strange," and "Superman" by '60s rockers the Clique), odd instrumentals, and inspired touches such as the echoed guitar that introduces the lead track on *Reconstruction of the Fables.* Produced by Joe Boyd, *Reconstruction* was later dismissed by the band as a failure, but opinion has shifted in recent years, and it stands as the last album shrouded in mystery before the band's subsequent move to more straightforward pop.

The Psychedelic Influence in Popular Culture
Jackson Pollock
Pogo
Pop Rocks
the PowerGlove
prisms
The Prisoner
Emilio Pucci
H. R. Puffinstuff
Thomas Pynchon
pyramids
Mary Quant
The Red Balloon
Ren and Stimpy
Tom Robbins
Ken Russell
scuba diving
sensory deprivation tanks
Maurice Sendak
Dr. Seuss
Sam Shepard
The Simpsons
sky diving
smiley faces
Terry Southern
spin art
Spirograf
the St. Louis arch
Star Trek
static generators
strobe lights
sunflowers
surfing
Tank Girl
tequila
Tetris
Hunter S. Thompson
tiger balm
J. R. R. Tolkein
tops
Amos Tutuola
The Twilight Zone
Twister
2001: A Space Odyessy
Ulysses
Un Chien Andalou

The Psychedelic Influence in Popular Culture

Jules Verne
virtual reality
volcanoes
Volkswagens
Kurt Vonnegut
wave machines
William Wegman
H. G. Wells
whale songs
Weel-O's
Robert Williams
Willy Wonka and the Chocolate Factory
Robert Anton Wilson
Winky Dink
Winnie the Pooh
Joel-Peter Witkin
The Wizard of Oz
Ed Wood
The X-Files
the X-Men
yo-yos
zebras

11. Tom Petty, "Don't Come Around Here No More," *Southern Accents* (1985)

A devoted Byrds fan, Petty borrowed the group's chiming, reverbed Rickenbackers many times early in his career, but he first explored the psychedelic implications of "Eight Miles High" on this single. Not that "Don't Come Around Here No More" is that graceful; one of Petty's talents is revisiting uglier or more complex sounds (say, *Exile on Main Street* or "Eight Miles High") and making them palatable for mainstream consumption. He does this with enough wit and melody that only the grumpiest purists can complain. In this case, lest anyone miss the echoed drums, droning sitar, Beatles-inspired cellos, and acid-freaked vocals, he paired the song with a sly and somewhat misogynistic video inspired by *Alice's Adventures in Wonderland.* (In fact, the clip is one of the first examples of a video being more psychedelic than the song it promotes, which would become increasingly common as MTV endeavored to provide an imagination for music fans who didn't have one of their own.) Petty went on to mine similar turf on "Free Fallin'" and "Mary Jane's Last Dance," while the 1994 B side "Girl on LSD" was a hokey, folkie drug spoof ("I was in love with a girl on LSD / She'd see things I'd never see / She broadened her perspective / Then I got more selective").

12. Cracker, "Low," *Kerosene Hat* (1993)

Before its bitter split in 1989, San Francisco's Camper Van Beethoven nodded at psychedelic rock several times, including on the enigmatic "Eye of Fatima" and relatively respectful covers of Pink Floyd's "Interstellar Overdrive" and Status Quo's "Pictures of Matchstick Men." But it was just one of many strains that the band explored while indulging a stubborn and annoying devotion to eclecticism; the group spent so much time being clever and showing its mastery of different genres that it rarely had time to write good songs. David Lowery took a different route in his solo career, focusing on tight country-tinged alternative rock, but the old fondness for space rock surfaced on the lead track of Cracker's second album. With a droning melody and languid rhythm that match the lyrical images of poppy fields and floating spacemen, "Low" creatively nods to Roxy Music's "Love Is the Drug" ("Being with you girl is like being stoned") and David Bowie's "Space Oddity" ("Don't you wanna go down like some junkie cosmonaut?"). It is Lowery's finest moment.

13. Soundgarden, "Black Hole Sun," *Superunknown* (1994)

Since grunge mixed punk and early Black Sabbath metal, and Sabbath mixed blues rock and psychedelia, it's surprising how long it took for a good psychedelic grunge tune to surface, but "Black Hole Sun" was worth the wait. It comes complete with a grinding riff, eerie, echoed guitar fills, processed vocals, and meaningless but fun brink-of-apocalypse lyrics ("Black hole sun won't you come and wash away the rain"). As in the case of "Don't Come Around Here No More," an effective video spells out everything for fans who might otherwise have missed the point—i.e., things aren't always what they seem.

CHAPTER 14

Reality Used to Be a Friend of Mine: Psychedelic Hip-Hop

Mirror, mirror on the wall / Tell me, mirror, what is wrong / Can it be my de la clothes / Or is it just my de la soul?

—De La Soul, "Me Myself and I"

Samplers emerged in the late 1970s as a logical progression of synthesizer and computer technology. Manufactured in Australia, the Fairlight Computer Musical Instrument allowed users to feed in a sound, digitally manipulate it, and replay it in a different context. It was joined in the '80s by the American-made Emu Emulator and a procession of increasingly less expensive and more user-friendly instruments. Some enthusiasts say that sampling brings *musique concrète* to the streets, making it possible to make music out of any sound, but that implies that the technology itself is magical, and that's the case only when it's used by imaginative technicians. Early Fairlight devotees such as Peter Gabriel and Mike Oldfield merely treated the machines like fancier synthesizers. "When the sampler first appeared, few people imagined it would have much effect—another new toy, a nine-days' wonder which would soon be put aside, a Mellotron for the digital age," sampling scholar Jeremy Beadle wrote. "Except that somewhere in the mid-1980s, the sampler's potential collided with the cutting and scratching techniques popular in the music of New York's hip-hop scene, and a whole range of pop musicians were inspired to create a different kind of music, a music which raided pop's past and put it in a new and modern—and sometimes quite unnerving—context."[1]

Rap began at street parties in the Bronx in the mid-'70s when DJs (many of them Jamaican immigrants) set up their turntables, mixed together the hottest sections of several records, and led the crowds in simple chants and call-and-response rhymes. The Sugar Hill Gang's 1979 novelty "Rapper's Delight" is generally considered the first rap record, but artists such as Kurtis Blow, Grandmaster Flash, and Afrika Bambaataa followed with music that signaled the birth of not only a genre, but a subculture. Hip-hop grew in popularity through the '80s as artists focused on harsh tales of life on the streets. Public Enemy constructed dense, sampled white-noise collages that abraded like the wildest free jazz or noise rock. Their political lyrics paved the way for a wave of gangsta rap, but the next big musical innovation came in 1989 when rappers began to sample mellower grooves in the first flowering of psychedelic hip-hop.

Robert Christgau called De La Soul "new wave" to Public Enemy's "punk rock." Like Chuck D., the three rappers were smart, middle-class African Americans who hailed from suburban Long Island. Posdnuos (Kelvin Mercer) and Trugoy the Dove (David Jolicouer) had been in a more conventional rap group called Easy Street before they linked up with Maseo (Vincent Mason) and producer Prince Paul, a veteran of Stetsasonic. Where Public Enemy urged its listeners to fight the power, De La Soul heralded the start of the Daisy Age, which, in the grand tradition of psychedelic acronyms, stood for "da inner self, y'all." "Many of the B-boys would say that our beats weren't hardcore enough," Maseo said. "But we're more about a vibe than coming up with hardcore beats. . . . Where we live is very open and mellow. Sure, there are rough neighborhoods. But people don't live one on top of the other. There's room to think about what's going on." Added Trugoy: "If our music reminds you of a hippie, bohemian vibe, that's okay. We want the music to speak for itself."[2]

Aside from a few scattered marijuana references, De La Soul wasn't vocal about its drug habits on its debut album. The samples on *3 Feet High and Rising* came from the Jarmels, Steely Dan, Prince, and a French language instruction record, and the lyrics were full of good-natured in-jokes and skits inspired by lazy afternoons spent goofing on bad TV. They combined to make a whole that was joyfully disorienting. "De La Soul create a kind of dance psychedelia, disrupting consciousness by rupturing stylistic integrity," critic Simon Reynolds wrote. "Splicing together grooves, beats and chants, licks and stray murmurings from unconnected pop periods, they create a friction, a rub that's both sensual and uncanny. Different auras, different vibes, different studio atmospheres, and different eras are placed in ghostly adjacence, like some strange composite organism sewn together out of a variety of vivisected limbs, or a Cronenberg dance monster."[3]

De La Soul never duplicated the crazy-quilt creativity of its debut. Stung by criticism from hardcore rappers, the members declared that the Daisy Age concept, clothing, and artwork had been forced on them by their label, Tommy Boy Records. *De La Soul Is Dead*, their sophomore effort proclaimed. Over harder beats and more traditional hip-hop samples, the group turned to the sort of gangsta tales it had previously avoided, including "Millie Pulled a Pistol on Santa." In an effort to thwart bootleggers, Tommy Boy issued advance cassettes of the album to reviewers with a sample of a braying donkey occasionally interrupting the music, and it's telling that many fans preferred this version to the final release. The trio was more ambitious on its jazzy 1993 effort, *Buhlōōne Mindstate*, but by then, its place as psychedelic-rap innovators had been forfeited.

Evolving from earlier incarnations as a New York hardcore punk band and snotty white rappers fighting for the right to party, the Beastie Boys moved west and chilled with the talented L.A. production team the Dust Brothers. A mellower and more sophisticated group emerged on 1989's sprawling double album *Paul's Boutique*. Curtis Mayfield's psychedelic soul rubbed elbows with the intro to Pink Floyd's "Time" and a thousand other sound bites that contributed to a funky, surreal collage. Musically and thematically, the album is a channel-flipping blur of junk-culture trivia.

The Beastie Boys get weird.

"If Raymond Carver wrote Kmart fiction, then the Beastie Boys create Salvation Army hip-hop," critics Havelock Nelson and Michael Gonzales wrote.[4] But the thrill of discovery in the Beasties' bargain bins was never as strong again.

By 1990, hip-hop was wide open for experimentation and cross-fertilization. Groups emerged with their own novel twists, caused a splash with a strong debut, then quickly lost inspiration or packed it in. Members of De La Soul's Native Tongues posse, the Jungle Brothers merged hip-hop and acid house on "I'll House You," and A Tribe Called Quest used well-chosen jazz and Lou Reed samples and scored a goofy hit with "I Left My Wallet in El Segundo." (The latter was one of the first acts to foreshadow a wave of "acid jazz," a merger of hip-hop and jazz that's generally devoid of the psychedelic influence that the name might imply.) Digital Underground one-upped other rappers' use of Funkadelic samples by also updating the vintage P-Funk stage show, complete with sex, science-fiction imagery, and druggy in-jokes. Arrested Development took its inspiration from upbeat Sly and the Family Stone; Digable Planets brought a new fluidity to its own merger of jazz and hip-hop; a self-styled psychedelic prophet from Brooklyn called the Divine Styler released a wonderfully weird but largely ignored stream-of-consciousness effort called *Spiral Walls Containing Autumns of Light*, and Cypress Hill pursued an obsessive devotion to droning melodies and *cannabis sativa*. But it fell to two brothers from Jersey City to make the next great psychedelic hip-hop albums and give the subgenre some staying power.

Set Adrift on Memory Bliss

Reality used to be a friend of mine / 'Cause complete control I don't take too kind.

> —PM Dawn, "Reality Used to Be a Friend of Mine"

Located just across the Hudson River from Manhattan and ten minutes away by PATH train, Jersey City is a schizophrenic town with all of the problems of its larger neighbor and none of its culture or charm. Run-down ghettoes abut tree-lined neighborhoods of aluminum-sided homes and gentrified historic districts of renovated brownstones. Political corruption, street crime, racism, and drugs are chronic problems, but more soul-shattering is a subtle but pervasive sense of despair and a chronic lack of vision. Growing up as an introverted, overweight misfit, Attrel Cordes Jr. decided that he could see a better way. Rechristening himself Prince Be and forming PM Dawn with his brother, Jarrett (a.k.a. DJ Minutemix), he announced that reality was an illusion and that anything could be changed if only one thought hard enough and had enough faith. In doing so, he joined a line of African-American musicians that included Jimi Hendrix and George Clinton, psychedelic rock visionaries who preached not escapism, but optimism and the power of positive thinking.

Infants when their father died of pneumonia in 1967, the Cordes brothers grew up surrounded by music and spirituality. Their mother sang in the church choir and taught them about Catholicism and Edgar Cayce, a Virginia Beach psychic and prophet who preached about karma, reincarnation, and the lost continent of Atlantis. At sixteen, Prince Be was kicked out of Jersey City's high school for the gifted and talented after he cursed at his gym teacher—"I thought I was a B-boy, and I wasn't," he said[5]—but he soon focused his adolescent energies on music. In addition to MTV stalwarts such as Prince and Culture Club, he was introduced to older sounds like the Beatles and Stevie Wonder by his stepfather, a sometimes conga player with Kool and the Gang. Prince Be toyed with guitar, and DJ Minutemix tried drums and piano, but they both gave up early on. It was in the sampler that they found their true calling.

Working as a security guard at a homeless shelter for the mentally ill, Prince Be saved up six hundred dollars and recorded a demo that attracted the attention of England's Gee Street Records, the label that launched the Jungle Brothers. PM Dawn was flown to London to record its debut, *Of the Heart, of the Soul and of the Cross: The Utopian Experience.* Prince Be alternated velvety smooth rapping and high, clear, soulful singing over hook-filled soundscapes that were lush, inviting, and extremely sophisticated. The brothers preferred the terms "sampling artists" or "songwriters" to rappers. The diverse ingredients in their musical collages included Chick Corea, the Doobie Brothers, Sly Stone, Hugh Masekela, and Spandau Ballet. Prince Be was crushed when he couldn't sample his heroes the Beatles, but he had musicians duplicate a snatch of "Baby You're a Rich Man" for "The Beautiful." (Permission is required to sample a song, but not to cover it.)

Although they're aware of the inspiration behind their favorite Beatles tracks, the Cordes brothers say they've never taken psychedelic drugs, and they aren't interested in trying. "To me, psychedelia is finding something tangible that you can hold on to in the unusual, and that's what any innovator does," Prince Be said. "That happened with the Beatles; they were trying to find something new because they were tired of just the guitars and drums. They started using sitars and xylophones and all kinds of stuff. It's just finding innovative ways of making music—to make it different—to make it sound more and more fresh at any point in time." "Whatever we do is just part of us," his brother added. "Prince Be, when he writes, is always asking questions about things. It's like physical therapy for the soul."

PM Dawn doesn't believe in utopia, but it does believe in the "utopian experience," in particular the idea that "heaven is within us all." Prince Be preaches transcending the outside world by accepting that reality is an illusion and that different realities can be created in the mind. ("When you open up your eyes / What's in front of you / Is what's supposed to be there / Really?") His faith in his own hodgepodge of religious ideas is strong, but he isn't seeking converts. When he addresses his "father," it's never clear whether he's writing to Attrel Sr. or penning what Brian Wilson called "teenage symphonies to God." In either case, people who aren't interested in his personal philosophy can read the poetic lyrics as simple love songs. Prince Be balances even his weightiest raps with simple, infectious melodies and a playful sense of humor. He's clearly having fun with his image as a dreadlocks-wearing, four-hundred-pound guru in psychedelic pajamas. When he and his brother posed for the album cover on an Antarctic iceberg, the image is as incongruous as Parliament-Funkadelic's brothers in outer space and it's just as striking.

The Utopian Experience was an impressive hit in the United States and England, where it won support in the mainstream as well as the underground rave culture, but like De La Soul, PM Dawn was criticized by hardcore rappers as a sellout. Even worse, Prince Be was called an Uncle Tom because of his talk of a "quest to become colorless," and he was subjected to homophobic slurs because of his effeminate mannerisms and high-pitched vocals. The Cordes brothers aren't wimps, and they came back swinging on *The Bliss Album . . . ? (Vibrations of Love and Anger and the Ponderance of Life and Existence)*. "Plastic" revived a '60s put-down to dis gangsta rappers who are "hard at first but melt in the heat," and Prince Be rightfully claimed that he was doing more to move hip-hop forward than his dogmatic peers. "If water can't go any-

PM Dawn: DJ Minutemix and Prince Be, psychedelic brothers from Jersey City.

place and it doesn't move, it goes stagnant, and I couldn't see that happening to myself or to hip-hop," he told me. But unlike De La Soul, PM Dawn didn't allow its anger to distract from its strengths, and the album offers two more beautiful, ethereal ballads, "I'd Die Without You" and "Looking Through Patient Eyes." There's also another tribute to the Beatles, a cover of "Norwegian Wood" that transforms John Lennon's wry tale of infidelity into something much stranger, with noises recalling the backward bird cries of "Tomorrow Never Knows."

PM Dawn flirted with touring after the second album's release, performing with a powerful thirteen-piece band as part of Peter Gabriel's first American WOMAD tour. But the ambitious stage show wound up costing the band half a million dollars, and Prince Be said he wasn't really comfortable outside the studio, anyway. PM Dawn retreated for two and a half years. Prince Be got married and had a son, Christian. Fans worried that PM Dawn had run its course, but in his new Jersey City home studio, Prince Be was crafting his strongest and most psychedelic album. "It's pop, with a slightly experimental edge," he said in his self-deprecating way. "It's not that far-out, it's just slightly . . . elevated."[6] Released in 1995, *Jesus Wept* is named for the shortest verse in the Bible, and one that Prince Be praises for offering insight into Jesus the man. The album opens with a snippet from the animated Charlie Brown TV special about "The Great Pumpkin"—"If you really are a fake, don't tell me; I don't want to know," Linus says— then traces what the singer calls "an individual's spiritual journey through human existence." "We wanted to do an album that was spiritual top-to-bottom without being religious," he said. "For me, the jury is still out about organized religion. I wanted to evoke the spirituality I feel *inside*."[7]

Using real instruments instead of samples on most of the tracks, the album climaxes in an unlikely trio of covers dubbed "Fantasia's Confidential Ghetto." The minisuite starts with a stripped-down version of Prince's "1999," shifts into the layered art funk of the Talking Heads' "Once in a Lifetime," and ends with a gonzo version of Harry Nilsson's

"Coconut" that incorporates the now-obligatory Beatles nod by quoting "Flying." "Put the lime in the coconut and drink it all up," Prince Be sings. His conviction is strong enough to convince any skeptic that this brew—or at least the act of singing about it—is indeed all that is needed to cure life's ills.

Trip Hop

Please can't you stay a while to share my grief? / It's such a lovely day to have to always feel this way.

—Portishead, "Wandering Star"

Separated geographically and culturally from the urban meccas of American hip-hop, English musicians were inspired by the music's energy and technological advances while being free from constrictions about what constitutes "real" rap music. English sampling artists freely mixed musical elements, as evidenced by the pioneering Justified Ancients of Mu Mu. Former Liverpool manager, scenester, and Julian Cope target Bill Drummond teamed with Jimmy Cauty and released a series of singles featuring bizarre Scottish rapping and samples of artists ranging from Sly Stone to Petula Clark. Under the pseudonym the Timelords, the duo had an English hit in 1988 with "Doctoring the Tardis," which was inspired by the long-running science-fiction television series *Doctor Who*. As the KLF, they roped country star Tammy Wynette into a surreal musical and video guest turn. But the pair's interest in hip-hop was short-lived—"I ain't no B-boy / I hate that shit," they declared—and they soon shifted their attention to ambient house music.

England's own strain of psychedelic hip-hop surfaced several years after the innovations of De La Soul and PM Dawn, and it came from the racially mixed, West Country port city of Bristol. The roots of what the London label Mo' Wax would eventually dub "trip hop" can be traced to a mid-'80s collective of DJs known as the Wild Bunch who combined dub reggae, jazz, and hip-hop influences. Nellee Hooper went on to produce Soul II Soul, Neneh Cherry, and Sugarcubes singer Björk, while Daddy G and Mushroom formed Massive Attack and released two wide-ranging albums, *Blue Lines* and *Protection*. Massive Attack in turn nurtured Tricky, who rapped on both of its albums, and Geoff Barrow of Portishead, who got his start as the group's studio gofer.

Laid-back, low-key, and claustrophobic, trip hop is steeped in paranoia and melodrama, a musical equivalent to film noir. Reynolds called it "an aural simulation of the urban environment," but it's the sounds of the city as heard through a fever dream. "There's no unifying force to my album except confusion," Tricky said. "It's totally coming from my mind, so it's filled with contradictions, chaos, paranoia, and happiness—all loosely linked—like a jigsaw with some of the pieces missing."[8] Tricky's 1995 solo bow, *Maxinquaye*, blurs the lines between genres, transforming Public Enemy's raging "Black Steel in the Hour of Chaos" into a sinister rock meditation. At the same time, it blurs sexual identities, pairing the gruff vocals of the cross-dressing Tricky with female diva Martina's breathy singing in lusty bisexual fantasies. "Hip-hop has always been trippy and weird," Tricky said. "We're just mutating what's been done before."[9]

Stronger melodically and even more cinematic conceptually, Portishead was formed by Barrow after he auditioned twenty vocalists and finally teamed with cover band veteran Beth Gibbons. Gibbons's vocals on spooky, sensual tunes such as "Sour Times" and "Wandering Star" are equal parts Billie Holiday and Nico. The backing tracks on *Dummy* combine the live sounds of a small jazz combo and samples from soul, lounge music, and soundtrack albums, but while it might not be apparent at first listen, hip-hop is the biggest influence, both in the sloweddown rhythms and in the way that the songs are constructed. "Hip-hop hit England like a ton of bricks," Barrow told me. "I would never pretend that I know anything about living in America as a black person, because that's disrespectful. But what I've really gotten from that music is the way to use samples and manipulate beats and sounds. You have to take technology by the horns and guide it. The trouble is, a lot of people let it dictate the way they write songs, and all the actual vibe has gone out of music." Portishead, Tricky, D.J. Shadow, Money Mark, and others put the vibe back in, but so far trip hop has yet to produce an album as masterfully psychedelic as *3 Feet High and Rising* or any of PM Dawn's efforts.

CHAPTER 15

Raving and Drooling:
Psychedelic Dance Music

What do techno, rave, and Ecstasy have to do with each other? Taken together, are they the basis for an actual youth movement? Is it entertainment? Is it pagan? Is it music? Is it a fad? Is it a drug culture? Is it a religion? Is it a trend? Is it the final decline of Western Civilization? The answer, of course, is yes to all of the above.

—*Reactor* rave zine[1]

The earth reverberated in time to the throbbing bass as the sweaty twentysomething bodies gyrated directly in front of a twelve-foot-high wall of speakers. The sound drew the dancers in like a powerful magnet, and they undulated in free-form movements that were both awkward and beautiful. Nobody danced in pairs. The crowd was like one giant bouncing organism, and the sexual tension usually present at discos was missing completely. Blacks and Asians danced beside whites and Hispanics, and that wasn't an issue, either. What some would call infantilism and others a nostalgic yearning for childhood ran rampant. Dancers wore pacifiers on strings around their necks, sucked on lollipops, waved glow-in-the-dark toys, and sported T-shirts bearing their favorite cartoon characters.

The message was clear: Do your own thing. For some, that was orange hair, multiple piercings, giant Cat in the Hat *chapeaux*, and fuzzy lime-green vests. For others, it was outfits purchased on Dad's American Express card at the nearest Gap. The giant tent was almost pitch black, but a light from the DJ booth illuminated a skinny young nude dancing wildly atop the speakers. (He turned out to be Chicago writer David Prince, one of the event's organizers.) Outside, the air was thick with the hazy smoke from two dozen campfires, which could be glimpsed flickering beside smaller tents or next to cars or vans parked in the mud. A powerful argon laser shot a strong green beam into the sky, announcing that for the night, this remote campground on a wooded hillside in rural Wisconsin was the center of the Rave New World.

Located near the Minnesota border, the town of Hixton has a population of 403 or 356, depending on which of the welcome signs you choose to believe. The promoters chose the CMJ Motocross Track because it was roughly equidistant from the Chicago, Milwaukee, Minneapolis, and St. Louis rave scenes that they hoped to unite. Some two thousand dancers descended on the town like a '90s version of the gang in a '60s biker freak-out flick. Freak out they did, but peacefully, dancing all night to the liberating sounds of techno, acid, and ambient house music. The May Day 1994 rave was dubbed "Furthur" in honor of the multicolored bus driven by Ken Kesey and his Merry Pranksters. When it was all over, the promoters faced a giant, muddy mess, legal threats from an angry sheriff, and having to arrange bail for a pair English journalists who were the only ravers to get busted. The organizers were ecstatic nonetheless, partly because the journalists said it was the closest thing they'd seen in the States to a "real" English rave, partly because guest DJ the Aphex Twin delivered a transcendent set, and partly because they couldn't believe that they'd pulled it all off. "What we vowed to do was bring everybody together to communicate with each other and create more of a family atmosphere similar to Dead shows," said Kurt Eckes of Milwaukee's Drop Bass Network, primary promoters of the event. "Financially, it wasn't a success. But everybody that I talked to was having the weekend of their lives, and hearing that from as many people as I did was exactly what I wanted to happen." Added David Prince: "The idea of people going five hours into the middle of nowhere to dance to cutting-edge electronic music—that's the way it should be."

The music Prince referred to is inextricably intertwined with the other elements of rave culture as it developed in the late '80s. First came

Ecstasy—or E, or Adam, or X—developed as an appetite suppressant by the German pharmaceutical company Merck and patented in 1914 under its proper chemical name, MDMA. It was ignored until 1953, when the U.S. Army began testing its toxicity on lab animals. Its psychedelic properties weren't noted until 1976, when biochemist Alexander Shulgin wrote a report that earned him the title of the "stepfather of Ecstasy." "You discover a secret doorway into a room in your house that you did not previously know existed," is how Ecstasy researcher Bruce Eisner described the experience. "It is a room in which both your inner experience and your relations with others seem magically transformed. You feel really good about yourself and your life. At the same time, everyone who comes into this room seems more lovable. You find your thoughts flowing, turning into words that previously were blocked by fear and inhibition."[2]

While some scientists consider Ecstasy separate from psychedelics, preferring the term "empathogen," most users view the trip as a milder form of the LSD or mescaline experience. "With classic psychedelics, transformations frequently are both extreme and, for the most part, internalized," Peter Stafford wrote. "MDMA seems to offer a benign route to many similar consequences."[3] It also allows users to maintain enough of a grip on reality to function responsibly. Unlike people on LSD, Ecstasy trippers can tell that the red light is a red light and the cop is a cop. Nevertheless, Ecstasy followed a similar path to LSD in terms of media-fueled paranoia and its eventual outlawing. Shulgin's report was followed by false stories that the drug drained spinal fluid and caused Parkinson's disease, that it was a potent aphrodisiac (actually, it physically slows amorous adventures), and that it caused drug-crazed partiers to dance until they dropped from heatstroke or exhaustion. As in the '60s, the official clampdown was spurred by the drug's increasing popularity in social settings. A large quantity somehow surfaced in Dallas and Fort Worth in 1984, and it became the rage at yuppie bars after work. It was banned in England and the States in 1985, just before it collided with a new musical movement and became more popular than ever.

In 1981 DJs in Chicago's gay dance clubs started pumping the bass on mid-tempo disco records and adding melodic snatches ranging from gospel to Kraftwerk. One of the masters at manipulating dancers' emotions was Frankie Knuckles, who worked at a club called the Warehouse. A shortened version of the club's name gave the music a moniker: house. "The windows of the Warehouse were painted black, the crowd would be high on the music and on drugs"—including Ecstasy sprinkled on slices of fruit—"I'd pump up the bass, then play this record, which was the soundtrack of an express train," Knuckles said. "People would scream—it was mixture of ecstasy and fear—and it sounded like a train was racing through the club."[4]

House was popularized by Chicago labels such as DJ International and Trax. Simultaneously, a sound called techno was being developed in Detroit by DJs Derrick May, Kevin Saunderson, and Juan Atkins. The three were influenced by a Detroit radio jock named the Electrifyin' Mojo whose sets mixed Kraftwerk, Gary Numan, disco, and Parliament-Funkadelic. Techno did the same, but all on one track. "We like to say it's tomorrow's soul music for the modern-day black man," May said. "We took the intellectual technology and ran it through the streets of Detroit."[5] The technology he was referring to was digital samplers and MIDI, which allowed a single DJ or producer to control any number of synthesizers.

Most accounts agree that house, techno, and Ecstasy were first combined in 1986 on the Spanish island of Ibiza, where working-class youth vacation in England's version of spring break. "Somewhere in this sparse technology-based music was a chord that linked the disenfranchised: black American gays and alienated British youth with few job prospects and even fewer expectations of life," Ernest Hardy wrote.[6] A harsh critic of the rave scene, Hardy missed the uplifting, addicting, and colorblind physicality of techno, which had an appeal that soon expanded beyond its core devotees. From their Spanish origins, raves moved back to Britain, finding a home in urban warehouses and rural outdoor locales. They spread to Los Angeles, New York, and San Francisco in 1988 and 1989, and by the early '90s, they were common throughout the Midwest, as well as in Germany and Belgium.

In the summer of 1988, a hybrid sound called acid house evolved, and critics are still debating what the "acid" refers to. Some DJs say the term came from the distinctive buzzing sound of one of the primary technical components, the Roland TB-303 bass synthesizer. ("Hear that?" Chicago DJs are fond of asking. "*That* is the sound of acid.") Genesis P-Orridge of Psychic TV claimed that he saw the description on a bin in a Chicago record store, was disappointed to find that it meant "acid" as in "corrosive," and set about making psychedelic music that really fit the bill. Paul Staines of England's Freedom to Party Campaign admitted that the story he told the British Parliament—that acid house came from the

Chicago street slang "acid burn," meaning to steal or sample another piece of music—was concocted in a public relations effort to separate the phrase from its drug connotation. But anyone who's been to a rave can tell you the psychedelic connection is entirely appropriate.

At any rave a significant portion of the crowd is likely to be tripping, and the rest feels as if it is thanks to the disorienting sounds, overpowering volume, and classic psychedelic light show. LSD is popular, and there have been bursts of enthusiasm for ketamine, or Special K, an anesthetic related to PCP that often prompts hallucinations of a decidedly dark nature. Marijuana is used by dancers who want to come down, but alcohol is rarely in evidence. Ecstasy is still the high of choice, and users often heighten its effects by sucking on balloons filled with nitrous oxide or taking a quick whiff of Vicks Vap-O-Rub, which opens up the bronchial tubes and allows a rush of oxygen. "When MDMA is experienced at raves, it lacks some of the subtle effects experienced in quiet surroundings, but has an extra quality not seen when the drug is taken in private," researcher Nicholas Saunders wrote. "The combination of the drug with music and dancing together produces an exhilarating trancelike state, perhaps similar to that experienced in tribal rituals or religious ceremonies."[7]

The difference between raves and ancient rituals or '60s Acid Tests is technology. Techno-shamanism, some ravers call it, referring to the electronic music-making machines (there is no such thing as acoustic rave music), computer communications (ravers network and post party announcements on the Internet), virtual reality (better than LSD, they say), and a general philosophy that technology will improve humanity and preserve the planet. "If ravers lionize anything, it's technology, which offers ways to circumvent the kinds of blockage that derailed countercultures of the past," author Dennis Cooper wrote. "Rave is not about destroying corrupt power structures; it's about general things like self-belief, open-mindedness, and faith. . . . Ravers have no particular enemies, so they're relatively invisible. And their invisibility is their strength."[8]

Cooper wasn't entirely correct. Ravers are certainly visible to local government officials who take joy in cracking down on a phenomenon that means easy headlines and no political fallout. But to a large extent, the *artists* who make rave music are invisible, or at least anonymous. The DJ at a rave isn't the focus of the room the way a band is, because the crowd itself is the star of the show. Artists record under different and ever-changing names, most of which don't matter to ravers. The forum of choice is the twelve-inch single, and those are often unavailable to the general public until they're rounded up on compilation discs. "Although it would be exaggerating to suggest that techno records are amelodic at heart, the fact is that most techno singles tend toward short, repetitive phrases—'tunettes,' if you will—more than fully realized themes," critic J. D. Considine wrote. "Moreover, the dearth of vocals on most of these singles leaves most techno records seemingly indistinguishable from one another."[9]

This belief has led many critics to conclude that techno and acid house can't be judged outside the raves where the music is conceived and played. But there are reasons why certain artists have distinguished themselves from the faceless ranks. The best techno performers succeed because of the same attributes of all of the best psychedelic rock: strong songs, inventive production, an elemental drive, and a distinctive vision.

James Brown Is Buggin'

The power of sound is almost an archetypal conceit of all theories of magic anywhere in the world. For us, magic means stagecraft and illusion, but for many people, it simply means another way of doing business with reality. Rave culture, to some degree, can be seen as a nostalgia for archaic and so-called primitive lifestyles. . . . Music has to be percussive to address the human physiology. I mean, you wouldn't want to listen to too much Schoenberg on acid.

—Terence McKenna

The first techno single to scrape the U.S. charts and dent the consciousness of mainstream listeners was the grinding novelty tune "James Brown Is Dead," a 1992 single by a pair of radio DJs. The title was meant not as homage in the style of the Moody Blues' "Legends of a Mind," but as an obnoxious pronouncement signaling the birth of a new dance music with no ties to the past. Of course, this wasn't remotely true. Amid the onslaught of techno, acid house, and the myriad subgenres that followed—including ambient house, intelligent techno, acid, tribal, trance, and breakbeat/jungle—some of the best artists built on the legacy of psychedelic rock and extended it into the '90s.

Often called "the face of techno," Richard Melville Hall was born and raised in Darien, Connecticut, an upper-class bedroom community fifty miles north of Manhattan. He was nicknamed Moby as a baby in a nod to his great-great-granduncle, *Moby-Dick* author Herman Melville. He studied music and classical guitar, dabbled with hardcore punk in the Vatican Commandos, majored in philosophy at the University of Connecticut, and graduated with two abiding fascinations: Christianity and dance music. "Up until college, I had the typical white, suburban attitude towards dance music," he said. "I'd been told I wasn't allowed to like it, so I didn't. It represented everything foreign and threatening about inner-city culture. It was very threatening to me, but I realized it was also very seductive."[10]

Moby, distant relative of the great white whale. (Photo by Jill Greenberg.)

Moby became a DJ in New York in the late '80s, and he began crafting imaginative collages that mixed samples of Stockhausen-style industrial noise, pop fluff like Samantha Fox, and James Brown beats. In 1991 he scored a million-selling hit with the catchy single "Go," which featured him playing (not sampling) composer Angelo Badalamenti's theme for David Lynch's *Twin Peaks*. Like the TV show, the song has a surreal and vaguely threatening undercurrent. The influence of psychedelic rock was obvious, even if psychedelic drugs weren't a factor. (Moby lives a drug-free vegan lifestyle.) "I've always liked drug music, subversive music," Moby said. "I love psychedelic stuff. I have strong psychedelic experiences, but they're not drug related. Dancing for three or four hours with great lights and great music, the body produces its own drugs."[11]

Touring relentlessly, Moby won notice for his energetic stage shows, which featured him hurling his body around like Iggy Pop. But even as he was labeled techno's best-known performer, he was rejecting the rave scene as stagnant, cliquish, and unimaginative. His major-label debut, 1995's *Everything Is Wrong*, tried to break down arbitrary boundaries by embracing industrial dance music, old-style house, and alternative rock. But the lyrics were preachy and the music was only partially successful, and it didn't win any new fans.

It's been said that Richard James—a.k.a. the Aphex Twin, AFX, and Polygon Window—makes the techno equivalent of *Nuggets*-style garage rock, but he's closer in spirit to Brian Eno. A native of Cornwall, England, James began experimenting with sound as a child, dismantling and

He was only joking: Richard James, a.k.a. the Aphex Twin, in a self-portrait.

rebuilding the piano in his parents' living room. He discovered house via a tape that a friend brought back from Chicago, but he was already crafting similar tracks using old analog synthesizers that he built or customized himself. Tape hiss, crackles, and pops are part of their charm, as are the improvised instruments. "I'd say to my friends, 'Pick any object in the room and I'll make a track out of it,'" James said. "I'd make complete tracks out of Coke cans and carpets. Coke cans are easy because they have a lot of good acoustic characteristics, but with things like carpets, it's very difficult to get a bass drum sound."[12]

Slower and spacier than more hardcore dance sounds, James's music functions as well on headphones as at raves. His best known track is "Didgeridoo," which uses electronic sounds to duplicate the drone of the Australian Aboriginal instrument. (The track made didgeridoos as popular in techno as sitars were in the psychedelic rock of the '60s, and it kicked off a wave of DJs incorporating other ethnic instruments, as evidenced by the Wax Trax! compilation, *Ethnotechno*.) Unlike Moby, James doesn't shy away from psychedelics, though he credits dreams as his major source of inspiration. "I've always had sounds in my dreams," he said. "I can almost always remember melodies. But sounds, you can't get them the same."[13]

Troubled by the bland nature of much of the ambient techno that he helped usher in, James turned toward more nightmarish sounds on his Sire debut, 1994's *Selected Ambient Works Volume II*, which is reminiscent at times of Stockhausen, Can, and Eno's more sinister tracks. Befitting his evil-scientist image, James bought a British Daimler Ferret Mark 3 tank and took to driving it around his parents' backyard. Naturally, the sound of its engines became part of the mix on 1995's . . . *I Care Because You Do*, a more diverse but equally dark effort featuring a cover with a self-portrait of its creator grinning demonically.

England's Shamen shifted gears in 1989 from postpunk psychedelic rock to more dance-oriented sounds, and "Move Any Mountain" was another acid-house single that breached the mainstream. In 1993 the group started a trend by recording *Boss Drum* with Terence McKenna, the American ethnobotanist who no less an authority than Timothy Leary called "the Timothy Leary of the '90s." The author of propsychedelic tracts such as *True Hallucinations, The Archaic Revival,* and *Food of the Gods,* McKenna is the closest thing rave culture has to a guru. Although ravers have failed to adopt all of his theories, he shows a keen understanding of the rock 'n' roll mindset with his central tenet that going to the grave without having a psychedelic experience is like going to the grave without ever having sex. (Samples of such pronouncements have shown up on tracks by Psychic TV, Coil, Youth, and the Orb, among other techno artists.)

London resident Mixmaster Morris—a.k.a. the Irresistible Force—was a psychedelic-rock fan whose horizons were broadened by dropping LSD at a concert by minimalist composer Steve Reich. Originally a member of the Shamen's sizable posse of DJs, musicians, and lighting technicians, he struck out on his own after founding member Will Sinnott drowned while filming a video. Morris scored a solo hit in 1991 with the Sun Ra–inspired "Space Is the Place," and he followed with *Flying High,* a double album with the word "high" in every title but one ("Symphony in E"). He is devoted to the idea of eliminating the artist as star. "I've always been into music that was antimusician," he said. "We got rid of musicians and replaced them with DJs. Now I want to get rid of the DJs, too."[14]

Until Morris accomplishes that task, it's well worth following the work of some of techno's other avatars. Orbital is English brothers Phil and Paul Hartnoll; they crafted several ambitious soundscapes, including *Snivilisation,* a danceable concept album about the decline of Western Civilization. Canadian Richie Hawtin, a.k.a. Plastikman, debuted with a crisp, clean techno tribute to LSD, *Sheet One,* and found himself at the center of a controversy when a fan was arrested for carrying the CD jacket, which was made to resemble a sheet of blotter acid. Rochester, New York's Mark Gage records under the name VapourSpace for England's Swim label, which was founded by Colin Newman of Wire. San Francisco's Jonah Sharp collaborated with McKenna and recorded a strong album of his own as Space Time Continuum. Chicago DJ Derrick Carter made an influential ambient-house disc under the name Symbols & Instruments and several techno records with a decidedly jazzy bend under the name Sound Patrol. The New York collective Deee-Lite offered a more old-fashioned brand of house music with delightful psychedelic overtones and guest bass from former P-Funk member

Bootsy Collins. Englishmen Paul Hammond and Ian Cooper, better known as Ultramarine, grew up on a steady diet of the Canterbury bands Soft Machine and Caravan, and their music fuses jazzy flutes and guitars with electronic backgrounds. On 1993's *United Kingdom* they were joined by one of the grand old men of psychedelic rock, Robert Wyatt of the Soft Machine.

This isn't the only example of the first-generation psychedelic rockers linking up with '90s techno artists. In 1993 Paul McCartney hooked up with DJ and former Killing Joke bassist Youth in a duo called the fireman. Although McCartney reportedly had a blast in the studio, the resulting album, *strawberries oceans ships forest*, isn't particularly inspired. Former Throbbing Gristle leader, industrial pioneer, and artistic terrorist Genesis P-Orridge turned his attention to acid house with Psychic TV releases such as *Tekno Acid Beat* (1989) and *Towards thee Infinite Beat* (1990); space-rock veterans Hawkwind dabbled in techno on 1995's *Spirit of the Age*, and Steve Hillage of Gong resurfaced as a techno artist under the name 777. Much more interesting are Hillage's collaborations with Alex Paterson, a.k.a. the Orb, the father of ambient house, and arguably psychedelic dance music's most consistent artist.

Little Fluffy Clouds Over Battersea

The Orb have a little game they play, designed to limit the consumption of drugs to those still coherent enough to get a spark across a synapse. Having had his fill of a joint, Thrash turns to Alex. "What's the capital of Peru?" "Lima," replies Alex with some satisfaction. Thrash surrenders the spliff. "The Orb," explains Alex hazily, "has become a very geographically conscious band. Mountain ranges in Africa, rivers in Russia, cities in South America—we know 'em all. Have to. No geography, no drugs."

—Adam Higginbotham[15]

Born in 1959, Alex Paterson was raised in the Battersea section of south London, home of the evil-looking power station immortalized on the cover of Pink Floyd's *Animals*. His interest in outer space was born early on, spurred by his father's work on the Telstar satellite. He attended Kingham Hill School in rural Oxfordshire with Youth and went on to spend a year and a half in art school before quitting to work as a roadie for his friend's band. Paterson spent six years with industrial punks

Killing Joke, occasionally joining them onstage for an encore of Sex Pistols covers. He wound up as an A&R man at the band's label, EG Records, but by all accounts, he was a lousy talent scout—he thought the music he heard in his head was better than everything else he encountered. "The Orb is in essence a collaboration of people I would have liked to work with on an A&R level anyway," he said later. "It's a completely different way of working in a band structure."[16]

Inspired by the sounds of Eno and others in the EG catalog, Paterson started recording ambient music as a hobby, but Youth encouraged him to get more serious. In 1988 he began working at the studio owned by Jimmy Cauty, Bill Drummond's partner in the KLF. The result was the *Kiss* EP, four songs based on house samples from New York radio station KISS-FM. It was released on WAU!/Mr. Modo, a label started by Paterson and Youth. At the same time, Paterson established an ambient/chill-out room at Land of Oz dance nights in the London club Heaven. Surrounded by billowing white sheets and spacey slide projections, he played a mix of EG ambient records, old progressive rock, and other soothing sounds so that people could relax and reenergize between trips to the dance floor. One night he was spinning "Rainbow Dome Music" by Steve Hillage when Hillage walked in. The two struck up a friendship, and the guitarist later appeared on several Orb recordings.

The Paterson-Cauty Orb started to garner more attention with a 1989 single called "A Huge Evergrowing Pulsating Brain That Rules from the Centre of the Ultraworld." The melody came from Minnie Riperton's 1975 hit "Lovin' You," and the title was a tip of the hat to Pink Floyd's "Several Species of Small Furry Animals Gathered Together in a Cave and Grooving With a Pict." (It wasn't the last Floyd homage: Another track was called "Back Side of the Moon," and the cover of *Live 93* featured a stuffed sheep flying over Battersea in place of the pig on *Animals.*) Paterson jokingly called the sound he was developing "ambient house for the E generation." The name stuck, though he would later say he preferred "ambient with attitude."

Unlike more static ambient or New Age sounds, you can dance to the Orb, even on tracks where there aren't any drums. Musically, Paterson mixes slowed-down and sometimes subliminal rhythms with melodic samples and the dub production techniques pioneered by producers Lee "Scratch" Perry and Adrian Sherwood. Philosophically, he combines Eno's ambient ideas with a psychedelic approach to the studio and a punkish sense of humor. "People should get into the album for what it is; have a bit of a laugh, and relax," Paterson said of the group's debut. "The ambient sides you can go off and cook dinner and listen to it, or water the plants, or make love. Whether it's the missing link after Pink Floyd, I don't know. Don't ask me, I'm just enjoying myself."[17]

Paterson appeared uncredited on the KLF's two ambient-house forays, *Chill Out* and another effort released under the moniker *Space*, but he and Cauty parted ways after the Orb scored a hit with "Little Fluffy Clouds," a catchy single featuring a sample of Rickie Lee Jones longing for the Southwestern skies of her youth. Cauty was replaced by the young engineer Kris Weston, a.k.a. Thrash, and the restructured Orb traced a voyage through the cosmos on 1991's ambitious double album, *Adventures Beyond the Ultraworld*. The group also developed into a powerful live unit with the most elaborate light show since Hawkwind. Paterson turned knobs, tweaked dials, and spun records as Thrash played the mixing console like an instrument. A jazzy rhythm section decorated the clock, blurring the lines between electronic and live instrumental sounds. "It's much like I'm a vocalist in a sense, but I don't actually have to have vocals," Paterson said. "I just *play* what I want to say. If I want to say 'Back off' or whatever, I have samples on my keyboards, or I just fuck about on top. There's so many ambient noises around."[18]

The Orb continued exploring outer space on the unprecedented forty-minute single, "The Blue Room," which used sound effects, Hillage's guitar, and Jah Wobble's bass to conjure the sounds of an alien abduction. (The track was named for a room at Ohio's Wright-Patterson Air Force Base, which is alleged to hold the remains of crashed UFOs.) The album that followed, *U.F. Orb*, entered the English charts at number 1, but Paterson seemed to be at a crossroads. He retreated to the studio for over a year, then released an abrasive six-song "little album" called *Pomme Fritz*. Like Moby, he was convinced that many new techno artists were mere noodlers and that listeners were unthinkingly accepting self-indulgent crap. "We were simply trying to piss off the people who we didn't want to like the Orb," he said.

The doctor is in: Alex Paterson, a.k.a. the Orb.

Famous for mapping the cosmos, the Orb returned to terra firma in 1995. *Orbus Terrarum* is Paterson's version of *Another*

Green World, an aural tour of various geographic locales. But what at first seems like a radical departure is actually tied to earlier efforts by the way Paterson uses sounds to create images. "From track to track, there may not be any similarity in any of the Orb's material, but the thing that's always connected is the ambience," Paterson said. "It's the most obvious link—textural noises and the idea of using natural sounds and turning them into rhythmic sounds." Considered by many fans to be a paradigm of '90s psychedelia, Paterson remains more committed to open-mindedness than to drugs. "People have to find their own source of psychedelia," he told me. "You could become a deep-sea diver in Thailand, and that could become the most psychedelic experience you could ever imagine. And that's just a natural thing as opposed to putting chemicals in your head." He also refuses to invest his music with higher purpose, despite the obvious care he takes in crafting it.

"It's pure escapism; that's all psychedelic music is," Paterson added. "That's what we are and that's what we want to be. At the end of the day, when you come and see us live or put a record of ours on, that's what you do: escape."

CHAPTER 16

Pigfuckers and Shoegazers: Psychedelic Guitar Bands in the '80s and '90s

"Bliss" and "noise" are the same thing—a rupture/disruption in the signifying system that holds a culture together. . . . The pleasure of noise lies in the fact that the obliteration of meaning and identity is ecstasy—literally, being out-of-oneself.
—Simon Reynolds[1]

Faced with the musical innovations and growing popularity of hip-hop and dance music, some critics in the mid-'80s announced that rock had run its course, and that everything that *could* be done with guitars, bass, and drums *had* been done. The *Village Voice* used the term "pigfuckers" to write off a particular strain of aggressive noise bands, but it was equally dismissive of a broad range of inventive groups that struggled to find an audience through fanzines, college radio, and independent labels. The English music weeklies were slightly more tolerant, but the guitar bands of the early '90s were dubbed "shoegazers" or members of "the scene that celebrates itself," branding them with brooding attitudes and superiority complexes that weren't always there. In fact, psychedelic rock lived on in dozens of bands on both sides of the Atlantic. The best referenced the past, often through covers, while setting their sights on the future, avoiding the self-imposed constraints of the revivalists. Some survived to thrive in the '90s as post-Nirvana "alternative" rock became a new mainstream specializing in quirkiness and novelty, while others fell by the wayside, leaving catalogs that stand with the most inspired and passionate psychedelic rock of any period.

Hardcore punk was generally considered in opposition to the psychedelic revival of the '80s, but the hyperactive subgenre produced several groups that evolved into more expansive sounds. California's straightedge-turned-pothead SST Records was at various times home to Arizona's psychedelic country rockers the Meat Puppets; Dinosaur Jr., whose guitar squalls could be traced back to hardcore punks Deep Wound; and Das Damen, whose high point was a demented cover of "Magical Mystery Tour." But SST's most influential band was the Minneapolis trio Hüsker Dü. Its cover of Donovan's "Sunshine Superman" on 1993's *Everything Falls Apart* should have been the tip-off, but its competing musical impulses—supermelodic psychedelic rock vs. supercharged hardcore punk—became crystal-clear with a version of "Eight Miles High" released as a single in 1984. The Byrds' original is invested with new meaning as Hüsker Dü tears through the song at breakneck speed with a guitar sound evoking a hundred jets at takeoff. Bob Mould's vocal cracks midway through, and by the end of the song, he's reduced to primal screaming. Where the Byrds celebrated the freedom of the '60s, Mould rages against the repression of the Reagan-Thatcher '80s, as well as the stifling cloak of '60s nostalgia.

Heirs to the twisted Texas tradition of the 13th Floor Elevators, the Butthole Surfers came together at Trinity College in San Antonio in 1981. Living a nomadic lifestyle, shifting personnel frequently, and recording prolifically, the Buttholes explored a noisy vision of psychedelia that was overwhelming, disorienting, full of crude humor, and obsessed with the aesthetics of ugliness. Live, the band revived Hawkwind's nude go-go dancers and light show, adding smoke, fire, and autopsy films checked out of the college library. On album, it created sonic collages with tape loops, samples, two drummers, feedback, distorted vocals, and covers of its heroes, including Black Sabbath and Donovan. The group eventually settled at a ranch outside Austin and built its own home studio, allowing main men Gibby Haynes and Paul Leary to indulge in solo projects such as the Jack Officers, a dance effort that Haynes dubbed "hick house." Signing to Capitol Records enabled an inspired pairing with producer John Paul Jones, but the band's later releases don't have the insane energy of the early recordings. Not that the

Just some good ol' Texas boys and gals: the Butthole Surfers. (Photo by Marty Perez.)

Buttholes worry about criticism; "Art is just the last three letters of fart," Haynes is fond of saying.[2]

In the wake of Wire-inspired art punks Mission of Burma, the Boston area produced one school of bands dedicated to focused, melodic guitar workouts (including the Neats, Dumptruck, Big Dipper, and the Blake Babies), and another that was more self-conscious in its ambitious eclecticism (including the Pixies, Throwing Muses, and Christmas). In a class of its own was Galaxie 500, a trio of friends who came together while studying at Harvard University. Taking off from the introspective, druggy grooves of the Velvet Underground's "Candy Says" and "Here She Comes Now" (which they covered), the group recorded three strong albums, although diversity isn't among their charms. "The whole band has just been like one long jam on the same theme—it's just that you discover a lot of what you can do with it," drummer Damon Krukowski said. The band split up in 1990, but its influence lives on in groups such as Low and Bedhead. Krukowski and bassist Naomi Yang went on to record two underrated albums as a duo and link up with the Soft Machine–inspired Magic Hour, while guitarist-vocalist Dean Wareham formed the more accomplished but sometimes sterile sounding Luna with former Feelies drummer Stanley Demeski and former Chills bassist Justin Harwood.

Galaxie 500's albums were all produced by Kramer, a New York underground mainstay whose own musical adventures included the psychedelic studio project Bongwater. Former punk Tim Sommer formed Hugo Largo, an ethereal combo dedicated to lilting music that was part ambient, part pop, and part opera. Across the Hudson River in Hoboken, New Jersey, Yo La Tengo progressed from Velvets- and Feelies-inspired jams, to acoustic folk rock, to hypnotic krautrock drones. On Long Island, musical prodigy Kurt Ralske forged a sound that merged bubblegum and sinister atmospherics, recording as a one-man band named Ultra Vivid Scene, and in Livonia, Michigan, a studio trio called His Name Is Alive paired two soaring female voices with Eno-style ambient backing. Both of these acts found outlets on the English independent label 4AD, which was also home to Scotland's influential Cocteau Twins.

Formed in 1981, the Cocteaus honed a distinctive sound based on shimmering walls of Robin Guthrie's heavily effected guitars, hypnotic drum machine patterns, and Elizabeth Fraser's swooping vocals. Melodies unfold leisurely over long musical passages, and Fraser sings in a mix of English, foreign phrases, and nonsense syllables. The result is soothing but erotic lullabies, their meanings left to the listener. "I've always assumed that psychedelic music was kind of to do with the hippie culture, drugs, and anything that was slightly left-field that you could sit in your bedroom, crank up to 10, and smoke a pipe to," bassist Simon Raymonde said. "In that respect, we are quite a psychedelic band, because a lot of people do that with our music, and we used to do that with our music. That's how we actually created half of it."

Echoes of the Cocteaus could be heard in the mid '90s work of the female-led psychedelic pop quartet Lush; the group were also kindred spirits to a class of English bands that critic Simon Reynolds dubbed "oceanic rockers." Guthrie remixed and produced A. R. Kane, a duo that, after serving as part of the team behind "Pump Up the Volume" by M/A/R/R/S, cut a path between techno and Miles Davis's psychedelic fusion. Working as Durutti Column, Vini Reilly made ambient instrumental music that updated Mike Oldfield. After starting out as a synth-pop band, Talk Talk moved to ethereal, orchestrated rock, and Dream Academy offered a more accessible take on a similar sound, scoring hits with "Life in a Northern Town" (produced by David Gilmour) and an acid-house cover of John Lennon's "Love" that was clearly inspired by the emergence of the so-called Madchester scene.

At the turn of the decade, the gloomy northern town of Manchester became the center for a wave of bands that straddled the line between psychedelic rock and psychedelic dance music, producing inferior versions of both. Chosen because of his work with the Dukes of Stratosphear, John Leckie produced the Stone Roses' self-titled 1989 debut, an impressive hit that its creators were unable to follow up. Inspiral Carpets put its twist on the formula of mechanical dance beats and chiming guitars by adding garage-punk organ, while Happy Mondays were distinguished by funkier grooves and some of the dopiest lyrics ever written. Only two Madchester groups developed beyond the original sound, but they had been only marginally connected to the scene in the first place. The Charlatans progressed from "The Only One I Know," a danceable rewrite of Deep Purple's "Hush," to more soulful and psychedelic R&B. Led by art-school product Damon Albarn, the son of Soft Machine's road manager, Blur moved from dance hits such as "She's So

High" to invigorating albums that put Syd Barrett, Ray Davies, Julian Cope, Wire, and XTC into a psychedelic Cuisinart.

Critic Rachel Felder noted the contrast between the Madchester bands and what she called the "miasma bands" that followed. "The point of enjoying bands like the Mondays was to get, as the British put it, out of your head—to take so many drugs you escape your reality," Felder wrote. "The miasmics aren't so much concerned with getting away from their problems as with somehow articulating them: actualizing angst and bewilderment with grizzled guitars instead of heavy lyrics."[3] Paving the way for miasma bands such as My Bloody Valentine and much of the Creation Records roster were Spacemen 3 and the Jesus and Mary Chain.

Formed by guitarists Peter Kember (a.k.a. Sonic Boom) and Jason Pierce (a.k.a. Jason Spaceman) at Rugby Art College, Spacemen 3 specialized in dark, droning, Velvets-style mantras. The group endorsed drugs and came to be associated with a new wave of heroin chic, but critic Greg Shaw argued, "They were one of the great psychedelic bands, capturing the essence of altered states of many varieties."[4] Released in 1989, *Playing With Fire* added a gospel influence—"It's as though, through sacramentalizing opiates, they've come to see God as the ultimate narcotic," Reynolds wrote[5]—while the band's final release, 1991's *Recurring*, embraced Kraftwerk-style synthesized rhythms.

A host of Spacemen-related projects followed. Bassist Pete Bassman led the Darkside, which emphasized the *Nuggets*-Doors element of his old group's sound. Sonic Boom formed Spectrum, which moved toward techno, and collaborated with Kevin Shields of My Bloody Valentine in Experimental Audio Research, which created atmospheric ambient music. *Recurring* veteran Mark Refoy formed Slipstream and released a strong debut that added acoustic folk to the formula, as well as paying tribute to Kraftwerk with a cover of "Computer Love." Tied to the family tree only as kindred spirits, Croydon's Loop mined similar influences and created brooding drones with the stated intention of evoking a nightmarish acid trip. ("It's been said that taking acid is the closest you can come to schizophrenia," said bandleader Robert. "But how do the doctors know? How can you find out what being mad is like?"[6]) But the most significant spin-off was Pierce's new band, Spiritualized.

Spiritualized's 1992 debut, *Lazer Guided Melodies*, features transcendent rock spirituals that combine the rolling rhythm of the Velvets' "Ocean" with gospel saxophone and a guitar sound somewhere between the Spacemen's drone and Gilmour's echoed slides. Live shows ebbed and flowed as members performed on fog-drenched stages lit by vertical columns of white light, evoking revival-tent hysteria with the loud passages and Roman Catholic solemnity with the quieter ones. After a four-year delay, *Pure Phase* added a minimalist string section and jazzier interplay. A studio perfectionist—"For us, it's about striving to make an *Electric Ladyland* every time you do a record," Pierce said—the album was released with two complete mixes done several months apart, one on the right channel, the other on the left. Despite titles such as "Electric Mainline" and "Medication," the songs advocate escape through the beauty of music rather than chemicals. "All the best things in life fuck you up the most, whether it's lovesickness or drug sickness," Pierce said. "I don't think using music as an escape is a bad thing."[7]

Formed in Glasgow by brothers Jim and William Reid, the Jesus and Mary Chain was another Velvets-inspired group, but the drug references and black attitude were underscored by an early Beach Boys–style pop sensibility. The group debuted with a dramatic single, "Upside Down," that married an indelible melody with some of the most brutal guitar feedback ever recorded. (It was backed by a twisted cover of Syd Barrett's "Vegetable Man.") The group varied this formula from album to album, sometimes taking a quiet, acoustic approach, and at other times stressing a mechanized dance beat. But although it created dozens of memorable tunes, it never topped that first violent explosion.

The Jesus and Mary Chain left Creation after "Upside Down," but that single put the label on the map, and it became one of England's biggest indie success stories. Most Creation releases reflect the psychedelic aesthetic of founder Alan McGee. Born in the Glasgow suburb of East Kilbride, McGee said he relocated to London in 1981 "because of the drugs." He booked a club called the Living Room and started Creation as a hobby, taking the name from his favorite '60s rockers. (He also played in a modish combo called Biff Bang Pow!, named for the Creation song.) "It's a totally selfish label," McGee said in his thick brogue. "The whole thing is just my taste." Not every Creation band is worth bragging about; the roster has included lightweights such as Swervedriver, House of Love, the

Like the Velvets, the Jesus and Mary Chain favor black.

Creation Records fave raves Ride go tripping.

Telescopes, and Primal Scream, the '60s-flavored dance group led by former Mary Chain drummer Bobby Gillespie. But the label was also the English home for the Big Star–inspired Teenage Fanclub and Velvet Crush; Bob Mould's new band, Sugar; genre-hopping, nitrous-inhaling New Jersey brothers Gene and Dean Ween; mod-dressing, venom-spewing Irish brothers Noel and Liam Gallagher (a.k.a. Oasis), and Eugenius, the psychedelic guitar band started by former Vaselines leader Eugene Kelly.

"The whole Creation aesthetic seems based in the sad conviction that rock is over, it's been and gone, and that all that's left is to uphold the legacy through the Dark Ages of Plastic Pop," Reynolds contended. "The result is bands like Primal Scream: a living, breathing archive of rock gesture; a mere footnote."[8] But while the best Creation bands lovingly cite their references, their music succeeds because it crackles with the energy of the present. The Boo Radleys are a charming Liverpool pop group whose swaggering trumpets and swirling guitars recall two earlier charming Liverpool pop groups, the *Revolver*-era Beatles and The Teardrop Explodes. The band's albums are powered by the smart, droll lyrics, unflagging enthusiasm, and an unerring way with a hook. Slowdive's elegant "cathedrals of sound" were modeled on the Cocteau Twins and Brian Eno (whom they worked with as a producer), but songs such as "Spanish Air" and "Alison" were as strong as anything written by their mentors. And Ride's reference points were so varied (Byrds, Who, Kraftwerk, Creation) that combining them created something new: cascading waves of sound that sweep you away with simple, emotionally charged choruses.

Creation served as a model for England's second great psychedelic indie, Too Pure, founded in 1990 by Richard Roberts and Paul Cox. With the exception of the bluesy PJ Harvey, the Too Pure bands were inspired by artier psychedelic sounds. Moonshake and th' faith healers were both influenced by Can's monster grooves—Moonshake took its name from the Can song—but they were quick to rail against nostalgia. "It's more the openings that groups like that created that no one's followed up since," said Moonshake guitarist David Callahan.[9] th' faith healers split up after two strong albums, and half of Moonshake left to form the jazzy techno unit Laika, named for the first dog in outer space. But Too Pure's catalog grew with releases by the poppy ambient group, See Feel, jazz-rock impressionists Pram, and the prolific Stereolab.

Like Fritz Lang's 1926 film *Metropolis*, Stereolab has a vision that's both antiquated and futuristic. The group was formed in 1990 by guitarist Tim Gane and French vocalist Laetitia Sadier after the demise of Gane's indie-pop band McCarthy. Gane embraces old analog synthesizers, the trademark *motorik* beat of Neu!, and the hi-fi production tricks of '50s space-age bachelor-pad records, while Sadier sings lyrics that, like the Cocteaus', mix real words with nonsense syllables. As with the Feelies' *Crazy Rhythms*, another big influence, Stereolab's songs seem to exist before the group starts playing and continue after it finishes. "Sometimes I feel like it's a big block of music and we just chip bits off and record them," Gane said.

Stereolab's enthusiasm for vintage synthesizers was shared in the mid-'90s by a wave of underground American bands, including the improvisational combos LaBradford, Cul de Sac, and Flowchart; space rockers Sabalon Glitz and Flying Saucer Attack, and Red Red Meat, which combined space-rock synthesizers and decadent *Exile on Main Street*–inspired blues on its third album, *Bunny Gets Paid*. At the same

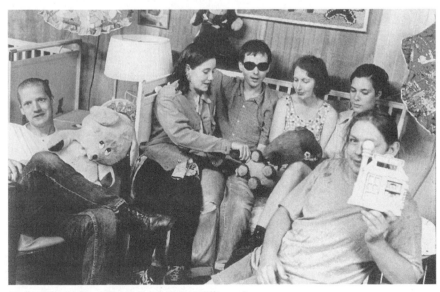

Stereolab at play. (Photo by Brooke Williams.)

time, the underground rock scene witnessed a resurgence in baroque psychedelic pop in the style of *Pet Sounds*, prompted in large part by the enormously talented Richard Davies, the man behind Australian rockers the Moles, but also including Eric Matthews (Davies' partner in Cardinal) and the Chicago group Yum-Yum.

Books could be written about many of these modern psychedelic rock groups, but two in particular deserve a closer look here. Both are led by auteurs who are products, not of privileged or art-school backgrounds, but of ordinary middle-class upbringings. They honed their sounds over long periods spent working in relative obscurity in the rock underground, recording quickly and cheaply in the punk D.I.Y. spirit. Both experimented with psychedelic drugs, but they have always been more impressed with the power of imagination, and they prefer a laid-back style of living and creating to more fast-paced "rock star" lives. Their stories are indicative of the experiences of psychedelic-rock bands in the '90s striving to sustain the "no rules" ideals of a genre over three decades old. But most importantly, their music shows just how much can still be done with guitars, bass, and drums.

To Here Knows When

Ultimately, where we're all heading in music is a sort of integration of the reality of what it's all about in the end, and that's extremely psychedelic in its purest sense. Music can remind you of what else is out there. It's a guidepost or a stepping-stone.

—Kevin Shields

Because several of the Shields children wound up in the arts, fans often assume that My Bloody Valentine's founder grew up in privilege. In fact, Kevin Shields had an ordinary upbringing remarkable only for its uprooting when he was eleven. Reversing the common trend in immigration, the family relocated from an Irish enclave of Queens, New York, to Dublin, and their father worked for the A&P grocery store chain. "We moved over to Ireland and were completely broke," Shields said. "We lived in a rented house in a row of rented houses with all the other employees from the store. We lived beside the car park, and that was our playground." School took a backseat to rock 'n' roll—Shields learned to play guitar by mimicking the downstrokes on the Ramones' *It's*

Alive—but his parents were supportive enough to let the band rehearse in the living room on Sunday afternoons.

My Bloody Valentine formed in 1983 as a gloomy, mascara-wearing band enamored of the Cramps, the Doors, and the Birthday Party. Dublin was unreceptive, so the group took the advice of Gavin Friday of the Virgin Prunes and lined up some shows in Europe. The band settled in Germany in 1985 and recorded the *This Is Your Bloody Valentine* EP in Berlin. "The first one was crap," Shields said frankly. Over the course of several more EPs, the group began to construct a wall of noise to rival the Jesus and Mary Chain's, but it was dragged down by David Conway's basso profundo crooning and posing. "The whole thing became a kind of intellectual project around '86, and by '87, it died," Shields said.

Relocating to England, Shields regrouped with veteran drummer Colm O'Ciosoig and new member Bilinda Butcher on guitar and vocals. The band started over with a pair of 1987 EPs, *Strawberry Wine* and *Ecstasy*. They ushered in a new, optimistic vibe reminiscent of Love's sunny psychedelia, but Shields was "still in this apologetic frame of mind, not just going for it, wherever your imagination takes you." In 1988 the band signed to Creation and finally went for it. *You Made Me Realise* was the first time Shields felt totally in control. The EP introduced what he called "glide guitar" (strumming the guitar while holding the tremolo arm, or whammy bar, a relic of the surf era, so that the tuning is shifting slightly all the time). "In '88 a lot of elements came together at the same time, and a lot of extreme things happened," Shields said. "What I did then was virtually invent my own way of playing. It didn't come about in any conscious way; it just came about from messing around on borrowed equipment. It felt playful, but on a much stronger level. Everything was adding up, and I was twenty five then. . . . Everything starts to come in and you go, 'God, what was I messing around with before?' "

This approach solidified on a subsequent EP and a 1988 album, *Isn't Anything*, engineered by Hawkwind and Amon Düül II veteran Dave Anderson. Felder proclaimed the group king of the miasma bands, while Reynolds credited it with developing "a new and private lexicon of sounds and effects—shapeless surges, swathes, precipices, vortices, wraiths, and detonations."[10] Shields was happy to explain his tools, including glide guitar and the backward reverb setting of his Yamaha digital effects machine, but he wasn't above a little impressionism himself. "The thing is, the sound literally isn't all there," he said. "It's actually the opposite of rock 'n' roll. It's taking all the guts out of it; there's no guts, just the rem-

My Bloody Valentine. From left, Kevin Shields, Colm O'Ciosoig, Debbie Googe, and Belinda Butcher.

nants, the outline. It's like—did you ever walk around in the city on a Sunday, somewhere like the East End or the Angel?—and there's this dead, where-is-everybody feel. . . . That kind of deserted feel. Not spooky; you are not made uncomfortable. But you're not comfortable either."[11]

Like the Cocteau Twins, the Valentines rarely write songs that are "about" anything. The words are often inaudible, and the vocals are placed behind the wall of guitars. Adding to the mystery is the lazy way that they're sung. "Often when we do vocals, it's seven-thirty in the morning; I've usually just fallen asleep and have to be woken up to sing," Butcher said. "I'm usually trying to remember what I've been dreaming about when I'm singing."[12] Song titles such as "Feed Me With Your Kiss," "Soft As Snow (But Warm Inside)," and "To Here Knows When" combine with the mood of the music to offer clues about the band's recurring themes: lustful yearning, the longing for blissful escape, and feelings of overwhelming alienation.

Repeating the pattern they had just established, the Valentines recorded two more work-in-progress EPs—1989's *Glider* and 1990's *Tremolo*—paving the way for the next full album. Released in 1991, *Loveless* was the culmination of everything the group had attempted. Critic David Sprague called it "part *Metal Machine Music* and part *Pet Sounds*."[13] Shields abandoned the near-mono mix of *Isn't Anything* in favor of a shifting and thoroughly disorienting stereo soundscape. It's the sound of bedspins—or a psychedelic rush. "I think it was influenced a little bit too much by Ecstasy culture," Shields said. "A lot of the melodies and the kind of hook lines that come from the instruments are extremely dinky and toylike. For me, that was the aftereffects of experiencing too much Ecstasy. . . . I love dance music; that was when De La Soul came out, and it was all such a happy sound." But not everybody was happy. The album was crafted over three years, requiring the services of sixteen engineers and costing Creation 250,000 pounds. "I don't cry, but it drove me to tears, just drove me insane," McGee said.[14]

Three months after *Loveless* was released, the Valentines and Creation parted ways. The group spent a year on the road, touring in support of *Loveless* and earning a reputation as the loudest band anyone had ever seen. "A lot of what we've done is perceived by people as coming from somebody who's not quite sane, or a bit woozy or dreamy," Shields said. "That's why when we play live, it's quite aggressive or confrontational. . . . What I do is about consciousness, being conscious of a feeling in my whole body. The trouble with the attitude toward psychedelic music is that it's about your head only. And to me, all non-Western people when they get into altered states of mind, it's the whole body that's involved."

When the Valentines finally returned to London, they signed to Island in England and invested their advance in building a home studio. The group ran into equipment problems, and time dragged on. There were rumors that Shields was making a jungle record, that bassist Debbie Googe had been seen driving a cab around London, and that the band would never finish whatever it was that it was working on. "That's one of the great misconceptions about this band, that everything is intellectual and there's an awful lot of time spent in the studio perfecting things," Shields told me in the summer of 1995. "Everything you ever hear on our records, virtually all the overdubs are first-take stuff, and all the guitar parts are first or second take. It's more like capturing the moment. For me, everything hinges on one critical thing, and that's being in an inspired state of mind."

My Bloody Valentine finally resurfaced in 1996 with a cover of Wire's "Map Ref. 41°N 93°W" on the Wire tribute album *Whore.* Shields promised a new album by the end of 1996, and a long career thereafter. "Too often when people make good records, there's an aftershock effect, and they collapse psychologically and emotionally, " he said. "Brian Wilson is a classic case of that. I'm trying to prove that you can make genuinely interesting music and come out with new ideas without an emotional drain to the point where you break down. I could make another record that would top the others we've made—I've been ready to for a while now—but to me it's extremely important to make that record in such a way that I'll be able to make another one. For lots of small, petty, human reasons that I won't go into, I'd like to be around in five years' time, making better and better records."

Turn It On

When people say psychedelia, it's been tainted by tie-dye shirts and people smoking dope. We think of it as cinematic music; it gives you something to think about, and there's imagery within it. People who record Christmas music have all this imagery: You hear bells and the swishing of sleighs and horse hooves and angels. These are visual references you can turn into sound because you're trying to get a mood across. That's us. We're the band that's always making a Christmas record.

—Wayne Coyne

In early April 1995, the Flaming Lips had been hunkered down for six weeks at Studio 7, a big, squat building located on the wrong side of the tracks dividing Oklahoma City's north and south sides. (The Murrah Federal Building, which would be torn apart by a bomb blast two weeks later, was only about a mile away.) Guitars, percussion toys, a pedal steel, orchestra bells, some old analog synthesizers, a Fender Rhodes piano, a Hammond organ, and even a hurdy-gurdy were all piled about the main recording room. Steven Drozd's drums were set up in another brick-walled room in front of a giant, tacky mural that looked like something from a hippie day-care center, and two dozen broken sticks littered the floor. (A monster drummer, Drozd has to duct-tape his headphones to his head so they won't fly off when he plays.) In a separate vocal booth were an impressive pile of cigarette butts, a big collection of Bob Dylan lyrics, and William Joyce's children's book *Santa Calls*. ("For inspiration," Coyne said.) In the cluttered lounge, Jean-Luc Godard's in-studio film about the Rolling Stones, *Sympathy for the Devil*, played on the VCR.

The night before I arrived, Coyne recorded vocals and acoustic guitar for "Brainville University, Tuition One Dollar," which started as a hokey tune that sounded a bit like Rick Nelson's "Garden Party." Over the course of the next sixteen-hour day, a dozen guitar and vocal overdubs turned the song into a two-minute, seventeen-second minisymphony. Time and again, band members stopped to ask, "That's not another song, is it?" or "This hasn't been done before, has it?" (They don't mind borrowing from rock history, but only as long as it fits into something that's 100 percent their own). At one point, everyone in the studio (including me) was pressed into recording some handclaps for the end of the tune. A passionate debate followed about how engineer David Fridmann should make the clapping sound. Lead guitarist Ronald Jones favored the giant handclaps of Queen and the Cars. Coyne preferred the loose clapping on the first Stooges album. Finally, Drozd pulled out a CD of David Bowie's *Hunky Dory* and played "Andy Warhol." Everyone agreed that *that* was the way handclaps should sound, and work moved on. "The best part about working the way we do is that you can never do anything wrong," Coyne said in his Okie drawl.

*The fabulous Flaming Lips. From left: Wayne Coyne, Steven Drozd, Michael Ivins, and Ronald Jones. (*Photo by J. Michelle Martin.)

The youngest of six children, Wayne grew up in a middle-class Catholic family surrounded by Baptists in what's often called the buckle of the Bible Belt. He didn't go to college, but he was drawn to the University of Oklahoma in neighboring Norman when some enterprising rock fans began hosting hardcore punk shows in the early '80s. He started the band with his brother, Mark, and bassist Michael Ivins. They bought a PA that had been stolen from a cowboy bar, and they hauled it to gigs by touring groups such as the Meat Puppets. In return, they got into shows for free and learned about the indie-rock ritual of making your own album and selling it at gigs while touring the country in a van. They chose the name Flaming Lips for its random weirdness, and they decided to join in the fun.

In 1985 Wayne's dad was selling office products, and he had accumulated credit under the barter system from a studio specializing in recording Christian jingles. Wayne, Mark, Ivins, and drummer Richard English went into the studio in the middle of the night and recorded a self-titled, six-song EP released on the band's own Lovely Sorts of Death Records. The label's name was borrowed from the poster for the '60s acid-exploitation flick *The Trip,* and though the initials spelled LSD, Coyne was never indulgent in his use of psychedelic drugs. "I've done acid probably three or four times, and one of them I don't think counted because it was shitty," he said with characteristic frankness. "I think that's the great misconception about our music. People think, 'The only way you could do that is to be on drugs.' If you look for the influence of drugs on our music, it's like looking for a UFO. You'll probably find it. But it has always been more about propelling the ideas away from what's boring."

None of the band members was a virtuoso, but that didn't bother them. "We've always figured that if we can't play our instruments, at least we can come up with some weird ideas no one's done before," Coyne said. The Lips toured for a while, Mark quit, and eventually the independent Restless Records offered the band a contract. The three-man Lips released three albums: *Hear It Is* (1986), *Oh My Gawd!!! . . . The Flaming Lips* (1987), and *Telepathic Surgery* (1989). The company never gave the Lips much money, so they had no choice but to make records in intense two- or three-day bursts. "We never called it punk rock, that was just all the money and all the time we had," Coyne said. For the most part, the Lips came across as a druggier version of the Replacements, but the albums hinted that the band was capable of more, including the Pink Floyd–inspired "One Million Billionth of a Millisecond on a Sunday Morning," the lulling "Jesus Shootin' Heroin," and the crushing "Godzilla Flick."

English quit midway through the tour supporting *Telepathic Surgery*, and Coyne and Ivins finished the remaining gigs as a duo. They considered packing it in, but Coyne had just signed a song publishing deal and gotten a $10,000 advance. They decided to spend it by going out in a blaze of glory. Jonathan Donahue, a Lips fan from Buffalo, New York, had hopped in the van during that last ill-fated tour, joining the group as soundman. When Coyne and Ivins reassembled the Lips, Donahue became the second guitarist and Nathan Roberts joined on drums. "We did *In a Priest Driven Ambulance* thinking it was the last record we were ever gonna do," Coyne said. "We really liked the idea of breaking free of that whole thing where independent bands spend fifty dollars making shitty-sounding records." The group worked at a studio in Buffalo staffed by students, including their producer, Fridmann. "These were guys who wanted to be engineers. They liked us giving them challenges. It wasn't like dreading going into the recording studio. We'd wake up every day, and ideas would be flying out of everybody's heads. We could set up an amp and put a mike sixty feet down the hall just to see how it sounded. After that, we didn't want to make a record ever again if we had to do it the old way."

Priest is the Lips' first masterpiece. It takes familiar influences such as the Stooges, the Velvets, and Pink Floyd and twists and contorts them like images in a fun-house mirror. Unfortunately, Restless nearly folded just as the album was released, and it was impossible to find in stores. Around the same time, longtime manager and booking agent Michele Vlasimsky threw up her hands and quit. Managing the band fell by default to Scott Booker, a fan who was running Oklahoma City's one cool record store. ("Basically, the Lips liked me 'cause I had a phone," he said.) Just when things were looking bleakest, Booker got a call from Warner Bros. executive Roberta Peterson, the woman who signed Jane's Addiction. Other staffers had been raving about the Lips' indie releases and wild stage shows featuring smoke and bubble machines and thousands of blinking Christmas lights. Peterson offered the group a contract.

"We were like, 'We're glad you like us and all that, but we just wanna make records like the last one,'" Coyne said. "They said, 'Sure.' But we kept thinking there had to be some catch." There was, and it came in the sort of corporate red tape that the Lips had never dealt with before. Working with Fridmann, they recorded another strong and twisted album, *Hit to Death in the Future Head.* They delivered it to Warners and then—nothing. The band waited for the better part of a year as lawyers tried to get copyright approval from conductor Michael Kamen. It seems the group was watching a videotape of Terry Gilliam's 1985 film *Brazil* during the recording, and a bit of the soundtrack made its way onto "You Have to Be Joking (Autopsy of the Devil's Brain)." The Lips liked it too much to remove it, but it took forever to get the sample cleared. (The band got their revenge on the company by tacking on a thirty-minute "bonus track" of grating noise and then following the album with an EP titled *Wastin' Pigs Is Still Radical,* released at the height of the Warners-Ice-T "Cop Killer" controversy.)

By the time *Hit to Death* was released in mid-1992, there was a new version of the band. Roberts quit, Donahue returned to Buffalo to form the equally weird but less tuneful Mercury Rev, and Jones and Drozd came onboard. Born in Hawaii to African-American and Filipino parents, Jones wound up in Oklahoma when his father was transferred by the air force. He taught himself to play guitar in his bedroom, developing a swirling calliope sound by using racks of effects and ingenious tricks such as placing a small speaker next to his pickups to create a roar like a million electric razors. (His role in the Lips is similar to Brian Eno's in Roxy Music or Allen Ravenstine's in Pere Ubu, transforming the ordinary into art by injecting the unexpected.) Drozd started playing drums with a polka band in Dallas. He attacks his kit with the bombastic ferocity of Led Zeppelin's John Bonham or Black Sabbath's Bill Ward, but he's also an accomplished pianist and guitar player. "Those guys are both such amazing musicians, I feel sorry that they're stuck with a singer like me," Coyne said, referring to his plaintive Neil Young whine.

The new Lips recorded *Transmissions From the Satellite Heart*, the band's most accessible collection. At their core, songs such as "She Don't Use Jelly" and "Pilot Can at the Queer of God" are simple, catchy rock tunes, albeit ones with highly impressionistic lyrics. The magic comes from the twists and turns and the band's dense wall of sound, which can hold surprises even after dozens of listens. "Moth in the Incubator" is a perfect example. It starts as a lonely acoustic number with Coyne singing, "Something in you / It titters like a moth." Soon, the band kicks into a grinding T. Rex–style riff full of sexual bravado. "Your incubator is so tight / Your incubator is alright," Coyne sings. "Been born before / I'm gettin' used to it / Brain-dead is how it always ends." The song launches into a wonderful hum-along instrumental that builds in intensity as Coyne and Jones pile on layers of harmonics with guitars that buzz like an army of insects on the march, until it finally climaxes in an explosion of dissonance, an epic evocation of nature's cycle of birth, death, and rebirth.

Transmissions was released in mid-1993, and when alternative-rock radio passed on the single "Turn It On," Warners shifted its attention to the next piece of product in the pipeline. "This was a dead, dead, dead record," one executive said. Coyne, thirty-four, and Ivins, thirty-two, knew that it was probably their last shot at making a major-label album. *Hit to Death* sold only sixteen thousand copies, which was dismal by indie standards, let alone a major's. The Lips were determined to convert fans one gig at a time, and so they toured relentlessly. The work began to pay off in the fall of '94 when novelty-starved modern rock radio started playing "She Don't Use Jelly," finally realizing the potential of an irresistibly catchy ditty about tangerines, toast, and Vaseline. The video that Warners rejected because it was directed by Coyne for a mere $12,000 wound up in MTV's Buzz Bin. The band was soon appearing on *The Late Show With David Letterman*, contributing a song to the *Batman Forever* soundtrack, and even guesting on *Beverly Hills 90210*, a move roughly comparable to Amon Düül II appearing on *The Brady Bunch*.

Having proven what they could do on their own, the Lips were in an enviable position when they started recording *Clouds Taste Metallic*.

"We're lucky in the regard that this time, if it flops, it's the record company's fault," Coyne said. "We can't lose now. If we sell a million records, fine. If we sell fifty thousand, it just looks like they fucked up. But it doesn't make doing records any easier, because all that shit really doesn't matter."

True enough. At Studio 7 no one ever mentioned Warner Bros., or MTV, or modern-rock radio. The band concentrated on having fun with the business at hand, crafting thirteen more brilliant and diverse songs for the alien hit parade. Less in-your-face than *Transmissions*, *Clouds* is the Lips' most ambitious album, a sprawling *Pet Sounds*–style work full of different moods and atmospheres but never lacking strong melodies or rock-'n'-roll drive. "The Flaming Lips' music, if it's done right, can reach some guy who walks in off the street liking Lynyrd Skynyrd, Led Zeppelin, and the Stone Temple Pilots," Coyne said. "He can hear Flaming Lips music and not understand that it's being subversive or weird and just think it's good rock 'n' roll. Whereas it's a stretch to be a normal guy and listen to some Sonic Youth or Pavement records."

This attitude may come from where the band lives: There's simply no room for pretension in Oklahoma City, and the band doesn't plan on moving. Coyne and his girlfriend Michelle Martin are the proud owners of a two-level brick building that's vaguely in the style of Frank Lloyd Wright. It stands out from the ramshackle ranch houses even before you notice the gargoyles on the roof and the giant flower sculptures on the balcony. Ivins and Booker share a sort of outbuilding in the back, and Drozd and Jones wind up there whenever they can't be bothered to drive home. The band rehearses there, and it's where Coyne silk-screens the group's posters and prepares its cover art. Most people call the house "the compound," but Wayne prefers "stately Wayne Manor." As unlikely as it seems, the Flaming Lips have created a sort of ideal community based on music, in the middle of Oklahoma in the 90s. "People always ask why we live here, and I say, 'Just look around,'" Coyne said. "You really can't separate the way we work from the way we live."

More than drug use or cosmic concerns, it's this philosophy that links the Flaming Lips to the thirty-year legacy of psychedelic rock. "Success is living a good life," Coyne said. "This is how we wanna live our lives. I don't think people have to agree with it or anything. We just do our trip. Hopefully, the main thing the Flaming Lips stand for is individuality in a sea of conformity—even if conformity isn't what it used to be."

A Select Psychedelic-Rock Discography

In listing releases, critical judgment has been applied for artists who have worked in a variety of styles, and only those albums that can be considered psychedelic rock or those that included important psychedelic-rock songs have been listed. In other cases, including many of the more obscure or less significant artists, only their most noteworthy efforts are included; in other words, the ones that are listed are the ones worth buying. When only one year is listed, it is generally either that of the album's original release or that of a later repackaging or significant CD reissue. A second date following a semicolon signifies the original release date of a rerelease. The label listed is the American company that issued the album on CD, unless otherwise noted.

Absolute Grey
   Green House (Midnight, 1986; 1984)
   What Remains (Midnight, 1986)
AFX
   Analogue Bubblebath EP (Wax Trax!/TVT, 1994)
   see also: The Aphex Twin
The Amboy Dukes
   Journey to the Center of the Mind (Mainstream, 1968)
Amon Düül I
   Airs on a Shoe String (Best of . . .) (Thunderbolt, 1994, Eng.)

Amon Düül II

Phallus Dei (Mantra, 1993, Fr.; 1969)

Yeti (Mantra, 1993, Fr.; 1970)

Dance of the Lemmings (Mantra, 1993, Fr.; 1971)

Wolf City (Mantra, 1993, Fr.; 1972)

Carnival in Babylon (Mantra, 1993, Fr.; 1973)

The Aphex Twin

Selected Ambient Works 82–92 (R&S, 1992, Ger.)

Selected Ambient Works Volume II (Sire, 1994)

Classics (R&S, 1994, Ger.)

. . . I Care Because You Do (Sire, 1995)

see also: AFX, Polygon Window

Arrested Development

3 Years, 5 Months & 2 Days in the Life of . . . (Chrysalis, 1992)

Zingalamaduni (Chrysalis, 1994)

A R Kane

Sixty Nine (Rough Trade, 1988, Eng.)

"i" (Rough Trade, 1989, Eng.)

Ash Ra Tempel

Ash Ra Tempel (Spalax, 1993, Fr.; 1971)

Schwingungen (Spalax, 1993, Fr.; 1971)

Seven Up (Spalax, 1993, Fr.; 1972)

A Tribe Called Quest

People's Instinctive Travels and the Paths of Rhythm (Jive, 1990)

The Low End Theory (Jive, 1991)

Kevin Ayers

Joy of a Toy (Harvest, 1970)

The Bangles

Bangles EP (Faulty Products/I.R.S., 1982)

All Over the Place (Columbia, 1984)

The Barracudas

Drop Out With the Barracudas (Voxx, 1981)

Syd Barrett

The Madcap Laughs (Capitol/EMI, 1990; 1970)

Barrett (Capitol/EMI, 1990; 1970)

The Peel Sessions EP (Strange Fruit, 1987)

Opel (Capitol/EMI, 1988)

Crazy Diamond box set (Capitol/EMI, 1994)

The Beach Boys

Pet Sounds (Capitol, 1966)

Good Vibrations box set (Capitol, 1993)

The Beastie Boys
Paul's Boutique (Capitol, 1989)
The Beatles
Rubber Soul (Capitol, 1965)
Revolver (Capitol, 1966)
Sgt. Pepper's Lonely Hearts Club Band (Capitol, 1967)
Magical Mystery Tour (Capitol, 1967)
The Beatles (Apple, 1968)
Yellow Submarine (Capitol, 1969)
Abbey Road (Apple, 1969)
Beaver and Krause
In a Wild Sanctuary/Gandharva (Warner Bros., 1994; 1970, 1971)
Bedhead
WhatFunLifeWas (Trance Syndicate, 1993)
Captain Beefheart
Safe As Milk/Mirror Man (Castle, 1988, Eng.; 1967)
Trout Mask Replica (Reprise, 1969)
Lick My Decals Off, Baby (Enigma Retro, 1989; 1970)
The Spotlight Kid/Clear Spot (Reprise, 1991; 1972)
Shiny Beast (Bat Chain Puller) (Rhino, 1991; 1978)
Doc at the Radar Station (Virgin, 1980)
Ice Cream for Crow (Blue Plate/Caroline, 1990; 1982)
Chris Bell
I Am the Cosmos (Rykodisc, 1992)
The Bevis Frond
Triptych (Reckless, 1988)
The Auntie Winnie Album (Reckless, 1989)
Big Star
#1 Record/Radio City (Stax, 1992; 1972, 1974)
Third (Rykodisc, 1992; 1978)
Black Sabbath
We Sold Our Soul for Rock 'n' Roll (Warner Bros., 1976)
Blue Cheer
Louder Than God: The Best of Blue Cheer (Rhino, 1986)
Blue Öyster Cult
Workshop of the Telescopes (Legacy/Columbia, 1995)
Blur
Leisure (Food/SBK, 1991)
Modern Life Is Rubbish (Food/SBK, 1993)
Parklife (Food/SBK, 1994)
The Great Escape (Virgin, 1995)

Bongwater
   Double Bummer+ box set (Shimmy-Disc, 1989)
The Boo Radleys
   Everything's Alright Forever (Columbia, 1992)
   Giant Steps (Columbia, 1993)
   Wake Up! (Columbia, 1995)
David Bowie
   Low (Rykodisc, 1991; 1977)
   "Heroes" (Rykodisc, 1991; 1977)
   Lodger (Rykodisc, 1991; 1979)
The Buffalo Springfield
   Retrospective: The Best of the Buffalo Springfield (Atco, 1969)
The Butthole Surfers
   *Psychic . . . Powerless . . . Another Man's Sac/Cream Corn From the Socket
      of Davis* (Touch and Go, 1985)
   Rembrandt Pussyhorse (Touch and Go, 1986)
   Locust Abortion Technician (Touch and Go, 1987)
   Hairway to Steven (Touch and Go, 1988)
   Piouhgd (Rough Trade, 1991)
   Independent Worm Saloon (Capitol, 1993)
   The Hole Truth and Nothing Butt! (Trance Syndicate, 1995)
   Electric Larryland (Capitol, 1996)
The Byrds
   Fifth Dimension (Columbia, 1966)
   Younger Than Yesterday (Columbia, 1967)
   The Byrds box set (Columbia, 1990)
David Byrne and Brian Eno
   My Life in the Bush of Ghosts (Sire, 1981)
John Cale
   Paris 1919 (Reprise, 1973)
   Fear (Island, 1974)
   Slow Dazzle (Island, 1975)
   Helen of Troy (Island, 1975)
   Fragments of a Rainy Season (Hannibal/Rykodisc, 1992)
   Seducing Down the Door: A Collection 1970–1990 (Rhino, 1994)
John Cale and Brian Eno
   Wrong Way Up (Opal/Warner Bros., 1990)
Robert Calvert
   Captain Lockheed and the Starfighters (BGO, 1987, Fr.; 1974)
   Lucky Lief and the Longships (BGO, 1987, Fr.; 1975)
Can
   Monster Movie (Mute/Spoon, 1990; 1969)

Tago Mago (Mute/Spoon, 1990; 1971)
Ege Bamyasi (Mute/Spoon, 1990; 1972)
Future Days (Mute/Spoon, 1990; 1973)
Soon Over Babaluma (Mute/Spoon, 1990; 1974)
Incandescence 1969–1977 (Virgin, 1981)

Cardinal
Cardinal (Flydaddy, 1994)

The Chambers Brothers
Goin' Uptown (Sony Music Special Products, 1991)

The Charlatans U.K.
Some Friendly (Beggars Banquet/RCA, 1990)
Between 10th and 11th (Beggars Banquet/RCA, 1992)
Up to Our Hips (Beggars Banquet/Atlantic, 1994)
The Charlatans U.K. (Beggars Banquet/Atlantic, 1995)

The Chills
Kaleidoscope World (Homestead, 1988)
Brave Words (Homestead, 1988)

The Chocolate Watchband
Rev-enge (SACEM, 1985, Fr.)

The Chud
Silhouettes of Sound (Love's Simple Dreams, 1986, Ger.)

George Clinton
Hey Man . . . Smell My Finger (Paisley Park, 1993)

Cluster
Cluster and Eno (Gyroscope, 1996; 1977)
After the Heat (Gyroscope, 1996; 1978)

The Cocteau Twins
Head Over Heels (4AD, 1983, Eng.)
Treasure (4AD/Capitol, 1984)
Victorialand (English 4AD, 1986)
Blue Bell Knoll (4AD/Capitol, 1988)
Heaven or Las Vegas (4AD/Capitol, 1990)
Milk and Kisses (Capitol, 1996)
Four-Calendar Café (Capitol, 1993)

Coil
Love's Secret Domain (Wax Trax!, 1991)

Bootsy Collins
Back in the Day: The Best of Bootsy Collins (Warner Archives, 1994)

Julian Cope
World Shut Your Mouth (Mercury, 1983)
Fried (Mercury, 1983)
Saint Julian (Island, 1987)

My Nation Underground (Island, 1988)

Peggy Suicide (Island, 1991)

Jehovahkill (Island, 1992)

Autogeddon (American, 1994)

Queen Elizabeth (Echo Special Products, 1994, Eng.)

20 Mothers (American, 1995)

The Count Five

Psychotic Reaction (Edsel, 1994, Eng.; 1966)

Cracker

Kerosene Hat (Virgin, 1993)

The Crazy World of Arthur Brown

The Crazy World of Arthur Brown (Polydor, 1991; 1968)

Strangelands (Reckless, 1988, Eng.)

The Creation

How Does It Feel to Feel? (Edsel, 1982, Eng.)

Lay the Ghost (Cohesion, 1993, Eng.)

Cul de Sac

I don't want to go to bed. (Flying Nun, 1995, New Zealand)

China Gate (Thirsty Ear, 1996)

Culture Club

At Worst . . . The Best of Boy George and Culture Club (SBK, 1993)

Cypress Hill

Black Sunday (Columbia, 1993)

Damon and Naomi

More Sad Hits (Shimmy-Disc, 1992)

The Wondrous World of Damon & Naomi (Sub Pop, 1995)

The Darkside

All That Noise (Beggars Banquet/RCA, 1991)

Das Damen

Jupiter Eye (SST, 1987)

Triskaidekaphobe (SST, 1988)

Marshmellow Conspiracy EP (SST, 1988)

Richard Davies

There's Never Been a Crowd Like This (Flydaddy, 1996)

Deee-Lite

World Clique (Elektra, 1990)

De La Soul

3 Feet High and Rising (Tommy Boy, 1989)

De La Soul Is Dead (Tommy Boy, 1991)

Buhlōōne Mind State (Tommy Boy, 1993)

Digable Planets

Reachin' (a new refutation of time and space) (Elektra, 1993)

Blowout Comb (Elektra, 1994)

Digital Underground
Sex Packets (Tommy Boy, 1990)

Dinosaur Jr
You're Living All Over Me (SST, 1987)
Bug (SST, 1988)

The Divine Styler
Spiral Walls Containing Autumns of Light (Giant, 1992)

Dome
Dome 1. 2. (Mute, 1992; 1980, 1981)
Dome 3. 4. (Mute, 1992; 1981, 1982)

Donovan
Troubadour: The Definitive Collection, 1964–1976 (Epic/Legacy, 1992)

Nick Drake
Fruit Tree: The Complete Works of Nick Drake box set
    (Hannibal/Rykodisc, 1986)

The Dream Academy
The Dream Academy (Warner Bros., 1985)
Remembrance Days (Reprise, 1987)
A Different Kind of Weather (Reprise, 1991)

The Dream Syndicate
The Days of Wine and Roses (Slash, 1993)

The Dukes of Stratosphear
Chips From the Chocolate Fireball (An Anthology) (Geffen, 1988)

Dumptruck
D Is for Dumptruck (Big Time, 1985; 1983)
Positively Dumptruck (Big Time, 1986)

Durutti Column
The First Four Albums box set (Factory, 1988, Eng.)

Echo and the Bunnymen
Crocodiles (Sire, 1980)

Elektric Music
Esperanto (Atlantic, 1993)

Brian Eno
Here Come the Warm Jets (EG, 1973)
Taking Tiger Mountain (By Strategy) (EG, 1974)
Another Green World (EG, 1975)
Discreet Music (EG, 1975)
Before and After Science (EG, 1977)
Music for Films (EG, 1978)
Music for Airports (EG, 1978)
On Land (EG, 1978)

Thursday Afternoon (EG, 1985)

Nerve Net (Opal/Warner Bros., 1992)

The Shutov Assembly (Opal/Warner Bros., 1992)

Roky Erickson

Roky Erickson and the Aliens (CBS International, 1980, Eng.)

Don't Slander Me (Pink Dust/Enigma, 1986)

You're Gonna Miss Me: The Best of Roky Erickson (Restless, 1991)

All That May Do My Rhyme (Trance Syndicate, 1995)

Eugenius

Oomalama (Atlantic, 1992)

Mary Queen of Scots (Atlantic, 1994)

Experimental Audio Research

Mesmerised (Sympathy for the Record Industry, 1994)

Beyond the Pale (Big Cat, 1996)

Fairport Convention

Heyday: BBC Radio Sessions 1968–69 (Hannibal, 1987)

th' faith healers

lido (Too Pure/Elektra, 1992)

imaginary friend (Too Pure/Elektra, 1994)

Faust

Faust (Polydor, 1971)

Faust So Far (Polydor, 1972)

The Faust Tapes (Virgin, 1973, Eng.)

Faust IV (Virgin, 1973, Eng.)

The Feelies

Crazy Rhythms (A&M, 1991; 1980)

The Good Earth (Twin/Tone-Coyote, 1986)

Only Life (Coyote-A&M, 1988)

Time for a Witness (Coyote-A&M, 1991)

see also: The Trypes, Wake Ooloo, Yung Wu

The Flaming Lips

Hear It Is (Pink Dust, 1986)

Oh My Gawd!!! . . . The Flaming Lips (Restless, 1987)

Telepathic Surgery (Restless, 1989)

In a Priest Driven Ambulance (Restless, 1990)

Hit to Death in the Future Head (Warner Bros., 1992)

Transmissions From the Satellite Heart (Warner Bros., 1993)

Clouds Taste Metallic (Warner Bros., 1995)

Flying Saucer Attack

Flying Saucer Attack (VHF, 1993)

CDs Destroy Music (VHF, 1994)

Chorus (Drag City, 1996)

John Frankovic

Under the Water Lilly (Midnight, 1994)

Robert Fripp and Brian Eno

The Essential Fripp and Eno (Caroline, 1994)

Funkadelic

Funkadelic (Westbound, 1970)

Free Your Mind and Your Ass Will Follow (Westbound, 1970)

Maggot Brain (Westbound, 1971)

America Eats Its Young (Westbound, 1972)

Cosmic Slop (Westbound, 1973)

Standing on the Verge of Getting It On (Westbound, 1974)

Tales of Kidd Funkadelic (Warner Bros., 1976)

Hardcore Jollies (Warner Bros., 1976)

One Nation Under a Groove (Warner Bros., 1978)

Uncle Jam Wants You (Warner Bros., 1979)

The Electric Spanking of War Babies (Warner Bros., 1981)

The Fuzztones

Lysergic Emanations (Pink Dust, 1985)

Peter Gabriel

Peter Gabriel (Atco, 1977)

Peter Gabriel (Atlantic, 1978)

Peter Gabriel (Mercury, 1980)

Peter Gabriel (Security) (Geffen, 1982)

Galaxie 500

Today (Rough Trade, 1991)

On Fire (Rough Trade, 1989)

This Is Our Music (Rough Trade, 1990)

Game Theory

The Big Shot Chronicles (Enigma, 1986)

Ron Geesin

A Raise of Eyebrows/As He Stands (See for Miles, 1995, Eng.; 1967, 1973)

Genesis

Trespass (MCA, 1980; 1970)

Nursery Cryme (MCA, 1980; 1971)

Foxtrot (Atlantic, 1972)

Genesis Live (Atlantic, 1973)

Selling England by the Pound (Atlantic, 1973)

The Lamb Lies Down on Broadway (Atco, 1974)

David Gilmour

David Gilmour (Columbia, 1978)

The Grateful Dead

The Grateful Dead (Warner Bros., 1967)

Anthem of the Sun (Warner Bros., 1968)

Aoxomoxoa (Warner Bros., 1969)

Live/Dead (Warner Bros., 1970)

Harmonia

Music Von Harmonia (Germanofon, 1994; 1974)

Harmonia Deluxe (Germanofon, 1994; 1975)

Harmony Rockets

Paralyzed Mind of the Archangel Void (Excelsior, 1995)

see also: Mercury Rev

George Harrison

Wonderwall Music (Capitol, 1968)

Hawkwind

In Search of Space (United Artists, 1971)

Doremi Fasol Latido (United Artists, 1972)

Space Ritual (United Artists, 1973)

Hall of the Mountain Grill (United Artists, 1974)

Warrior on the Edge of Time (Atco, 1975)

25 Years On 1973–1977 box set (Griffin Music, 1994)

Jimi Hendrix

Are You Experienced? (MCA, 1993; 1967)

Axis: Bold as Love (MCA, 1993; 1968)

Electric Ladyland (MCA, 1993; 1968)

Band of Gypsys (MCA, 1995; 1970)

His Name Is Alive

Livonia (4AD, 1990, Eng.)

Robyn Hitchcock

Black Snake Diamond Röle (Rhino, 1995; 1985)

I Often Dream of Trains (Rhino, 1995; 1984)

Fegmania! (Rhino, 1995; 1985), with the Egyptians

Element of Light (Rhino, 1995; 1986), with the Egyptians

Invisible Hitchock (Rhino, 1995; 1986)

Globe of Frogs (A&M, 1988), with the Egyptians

Queen Elvis (A&M, 1989), with the Egyptians

Eye (Rhino, 1995; 1990)

Perspex Island (A&M, 1991), with the Egyptians

Respect (A&M, 1993), with the Egyptians

You & Oblivion (Rhino, 1995)

The Hoodoo Gurus

Stoneage Romeos (Big Time/A&M, 1983)

Hugo Largo

Drum (Opal/Warner Bros., 1988; 1987)

Mettle (Opal/Warner Bros., 1989)

Hüsker Dü
Everything Falls Apart (Reflex, 1982)
Metal Circus (Reflex/SST, 1983)
Zen Arcade (SST, 1984)
New Day Rising (SST, 1985)
Flip Your Wig (SST, 1985)
Candy Apple Grey (Warner Bros., 1986)
Warehouse: Songs and Stories (Warner Bros., 1987)
Everything Falls Apart and More (Rhino, 1993)

The Hypstrz
Hypstrization! (Voxx, 1980)
see also: The Mighty Mofos

The Incredible String Band
The Incredible String Band (Rykodisc, 1994; 1966)
The 5000 Spirits or the Layers of the Onion (Rykodisc, 1994; 1967)
The Hangman's Beautiful Daughter (Rykodisc, 1994; 1967)
Wee Tam & The Big Huge (Rykodisc, 1994; 1968)

The Irresistible Force
Dream Fish (Big High Productions, 1993)
Chill Out or Die! (Big High Productions, 1993)
Flying High (Rising High/Instinct, 1993)

The Jefferson Airplane
Jefferson Airplane Loves You box set (RCA, 1992)

The Jesus and Mary Chain
Psychocandy (Reprise, 1985)
Darklands (Blanco y Negro/Warner Bros., 1987)
Barbed Wire Kisses (Blanco y Negro/Warner Bros., 1988)
Stoned & Dethroned (American, 1994)
The Jesus and Mary Chain Hate Rock 'n' Roll (American, 1995)

Janis Joplin
18 Essential Songs (Legacy/Columbia, 1995)

The Jungle Brothers
Straight Out the Jungle (Warlock, 1988)

Kaleidoscope
Egyptian Candy (A Collection) (Epic/Legacy, 1991)

Katrina and the Waves
Shock Horror! (Aftermath, 1983, Eng.), as the Waves
Katrina and the Waves (Capitol, 1985)

King Crimson
In the Court of the Crimson King (EG, 1989; 1969)
Sleepless/The Concise King Crimson (Caroline, 1993)

The Kinks
(The Kinks Are) The Village Green Preservation Society (Reprise, 1969)

Kraftwerk

Kraftwerk (Germanofon, 1994; 1972)

Kraftwerk 2 (Germanofon, 1994; 1972)

Ralf and Florian (Germanofon, 1994; 1973)

Autobahn (Elektra, 1974)

Radio-Activity (Capitol, 1975)

Trans-Europe Express (Capitol, 1977)

The Man Machine (Capitol, 1978)

Computer World (Elektra, 1981)

Electric Café (Elektra, 1986)

see also: Organisation

LaBradford

Prazision LP (Kranky, 1994)

A Stable Reference Point (Kranky, 1995)

La Düsseldorf

La Düsseldorf (Nova, 1976)

Laika

Silver Apples of the Moon (Too Pure/American, 1995)

Peter Laughner

Take the Guitar Player for a Ride (Tim/Kerr, 1994)

Led Zeppelin

Led Zeppelin (Atlantic, 1969)

Untitled (Atlantic, 1971)

Houses of the Holy (Atlantic, 1973)

Physical Graffiti (Atlantic, 1975)

The Lime Spiders

The Cave Comes Alive! (Virgin, 1987)

The Long Ryders

10–5–60/Native Sons (Frontier, 1992; 1983, 1984)

Loop

Heaven's End (Head, 1987, Eng.)

The World in Your Eyes (Head, 1988, Eng.)

Fade Out (Rough Trade, 1989; 1988)

A Gilded Eternity (Beggars Banquet/RCA, 1990)

Lothar and the Hand People

Presenting . . . Lothar and the Hand People (CEMA Special Markets, 1994; 1968)

Love

Love (Elektra, 1966)

Da Capo (Elektra, 1967)

Forever Changes (Elektra, 1968)

Love Story 1966–1972 box set (Elektra Traditions/Rhino, 1995)

Low
> *I Could Live in Hope* (Vernon Yard, 1994)
> *Long Division* (Vernon Yard, 1995)

Luna
> *Lunapark* (Elektra, 1992)
> *Bewitched* (Elektra, 1994)
> *Penthouse* (Elektra, 1995)

Lush
> *Gala* (Reprise, 1990)
> *Split* (Reprise, 1994)
> *Lovelife* (Reprise, 1996)

Magic Hour
> *No Excess Is Absurd* (Twisted Village, 1994)
> *Will They Turn You On or Will They Turn on You* (Twisted
>   Village, 1995)

Phil Manzanera
> *The Manzanera Collection* (Caroline, 1995)

The Marshmallow Overcoat
> *The Marshmallow Overcoat: 1986–1990* (Get Hip, 1990)

Nick Mason
> *Nick Mason's Fictitious Sports* (Columbia, 1981)

Massive Attack
> *Blue Lines* (Virgin, 1992)
> *Protection* (Virgin, 1995)

The Master Musicians of Joujouka
> *Brian Jones Presents the Pipes of Pan at Joujouka* (Virgin, 1971)

Matching Mole
> *Matching Mole* (BGO, 1972, Fr.)
> *Matching Mole's Little Red Record* (BGO, 1972, Fr.)

Eric Matthews
> *It's Heavy in Here* (Sub Pop, 1994)

The MC5
> *Kick out the Jams* (Elektra, 1969)
> *Back in the USA* (Rhino, 1992; 1970)
> *High Time* (Rhino, 1992; 1971)

The Meat Puppets
> *Up on the Sun* (SST, 1985)
> *Mirage* (SST, 1987)
> *Huevos* (SST, 1987)

Mercury Rev
> *Yerself Is Steam* (Columbia, 1992; 1991)
> *Boces* (Columbia, 1993)

See You on the Other Side (Work/Columbia, 1995)
see also: Harmony Rockets

The Mighty Mofos

Sho' Hard! (Treehouse, 1988)
see also: The Hypstrz

The Miracle Workers

Inside Out (Voxx, 1985)
Primary Domain (Glitterhouse, 1989, Ger.)
Moxie's Revenge (Get Hip, 1990)

Mission of Burma

Mission of Burma (Rykodisc, 1988)

Moby

Go Remixes (Instinct, 1991)
Moby (Instinct, 1992)
Move EP (Elektra, 1993)
Early Underground (Instinct, 1993)
Everything Is Wrong (Elektra, 1995)

Moby Grape

Vintage: The Very Best of Moby Grape (Columbia/Legacy, 1993)

The Mod Fun

Dorothy's Dream (Midnight, 1986)
Past Forward (Get Hip, 1995)

The Moles

Untune the Sky (Seaside, 1992, Eng.)
Instinct (Flydaddy, 1994)

The Monkees

Greatest Hits (Rhino, 1995)

The Moody Blues

In Search of the Lost Chord (Deram, 1968)

Moonshake

Eva Luna (Too Pure/Matador/Atlantic, 1993)
Big Good Angel (Too Pure/Matador, 1994)
The Sound Your Eyes Can Follow (Too Pure/American, 1994)

The Move

The Early Years (Earl, 1992, Fr.)

My Bloody Valentine

Ecstasy and Strawberry Wine (Lazy, 1987, Eng.)
Isn't Anything (Sire/Warner Bros., 1988)
Glider EP (Sire, 1989)
Tremolo EP (Sire/Warner Bros., 1991)
Loveless (Sire/Warner Bros., 1991)

Neu!
  Neu! (I) (Germanofon, 1994; 1972)
  Neu! (II) (Germanofon, 1994; 1973)
  Neu! (III) (Germanofon, 1994; 1975)
Colin Newman
  A-Z (Beggars Banquet, 1980)
  provisionally entitled the singing fish (4AD, 1981, Eng.)
  Not To (4AD, 1982, Eng.)
  Commercial Suicide (Restless, 1986)
  It Seems (Restless, 1988)
Nico
  Chelsea Girl (Verve, 1968)
  The Marble Index (Elektra, 1969)
  Desert Shore (Reprise, 1971)
The Nomads
  Outburst (Homestead, 1984)
Oasis
  Definitely Maybe (Creation/Epic, 1994)
  (What's the Story) Morning Glory (Creation/Epic, 1995)
Mike Oldfield
  Tubular Bells (Virgin, 1973)
  Hergest Ridge (Virgin, 1974)
  Ommadawn (Virgin, 1975)
  Exposed (Virgin, 1979)
  Elements box set (Virgin, 1993)
Yoko Ono
  Onobox (Rykodisc, 1992)
Opal
  Happy Nightmare Baby LP (SST, 1987)
The Orb
  Adventures Beyond the Ultraworld (Big Life/Mercury, 1991)
  Peel Sessions EP (Dutch East India, 1991)
  U.F.Orb (Big Life/Mercury, 1992)
  Live 93 (Island, 1993)
  Pomme Fritz (Island, 1994)
  Orbus Terrarum (Island, 1995)
Orbital
  Orbital I (ffrr, 1992)
  Orbital II (ffrr, 1993)
  Snivilisation (ffrr, 1994)
Organisation
  Tone Float (Germanofon, 1994; 1970)
  see also: Kraftwerk

Parliament
Up for the Down Stroke (Casablanca, 1974)
Chocolate City (Casablanca, 1975)
Mothership Connection (Casablanca, 1976)
The Clones of Dr. Funkenstein (Casablanca, 1976)
Funkentelechy vs. the Placebo Syndrome (Casablanca, 1977)
Motor-Booty Affair (Casablanca, 1978)
Gloryhallastoopid—or Pin the Tail on the Funky (Casablanca, 1979)
Trombipulation (Casablanca, 1981)

The Peanut Butter Conspiracy
The Great Peanut Butter Conspiracy (Sony Music Special
    Products, 1992)

Pere Ubu
The Modern Dance (Rough Trade, 1981; 1977)
Dub Housing (Rough Trade, 1981; 1977)
Terminal Tower: An Archival Collection (Twin/Tone, 1985)
The Tenement Year (Enigma, 1988)
Cloudland (Mercury/Fontana, 1989)
Story of My Life (Imago, 1993)
Raygun Suitcase (Tim/Kerr, 1995)

Lee "Scratch" Perry
The Upsetter Compact Set (Trojan, 1988)

Tom Petty and the Heartbreakers
Greatest Hits (MCA, 1993)

Pink Floyd
The Piper at the Gates of Dawn (Capitol, 1967)
A Saucerful of Secrets (Capitol, 1968)
Ummagumma (Capitol, 1969)
More (Capitol, 1969)
Atom Heart Mother (Capitol, 1970)
Meddle (Capitol, 1971)
The Dark Side of the Moon (Capitol, 1973)
Wish You Were Here (Columbia, 1975)
Animals (Columbia, 1977)
The Wall (Columbia, 1979)
Shine On box set (Columbia, 1992)

Plan 9
Dealing With the Dead (Midnight, 1984)

Plasticland
Plasticland (Pink Dust/Enigma, 1985)
Wonder Wonderful Wonderland (Pink Dust/Enigma, 1985)
Salon (Pink Dust/Enigma, 1987)
Dapper Snappings (German Repulsion, 1994)

Plastikman

Sheet One (Novamute, 1994)

Musik (Novamute, 1995)

PM Dawn

Of the Heart, of the Soul and of the Cross: The Utopian Experience (Island, 1991)

The Bliss Album . . . ? (Vibrations of Love and Anger and the Ponderance of Life and Existence) (Island, 1993)

Jesus Wept (Island, 1995)

Polara

Polara (Clean, 1995)

Polygon Window

Surfing on the Sine Waves (Wax Trax!/TVT, 1993)

see also: The Aphex Twin

Popol Vuh

Affenstunde (Spalax, 1993, Fr.; 1971)

Aguirre/In Den Gärten Pharaos (Spalax, 1992, Fr.; 1975, 1972)

Best of Popol Vuh From the Films of Werner Herzog (Milan, 1993)

Porno for Pyros

Porno for Pyros (Warner Bros., 1993)

Good Gods-Urge (Warner Bros., 1996)

Portishead

Dummy (Go! Discs/London, 1994)

Pram

The Stars Are So Big the Earth Is So Small (English Too Pure, 1993)

Helium (Too Pure/American, 1995)

Sargasso Sea (Too Pure/American, 1995)

The Pretty Things

Emotions (Edsel, 1987, Eng.; 1967)

S.F. Sorrow (Edsel, 1987, Eng.; 1969)

Parachute (Edsel, 1987, Eng.; 1970)

Prince

Purple Rain (Warner Bros., 1984)

Around the World in a Day (Warner Bros., 1985)

The Prisoners

Revenge of the Prisoners (Pink Dust, 1984)

Procol Harum

Chapter One: Turning Back the Page 1967–1991 (Zoo, 1991)

The Psychedelic Furs

The Psychedelic Furs (Columbia, 1980)

Talk Talk Talk (Columbia, 1981)

Forever Now (Columbia, 1982)

Quicksilver Messenger Service
Sons of Mercury (1968–1975) (Rhino, 1991)
The Rain Parade
Emergency Third Rail Power Trip/Explosions in the Glass Palace (Restless, 1984; 1983, 1984)
Crashing Dream (Island, 1986)
The Ramones
Acid Eaters (Radioactive, 1994)
The Red Crayola
The Parable of Arable Land/God Bless the Red Crayola and All Who Sail on Her (Decal, 1990, Fr.; 1967, 1968)
Red Red Meat
Jimmywine Majestic (Sub Pop, 1994)
Bunny Gets Paid (Sub Pop, 1995)
Lou Reed
Berlin (RCA, 1973)
Metal Machine Music (RCA, 1975)
The Blue Mask (RCA, 1982)
R.E.M.
Chronic Town EP (I.R.S., 1982)
Murmur (I.R.S., 1983)
Fables of the Reconstruction (I.R.S., 1985)
Kimberley Rew
The Bible of Bop (Press, 1982)
Ride
Smile (Sire/Reprise, 1990)
Nowhere (Sire/Reprise, 1990)
Going Blank Again (Sire/Reprise, 1992)
Carnival of Light (Sire/Reprise, 1994)
Tarantula (Sire, 1996)
Paul Roland
Danse Macabre (Bam Caruso, 1987)
The Rolling Stones
Aftermath (Abkco, 1966)
Between the Buttons (Abkco, 1967)
Their Satanic Majesties Request (Abkco, 1967)
Exile on Main Street (Abkco, 1972)
Hot Rocks 1964–71 (Abkco, 1972)
More Hot Rocks: Big Hits and Fazed Cookies (Abkco, 1972)
Michael Rother
Flammende Herzen (Sky, 1976)
Fernwarme (Polydor, 1981)

Roxy Music

Roxy Music (Island, 1972)

For Your Pleasure (Island, 1973)

Stranded (Island, 1974)

Country Life (Island, 1974)

Siren (Island, 1975)

Todd Rundgren

Something/Anything? (Warner Bros., 1972)

A Wizard/A True Star (Warner Bros., 1973)

Hermit of Mink Hollow (Warner Bros., 1978)

Sabalon Glitz

Ufonic (Trixie, 1994)

The Salvation Army

Befour Three O'Clock (Frontier, 1985)

see also: The Three O'Clock

Santana

Dance of the Rainbow Serpent box set (Legacy/Columbia, 1995)

Klaus Schulze

Kluas Schulze: The Essential '72–'93 (Caroline, 1993)

The Seeds

The Seeds/A Web of Sound (GNP/Crescendo, 1987; 1966)

See Feel

Quique (Too Pure/Caroline, 1994)

The Shamen

What's Going Down? EP (Moksha-Communion, 1988)

In Gorbachev We Trust (Moksha-Demon, 1989)

En-Tact (Epic, 1991)

Boss Drum (Epic, 1993)

Silver Apples

Silver Apples/Contact (TRC, 1994, Ger.; 1968, 1969)

Slipstream

Slipstream (Carrot Top, 1995)

Slowdive

Just for a Day (Creation, 1991, Eng.)

Souvlaki (Creation/SBK, 1994)

Sly and the Family Stone

Anthology (Epic, 1973)

There's a Riot Goin' On (Epic, 1971)

The Small Faces

There Are But Four Small Faces (Sony, 1991; 1967)

Ogden's Nut Gone Flake (Sony, 1991; 1968)

Kendra Smith
  Five Ways of Disappearing (4AD, 1995)
The Soft Boys
  A Can of Bees (Rykodisc, 1992; 1979)
  Underwater Moonlight (Rykodisc, 1992; 1980)
  Invisible Hits (Rykodisc, 1992; 1983)
  1976–91 (Rykodisc, 1993)
The Soft Machine
  Volumes One and Two (Big Beat, 1989, Eng.; 1968)
Sonic Youth
  Bad Moon Rising (Homestead, 1985)
  EVOL (SST, 1986)
  Sister (SST, 1987)
  Daydream Nation (Enigma/Blast First, 1988)
Soundgarden
  Superunknown (A&M, 1994)
Sound Patrol
  Sweetened—No Lemon (Organico, 1995)
  see also: Symbols & Instruments
Spacemen 3
  Sound of Confusion (Taang!, 1994; 1986)
  The Perfect Prescription (Taang!, 1994; 1987)
  Performance (Taang!, 1994; 1988)
  Playing With Fire (Taang!, 1994; 1989)
  Recurring (Dedicated/RCA, 1991)
  Taking Drugs to Make Music to Take Drugs to (Bomp, 1994)
Space Time Continuum
  Sea Biscuit (Caroline, 1994)
  Alien Dreamtime (Caroline, 1994)
  Emit Ecaps (Caroline, 1996)
Spectrum
  Spectrum (Silvertone, 1990)
  Soul Kiss (Glide Divine) (Silvertone, 1994)
Speed the Plough
  Speed the Plough (East Side Digital, 1991; 1989)
  Wonder Wheel (East Side Digital, 1991)
  Mason's Box (East Side Digital, 1993)
  Marina (East Side Digital, 1995)
  see also: The Trypes
Skip Spence
  Oar (Sony Music Special Products, 1991; 1969)

Spiritualized

Lazer Guided Melodies (Dedicated/RCA, 1992)

Pure Phase (Dedicated/RCA, 1992)

Stereolab

Peng! (Too Pure/American, 1992)

Switched On Stereolab (Too Pure/American, 1992)

The Groop Played Space Age Batchelor Pad Music (Too Pure/American, 1993)

Transient Random Noise Bursts With Announcements (Elektra, 1993)

Mars Audiac Quintet (Elektra, 1994)

Refried Ectoplasm [Switched On Volume 2] (Drag City, 1995)

Emperor Tomato Ketchup (Elektra, 1996)

The Stooges

The Stooges (Elektra, 1969)

Fun House (Elektra, 1970)

Donna Summer

The Donna Summer Anthology (Polygram, 1993)

Sun Ra

The Heliocentric Worlds of Sun Ra, I (ESP, 1965)

The Heliocentric Worlds of Sun Ra II (ESP, 1966)

Symbols & Instruments

Mood EP (KMS, 1988)

see also: Sound Patrol

Talking Heads

More Songs About Buildings and Food (Sire, 1978)

Fear of Music (Sire, 1979)

Remain in Light (Sire, 1980)

Talk Talk

Spirit of Eden (EMI, 1988)

Natural History: The Very Best of Talk Talk (EMI, 1990)

Tangerine Dream

In the Beginning box set (Relativity, 1985)

The Teardrop Explodes

Kilimanjaro (Skyclad, 1988; 1980)

Wilder (Skyclad, 1989; 1981)

Everybody Wants to Shag . . . The Teardrop Explodes (Fontana, 1990)

Teenage Fanclub

A Catholic Education (Matador, 1990)

The King (Creation, 1991; Eng.)

Bandwagonesque (DGC, 1991)

Television

Marquee Moon (Elektra, 1977)

The Television Personalities
. . . And Don't the Kids Just Love It (Razor & Tie, 1995; 1980)
The Painted World (Illuminated, 1984, Eng.)
Yes Darling, But Is It Art? (Early Singles and Rarities) (Seed, 1995)

The Temptations
Cloud Nine/Puzzle People (Gordy, 1986; 1969)
Psychedelic Shack (Motown, 1970)

Thin White Rope
Exploring the Axis (Frontier, 1985)
Moonhead (Frontier, 1987)

The 13th Floor Elevators
The Psychedelic Sounds of the 13th Floor Elevators/Live (Decal, 1988, Fr.;
    1967, 1968)
Easter Everywhere/Bull of the Woods (Decal, 1988; 1967, 1968)

The Three O'Clock
Sixteen Tambourines/Baroque Hoedown (Frontier, 1991; 1982, 1983)
Arrive Without Travelling (I.R.S., 1985)
see also: The Salvation Army

Tiny Lights
Hot Chocolate Massage (Uriel, 1986)
Hazel's Wreath (Gaia, 1988)
Prayer for the Halcyon Fear (Absolute A Go Go, 1990; 1986)
Stop the Sun I Want to Go Home (Dr. Dream, 1992)
Milky Juicy (Dr. Dream, 1994)
The Young Person's Guide to Tiny Lights (Bar/None, 1995)

Tomorrow
Tomorrow (See for Miles, 1991, Eng.; 1968)

The Troggs
Archeology (1967–1977) (Mercury, 1992)

Tricky
Maxinquaye (Island, 1995)

The Trypes
The Explorers Hold EP (Coyote, 1984)
see also: The Feelies, Speed the Plough

Nik Turner
Space Ritual 1994 Live (Cleopatra, 1995)

The 27 Various
Hi. (Susstones, 1987)
Yes, Indeed (Susstones, 1989)
Approximately (Clean, 1990)
Up (Clean, 1992)
Fine (Clean, 1992)
see also: Polara

Ultramarine

Every Man and Woman Is a Star (Rough Trade, 1992)

United Kingdom (Sire/Giant, 1993)

Ultra Vivid Scene

Ultra Vivid Scene (4AD/Rough Trade, 1988)

Joy 1967–1990 (4AD/Columbia, 1990)

The United States of America

The United States of America (Sony Music Special Products, 1992; 1968)

U2

Achtung Baby (Island, 1991)

Zooropa (Island, 1993)

VapourSpace

Gravitational Arch of 10 (ffrr, 1993)

Various Artists: Compilations and Tributes

Battle of the Garages 1 & 2 (Voxx, 1994; 1981, 1982)

Best of Techno, volumes 1–3 (Profile, 1993)

California Dreaming (ffrr, 1993)

Ethnotechno (Wax Trax!/TVT, 1994)

Excursions in Ambience (Caroline, 1993)

Excursions in Ambience: The Second Orbit (Caroline, 1993)

Excursions in Ambience: The Third Dimension (Caroline, 1994)

Excursions in Ambience: The Fourth Frontier (Caroline, 1995)

Garage Sale cassette compilation (ROIR, 1985)

Nuggets: Original Artyfacts From the First Psychedelic Era, 1965–1968 (Sire, 1976; 1972)

Rainy Day (Rough Trade, 1989)

Where the Pyramid Meets the Eye: A Tribute to Roky Erickson (Sire/Warner Bros., 1991)

Whore: Various Artists Play Wire (WMO, 1996)

Velvet Crush

In the Presence of Greatness (Ringers Lactate, 1991)

Teenage Symphonies to God (Creation/Epic, 1994)

The Velvet Monkeys

Future (Fountain of Youth, 1983)

Rotting Corpse au Go-Go (Shimmy-Disc, 1989)

The Velvet Underground

The Velvet Underground and Nico (Verve/Polygram, 1985; 1967)

White Light/White Heat (Verve/Polygram, 1985; 1967)

The Velvet Underground (Verve/Polygram, 1985; 1969)

Loaded (Cotillion, 1970)

V.U. (Polygram, 1985)

Another View (Polygram, 1986)

The Vipers
Outta the Nest (PVC, 1984)
Viva Saturn
Viva Saturn (Heyday, 1990)
Brightside (Restless, 1995)
Wake Ooloo
Hear No Evil (Pravda, 1994)
What About It (Pravda, 1995)
see also: The Feelies
Ween
God Ween Satan—The Oneness (Twin/Tone, 1990)
The Pod (Shimmy-Disc, 1991)
The Who
The Who Sell Out (MCA, 1967)
Wild Carnation
Tricycle (Delmore, 1995)
Wire
Pink Flag (Restless Retro, 1989; 1977)
Chairs Missing (Restless Retro, 1989; 1978)
154 (Restless, Retro, 1989; 1979)
Behind the Curtain (EMI, 1995, Eng.)
Stevie Wonder
Music of My Mind (Motown, 1972)
Talking Book (Tamla, 1972)
Innervisions (Motown, 1973)
Songs in the Key of Life (Tamla, 1976)
Rick Wright
Wet Dream (Columbia, 1978)
Robert Wyatt
Rock Bottom (Virgin, 1974)
Ruth Is Stranger Than Richard (Virgin, 1975)
XTC
Drums and Wires (Geffen, 1984; 1979)
Black Sea (Geffen, 1984; 1980)
English Settlement (Geffen, 1984; 1982)
Mummer (Geffen, 1984)
The Big Express (Geffen, 1984)
Skylarking (Geffen, 1986)
Oranges & Lemons (Geffen, 1989)
Nonsuch (Geffen, 1992)
The Yardbirds
Over Under Sideways Down (Epic, 1966)
The Yardbirds, Vol. 2: Blues, Backtracks and Shapes of Things (Sony, 1991)

Yard Trauma
    Must've Been Something I Took Last Night (Dionysius, 1985)
The Yellow Sunshine Explosion
    The Yellow Sunshine Explosion (Love's Simple Dreams, 1987, Ger.)
Yo La Tengo
    New Wave Hot Dogs/President Yo La Tengo (Coyote-Twin/Tone, 1989;
       1987, 1989)
    May I Sing With Me (Alias, 1992)
    Painful (Matador/Atlantic, 1993)
    Electr-O-Pura (Matador/Atlantic, 1995)
Neil Young
    Decade (Reprise, 1977)
Yum-Yum
    Dan Loves Patti (TAG, 1996)
Yung Wu
    Shore Leave (Coyotoe-Twin/Tone, 1987)
    see also: The Feelies
Frank Zappa and the Mothers of Invention
    Freak Out! (Rykodisc, 1995; 1966)
    Absolutely Free (Rykodisc, 1995; 1967)
    We're Only in It for the Money (Rykodisc, 1995; 1968)
The Zombies
    Odyssey and Oracle (Rhino, 1987; 1968)

Endnotes

Throughout the text, quotations that are not otherwise cited have been taken from interviews with the author, most of which were conducted between 1993 and 1995. Complete information on all booklength works cited below appears in the Bibliography.

Chapter 1   My White Bicycle: The Origins and Hallmarks of Psychedelic Rock

1. Peter Stafford, *Psychedelics Encyclopedia*, p. 1.
2. Albert Hofmann, *LSD, My Problem Child*, p. 15.
3. Ibid., p. 19.
4. Stafford, *Psychedelics Encyclopedia*, pp. 4–5.
5. Marion A. Lee and Bruce Shlain, *Acid Dreams*, p. 57.
6. Stafford, *Psychedelics Encyclopedia*, p. 49.
7. Charles Perry, *The Haight-Ashbury*, p. 7.
8. David Crosby and Carl Gottlieb, *Long Time Gone*, p. 76.
9. Tom Wolfe, *The Electric Kool-Aid Acid Test*, p. 247.
10. Leigh A. Henderson and William J. Glass, *LSD: Still With Us After All These Years*, p. 4.

11. Hofmann, *LSD, My Problem Child*, p. 15.
12. Alan Watts, *The Joyous Cosmology*, p. 33.
13. Timothy Leary, *Flashbacks*, p. 34.
14. Eric Tamm, *Brian Eno: His Music and the Vertical Color of Sound*, p. 17.
15. Nick Tosches, *Unsung Heroes of Rock 'n' Roll*, p. 160.
16. R. A. Durr, *Poetic Vision and the Psychedelic Experience*, p. ix.
17. Leary, *Flashbacks*, p. 32.
18. Stafford, *Psychedelics Encyclopedia*, p. 5.
19. Camille Paglia, *Vamps & Tramps*, p. 20.
20. Jay Stevens, *Storming Heaven*, p. 368.

Chapter 2   Why Don't We Sing This Song All Together?: The Psychedelic Beach Boys, Beatles, and Rolling Stones

1. Peter Brown and Steven Gaines, *The Love You Make*, pp. 226–27.
2. Steven Gaines, *Heroes & Villains*, p. 133.
3. Brian Wilson and Todd Gold, *Wouldn't It Be Nice*, p. 117.
4. Ibid., p. 205.

5. Ibid., p. 141.

6. Timothy White, *The Nearest Faraway Place*, p. 258.

7. Gaines, *Heroes & Villains*, p. 142.

8. Wilson and Gold, *Wouldn't It Be Nice*, p. 138.

9. Richard Goldstein, *Goldstein's Greatest Hits*, p. 148.

10. Mark Lewisohn, *The Beatles Recording Sessions*, p. 69.

11. Greil Marcus, "The Beatles," in *The Rolling Stone Illustrated History of Rock & Roll*, ed. Miller, p. 183.

12. Goldstein, *Goldstein's Greatest Hits*, p. 148.

13. Brown and Gaines, *The Love You Make*, pp. 226–27.

14. Stanley Booth, *The True Adventures of the Rolling Stones*, pp. 491–92.

15. Bill Wyman, *Stone Alone*, pp. 395–96.

16. Booth, *The True Adventures of the Rolling Stones*, p. 272.

17. Robert Christgau, "The Rolling Stones," in *The Rolling Stone Illustrated History of Rock & Roll*, ed. Miller, p. 197.

18. Christopher Andersen, *Jagger Unauthorized*, p. 138.

19. Booth, *The True Adventures of the Rolling Stones*, p. 366.

20. Wyman, *Stone Alone*, p. 474.

21. Ibid., p. 509.

22. Christgau, "The Rolling Stones," in *The Rolling Stone Illustrated History of Rock & Roll*, ed. Miller, p. 196.

23. Wyman, *Stone Alone*, p. 509.

24. Lillian Roxon, *Rock Encyclopedia*, p. 424.

Chapter 3 Drugs, Dementia, and Amplified Jugs: Psychedelic Punk

1. Lester Bangs, "The Roots of Punk," *New Wave*, November 1978.

2. Lester Bangs, "Protopunk: The Garage Bands," in *The Rolling Stone Illustrated History of Rock & Roll*, ed. Miller, p. 262.

3. Stafford, *Psychedelics Encyclopedia*, p. 58.

4. Howard Becker, "History, Culture, and Subjective Experience," *Journal of Health and Social Behavior*, 1967.

5. Alan Vorda, *Psychedelic Psounds*, pp. 6–7.

6. Bill Bentley, "Tommy Hall's Trip Through the Revolving Doors of Perception," *The Austin Chronicle*, 24 Oct. 1990.

7. Doug Hanners, Joe Nick Patoski, and Kirby McDaniel, "Roky '75," *Third Coast*, November 1984.

8. Vorda, *Psychedelic Psounds*, p. 192.

9. Richard Leiby, "The Elevator Doesn't Stop Here Anymore," *Washington Post*, 23 June 1991.

10. Hanners et al., "Roky '75."

11. Ibid.

12. Leiby, "The Elevator Doesn't Stop Here Anymore."

13. Hanners et al., "Roky '75."

14. Gregg Turner, "Roky: On the Line With God and His Mom," *Forced Exposure* no. 9, 1986.

15. John Morthland, liner notes, *You're Gonna Miss Me: The Best of Roky Erickson*, Restless, 1991.

16. Hanners et al., "Roky '75."

17. Goldstein, *Goldstein's Greatest Hits*, p. 18.

18. Clinton Heylin, *From the Velvets to the Voidoids*, pp. xiii–xiv.

19. Ibid., p. 3.

20. Victor Bockris and Gerard Malanga, *Up-Tight: The Velvet Underground Story*, p. 18.

21. Ibid., p. 11.

22. Ibid., p. 47.

23. Ibid.

24. Lester Bangs, *Psychotic Reactions and Carburetor Dung*, p. 167.

Chapter 4 Eight Miles High: Folk Rock Turns Psychedelic

1. Geoffrey Stokes, "The Sixties," in Ward, Stokes, and Tucker, *Rock of Ages: The Rolling Stone History of Rock & Roll*, p. 312.

2. Bud Scoppa, *The Byrds*, p. 157.

3. David Fricke, liner notes, *The Byrds* CD box set, Columbia, 1990.

4. Ibid., p. 40.

5. Tim Riley, *Hard Rain: A Dylan Commentary*, pp. 104–105.

6. Fricke, *The Byrds*, p. 16.

7. Crosby and Gottlieb, *Long Time Gone*, p. 121.

8. Roxon, *Rock Encyclopedia*, p. 78.

9. David Sprague, "Don't Write Him Off," *Request*, May 1991.

10. Vorda, *Psychedelic Psounds*, p. 150.

11. Ibid., p. 149.

12. Ibid., p. 139.

13. Frank Beeson, "Arthur Lee Loves You," *The Bob*, no. 49.

14. Dave DiMartino, "Love Through the Ages (Of Prophets, Seers and Sages): Arthur Lee's Legend Lingers," *Creem*, April 1981.

15. Joel Selvin, *Summer of Love*, p. 92.

16. Perry, *The Haight-Ashbury*, pp. 70–71.

17. Charles Perry, "The Sound of San Francisco," in *The Rolling Stone Illustrated History of Rock & Roll*, ed. Miller, p. 271.

18. Perry, *The Haight-Ashbury*, p. 256.

19. Goldstein, *Goldstein's Greatest Hits*, p. 115.

20. Roxon, *Rock Encyclopedia*, p. 209.

21. David Fricke, liner notes, *Vintage: The Very Best of Moby Grape*, Columbia/Legacy, 1993.

22. Goldstein, *Goldstein's Greatest Hits*, p. 119

23. Perry, *The Haight-Ashbury*, p. 288.

24. Geoffrey Himes, "Williamson's Celtic Connection," *Washington Post*, 9 April 1987.

25. Ibid.

Chapter 5   Pipers at the Gates of Dawn: The Pink Floyd

1. Kenneth Grahame, *The Wind in the Willows*, p. 115.

2. Nicholas Schaffner, *Saucerful of Secrets*, p. 6.

3. Brian Hoss, liner notes, *Syd Barrett: Crazy Diamond* box set, EMI, 1993.

4. Schaffner, *Saucerful of Secrets*, p. 11.

5. Karl Dallas, *Pink Floyd: Bricks in the Wall*, p. 64.

6. Schaffner, *Saucerful of Secrets*, p. xv.

7. Dallas, *Pink Floyd: Bricks in the Wall*, p. 20.

8. Schaffner, *Saucerful of Secrets*, p. 143.

9. Ibid., p. 75.

10. Ibid., p. 203.

11. Ibid., p. 184.

12. Deena Weinstein, *Serious Rock*, pp. 11–12.

13. Schaffner, *Saucerful of Secrets*, p. 213.

14. Mike Watkinson and Peter Anderson, *Crazy Diamond*, pp. 151–52.

Chapter 6   The 14-Hour Technicolour Dream and the Art-Rock Nightmare

1. Angus Strychn, "The Return of Hellfire: An Interview with Arthur Brown," *Your Flesh*, no. 29, 1993.

2. Christgau, *Christgau's Record Guide*, p. 446.

3. John Rockwell, "Art Rock," in *The Rolling Stone Illustrated History of Rock & Roll*, ed. Miller, pp. 347–48.

4. Roxon, *Rock Encyclopedia*, pp. 353–54.

5. Richard Newman and Dave Laing, liner notes, *Mike Oldfield: Elements* box set, Virgin 1993.

6. Armando Gallo, *Genesis: I Know What I Like*, p. 33.

7. Ibid., p. 49.

8. Ibid., pp. 68–69.

Chapter 7   Just Say Yes: Psychedelia Stretches Out

1. John Morthland, "Jimi Hendrix," in *The Rolling Stone Illustrated History of Rock & Roll*, ed. Miller, p. 297.

2. Charles Shaar Murray, *Crosstown Traffic*, p. 2.

3. Ibid., p. 3.

4. Ibid., p. 7.

5. Ibid., p. 161.

6. Michael Fairchild, liner notes, *Are You Experienced?*, MCA, 1993.

7. Murray, *Crosstown Traffic*, p. 138.

8. Ibid., p. 181.

9. Dave Marsh, "Sly and the Family Stone," in *The Rolling Stone Illustrated History of Rock & Roll*, ed. Miller, pp. 317–18.

10. John Corbett, *Extended Play*, p. 148.

11. Christgau, *Christgau's Record Guide: Rock Albums of the '70s*, p. 292.

12. Corbett, *Extended Play*, p. 7.

13. Ibid., p. 17.

14. Dave Thompson, *Space Daze*, p. 7.

15. Deena Weinstein, *Heavy Metal: A Cultural Sociology*, p. 17.

16. Robert Godwin, *The Illustrated Collector's Guide to Hawkwind*, p. 172.

17. Thompson, *Space Daze*, p. 10.

18. Godwin, *The Illustrated Collector's Guide to Hawkwind*, pp. 165–66.

19. Thompson, *Space Daze*, p. 14.

20. Ed Ward, review of *Lick My Decals Off, Baby*, in *The Rolling Stone Record Review, Volume II*, p. 400.

21. Ben Watson, *Frank Zappa: The Negative Dialectics of Poodle Play*, p. 74.

22. Barret Hansen, review of *We're Only in It for the Money*, in *The Rolling Stone Record Review*, p. 350.

23. Lester Bangs, review of *Fillmore East*, in *The Rolling Stone Record Review, Volume II*, pp. 387–88.

24. Watson, *Frank Zappa*, p. 154.

Chapter 8   Broken Head (Quiet, Super Genius at Work)

1. Brian Eno and Peter Schmidt, Oblique Strategies, 1975.

2. Brian Eno, Russell Mills, and Rick Poynor, *More Dark Than Shark*, pp. 40–41.

3. Barry Lazell and Dafydd Rees, *Bryan Ferry & Roxy Music*, p. 8.

4. Ibid., p. 13.

5. Tamm, *Brian Eno: His Music and the Vertical Color of Sound*, p. 30.

6. Ibid., pp. 89–90.

7. Lazell and Rees, *Bryan Ferry & Roxy Music*, p. 57.

8. Ibid.

9. Eno and Schmidt, Oblique Strategies.

10. Tamm, *Brian Eno*, p. 55.

11. Ibid., pp. 46–47.

12. Eno, et al. *More Dark Than Shark*, p. 101.

13. Tamm, *Brian Eno*, p. 81.

14. Ibid., p. 80.

15. Eno et al. *More Dark Than Shark*, p. 76.

16. Tamm, *Brian Eno*, p. 43.

17. Ibid., p. 46.

18. Eno and Schmidt, Oblique Strategies.

19. Tamm, *Brian Eno*, p. 43.

20. Eno, liner notes, *Discreet Music*, EG Records, 1975.

21. Eno, liner notes, *On Land*, EG Records, 1982.

22. Ted Greenwald, "Brian Eno: Taking the Recording Studio by Strategy," *Musician*, November 1993.

23. Scott Cohen, *Yakety Yak*, p. 39.

24. Tamm, *Brian Eno*, p. 161.

25. Eno and Schmidt, Oblique Strategies.

Chapter 9   Yoo Doo Right: The Krautrock Invasion

1. Bangs, *Psychotic Reactions and Carburetor Dung*, p. 154.

2. Pascal Bussy, *Kraftwerk: Man, Machine and Music*, p. 12.

3. Simon Reynolds, review of *Faust So Far*, *Melody Maker*, 7 November 1992.

4. Faust press release, Polydor Records, 1971.

5. Pascal Bussy and Andy Hall, *The Can Book*, p. 155.

6. Armstrong Whitworth, "Deutsch Nepal," *Strange Things Are Happening*, September-October, 1988

7. Thompson, *Space Daze*, p. 90.

8. Greg Kot, "The Experiment Continues," *Chicago Tribune*, 1 May 1994.

9. Reynolds, *Melody Maker*, 7 November 1992.

10. Jason Ferguson, "White Flags Over Georgia," *Alternative Press*, August 1994.

11. Dave Morrison, "First Things Faust," *The Wire*, February 1994.

12. Bussy and Hall, *The Can Book*, p. 30.

13. Ibid., pp. 65–66.

14. Ibid., p. 17.

15. Ibid., p. 42.

16. Ibid., p. 71.

17. Ibid., p. 77.

18. Ibid., p. 179.

19. Bussy, *Kraftwerk*, p. 96.

20. Ibid., p. 33.

21. Ibid., p. 78.

22. Ibid., p. 169.

23. Ibid., p. 87.

24. Ibid., p. 146.

25. Ibid., p. 155.

26. Simon Witter, "Robopop!" *New Musical Express*, 9 June 1991.

27. David Elliott, liner notes, *Black Forest Gateu*, Cherry Red, 1982.

28. Liner notes, *Neu!*, Billingsgate, 1972.

Chapter 10   An Evening of Fun in the Metropolis of Your Dreams: Psychedelic Punk Return

1. Heylin, *From the Velvets to the Voidoids*, p. 219.

2. Ibid., pp. 147–48.

3. Lester Bangs, "A Bellyful of Wire," *Village Voice*, 23 April 1979.

4. Kevin S. Eden, *Wire . . . Everybody Loves a History*, p. 37.

5. Ibid., p. 37.

6. Ibid., p. 29.

7. Robert Christgau, *Christgau's Record Guide: Rock Albums of the '70s*, p. 426.

8. Eden, *Wire*, p. 38.

9. Aldous Huxley, *Brave New World*, p. 23.

10. Greg McLean, "Up & Down With the Feelies," *New York Rocker*, June 1980.

11. Interview with *Jersey Beat* editor Jim Testa, 1984.

Chapter 11   Passionate Friends: The English Psychedelic Eccentrics

1. Tom Hibbert, "Mad Dog and Englishman," *Details*, March 1993.

2. Julian Cope, *Head-On*, p. 130.

3. Randy Bookasta, "Julian Cope: The Saint Came Marching In," *Contrast* no. 3, Fall 1987.

4. Hibbert, "Mad Dog and Englishman."

5. Bookasta, "Julian Cope."

6. Nigel Cross, "A Boring Midday Chat with Robyn Hitchcock," *Forced Exposure* no. 13, 1987.

7. Ibid.

8. Robert Christgau, *Christgau's Record Guide: The '80s*, p. 465.

9. Chris Twomey, *XTC: Chalkhills and Children*, p. 5.

10. Scott Isler, "The Dukes of Swindon," *Musician*, January 1987.

11. Twomey, *XTC*, p. 124.

12. Ibid.

13. "XTC Talk to *The Little Express*," June 1985.

14. Twomey, *XTC*, p. 144.

15. Ibid., p. 151.

16. Isler, "The Dukes of Swindon."

17. Twomey, *XTC*, p. 178.

Chapter 12   Retrodelic: The American Psychedelic Revival

1. Gregg Turner, "Cavern Club Psych-Out: The '60s are Alive and Well (Sort Of)," *Creem*, March 1986.

2. Ibid.

3. Timothy Gassen, *Echoes in Time*, p. 3.

4. Pat Thomas, "Dream On: Steve Wynn Gets Down & Dirty . . . Er, Dusty," *The Bob*, 1985.

5. Elizabeth Phillip, "Rain Parade: Flashback or Stand Still?" *Matter*, February 1984.

Chapter 13   Bad Trips and One-Hit Wonders

1. Goldstein, *Goldstein's Greatest Hits*, p. 103.

2. Lester Bangs, "The Doors," in *The Rolling Stone Illustrated History of Rock & Roll*, ed. Miller, p. 280.

3. Dave Marsh, "Eric Clapton," in *The Rolling Stone Illustrated History of Rock & Roll*, ed. Miller, p. 293.

4. Jerry Garcia obituary, Reuters news wire, 9 August 1995.

5. Mickey Dolenz and Mark Bego, *I'm a Believer*, p. 146.

6. Watkinson and Anderson, *Crazy Diamond*, p. 141.

7. Ray Davies, *X-Ray*, p. 361.

8. Cameron Crowe, review of *Zuma*, in *Neil Young: The Rolling Stone Files*, Editors of *Rolling Stone*, p. 124.

Chapter 14   Reality Used to Be a Friend of Mine: Psychedelic Hip-Hop

1. Jeremy J. Beadle, *Will Pop Eat Itself?*, p. 2.

2. Marisa Fox, "Others From a Brother Planet," *New Musical Express*, 13 April 1991.

3. Simon Reynolds, *Blissed Out*, p. 167.

4. Havelock Nelson and Michael A. Gonzales, *Bring the Noise*, p. 17.

5. Helene Stapinski, "Nothing Is Real," *Request*, April 1992.

6. David Sprague, "Soul Brothers," *Request*, December 1995.

7. Ibid.

8. Island Records biography, 1995.

Chapter 15 Raving and Drooling: Psychedelic Dance Music

1. David Prince, editorial, *Reactor* 0.0, August 1992.

2. Bruce Eisner, *Ecstasy: The MDMA Story*, p. 1.

3. Ibid., p. xxxviii.

4. Sue Cummings, "Welcome to the Machine," *Rolling Stone*, 7 April 1994.

5. Yuri Kageyama, "Soul Meets Technology in New Detroit Dance Music," Associated Press, 31 October 1994.

6. Ernest Hardy, "Why I Hate Techno," *Request*, July 1994.

7. Nicholas Saunders, *E for Ecstasy*, p. 20.

8. Dennis Cooper, "A Raver Runs Through It," *Spin,* March 1995.

9. J. D. Considine, "When Techno Music Pulsates, There Is Just No Sitting Still," *Baltimore Sun*, 20 September 1992.

10. David Prince, "Moby Feature," *Request*, April 1995.

11. David Prince, Matt Adell, and Geno Andrews, "Moby in Chicago," *Reactor*, September 1992.

12. Neil Strauss, "Beat Generation," *Option*, January 1994.

13. David Prince, "Head Music," *Request*, July 1994.

14. Strauss, "Beat Generation."

15. Adam Higginbotham, "Music for Spaceports," *Details*, April 1993.

16. David Prince, "Interstellar Overdrive: Reaching Escape Velocity With the Orb," *Option*, January 1994.

17. Roger Morton, "Cloud Cuckoo Man," *New Musical Express*, 5 January 1991.

18. Strauss, "Beat Generation."

Chapter 16 Pigfuckers and Shoegazers: Psychedelic Guitar Bands in the '80s and '90s

1. Reynolds, *Blissed Out*, pp. 13, 57.

2. Gina Arnold, *Route 666*, p. 100.

3. Rachel Felder, *Manic Pop Thrill*, p. 21.

4. Liner notes, *Losing Touch With Your Mind*, Tecno, 1995.

5. Reynolds, *Blissed Out*, p. 145.

6. Ibid., p. 137.

7. Roger Morton, "The Correct Use of Soup," *New Musical Express*, 21 January 1995.

8. Reynolds, *Blissed Out*, p. 44.

9. Eric Gladstone, "Moonshake: Standing Naked in This Back of the Woods," *Alternative Press*, December 1993.

10. Reynolds, *Blissed Out*, p. 120.

11. Ibid., p. 121.

12. Ibid., p. 123.

13. David Sprague, "Pop Shredded Through the Looking Glass," *Request*, February 1992.

14. Keith Cameron, "(No) Sign of the Valentines," *New Musical Express*, 15 April 1995.

Bibliography

Andersen, Christopher. *Jagger Unauthorized*. New York: Delacorte, 1993.

Arnold, Gina. *Route 666: On the Road to Nirvana*. New York: St. Martin's, 1993.

Bangs, Lester. *Psychotic Reactions and Carburetor Dung*. New York: Knopf, 1987.

Beadle, Jeremy J. *Will Pop Eat Itself? Pop Music in the Soundbite Era*. London: Faber and Faber, 1993.

Bockris, Victor, and Gerard Malanga. *Up-Tight: The Velvet Underground Story*. New York: Omnibus Press, 1983.

Booth, Stanley. *The True Adventures of the Rolling Stones*. New York: Vintage, 1985.

Brown, Peter, and Steven Gaines. *The Love You Make: An Insider's Story of the Beatles*. New York: Signet, 1984.

Bussy, Pascal. *Kraftwerk: Man, Machine and Music*. London: S.A.F., 1993.

Bussy, Pascal, and Andy Hall. *The Can Book*. London: S.A.F., 1989.

Carducci, Joe. *Rock and the Pop Narcotic*. San Francisco: Redoubt Press, 1990.

Christgau, Robert. *Christgau's Record Guide: Rock Albums of the '70s*. New Haven and New York: Ticknor & Fields, 1981.

———. *Christgau's Record Guide: The '80s*. New York: Pantheon, 1990.

Clapton, Diana. *Lou Reed and the Velvet Underground*. New York: Proteus, 1982.

Cohen, Scott. *Yakety Yak: The Midnight Confessions and Revelations of Thirty-seven Rock Stars and Legends*. New York: Fireside, 1994.

Cope, Julian. *Head-On: Memories of the Liverpool Punk Scene and the Story of the Teardrop Explodes, 1976–82*. London: Ma-Gog Books, 1994.

———. *Krautrocksampler*. London: Head Heritage, 1995.

Corbett, John. *Extended Play: Sounding Off From John Cage to Dr. Funkenstein*. Chapel Hill, N.C.: Duke University Press, 1994.

Crosby, David, and Carl Gottlieb. *Long Time Gone: The Autobiography of David Crosby*. New York: Dell, 1988.

Dallas, Karl. *Pink Floyd: Bricks in the Wall*. New York: S.P.I., 1994.

Davies, Ray. *X-Ray: The Unauthorized Autobiography*. Woodstock, N.Y.: Overlook Press, 1994.

DeCurtis, Anthony, James Henke and Holly George-Warren, eds. *The Rolling Stone Album Guide*. New York: Random House, 1992.

Dolenz, Mickey, and Mark Bego. *I'm a Believer: My Life of Monkees, Music and Madness*. New York: Hyperion, 1993.

Durr, R. A. *Poetic Vision and the Psychedelic Experience*. Syracuse, N.Y.: Syracuse University Press, 1970.

Eden, Kevin S. *Wire . . . Everybody Loves a History*. London: S.A.F., 1991.

The editors of *Rolling Stone. Neil Young: The Rolling Stone Files*. New York: Hyperion, 1994.

———. *The Rolling Stone Record Review*. New York: Pocket Books, 1971.

———. *The Rolling Stone Record Review, Volume II*. New York: Pocket Books, 1974.

Eisner, Bruce. *Ecstasy: The MDMA Story*. Berkeley, Calif.: Ronin, 1994.

Eno, Brian, and Russell Mills with Rick Poynor. *More Dark Than Shark*. London: Faber and Faber, 1986.

Eno, Brian, and Peter Schmidt. *Oblique Strategies*. London: Opal Information, Ltd., 1992.

Erickson, Roky. *Openers II: The Lyrics of Roky Erickson*. Los Angeles: 2.13.61, 1995.

Felder, Rachel. *Manic Pop Thrill*. Hopewell, N.J.: Ecco Press, 1993.

Gaines, Steven. *Heroes & Villains: The True Story of the Beach Boys*. New York: NAL, 1986.

Gallo, Armando. *Genesis: I Know What I Like*. New York: Omnibus, 1984.

Gans, David. *Conversations With the Grateful Dead*. Secaucus, N.J.: Citadel Underground, 1993.

Gassen, Timothy. *Echoes in Time: The Garage and Psychedelic Music Explosion 1980–1990*. Telford, England: Borderline, 1991.

George, Leonard. *Alternative Realities: The Paranormal, the Mystic and the Transcendent in Human Experience*. New York: Facts on File, 1995.

Godwin, Robert. *The Illustrated Collector's Guide to Hawkwind*. Burlington, Ontario: Collector's Guide Publishing, 1993.

Goldman, Albert. *The Lives of John Lennon*. New York: William Morrow, 1988.

Goldstein, Richard. *Goldstein's Greatest Hits: A Book Mostly About Rock 'n' Roll*. New York: Prentice-Hall, 1970.

Grahame, Kenneth. *The Wind in the Willows*. New York: Bantam Classic, 1982.

Henderson, David. *'Scuse Me While I Kiss the Sky: The Life of Jimi Hendrix*. New York: Bantam, 1983.

Henderson, Leigh A., and William J. Glass. *LSD: Still With Us After All These Years*. New York: Lexington Books, 1994.

Heylin, Clinton. *From the Velvets to the Voidoids: A Pre-Punk History for a Post-Punk World*. New York: Penguin, 1993.

Hofmann, Albert. *LSD, My Problem Child: Reflections on Sacred Drugs, Mysticism, and Science*. Los Angeles: J. P. Tarcher, 1983.

Howe, Steve, with Tony Bacon. *The Steve Howe Guitar Collection*. New York: GPI, 1993.

Huxley, Aldous. *The Doors of Perception and Heaven and Hell*. New York: Harper Perennial, 1990.

———. *Brave New World*. New York: Harper & Row, 1969.

Joynson, Vernon. *The Flashback: The Ultimate Psychedelic Music Guide*. Telford, Eng.: Borderline, 1993.

———. *Fuzz, Acid and Flowers: A Comprehensive Guide to American Garage, Psychedelic and Hippie Rock 1964–1975*. Telford, Eng.: Borderline, 1993.

Kadrey, Richard. *Covert Culture Sourcebook*. New York: St. Martin's, 1993.

Lazell, Barry, and Dafydd Rees. *Bryan Ferry & Roxy Music*. New York: Proteus Books, 1982.

Leary, Timothy. *Flashbacks: An Autobiography*. Los Angeles: J. P. Tarcher, 1983.

———. *Chaos & Cyber Culture*. Berkeley, Calif.: Ronin, 1994.

Leary, Timothy, Ralph Metzner and Richard Alpert. *The Psychedelic Experience: A Manual Based on the Tibetan Book of the Dead*. Secaucus, N.J.: Citadel Press, 1990.

Lee, Martin A., and Bruce Shlain. *The Complete Social History of LSD: The CIA, the Sixties, and Beyond.* San Francisco: Grove Weidenfeld, 1985.

Lewisohn, Mark. *The Beatles Recording Sessions: The Official Abbey Road Studio Session Notes, 1962–1970.* New York: Harmony Books, 1988.

MacDonald, Ian. *Revolution in the Head: The Beatles' Records and the Sixties.* New York: Henry Holt, 1994.

Mackay, Andy. *Electronic Music: The Instruments, the Music & the Musicians.* London: Harrow House, 1981.

McKenna, Terence. *The Archaic Revival.* New York: HarperCollins, 1991.

———. *The Food of the Gods: The Search for the Original Tree of Knowledge.* New York: Bantam, 1992.

———. *True Hallucinations.* New York: HarperCollins, 1993.

Miles, Barry. *Pink Floyd: A Visual Documentary.* New York: Quick Fox, 1980.

Miller, Jim, ed. *The Rolling Stone Illustrated History of Rock & Roll.* 3d ed. New York: Random House, 1980.

Murray, Charles Shaar. *Crosstown Traffic: Jimi Hendrix and the Rock 'n' Roll Revolution.* New York: St. Martin's, 1989.

Nelson, Havelock, and Michael A. Gonzales. *Bring the Noise: A Guide to Rap Music and Hip-Hop Culture.* New York: Harmony Books, 1991.

Paglia, Camille. *Vamps & Tramps.* New York: Vintage, 1994.

Perry, Charles. *The Haight-Ashbury: A History.* New York: Vintage, 1985.

Reynolds, Simon. *Blissed Out: The Raptures of Rock.* New York: Serpent's Tail, 1990.

Reynolds, Simon, and Joy Press. *The Sex Revolts: Gender, Rebellion, and Rock 'n' Roll.* Cambridge, Mass.: Harvard University Press, 1995.

Riley, Tim. *Hard Rain: A Dylan Commentary.* New York: Vintage, 1993.

———. *Tell Me Why: A Beatles Commentary.* New York: Vintage, 1989.

Robbins, Ira, ed. *The Trouser Press Record Guide.* New York: Collier Books, 1991.

Romanowski, Patricia, and Holly George-Warren with Jon Pareles, eds. *The New Rolling Stone Encyclopedia of Rock & Roll.* New York: Fireside, 1995.

Rose, Cynthia. *Design After Dark: The Story of Dancefloor Style.* London: Thames and Hudson Ltd., 1991.

Roxon, Lillian. *Rock Encyclopedia.* New York: Grosset & Dunlap, 1969.

Rushkoff, Douglas. *Cyberia: Life in the Trenches of Hyperspace.* San Francisco: Harper San Francisco, 1994.

Saunders, Nicholas. *E for Ecstasy.* London: Nicholas Saunders, 1993.

Schaffner, Nicholas. *Saucerful of Secrets.* New York: Harmony Books, 1991.

Scoppa, Bud. *The Byrds.* New York: Scholastic Book Services, 1971.

Selvin, Joel. *Summer of Love: The Inside Story of LSD, Rock & Roll, Free Love and High Times in the Wild West.* New York: Dutton, 1994.

Stafford, Peter. *Psychedelics Encyclopedia.* Berkeley, Calif.: Ronin, 1992.

Stevens, Jay. *Storming Heaven: LSD and the American Dream.* New York: Harper & Row, 1988.

Tamm, Eric. *Brian Eno: His Music and the Vertical Color of Sound.* London: Faber and Faber, 1989.

Thompson, Dave. *Space Daze: The History & Mystery of Electronic Ambient Space Rock.* Los Angeles: Cleopatra, 1994.

Tosches, Nick. *Unsung Heroes of Rock 'n' Roll: The Birth of Rock in the Wild Years Before Elvis.* New York: Harmony Books, 1991.

Troy, Sandy. *One More Saturday Night: Reflections With the Grateful Dead, Dead Family, and Dead Heads.* New York: St. Martin's, 1991.

Twomey, Chris. *XTC: Chalkhills and Children.* London: Omnibus Press, 1992.

Vassal, Jacques. *Electric Children: Roots and Branches of Modern Folk Rock.* New York: Taplinger, 1976.

Vorda, Alan. *Psychedelic Psounds: Interviews From A to Z with '60s Psychedelic and Garage Bands.* Telford, Eng.: Borderline Productions, 1994.

Ward, Ed, Geoffrey Stokes, and Ken Tucker, *Rock of Ages: The Rolling Stone History of Rock & Roll.* New York: Rolling Stone Press/Summit Books, 1986.

Watkinson, Mike, and Pete Anderson. *Crazy Diamond: Syd Barrett and the Dawn of Pink Floyd.* London: Omnibus Press, 1991.

Watts, Alan. *The Joyous Cosmology.* New York: Vintage, 1962.

Watson, Ben. *Frank Zappa: The Negative Dialectics of Poodle Play.* New York: St. Martin's, 1995.

Weinstein, Deena. *Heavy Metal: A Cultural Sociology.* New York: Lexington Books, 1991.

———. *Serious Rock: Bruce Springsteen/Rush/Pink Floyd.* Montreal: Culture Texts, 1985.

Whitburn, Joel. *The Billboard Book of Top 40 Hits.* New York: Billboard, 1989.

White, Timothy. *The Nearest Faraway Place: Brian Wilson, the Beach Boys, and the Southern California Experience.* New York: Henry Holt, 1994.

Wilson, Brian, with Todd Gold. *Wouldn't It Be Nice: My Own Story.* New York: HarperCollins, 1991.

Wolfe, Tom. *The Electric Kool-Aid Acid Test.* New York: Quality Paperback, 1990.

Wyman, Bill, with Ray Coleman. *Stone Alone: The Story of a Rock 'n' Roll Band.* New York: Viking, 1990.

Index

A Tribe Called Quest, 197
Absolute Grey, 172
acid house, 184, 190, 197, 206–208, 210, 212, 219
Acid Tests, xv, 8, 14, 30, 55, 56, 127, 207
Ainslinger, Harry, 11–12, 33
Alice's Adventures in Wonderland, 9, 55, 180, 192
Allman Brothers, 104
Alpert, Richard, 6, 13, 59
ambient music,
    ambient house/techno, 27, 147, 201, 204, 208, 210, 211, 212–15; Brian Eno and, 117–20; New Age music and, 118, 213
Amboy Dukes, 35, 97, 100, 167
Amon Düül, 101, 126–27, 225, 232
Anderson, Dave, 101, 127, 225
Anderson, Pete, and Mike Watkinson, 76
Angel, Johnny, 57
Animals, 80, 83, 94
Aphex Twin, 204, 209–210
A R Kane, 219
Arrested Development, 197
art rock, 26, 83–86, 89, 91, 100, 112, 141, 146
art school, 6, 13, 28, 64, 80, 84, 145, 212, 219, 224
Ash Ra Tempel, 127
Ayers, Kevin, 80, 87, 88, 117, 142
Ayler, Albert, 106

Bacharach, Burt, and Hal David, 52
Badalamenti, Angelo, 209
Bambaataa, Afrika, 137, 195

Bangles, 174–76, 191
Bangs, Lester, xv, 32, 33, 34, 42, 46, 105, 106, 124, 145, 158, 183
Barracudas, 173
Barrett, Syd, 15, 41, 53, 63–67, 69, 70–71, 72, 74–77, 174, 175, 181, 220, 221
Baxter, Les, 48, 50
Beach Boys, 5, 7, 8, 11, 17–22, 23, 44, 67, 133, 135, 168, 174, 221
Beadle, Jeremy, 194
Beastie Boys, 196–97
Beatles, xv, 7, 11, 12, 15, 17, 19, 22–27, 29, 44, 48–52, 64–66, 69, 80, 81, 86, 89, 97, 98, 110, 111, 117, 125, 130, 135, 151, 161, 165, 167, 168, 170, 172, 191, 192, 198, 199–222
Beat movement, 7, 9, 10, 12, 13, 23, 30, 36, 47, 49, 54, 56, 58, 85, 112
Beaver and Krause, 110
Beck, Jeff, 59, 82
Becker, Howard, 34
Bedhead, 218
Berry, Chuck, 18, 135
Bevis Frond, 173
Big Dipper, 218
Big Star, 104, 174, 222
Birds, 82
Black Sabbath, 101, 188, 193, 217
Blake Babies, 218
Blake, William, 6, 8, 47, 71
Blegvad, Peter, 129, 169
Blue Cheer, 101
Blue Öyster Cult, 188

Blues Magoos, 183
Blur, 219–20
Bolan, Marc, 82, 112
Bongwater, 218
Boo Radleys, 222
Booth, Stanley, 28
Bowie, David, 112, 120, 122, 136, 154, 192, 228
Boyd, Joe, 14, 59–62, 64, 82, 191
Brown, Arthur, 64, 79, 86
Brown, Peter, and Steven Gaines, 17
Bubble Puppy, 37–38
Buck, Peter, 152, 163, 191
Buckley, Tim, 51
Budd, Harold, 119, 169
Buffalo Springfield, 47, 51
Burroughs, William S., 10, 80, 116, 160, 188
Bussy, Pascal, 124, 137
Butterfield, Paul, 54
Butthole Surfers, 41, 217–18
Byrds, 7, 8, 12, 23, 32, 39, 43, 44, 48–51, 52, 60,
    64, 81, 154, 162, 163, 170, 174, 177, 188,
    191, 192, 217, 222

Cage, John, 8, 42, 56, 109, 112
Cale, John, 41–46, 60, 88, 117, 119, 122
Calvert, Robert, 15, 101–103
Camel, 80
Camper Van Beethoven, 192
Can, 125, 126, 129–33, 140, 142, 178, 185, 210,
    222
Captain Beefheart, 105–107, 144, 145, 155, 161
Caravan, 80
Cardinal, 224
Carlos, Walter/Wendy, 110
Chambers Brothers, 97
Chandler, Chas, 80, 94
Charlatans,
    American group, 55; British group, 219
Charlesworth, Chris, 72
Chesterfield Kings, 171
Chills, 172, 218
Chocolate Watchband, 35
Christgau, Robert, 29, 31, 83, 95, 99, 146, 164,
    195
Christmas, 218
Chud, 172
Clark, Gene, 48–51, 177
Clay Allison, 177
Clinton, George, 97–100, 198
Clique, 191
Cluster, 119, 120, 128, 139
Cocteau Twins, 218–19, 222, 223, 226
Coil, 184
Coleman, Ornette, 80, 94, 100
Collins, William "Bootsy," 98, 212
Coltrane, John, 37, 50, 94, 100
Conrad, Tony, 42–43
Considine, J. D., 208
Cooper, Dennis, 207
Cope, Julian, 16, 40, 126, 155–59, 165, 201, 220
Corbett, John, 99–100

Count Five, 32, 34, 141
Cracker, 192
Craddock, Bill, 58
Cream, 130, 183–84
Creation,
    group, 79, 80–81, 89, 154, 170, 178, 179, 187,
    222; label, 220–22, 225–26
Creeping Pumpkins, 170
Crosby, David, 48–51, 56, 83
Crowe, Cameron, 189
Crowley, Aleister, 132
Cul de Sac, 223
Culture Club, 190, 198
Cure, 184
Cypress Hill, 197

dada movement/surrealism, 9–10, 27, 106, 109,
    115, 127, 142, 146, 161, 196, 201, 209
Dale, Dick, 11
Dalí, Salvador, 10, 127, 188
Damned, 142, 163
Darkside, 220
Das Damen, 217
Davies, Ray, 188, 220
Davis, Miles, 96, 219
Deee-Lite, 211
De La Soul, 12, 194–96, 226
Demeski, Stanley, 151–53, 218
Depeche Mode, 184
Diddley, Bo, 43, 57, 82, 150
didgeridoo, 14, 210
Digable Planets, 197
Digital Underground, 197
Dinosaur Jr., 217
Divine Styler, 197
Donovan, 58–59, 89, 188, 189, 217
Doors, 53, 117, 156, 183, 220, 225
Drake, Nick, 60
Dream Academy, 219
Dream Syndicate,
    avant-garde group, 42; paisley underground
    group, 173–74, 177, 180
Drummond, Bill, 156, 201, 213
dub, 100, 134, 201, 213
Dukes of Stratosphear, 165, 167–69, 219
Dumptruck, 218
Durr, R. A., 12
Durutti Column, 219
Dylan, Bob, 7, 8, 12, 23, 39, 47–51, 58,
    59, 97, 115, 120, 154, 161, 165, 174, 177,
    228

Echo and the Bunnymen, 156
Eisner, Bruce, 205
Electric Light Orchestra, 86
Electric Prunes, 34, 167
Emerson, Lake & Palmer, 86, 90
Eno, Brian, 10, 12, 13, 42, 88, 103, 108–23, 128,
    135, 141, 142, 147, 151, 154, 165, 166, 209,
    210, 213, 218, 222, 231
Erickson, Roky, 15, 36–41, 53

Eugenius, 222
Evans, Paul, 56, 61

Fairport Convention, 59–60, 162
faith healers, 222
fashion, 9, 55, 65, 98, 112, 136, 137, 140, 154, 171, 173, 175, 179, 183, 194
Faust, 125, 128–29
Feelies, 14, 126, 147, 149–53, 218, 223
Felder, Rachel, 220, 225
Ferry, Bryan, 108–13, 122
fireman, 212
Flaming Lips, xv, 227–33
Fleshtones, 171
Floh De Cologne, 128
Flowchart, 223
Flying Saucer Attack, 223
FM radio, 9, 86, 213
Focus, 86
folk rock, 12, 47–62, 162, 175, 190, 191, 192, 218
14-Hour Technicolour Dream, 27, 65, 78–79
Fricke, David, 49
Fricke, Florian, 128
Fripp, Robert, 91, 11, 118, 119
Frith, Fred, 88, 119
Fugs, 47, 94, 105, 126
Fuzztones, 173

Gabriel, Peter, 89–91, 194, 200
Gaines, Steven, 17, 18
Galaxie 500, 153, 218
Gamblers, 7, 19
Game Theory, 175
Garcia, Jerry, 15, 54, 56, 141, 185–86
Gassen, Timothy, 171, 172
Geesin, Ron, 68, 75, 78
Genesis, 89–92, 119, 141, 155
Gentle Giant, 86
Gilmour, David, 63, 67–77, 219, 220
Ginsberg, Allen, 6, 13, 189
Glass, Phillip, 151
Gleason, Ralph, 55
Glover, Tony, 96
Golden Dawn, 37
Goldman, Albert, 26
Goldstein, Richard, 22, 26, 44, 58, 182
Gong, 80, 88, 163, 212
Graham, Bill, 14, 55
Grahame, Kenneth, 63, 66
Granny Takes a Trip, 35, 78
Grateful Dead, 8, 15, 16, 43, 54, 56–57, 68, 104, 130, 172, 185–6
Green on Red, 173, 177–78
Griffin, Sid, 171, 177–78
Grinspoon, Lester, and James B. Bakalar, 3
Grogan, Larry, 33
Guru Guru, 128

Haight-Ashbury, xv, 14, 44, 54
Hansen, Barret, 105

Happy Mondays, 219
Hardy, Ernest, 206
Harmonia, 128, 139
Harrison, George, 17, 23, 25, 27, 30, 49, 66, 151
Hawkins, Screamin' Jay, 10, 11, 34, 89, 109
Hawkwind, 12, 79, 101–103, 127, 185, 212, 214, 217, 225
heavy metal, 100–101, 102, 184, 188, 193
Hendrix, Jimi, 21, 53, 66, 93–96, 97, 98, 99, 100, 102, 104, 110, 134, 161, 174, 198
heroin, 9, 44, 52, 58, 189, 220
Heylin, Clinton, 142
Higginbotham, Adam, 212
Hillage, Steve, 88, 163, 212, 213–14
hip hop, 137, 194–202, 216
His Name Is Alive, 218
Hitchcock, Robyn, 155, 159–64, 165
Hoffs, Susanna, 175, 176, 191
Hofmann, Albert, 3–5, 9, 10–12, 17, 79
Hollies, 83
Hollingshead, Michael, 6–7, 23, 59
Holly, Buddy, 37, 39, 64, 159
Hoodoo Gurus, 172
house music, 137, 205, 206, 209, 210, 211, 213
House of Love, 221
Howe, Steve, 78–79, 81, 86
Hubbard, Al, 6, 12
Hugo Largo, 218
Hüsker Dü, 171, 185, 217
Huxley, Aldous, 5–6, 10–13, 24, 36, 149, 183

I Ching, 66, 116
Incredible String Band, 14, 58, 60–62, 66, 82, 161, 189
insanity, 13, 15, 33–34, 41, 71, 157
Inspiral Carpets, 219
International Artists label, 37, 39
Iron Butterfly, 101
Irresistible Force, 211

Jajouka, Master Musicians of, 28
Janiger, Oscar, 6, 12
Jansch, Bert, 58, 59, 87
Jarry, Alfred, 9, 27, 142
Jefferson Airplane, 43, 54, 55–56
Jenner, Peter, 64, 67, 70, 71, 74, 163
Jesus and Mary Chain, 40, 220, 221, 225
Jethro Tull, 86
John's Children, 82
Johnston, Bruce, 7, 19, 75
Jones, Brian, 28–30, 31, 48, 67, 161
Jones, John Paul, 30, 59, 189, 217
Joplin, Janis, 57
Judas Priest, 101
Jungle Brothers, 197

Kaleidoscope,
    American group, 51; British group, 82
Kansas, 86
Katrina and the Waves, 162
Kaye, Lenny, 33, 42, 141

Kerouac, Jack, 13, 60
Kesey, Ken, xv, 7–9, 13, 14, 27, 28, 30, 31, 43, 54,
    55, 56, 127, 204
King, Carole, 187
King, Jonathan, 89
King Crimson, 84–86, 111
Kingsmen, xv
Kinks, 80, 188
Kirk, Roland, 94
KLF, 201, 213–14
Knuckles, Frankie, 205–206
Koobas, 82
Kraftwerk, 125, 126, 128, 133–38, 148, 166, 190,
    205, 206, 220, 222
krautrock, 37, 125–29, 134, 155,159, 178, 218
Kravitz, Lenny, 185

LaBradford, 223
Laika, 223
Lake, Greg, 86
Landau, Jon, 31
Leary, Timothy, 6, 7, 9, 10, 13, 14, 24, 36, 58, 59,
    85, 98, 127, 182, 211
Leaves, 52
Leaving Trains, 178
Led Zeppelin, 59, 81, 188–89, 233
Lee, Arthur, 51–53, 64, 164
Left Banke, 51
Lemon Pipers, 183
Lennon, John, 8, 13, 15, 23–27, 48, 61. 64, 127,
    190, 191, 200, 219
Lesh, Phil,16
light shows, 55, 66, 183, 207, 214, 217
Lime Spiders, 172
Lindisfarne, 86
Linkletter, Art and Diane, 34
Little Richard, 37, 94, 105
Long Ryders, 177, 178
Loop, 220
Lost & Found, 37
Lothar and the Hand People, 110
Love, 51–53, 64, 164, 225
Lovin' Spoonful, 47, 55
Low, 218
LSD, xv, 3–16, 17–31, 34, 35, 39, 44, 49, 52, 54,
    55, 59, 61, 64, 66, 71, 81, 83, 94, 96, 98,
    102, 106, 127, 128, 133, 156, 172, 182, 184,
    185, 192, 205, 207, 229
Luna, 153, 218
Lush, 14, 219
Lyres, 171

Madonna, 190
Magic Hour, 218
Mamas and the Papas, 51, 175
Manchester scene, 163, 219
Manson, Charles, 15, 58, 184
Marcus, Griel, 22
marijuana, 11, 12, 14, 19, 21, 23, 24, 28, 29, 30,
    33, 35, 36, 37, 39, 49, 54, 65, 66, 68, 87, 88,
    156, 158, 195, 207, 217

Marsh, Dave, 97, 184
Marshmallow Overcoat, 172
Martin, George, 23, 26, 65
Mason, Nick, 63–77, 80, 142
Massive Attack, 201
Matching Mole, 80
May, Derrick, 206
Mayfield, Curtis, 97, 196
Mazzy Star, 177
McCartney, Paul, 22–27, 59, 191, 212
MC5, 98, 100, 105
McGee, Alan, 81, 221–22, 226
McGuire, Barry, 51
McKenna, Terence, 190, 208, 210–11
Meat Puppets, 217, 229
Merry Pranksters, 8, 55, 204
Mighty Mofos, 172
Miller, Steve, 57
Ministry, 184
Minor Threat, 146
Minutemen, 171, 174, 185
Miracle Workers, 172
Mission of Burma, 218
Mo' Wax label, 201
Moby, 122, 208–209, 210, 214
Moby Grape, 57–58
Mod Fun, 170, 172, 173
Moles, 224
Monahan, Casey, 40–41
Monkees, 186–87
Monterey Pop Festival, 21, 53, 95, 105
Moody Blues, 29, 84–85, 208
Moonshake, 222–23
Move, 82, 86
Morrison, Van, 60
Morthland, John, 40, 93
MTV, 91,144, 157, 192, 198, 232, 233
Murray, Charles Shaar, 94, 95, 96
Music Machine, 32, 35, 174
musique concrète, 105, 118, 125, 194
My Bloody Valentine, xv, 13, 14, 220, 224–27

Neats, 218
Nelson, Havelock, and Michael Gonzales, 197
Nelson, Paul, 59
Neu!, 125, 126, 128, 134, 135, 138–40, 159, 223
New Age, 4, 15, 22, 87, 118, 127, 128, 187, 213
Nice, 84, 85, 86, 111
Nico, 43, 44, 46, 117, 202
Nine Inch Nails, 184
Nirvana, xv, 174, 217
Nomads, 173
Nuggets, 33–35, 42, 82, 94, 104, 141, 171, 172,
    186, 209, 220
Numan, Gary, 126, 166, 206

Oasis, 222
Oblique Strategies, 108, 113, 116, 117, 121
Oldfield, Mike, 87–89, 115, 117, 194, 219
Oldham, Andrew Loog, 28, 30, 85
Ono, Yoko, 78

Opal, 177
Open Mind, 82
Optic Nerve, 170
Orb, 12, 122, 211, 212–15
Orbital, 211
Osmond, Humphry, 5–6, 12
Ozric Tentacles, 185

Page, Jimmy, 21, 59, 80, 82, 189
Paglia, Camille, 15
paisley underground, 160, 173–78, 180
Palmer, Carl, 79, 86
Pandoras, 170, 178
Pareles, Jon, 83, 121
Parliament-Funkadelic, 97–100, 199, 206
Parks, Van Dyke, 21, 22
Parsons, Alan, 72
Patterson, Rob, 41
Pavement, 233
Peanut Butter Conspiracy, 51
Peel, John, 111
Penguin Cafe Orchestra, 119
Pentangle, 58
Pere Ubu, 12, 37, 142–45, 147, 150, 231
Perry, Charles, 7, 54, 55, 58
Perry, Lee "Scratch," 99–100, 134, 213
Petty, Tom, 192
Phillips, Eddie, 80–81, 188
Phish, 185
Pink Fairies, 101
Pink Floyd, 5, 12, 14, 38, 63–77, 79–82, 101,
    120, 127, 128, 142, 145, 154, 155, 163, 165,
    174, 178, 192, 196, 212, 213, 214, 230, 231
Pixies, 218
Plan 9, 172
Plank, Conrad, 125, 133, 134, 135, 138, 139
Plasticland, 173, 178–81
Plastikman, 211
PM Dawn, xv, 12, 197–201, 201, 202
P-Orridge, Genesis, 184, 207, 212
Poe, Edgar Allan, 5, 8, 188
politics, 47, 100, 115, 171
    anarchism, 79, 124, 126, 131, 145;
    apathy toward, 158; communism, 131,
    144
Pop, Iggy, 136, 155, 209
Popol Vuh, 128
Portishead, 201–202
Pram, 223
Presley, Elvis, 10, 64
Press, Joy, 13
Pretty Things, 79, 80, 101, 170, 178, 179, 181
Primal Scream, 222
Prince, 175, 190–91, 195, 198, 200
Prince, David, 204
Prisoners, 173
Procul Harum, 84
psychedelic drugs, 7–11, 13, 19, 26, 27, 30, 32,
    36, 38, 44, 58, 69, 80, 83, 86, 93, 96, 100,
    106, 125, 142, 176, 184, 187, 198, 209, 224,
    229

derivation of the term "psychedelic," 6; DMT,
    13, 38; influence on popular culture,
    xv–xvi, 8–9, 182–83, 188–92;
    ketamine/Special K, 187, 207; lampooning
    of, 31, 52, 105; MDMA/Ecstasy, 3, 121, 172,
    203, 204–206, 207, 226; mescaline, 5, 6, 9,
    12, 205; PCP, 207; psilocybin/magic
    mushrooms, 13, 39, 104, 132, 172; ritual
    use of; 3. See also LSD, marijuana
psychedelic poster art, 55, 229
psychedelic rock,
    Albert Hofmann's bike ride and, 5; birth of,
    8, 11; blues influence in, 14, 28, 54, 58, 63,
    70, 82, 93, 96, 101, 104, 130, 180, 185, 188,
    189, 193, 223; embrace of technology by,
    xv, 11–12, 42, 120, 125, 133, 136, 137, 194,
    201, 202, 206, 207; gender roles and, 13,
    161; as a genre, xv–xvi, 3, 11, 12, 13, 16, 84,
    182–83, 186, 224; improvisation in, 10, 14,
    54, 56, 82, 85, 99, 106, 110, 127, 130, 133,
    139, 190, 210, 223, 226, 228; jazz influence
    in, 28, 50, 54, 56, 58, 80, 83, 85, 93, 94, 96,
    99, 101, 104–105, 127, 129, 130, 185, 196,
    197, 201, 211, 214, 221, 223; philosophy of,
    xv–xvi, 12–13, 26, 47, 86, 108, 110, 142,
    208, 216, 224, 233; drug influence in, xvi,
    3, 7–9, 14–15, 18–19, 22–24, 28–29, 33–35,
    36–37, 44, 49–50, 52–53, 54, 61, 66, 69, 80,
    94, 98, 102, 112, 125, 128, 133, 142, 156,
    181, 172, 199, 215, 219, 226, 229–30; sonic
    hallmarks of, xvi, 10, 95
Psychedelic Furs, 154, 162
Psychic TV, 184, 207, 211, 212
Public Enemy, 195, 202
Public Image, 126
punk rock, xv, 13, 16, 26, 33–35, 42–43, 52,
    74–75, 83, 89, 91, 100, 102, 108, 118, 136,
    140, 141–42, 143, 145, 150, 155, 162–63,
    165, 171, 172, 173–74, 176, 195, 209,
    212–13, 217, 218, 224, 229, 230
Puxley, Simon, 112

Quant, Mary, 170, 191
? and the Mysterians, 32, 35
Quicksilver Messenger Service, 57
Quine, Robert, 46

ragas, 25, 50, 54, 78, 101, 157
Rain Parade, 173, 174, 176–77, 178
Ramones, xv, 140, 141, 146, 224
raves, xv, 172, 199, 203–208, 209, 210, 211
Red Crayola/Krayola, 38, 144
Red Red Meat, 223
Reed, Lou, 15, 42–46, 150, 197
Reich, Steve, 211
religion/spirituality,
    as a panacea, 20, 75; Buddhism/Eastern
    philosophy, 66, 114, 116, 127, 136;
    Catholicism, 15, 167, 198, 221, 229;
    Christianity, 14, 15, 20, 50, 53, 209, 229;

drug use and "seeing God," 18, 26; Edgar
Cayce, 198; "God" in song titles and band
names, 15, 20, 126, 127, 168, 232; Jehovah's
Witnesses, 132, 144; "Jesus" in song titles
and band names, 15, 39, 40, 45, 200, 221,
230; League for Spiritual Discovery, 6, 14,
182; Moslem religion, 50, 121; paganism,
61, 159, 203; psychedelic rock and, 12,
14–15, 20, 97, 200, 203, 220; Scientology,
61; "teenage symphonies to God," 21, 199;
witches, 5, 57, 59, 188
R.E.M., 40, 146, 151–52, 163, 174, 191
Renaissance, 86
Renbourn, John, 58, 87
Reynolds, Simon, 13, 125, 129, 196, 202, 216,
219, 220, 222, 225
Ride, 222
Riley, Terry, 125
Riley, Tim, 26, 49
Rimsite, Ron, 172
Rockwell, John, 84
Roland, Paul, 173
Rogers, Kenny, 37, 183
Rolling Stone, 9, 31, 105, 118, 171
Rolling Stones, 8–9, 17, 28–31, 35, 36, 38, 52,
54, 64, 82, 85, 88, 125, 161, 176, 189
romantic movement, 8, 12–15, 34, 70, 71, 73,
77, 90, 112
Roxon, Lillian, 31, 51, 56, 85
Roxy Music, 37, 108–13, 114, 116, 117, 142, 145,
146, 161, 192, 231
Rundgren, Todd, 154, 168, 169
Rush, 86

Sabalon Glitz, 223
St.-Marie, Buffy, 57
sampling, xv, 12, 69, 73, 89, 102, 117, 121, 126,
137, 194–97, 198, 200, 201, 202, 206, 207,
209, 211, 213–15, 217, 231
Sandoz Pharmaceuticals Company, 4–7, 11, 12,
14, 83, 127
Santana, 57
Santo & Johnny, 11
Satie, Erik, 118
Saunders, Nicholas, 207
Saunderson, Kevin, 206
Schaffner, Nicholas, 23, 64, 66, 69
Schmidt, Peter, 116
Schwitters, Kurt, 115
science fiction, 21, 50, 56, 69, 90, 96, 99, 101,
102, 165, 197
See Feel, 223
Seeds, 32, 35, 156, 174
Sex Pistols, 140, 166, 213
sex/sexuality, 9, 13, 31, 52, 99, 172, 203, 232
bisexuality, 13, 120, 175, 202;
crossdressing/transvestism, 65, 81, 112,
178, 190, 202; homosexuality, 13, 42, 179,
189, 205, 206
Shadows of Knight, 32

Shamen, 210–11
Shankar, Ravi, 50, 54
Shaw, Greg, 171, 220
Sherwood, Adrian, 213
Shields, Kevin, 13, 220, 224–27
Shulgin, Alexander, 205
Silver Apples, 110
Sinclair, John, 35, 100
sitars, 14, 23, 25, 28, 35, 50, 61, 82, 162, 176,
192, 199, 210
Slickee Boys, 171
Slipstream, 220
Slowdive, 222
Sly and the Family Stone, 97–99,114, 158, 172,
191, 197, 198, 201
Small Faces, 82–83, 165
Smashing Pumpkins, 184
Smith, Norman "Hurricane," 65, 80
Smith, Patti, 46, 141
Smiths, 184
Social Deviants, 101
Soft Boys, 154, 160–63
Soft Machine, 64, 70, 79–80, 82, 87, 104, 115,
117, 142, 212, 218, 219
Sonic Youth, 126, 184–85, 233
Sopwith Camel, 55
Soundgarden, 193
space, 11, 30, 69, 96, 99–100, 127, 145, 192, 199,
212, 214, 223
influence on rock/space rock, 51, 64, 79, 192,
212, 223
Space Time Continuum, 211
Spacemen 3, 185, 220–21
Spector, Phil, 7, 11, 21, 146
Spectrum, 220
Speed the Plough, 151
Spence, Skip, 15, 57–58
Spiritualized, 14, 220–21
Sprague, David, 226
Stafford, Peter, 14, 205
Stampfel, Peter, 7
Standells, 35
Stanley, Augustus Owsley, 8, 19, 54, 56, 101, 104
Status Quo, 82, 192
Stereolab, 14, 126, 223
Stevens, Jay, 15
Stockhausen, Karlheinz, 42, 56, 104, 109, 125,
129, 130, 133, 209, 210
Stokes, Geoffrey, 47
Stone Roses, 219
Stooges, xv, 42, 46, 97, 100–101, 149,
228, 231
Strawberry Alarm Clock, 35
Styx, 86
Subotnick, Morton, 109
Sugarcubes, 201
Summer, Donna, 189–90
Sun Ra, 99–100, 211
Swervedriver, 221
Syn, 86

synthesizers, 12, 21, 28, 30, 37, 42, 69, 72, 74, 86,
    90, 93, 97, 99, 101, 102, 104, 139, 140, 146,
    154, 158, 166, 184, 194, 206, 207, 210, 219,
    220, 223, 228
  Eno and, 108–18, 122; Kraftwerk and,
    133–38; krautrock and, 125–29; Moogs,
    110, 112, 135; Pere Ubu and, 142–44;
    Roland TB303, 207; Yamaha DX7, 118

Talk Talk, 219
Talking Heads, 117, 120–21, 126, 149, 166, 200
Tall Dwarfs, 172
Tamm, Eric, 115, 116
Tangerine Dream, 127
techno music, 79, 103, 122, 137, 190, 203–15,
    219, 220, 223
Teenage Fanclub, 222
Telescopes, 222
Television, 141, 161
Television Personalities, 154
Temptations, 97
theremins, 21, 30, 110
The Teardrop Explodes, 154–156, 222
Thin White Rope, 178
13th Floor Elevators, xv, 8, 13, 36–39, 44, 57, 85,
    110, 141, 156, 157, 217
Thomas, David, 12, 139, 141–45
Thompson, Mayo, 38, 144
Three O'Clock, 173, 174–75
Throbbing Gristle, 128, 184, 212
Throwing Muses, 218
Tiny Lights, 172
Tomorrow, 5, 64, 78–79, 81, 86, 181
Too Pure label, 126, 222–23
Tornadoes, 11
Townshend, Pete, 64, 79, 95, 109, 187
Traffic, 83, 132
T. Rex, 82, 232
Tricky, 201–202
trip hop, 201–202
Troggs, 32, 188
True West, 178
Tryfles, 170
Trypes, 151
Turtles, 51
Tutuola, Amos, 121, 191
27 Various, 172
Twink, 78–79, 82, 101, 181
Twomey, Chris, 165

UFO,
    group, 101; psychedelic rock club, 59–60, 64,
    66, 81, 101
Ultramarine, 212
Ultra Vivid Scene, 218
Unclaimed, 171, 174, 177

United States of America, 110
U2, 121, 122

Valens, Ritchie, xv, 7
Van Der Graaf Generator, 83, 86
Vanilla Fudge, 98
VapourSpace, 211
Varese, Edgard, 104
Velvet Crush, 222
Velvet Monkeys, 172
Velvet Underground, xv, 9, 14, 15, 41–46, 60, 85,
    104, 106, 110, 114, 117, 125, 129, 130, 134,
    145, 149, 150, 151, 154, 174, 177, 185, 191,
    218, 220, 221, 231
Verlaines, 172
Village Voice, 26, 182, 216
Vipers, 173
virtual reality, 121, 207
Viva Saturn, 177

Wake Ooloo, 152–53
War, 97
Ward, Ed, 103
Warhol, Andy, 9, 43–46, 106, 228
Watson, Ben, 106
Watts, Alan, 6, 10, 24
Ween, 222
Weinstein, Deena, 71, 101
Weinstein, Michael, 186
Wenner, Jann, 31
Whitworth, Armstrong, 126
Who, 62, 80, 82, 187–88, 188, 222
Wild Carnation, 153
Wilson, Brian, 7, 8, 15, 18–22, 40, 41, 53, 67, 80,
    199, 227
Winner, Langdon, 26
Wire, 145–48, 160, 191, 211, 218, 220, 227
Wolfe, Tom, 8, 9
Wonder, Stevie, 97, 198
Woodentops, 155, 169
Woodstock, 61, 97
Wray, Link, 11
Wyatt, Robert, 80, 115, 120, 212

XTC, 91, 154, 160, 164–69, 220

Yardbirds, 32, 34, 82, 85, 189
Yard Trauma, 172
Yellow Sunshine Explosion, 172
Yes, 86, 90, 141
Yo La Tengo, 218
Young, La Monte, 42, 114, 125
Young, Neil, 51, 52, 174, 176, 177, 189, 232
Yung Wu, 151

Zager and Evans, 183
Zappa, Frank, 104–106
Zombies, 83

About the Author

Jim DeRogatis was born in Jersey City, New Jersey, the year the Beatles arrived in America, and he began voicing his opinions about rock 'n' roll shortly thereafter. He jokes that he is not a musician, but he *is* a drummer. He started writing about music in fanzines as a teenager, and went on to become assistant editor at *Request* magazine in Minneapolis, pop music editor at the *Chicago Sun-Times,* and senior editor at *Rolling Stone. Kaleidoscope Eyes* is his first book. He is working on a biography of Lester Bangs, an anthology of Generation X rock writers, and a book about rock 'n' roll and aging. He welcomes e-mail at jimdero@aol.com.